100 BATTLES

'100 BATTLES

General Editor: Martin J. Dougherty

Bath · New York · Singapore · Hong Kong · Cologne · Delhi
Melbourne · Amsterdam · Johannesburg · Auckland · Shenzhen

First published by Parragon in 2012
Parragon
4 Queen Street
Bath BA1 1HE, UK
www.parragon.com

ISBN: 978-1-4454-6680-4

Editorial and design by
Amber Books Ltd
Bradley's Close, 74–77 White Lion Street
London N1 9PF – United Kingdom
www.amberbooks.co.uk

Project Editor: Michael Spilling
Picture Research: Terry Forshaw
Designer: Joe Conneally
Text: Rupert Butler, Martin J. Dougherty,
Michael E. Haskew, Christer Jorgensen, Chris Mann,
Chris McNab, Michael Neiberg, and Michael Pavkovic

Printed in China

CONTENTS

INTRODUCTION

Victory or defeat on the battlefield can, from the safe distance of time, appear to have a clear rationale. Most commonly, the outcome of an engagement is ascribed to a leader's command decisions, and such can indeed have a critical effect. There are few historians who can deny, for example, that Major-General William Elphinstone's incompetence wasn't central to the disastrous British retreat from Kabul to Jalalabad in January 1842, or that Miltiades' disposition of troops at Marathon in September 490 B.C.E. made a signal contribution to the defeat of the Persian army. In strict tactical terms, good decisions result in the favorable mismatch of allied strengths to enemy weaknesses, and poor decisions do the reverse, while also breeding uncertainty and eroding morale.

There is something intrinsically appealing about looking to prominent commanders as the arbiters of battles, not least because they bring a clarity from the "fog of war." And yet, as the clashes discussed in this book will reveal, a battle is a struggle of more than just great minds and tactical education. In fact, the outcome of battle is determined by a host of factors large and small, many doubtless hidden from the historian. That seminal Prussian philosopher of war, Carl von Clausewitz, explained the truth that "Everything in war is simple, but the simplest thing is difficult. The difficulties accumulate and end by producing a kind of friction that is inconceivable unless one has experienced war."

A U.S. INFANTRY REGIMENT GUN CREW FIRE *a 1.4 in (37 mm) gun in support of an advance against German trenches, 1918. Technology proved king in the attritional campaigns of World War I.*

Some causes of "friction" are powerful and obvious. Climate, for instance, can bring an army to its knees if it does not have the resources, experience or technology to cope with it. Both Napoleon's and Hitler's campaigns against Moscow were dramatically curtailed by the Russian winter and the seasonal *rasputitsa* rain and mud. Conversely, the Battle of Hattin in July 1187 saw a Crusader army devastated not only by Arab cavalry, but also by scorching Middle Eastern sun.

An ancillary of climate is terrain. Adverse terrain, ranging from soft deserts to towering granite mountains, retards maneuver and can create near impenetrable obstacles, restricting tactical options. In mountainous regions, for example, passes are typically the only avenues for advance, while high-altitude ground favors defense and makes attack an additional torture (see Monte Cassino and Dien Bien Phu for examples). Terrain is also complicated

by sheer distance. The fighting efficiency of any army relies on the long train of logistics running up to the frontline. As a general rule, the farther that train runs, the more tenuous, expensive, and overworked the supply line. The German Army found this to its cost in North Africa and the Eastern Front during World War II, as did the Japanese Army in Burma.

FIREPOWER

Henry V's army moving through France in 1415 also experienced critical supply shortages, but at Agincourt their fortunes were partly restored through another major factor in battlefield success—firepower. In the case of Agincourt, the firepower came in the form of arrows, but history went on to produce far more destructive systems.

During World War I, for example, three men and a heavy machine gun could virtually destroy an entire company, and by World War II artillery was responsible for 70 percent of all battlefield casualties. If one side has a clear superiority in standoff firepower, a battle-winning option might simply be to hammer the enemy from a distance until he crumbles.

Yet firepower alone is rarely the ultimate arbiter of an entire campaign, as recent experience in Vietnam, Afghanistan, and Iraq have illustrated. In fact, battles and wars are won by a vast number of factors coalescing in an army's favor. As the examples in this book will show, each battle brings its own unique conditions. The one constant, perhaps, is the soldier himself, focused primarily on survival amid forces far greater than himself.

ABOVE: U.S. MARINE ARTILLERY BOMBARD JAPANESE POSITIONS *on the Philippine island of Luzon during the reconquest of the islands, April 1945.*

BELOW: NAPOLEON AND HIS MARSHALLS *on the march in France, 1814. Napoleon successfully beat the Russian army at Borodino and occupied Moscow, but struggled to keep his troops supplied across the vast Russian steppe during the harsh winter months.*

CHAPTER ONE

Ancient Times to the Middle Ages

The wars of the ancient world, although utterly dissimilar to the battles of today, nevertheless established some of the core tactical principles of warfare. Mass, momentum, flanking maneuvers, and the need for good logistics were at the heart of a victory.

The growth of great empires—Mesopotamian, Egyptian, Assyrian, Chinese, Greek, Roman, and others—meant warfare became a persistent feature of the ancient world. On land, the battles were fought with a mix of infantry, cavalry, and missile soldiers, plus the talents and technologies of siege warfare specialists, while at sea the oar and the ram were central. In many ways, the engagements were crude exercises in muscle, blade, and spear, the two sides moving to close quarters and hacking out a conclusion. Yet as this chapter shows, a talented commander could still tip the balance in his favor through intelligent maneuver, and the lessons of the ancients were carried through into the battles of the medieval world.

LEFT: THIS ROMANTICIZED EIGHTEENTH-CENTURY *depiction of the death of Paulus at the Battle of Cannae shows legionaries wearing armor that would not, in actual fact, be in service for at least another three centuries.*

AN ENEMY PLEADS FOR PHARAOH'S MERCY. *A generic foe dies under a blow from Ramses II's javelin in this 1257 B.C.E. wall relief at Abu Simbel.*

Kadesh 1294 B.C.E.

THE BATTLE OF KADESH PITTED TWO OF THE ANCIENT WORLD'S GREAT POWERS, EGYPT AND THE HITTITES, AGAINST EACH OTHER. EGYPT'S DEGREE OF CONTROL OVER SYRIA AND CANAAN VARIED OVER TIME. IT WAS NOT POSSIBLE TO KEEP THE LARGE GARRISONS IN THE AREA THAT WOULD BE NECESSARY TO MAINTAIN CLOSE CONTROL, SO INSTEAD A SERIES OF MILITARY CAMPAIGNS WERE FOUGHT TO RESTORE EGYPTIAN SOVEREIGNTY WHEN IT WAS CHALLENGED.

As the Hittites grew in power, they pushed into Syria and took control of the city of Kadesh. Determined to regain the city, Pharaoh Ramses II assembled an army of about 20,000 men organized into four divisions and marched northward. The march was completed with impressive speed by the well-organized Egyptians, who established a fortified camp near their objective.

However, the Hittites were prepared. Their king, Muwatallis, concealed his army behind the city rather than taking refuge inside the walls. The illusion that the city was undefended was strengthened by placing two agents

BATTLE FACTS

Who: An Egyptian army numbering approximately 18,000 infantry and 2,000 chariots under the command of Pharaoh Ramses II (d. 1213 B.C.E.), opposed by around 20,000 Hittite infantry and 3,000 chariots under the command of King Muwatallis (d. 1273 B.C.E.).

What: Part of the Egyptian army was ambushed and suffered heavy casualties before the arrival of the remainder permitted a successful counterattack.

Where: Kadesh on the Orontes River in Syria.

When: 1294 B.C.E.

Why: The Hittite empire had taken control of Kadesh, a former Egyptian possession.

Outcome: Although both sides proclaimed a victory, the result was a negotiated peace treaty.

pretending to be Hittite soldiers where they would be easily captured by the Egyptians. These men told Ramses that the Hittite army was some distance away.

RAMSES ADVANCES

Ramses' army had marched with its four divisions somewhat separated for logistical reasons, and only part of the force was available. However, with his objective seemingly ripe for the taking he saw no point in waiting and advanced with two of his four divisions.

As the Egyptians approached Kadesh, the division of Ra was suddenly attacked by Hittite chariots, causing a panic that quickly spread. The division of Ra disintegrated, with many men fleeing toward the division of Amon, Ramses' personal command. They hoped to find safety in its ranks but only caused confusion at a time when order and discipline were of paramount importance.

The desperate situation was alleviated somewhat as the Hittite troops plundered Ramses' camp instead of attacking his remaining division. Ramses was able to rally his force and launch a counterattack. In an age before instantaneous long-distance communications, sometimes the only way subordinates could tell what their commander-in-chief wanted them to do was to observe his actions. Ramses' attack was not only the only real chance he had to escape the Hittite trap, it was also a clear signal to his subordinate commanders that he wanted them to launch an attack of their own.

REINFORCEMENTS ARRIVE

Ramses' remaining divisions, Ptah and Sutekh, were approaching Kadesh from the south as the counterattack began. They rapidly advanced against the Hittite force and were joined by a mercenary

contingent hired by Ramses, which had been marching to rendezvous with the main army.

With his full attention on Ramses' two divisions, Muwatallis had failed to watch his army's rear, and was caught by surprise by the new arrivals. Thrown into confusion, the Hittite army was nevertheless able to retire into Kadesh and remained in fighting condition.

Both armies had suffered serious casualties and morale was shaken on both sides by near-defeat. It had become apparent that the Hittites' iron weapons were more effective than the bronze ones used by the Egyptians. However, the Egyptian chariots were superior, being faster and carrying archers instead of javelinmen. Neither side was sure of victory if battle was resumed, so negotiations began.

CONCLUSION

The outcome was a peace treaty that allowed both rulers to return home claiming a great victory. In reality, neither side really won; the Egyptians could boast that they drove the enemy from the battlefield, indicating a tactical victory, but the strategic picture was unchanged. Ramses II had gone to Kadesh to take it from the Hittites and in that he failed. However, the treaty was beneficial because it improved stability by preventing further conflict for a time.

EGYPTIAN CHARIOT

Primarily used as missile platforms, Egyptian chariots were of a light construction and offered little protection to their crews. The main means of defense was speed, making the vehicle a difficult target for opposing archers and keeping the crew out of reach of enemy troops armed with hand weapons.

AT THE BATTLE OF MARATHON *Miltiades, with 10,000 Athenian and 400 Plataean hoplites, defeated a Persian force nearly double their size, including 10,000 elite Immortals.*

Marathon 490 B.C.E.

AT MARATHON, AN OUTNUMBERED FORCE OF GREEK HOPLITES SEIZED A CHANCE TO DEFEAT THEIR PERSIAN FOES, EXPLOITING THEIR SUPERIOR ARMOR AND DISCIPLINE TO WIN ONE OF THE MOST FAMOUS TACTICAL VICTORIES OF THE ANCIENT WORLD. IT WAS, HOWEVER, NOT THE END OF THE PERSIAN THREAT TO THE INDEPENDENT GREEK CITY-STATES.

In 490 B.C.E., the Persian Great King, Darius I (circa 550–486 B.C.E.), decided once again to attempt to settle long-standing scores with the Athenians, who had resisted incorporation into the Persian Empire and had supported the Ionian revolt against Persian rule in 499 B.C.E. The Persian invasion force would be entirely transported by sea, thereby avoiding the problems that had beset a similarly minded expedition two years previously. The naval component of the force was composed of nearly 600 ships, transporting a landing force numbered at perhaps 25,000 fighting men including a small cavalry contingent, probably about 1,000 strong. This force was commanded by Darius' nephew Artaphernes and Datis, a nobleman of Median descent. The Persians burned a destructive trail across the Aegean and the Greek coastline,

BATTLE FACTS

Who: Nearly 11,000 Athenians and Plataean hoplites, led by Athenian general Miltiades, were opposed by a Persian army numbering perhaps 25,000 under the command of the Persian Artaphernes and the Median noble Datis.

What: The Athenians weakened the center of their line and strengthened their wings, drawing the Persians into the center then defeating them on the flanks and enveloping their center.

Where: The Plain of Marathon, about 26 miles (42 km) from Athens.

When: August 12, 490 B.C.E.

Why: The Persians wanted to attack Athens to punish the city for its support for the rebellion of the Ionian Greek cities.

Outcome: Following defeat the Persians were driven from Greece for ten years.

but their principal destination was the plain of Marathon, nearly 26 miles (42 km) from Athens. In response, an Athenian army of nearly 10,000 hoplites—heavily-armed infantry—marched out to Marathon. They were joined by a force of between 600 and 1,000 hoplites from the city of Plataea, a longtime ally of Athens.

THE BATTLE

The two armies faced each other for perhaps four days. By the evening of August 11, however, time was running out for the Persians. Expectations of a pro-Persian uprising in Athens remained unfulfilled, and the Athenians might soon be receiving Spartan reinforcements. As a result, the Persians embarked some of their forces on transports, which sailed for Athens the next morning while the remainder of their troops kept a watch on the Athenian and Plataean hoplites at Marathon. This mobile unit was under the command of Datis, and seems to have included the majority of the Persian cavalry, who would be very useful in making a dash for Athens once the task force made landfall at Phaleron Bay. Artaphernes would stay at Marathon and maintain a close blockade of the Athenian camp. He probably had about 15,000 men with him, almost exclusively infantry. Fortunately for the Athenians, they were alerted to the Persian plan by some sympathetic Ionians who were serving with the Persians. They sent the famous message "the cavalry are away," which galvanized the resolve of the Athenian commanders to offer battle. The next morning, therefore, saw the opposing forces arrayed for battle.

The Athenian general Miltiades, who understood Persian tactics, was in command that day, and deployed the Greek forces. He knew that the Persians were likely to put their best troops in the center of their battle line and that the Persian numbers would make it likely that if he arrayed his phalanx eight-deep along the entire front, they would be outflanked. In order to prevent this he made the center of his line thinner, knowing that the Persians would initially have success there.

However, Miltiades also knew that the wings of the Persian formation would be formed from lighter-armed and less enthusiastic levies and that the more heavily armed wings of the Greek army would be victorious. He therefore ordered that the wings not pursue the defeated levies, but once they had been driven off, to wheel

inward on the Persian center. The right wing was under the command of the leader Callimachus and the left was formed by the Plataeans.

Artaphernes deployed his troops as Miltiades had expected. His best troops, Iranian soldiers from the standing army and tough Saka mercenaries, formed the center of his formation with various levies, including unenthusiastic Ionian Greeks, on the flanks. In order to maintain his close blockade of the Athenian camp, he advanced to within eight *stades*, or 1 mile (1.6 km), of the Greek positions.

GREEK VICTORY

The Greeks advanced from their camp toward the Persian lines. The battle lines came together in brutal combat, and the Persians quickly had the better of it in the center, where the best of their troops were posted, and the Athenians were pushed back. On the wings, however, the levies were routed. Following their orders, the victorious Greeks wheeled in against the Persian center, catching it in a double envelopment. A slaughter followed that resulted in 6,400 Persian casualties, mostly Iranian and Saka troops, and only 192 Athenians (including Callimachus), and a handful of Plataeans killed. The Athenians could not, however, rest after their victory. While one tribal division held the field, the remainder made a forced march back to Athens. They arrived in time to deter the Persians from landing and so Datis, now joined by Artaphernes' survivors, was forced to return home.

GREEK HOPLITE

A typical hoplite of the Persian War era. His primary weapon was a long iron-headed spear, which could be between 6–10 ft (2–3 m) in length. It was usually held overarm in combat, and underarm when maneuvering. He also carried a short sword about 2 ft (60 cm) in length, made of iron with bronze fittings. The sword was used in both a cutting and thrusting motion. For protection he carries a hoplon (shield) made of wood with a bronze face and leather inner lining. The hoplon was secured to the hoplite's forearm by a band, and he held a grip in his left fist. His Corinthian helmet is topped with a plume of horsehair, which could be dyed for effect. His torso is protected by a cuirass of stiffened linen with metal scales added for greater protection. On his shins are molded bronze greaves, while simple leather sandals are worn on his feet.

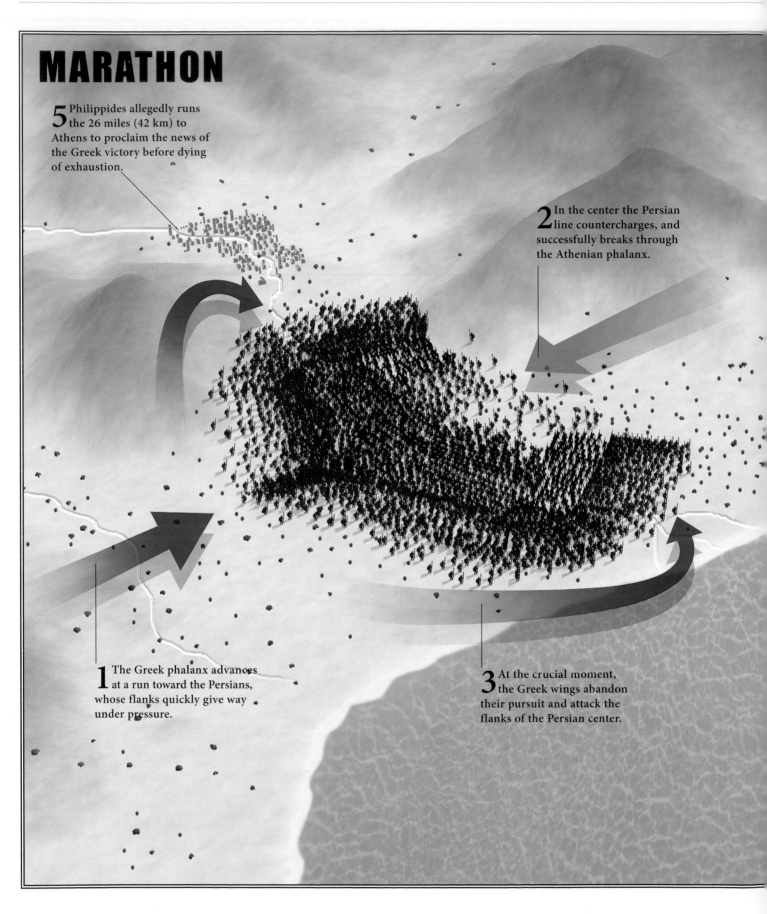

MARATHON

5 Philippides allegedly runs the 26 miles (42 km) to Athens to proclaim the news of the Greek victory before dying of exhaustion.

2 In the center the Persian line countercharges, and successfully breaks through the Athenian phalanx.

1 The Greek phalanx advances at a run toward the Persians, whose flanks quickly give way under pressure.

3 At the crucial moment, the Greek wings abandon their pursuit and attack the flanks of the Persian center.

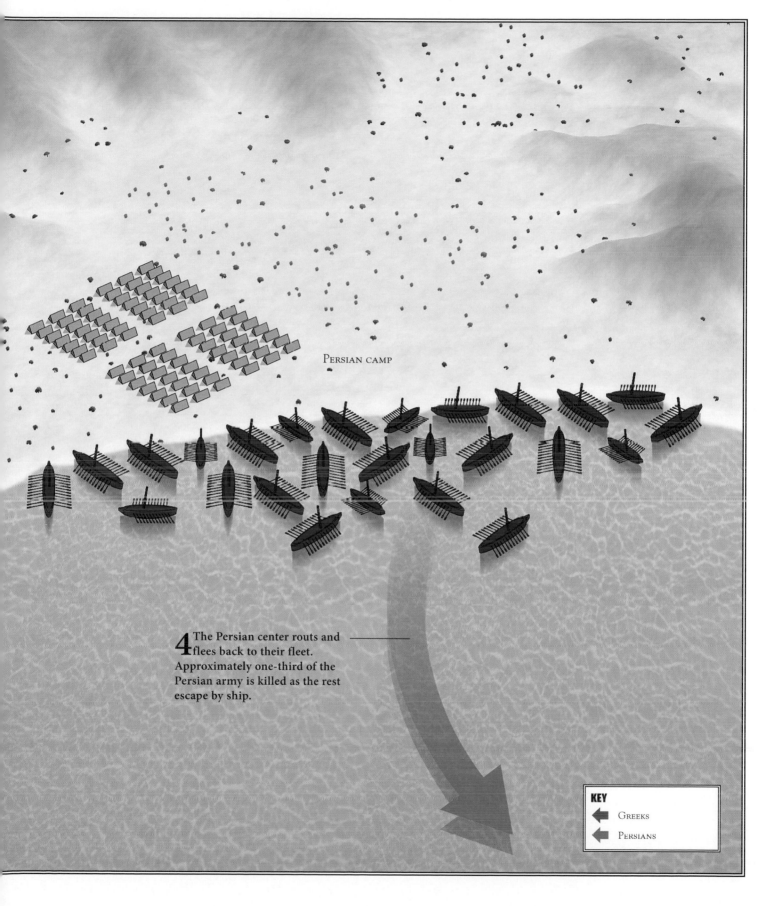

Persian camp

4 The Persian center routs and flees back to their fleet. Approximately one-third of the Persian army is killed as the rest escape by ship.

KEY
Greeks
Persians

THE GREEKS CELEBRATE THEIR VICTORY over the Persian navy in the Battle of Salamis, September 480 B.C.E., as depicted by eighteenth-century painter F. Cormon.

Salamis 480 B.C.E.

ON LAND AND SEA, THE PERSIAN KING XERXES THE GREAT MOVED WITH MASSIVE FORCE AGAINST THE GREEK CITY-STATES, PRINCIPALLY ATHENS AND SPARTA. AT THERMOPYLAE, A MERE 300 SPARTAN HOPLITES SACRIFICED THEMSELVES TO BUY PRECIOUS TIME. AT SALAMIS, THE GREEKS INFLICTED A CRUSHING NAVAL DEFEAT UPON THE INVADERS AND PRESERVED THE FLOWER OF WESTERN CULTURE.

During the fifth century B.C.E., the vast empire of Persia was at the height of its glory and its power. The realm of King Darius I (521–486 B.C.E.) extended from the Caucasus to the Indian Ocean and from the shores of the Mediterranean Sea to the Indus River, and his subjects included a great diversity of peoples.

Yet the city-state of Athens remained a resistant thorn in the Persian side. In 480 B.C.E., therefore, Darius' son, the Persian king Xerxes (reigned 486–465 B.C.E.) called his advisers together to discuss another military move against

BATTLE FACTS

Who: A Greek naval force under the Athenian Themistocles numbering 300 triremes opposed 400 Persian ships as Persian king Xerxes (d. 465 B.C.E.) watched from nearby heights.

What: The Persian fleet was routed and fled after being lured into shallow waters and set upon by the rams of the Greek vessels.

Where: In the Saronic Gulf near the island of Salamis, west of modern Athens.

When: September 20, 480 B.C.E.

Why: Xerxes wanted to avenge the defeat of his father, Darius, at Marathon a decade earlier and extend his empire into Europe.

Outcome: The Persians suffered grievous losses and were compelled to withdraw. Greek civilization was preserved and flourished.

A GREEK BIREME DATING FROM THE FIFTH CENTURY B.C.E. *It has a prominent ram at its prow. Note the chair provided for the helmsman, who has two large paddles to act as a rudder.*

Athens and an expansion of the Persian empire.

The Greeks certainly faced a powerful threat. The Persian army numbered approximately 500,000 men, while the Persian fleet was said to consist of 1,207 triremes. Early in the campaign, which began in the summer of 480 B.C.E., a number of Greek cities pledged allegiance to Xerxes as his juggernaut advanced inexorably toward them. Athens and Sparta, however, remained defiant against overwhelming odds. On August 18, the advancing Persians reached the pass at Thermopylae, through which the force had to move in order to reach Athens. The Persians drew up before the pass, which was barely 50 ft (15 m) wide and defended by 6,000 Greek hoplites, including 300 Spartans, under the command of the Spartan king, Leonidas. The Spartans were killed to the last man, mainly by vast clouds of arrows fired from the Persian lines. The heroic Spartans of Thermopylae did not sacrifice themselves in vain. Their stand cost the Persians precious time, and a pair of violent storms sank more than 200 Persian ships. When he received the news that the Persians had taken Thermopylae, the great Greek commander Themistocles (circa 528–462 B.C.E.) withdrew his fleet to the island of Salamis.

DELAY AND DECEPTION

By the time the Persian army reached Athens, most of the citizenry had fled. Those who had not were put to the sword. Still, in order to win a decisive victory, Xerxes had to defeat the Greek army on land. To defeat the Greek army, his triremes had to be able to maneuver in safety. Therefore, a victory over the Greek fleet became a necessity. Xerxes planned simply to overwhelm the 300 Greek triremes that opposed his force of 400 vessels in the narrow waters around Salamis. Themistocles, however, had other ideas. He deployed his fleet with the Athenians and Corinthians on the left, the

Aegenitans and Spartans on the right, hoping that the Persians would be drawn into the shallow and confined waters near the Bay of Eleusis. The Persian triremes, apparently constructed for combat on the open sea, would find maneuvering virtually impossible in the narrows.

On the morning of September 20, 480 B.C.E., Themistocles' plan worked perfectly. When the commanders of the leading Persian ships realized they had fallen into a trap, they ordered a backwater maneuver. But those vessels behind them had nowhere to go, throwing the fleet into confusion. The Persians' superior numbers had now become a hindrance rather than an advantage.

A line of Greek triremes moved in orderly fashion to encircle the confused enemy, and their bronze rams inflicted deadly punishment on the foundering Persian ships. The playwright Aeschylus, who is remembered as the father of literary tragedy, fought at both Marathon and Salamis. He described the scene as reminiscent of the mass netting and killing of fish on the shores of the Mediterranean. "At first the torrent of the Persians' fleet bore up," Aeschylus wrote. "But then with the press of the shipping hemmed there in the narrows, none could help another."

The Persian fleet was crippled at Salamis, losing 200 triremes, roughly half its strength, to a mere 40 for the Greeks. In the wake of the disaster, Xerxes had little choice but to retire to safety. Greece was at last free from the threat of Eastern domination. For half a century Athens maintained the strongest fleet in the Ancient World, while the army of Sparta was the preeminent force on land.

PERSIAN MARINE

At the Battle of Salamis, Xerxes relied heavily on marines, placing at least 30 on each vessel. At the heart of this decision was probably Persian distrust of sea power and failure to recognize the effectiveness of the ship itself as the primary weapon. Xerxes may also have distrusted his Egyptian, Phoenician, and Ionian-Greek subjects who manned the ships, and sought to assure their loyalty with a strong Persian marine presence. Impressive as they appeared, the marines probably did Xerxes' cause more harm than good. They were so tightly packed on the ships that they could not fight effectively and their lack of body armor and light weapons were no match for the Greeks.

Leuctra 371 B.C.E.

AT THE BATTLE OF LEUCTRA, THE THEBAN ARMY USED INNOVATIVE NEW TACTICS TO DEFEAT A SIGNIFICANTLY LARGER FORCE OF SPARTANS, AT THE TIME SUPPOSEDLY THE GREATEST WARRIORS IN GREECE.

The growing power of Thebes was a threat to Sparta's preeminent position in Greece at the time, and so when some of the cities of Boeotia asked for assistance in breaking away from their Theban overlords, Sparta sent an army to help. This was not the first conflict between Sparta and Thebes but part of an ongoing rivalry.

THEBES RESPONDS

The Spartan army of the day was one of the finest fighting forces in Greece. Traditionally the best elements were placed on the right of the line, but even the Spartans' left-flank units were considered a match for the best in anyone else's army. It was thus with confidence that King Cleombrotus led his army into Theban territory. Epaminondas of Thebes had no choice but to intercept the Spartans, but he faced certain defeat if he fought a

THEBAN GENERAL EPAMINONDAS RALLIES HIS TROOPS *at Leuctra. By concentrating his forces on a part of the Spartan line, he was able to win a great victory over the invincible Spartans.*

traditional line battle. The only troops in the Theban army that could take on Spartans on equal terms were the 300-strong Sacred Band.

Even if he had not been outnumbered, Epaminondas would still have been in a difficult position. His solution was to concentrate his infantry in a deep and powerful phalanx on the left wing, and to refuse his right. By bending his line back and defending it with light troops and cavalry, Epaminondas hoped to prevent the Spartans from engaging the weak wing until his powerful left-wing phalanx had done its work.

A DECISIVE CLASH

The Spartan attack on Epaminondas' refused right flank went badly. First their cavalry were driven off by a counterattack, throwing the line into disorder as they fled. Then the disorganized attack was beaten off by Theban light troops and cavalry.

Meanwhile, on the Theban left flank the phalanx rolled into the Spartan line, crushing the best of the Spartan troops, including the Royal Bodyguard. King Cleombrotus was killed as the right wing of his army disintegrated. The Thebans then wheeled to roll up the Spartan line, completing their victory. The ensuing Spartan retreat left Boeotia in Theban hands and inspired rebellions among Sparta's previous conquests.

BATTLE FACTS

Who: A Spartan army numbering around 12,000, commanded by King Cleombrotus (d. 371 B.C.E.), opposed by a Theban force of around 7,000–9,000 troops commanded by Epaminondas (d. 362 B.C.E.).

What: The Thebans concentrated their strength on one wing, gaining a decisive advantage.

Where: 10 miles (16 km) to the west of Thebes, on the Greek mainland.

When: July 371 B.C.E.

Why: Several Boeotian cities requested Spartan aid in becoming independent from Thebes, leading to a Spartan invasion of Theban territory.

Outcome: The Spartan army was decisively defeated and their king killed in action.

GREECE

Thebes · ⊹ Leuctra
Sparta · · Athens

PERSIAN EMPIRE

Mediterranean Sea

Granicus River 334 B.C.E.

THE RIVER GRANICUS WAS A SIGNIFICANT OBSTACLE TO ALEXANDER THE GREAT'S PROGRESS, AND OFFERED THE PERSIANS THEIR BEST CHANCE TO HALT HIS ADVANCE.

ALEXANDER LEADS HIS ELITE COMPANION CAVALRY *across the Granicus River, seizing the initiative from the Persians. The Companions were all handpicked sons of Macedonian nobles.*

Having brought Greece under his control, Alexander of Macedon launched a campaign into Asia Minor. This was opposed by the Persian Satraps whose territory was threatened, assisted by a Greek mercenary commander, Memnon of Rhodes. Memnon suggested a delaying strategy in the hope that the Macedonians' supplies would run out, but was overruled.

The Persian army moved to intercept Alexander's expedition and established a blocking position at the Granicus River, which could only be crossed by an army at certain points. The Persian force was superior in cavalry, and drew up with its cavalry to the fore. The infantry, composed mainly of Greek mercenaries, was placed in support.

ALEXANDER ATTACKS

Disregarding suggestions of a more cautious strategy made by his subordinates, Alexander decided to force a crossing.

BATTLE FACTS

Who: A Macedonian army under Alexander the Great (356–323 B.C.E.) numbering around 18,000 troops, opposed by a force of 10,000 Persian cavalry and 5,000 Greek mercenaries.

What: The Persian cavalry was driven off, after which the Greek mercenaries were overwhelmed by far superior numbers.

Where: The Granicus River, in modern-day Turkey.

When: May 334 B.C.E.

Why: The Persian army tried to halt Alexander's expedition into Asia Minor by preventing a crossing of the Granicus River.

Outcome: Alexander was able to continue his advance into Asia Minor.

His attack opened with a feint by his right-flank forces, which drew Persian reinforcements off to their left flank.

Alexander personally led the attack on the Persian center while his left-flank formations also advanced. The Persians initially held the advantage, defending a steep riverbank while their opponents had to struggle across the river and then attack uphill. The Macedonians' long spears gave them an advantage over the Persian cavalry, and the fight increasingly turned in Alexander's favor once his troops reached more level ground.

As the Persians were pushed back, Alexander himself was a prime target for their best cavalry. Indeed, it has been suggested that the crux of the Persian strategy was to kill him, which would likely cause the Macedonian army to fall apart. The attempt almost succeeded, but eventually the Persian center gave way. The flanks soon followed, leaving only the Greek mercenaries to oppose the Macedonian advance.

THE GREEKS FIGHT ON

Abandoned by their cavalry, the experienced Greek mercenaries were unable to withdraw but made a stubborn stand. Their request for surrender terms was denied, with Macedonian attacks continuing until the mercenaries agreed to an unconditional surrender. With the Persian army scattered and his own forces now established across the river, Alexander was able to resume his march into Asia Minor.

THIS PAINTING BY SEBASTIANO RICCI, *entitled* ALEXANDER AND THE FAMILY OF DARIUS, *shows Alexander meeting the widow and family of Darius following his victory.*

Gaugamela 331 B.C.E.

IN 334 B.C.E., ALEXANDER THE GREAT OF MACEDON REINFORCED HIS ALREADY MIGHTY ARMY, MARCHED INTO ASIA MINOR, AND BEGAN HIS GREAT CAMPAIGN TO CONQUER THE PERSIAN EMPIRE. WITHIN TWO YEARS HE HELD HALF THAT EMPIRE, HAD ELIMINATED THE PERSIAN FLEET'S MEDITERRANEAN BASES AND BRAZENLY SEIZED EGYPT.

As Alexander (356–323 B.C.E.) advanced into Mesopotamia in 331 B.C.E., Persia's King Darius (d. 330 B.C.E.) considered retreating farther into his territory and perhaps scorching the earth behind him, but instead decided to give battle.

Darius chose his ground near the modern city of Mosul in Iraq. Darius' initial attack would be made by his first line, which was composed mostly of cavalry with a few of the best Persian infantry units mixed in. Darius himself was in the Persian center with the cavalry and infantry of his personal guard. In front of them were arrayed some 200 scythed chariots. A second line, composed of enormous

BATTLE FACTS

Who: Alexander the Great (356–323 B.C.E.) led 47,000 Greek/Macedonian troops against a 240,000-strong Persian army under King Darius the Great (reigned 336–330 B.C.E.).

What: Alexander used an oblique formation to break the Persian front, Darius fled, and the Persian army subsequently collapsed.

Where: Near Tel Gomel, in what is now northern Iraq.

When: October 1, 331 B.C.E.

Why: Alexander sought to finally defeat Darius in battle and complete his conquest of the Persian empire.

Outcome: Darius was murdered, possibly by his own generals. Alexander became master of Persia.

MOUNTED ARCHERS *such as this Scythian (left) posed one of the Ancient Near East's most deadly threats to Western infantry, such as Alexander's phalanx. Riding close to fire into the ranks on foot, horse archers would then retire to a safe distance. But pursuit by other cavalry could negate the threat of such archers. Alexander had his own Thracian cavalry, and successfully thwarted this Persian threat at the Battle of Gaugamela.*

numbers of infantry, was positioned behind the first. Darius expected to be able to envelop both of Alexander's flanks with his vastly superior numbers and to crush his army from all sides.

BATTLE COMMENCES

To help protect his flanks from envelopment, Alexander positioned his cavalry on the flanks, with each unit echeloned back from the last, creating "refused" flanks that required the enemy to move farther if he wanted to engage them. His phalanx of well-drilled Macedonian infantry was positioned in the center of the Greek line. A reserve phalanx formed Alexander's second line.

Alexander's plan called for his left flank, under the veteran general Parmenio, to fight a holding action while Alexander led the right wing to victory. He was assisted in this by the Persians themselves, who sent their left-flank cavalry far around Alexander's right, opening up a gap in their line. The Macedonian army was drifting to the right. If Darius delayed too long his chariots might not gain the benefit of their prepared run.

So the attack was launched. Darius' cavalry swept around the flanks of the Macedonian force as the chariots (and, in some accounts, 15 war elephants) made their initial frontal attack. The Macedonian line was able to fend off the chariots and weather the initial onslaught, though some of the Persian cavalry were able to break through. They were engaged by the reserve phalanx and by light troops, which had been briefed for the task.

As he had planned, Alexander now led his elite Companion Cavalry and other units against the Persian left. Exploiting the gap that was opening between the Persian cavalry on the left and the center of their army, the Companions inflicted a savage blow on the forces in front

of them. They were followed by a great wedge of infantry and light troops, which fell on the disorganized Persians. Fearing that he would be cut off, the commander of the Persian left wing, Bessus, began to retire, which eased the pressure on Alexander's refused right flank. Meanwhile, Darius himself was feeling the pressure, and began to retreat. The withdrawal became a rout as Darius' bodyguards followed their leader in fleeing the field.

Alexander was not able to pursue because the situation on his left was becoming desperate. Parmenio's forces were hard-pressed on the left but had done their job, tying down the Persians' forces. Now Alexander fell upon the rear of the Persians engaging Parmenio, forcing them to retreat. The Persian right-wing commander, Mazaeus, tried to conduct an orderly retreat but was vigorously attacked and his troops thrown into confusion. This moment represented the end of organized Persian resistance at Gaugamela. Behind the fleeing Darius were left 40,000 dead Persian troops, 4,000 more as prisoners and the remainder of the army scattered around the countryside.

COMPANION CAVALRY

Companion Cavalry (below) were literally that, the sons of the Macedonian nobility, raised along with Alexander under Philip's supervision and trained in the tactics Philip had learned from the Theban Epaminondas. Many of them were personal friends to whom he owed his life. Companion Cavalry carried the shorter cavalry spear and lighter armor, and always fought under Alexander's personal command. To the cavalry was given the decisive role in Alexander's battles. When the lumbering phalanx created a gap in the enemy's line, the cavalry would charge through and carry out flanking attacks.

GAUGAMELA

3 The Persian left tries to outflank the Macedonians, but they cannot get past the light troops and cavalry.

1 The Macedonian phalanx marches obliquely toward the Persian line. The Persian chariots are repulsed by javelins.

4 Alexander and the Companions break through a weak spot in the Persian line and swing leftward.

2 Darius' secret weapons, his Indian war elephants and scythe-armed chariots, prove to be a disappointment.

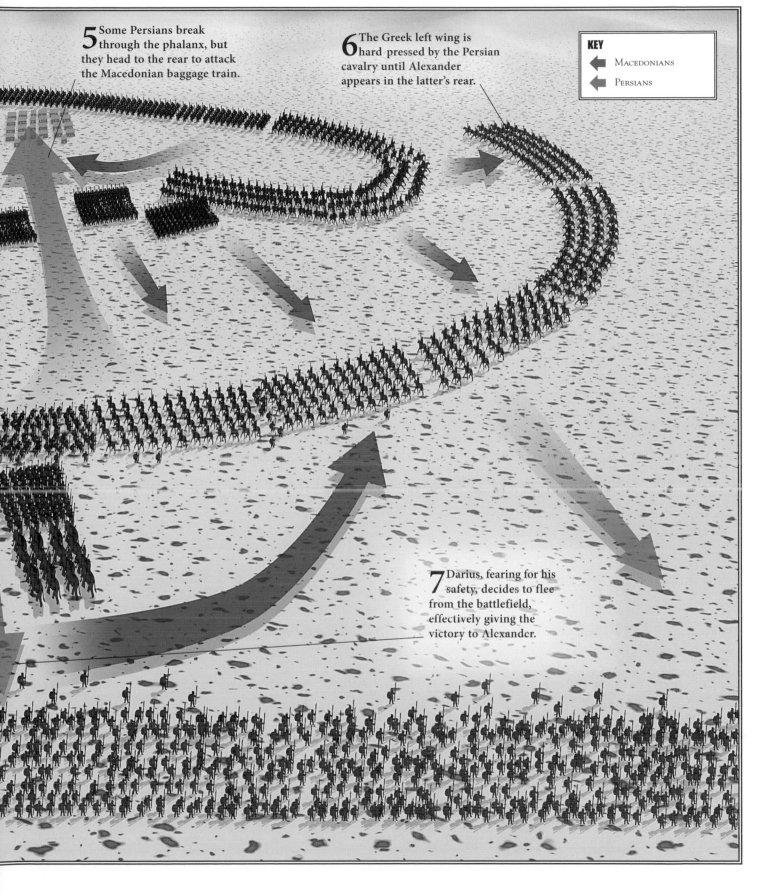

5 Some Persians break through the phalanx, but they head to the rear to attack the Macedonian baggage train.

6 The Greek left wing is hard pressed by the Persian cavalry until Alexander appears in the latter's rear.

KEY

← MACEDONIANS

← PERSIANS

7 Darius, fearing for his safety, decides to flee from the battlefield, effectively giving the victory to Alexander.

Hydaspes   326 B.C.E.

THE BATTLE OF THE HYDASPES RIVER WAS A TACTICAL MASTERSTROKE, ALEXANDER OUTFLANKING THE SUPERIOR INDIAN FORCE AND INFLICTING A SEVERE DEFEAT.

Alexander's ambitions drew him ever eastward, adding new territories to his empire as he went. His force of veteran infantry and cavalry was becoming increasingly war-weary as they approached India. They had defeated every foe they encountered, but were deep in unfamiliar territory and facing a highly organized and well-equipped army under the command of King Porus.

ALEXANDER CROSSES THE HYDASPES

Porus chose to take up a defensive position behind the Hydaspes River. He did not need to defeat Alexander decisively, only to keep him out of his territory. His intent was to prevent a crossing of the Hydaspes, which would be entirely sufficient to achieve his strategic aims. He was also operating at the end of a shorter supply line than Alexander and could afford to outwait his opponent. Never one for inaction even if he could afford to remain static, Alexander

INDIAN WAR ELEPHANTS *engage with Alexander's forces at the Hydaspes River in this Dutch Golden-Age painting by Nicolaes Berchem (1620–83 C.E.).*

BATTLE FACTS

Who: A Macedonian army probably numbering around 44,000 under the command of Alexander the Great (356–323 B.C.E.), opposed by 35,000 Indian troops loyal to King Porus (d. 317 B.C.E.).

What: Alexander distracted his opponent and crossed the river unopposed before attacking the Indian force.

Where: The Hydaspes River (now the Jhelum) in modern-day Pakistan.

When: June 326 B.C.E.

Why: Alexander intended to invade India and was opposed by the local ruler.

Outcome: Alexander won a complete victory but his army mutinied soon afterward, forcing him to withdraw westward.

ordered part of his army to demonstrate across the river from Porus while the majority made a crossing upstream. A thunderstorm helped conceal the movement, allowing Alexander to assemble his force and begin marching along the riverbank.

Knowing that his cavalry could not face Porus' war elephants, Alexander sent the majority of it against Porus' left flank, drawing reinforcements to the area. The Macedonian phalanx advanced against Porus' elephants, using their long pikes to good effect. The elephants were driven into the Indian infantry and created severe disorder.

ALEXANDER'S MASTERSTROKE

The remainder of Alexander's cavalry, which had made a flank march, attacked Porus' left-flank cavalry in the rear. Meanwhile, the Macedonian forces left on the far bank began to cross the river and join the fight. The Indian army, which had fought stubbornly, eventually collapsed.

King Porus himself was captured, but so impressed was Alexander with his conduct that he returned Porus to power as a client of Alexander's empire in much the same way that Alexander had installed some of his generals as rulers of conquered areas.

The weary Macedonian army demanded a return home soon afterward, and Alexander was forced to concede, bringing his great campaign of conquest to an end.

Trebbia   218 B.C.E.

AT THE TREBBIA RIVER, HANNIBAL BARCA EXPLOITED THE RASHNESS OF HIS EAGER OPPONENT TO OVERCOME THE FIGHTING POWER OF THE ROMAN LEGIONS.

Having successfully crossed the Alps and won an engagement against Publius Scipio at the Ticinus River, Hannibal was set to advance deep into Italy, perhaps even on Rome itself. This derailed plans to send legions to invade North Africa and thereby take the war to the Carthaginians. Instead the forces originally intended for the expedition were hurriedly sent north under Sempronius to reinforce Scipio's command.

OVERCONFIDENCE

Although Scipio had already been bested by Hannibal, Sempronius was confident. A successful skirmish with the Carthaginian advance guard seemed to confirm his sense of superiority. Scipio counseled caution but Sempronius sought glory. Correctly reading his character, Hannibal provoked Sempronius by sending cavalry to attack the Roman camp. Sempronius gave orders to pursue the

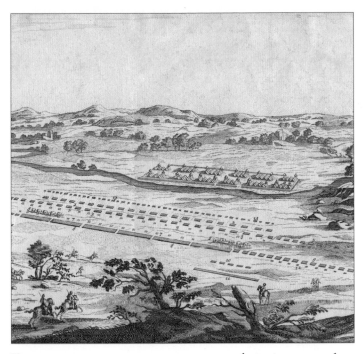

THIS EIGHTEENTH-CENTURY ILLUSTRATION *depicts in very neat form the Carthaginian and Roman armies lining up for battle beside the Trebbia River. The reality of ancient warfare was much messier.*

BATTLE FACTS

Who: A Roman army consisting of four Roman and four allied legions under the command of Publius Scipio (d. 211 B.C.E.) and Tiberius Sempronius Longus (260–210 B.C.E.), opposed by the army of Carthaginian general Hannibal Barca (247–182 B.C.E.).

What: The Roman force attacked across the Trebbia River and was drawn into a trap

Where: The Trebbia River southwest of Piacenza, in modern-day northern Italy.

When: December 218 B.C.E.

Why: Hannibal intended invading Italy, and needed to eliminate the army sent to stop him.

Outcome: The Roman force was decisively defeated in what was at the time the worst defeat ever suffered by Rome.

Carthaginians as they retired, which necessitated crossing the icy Trebbia River. As the chilled Romans advanced, Hannibal's force retired before them, wearing down the Romans with missile fire. Hannibal's superior cavalry, along with his war elephants, defeated the Roman cavalry and thus exposed the Roman flanks to attack.

Although it was by now apparent that things were going badly awry, Sempronius forged ahead. His lead elements were able to make some progress, but much of the Roman force became disorganized and trapped against the river. Perhaps unaware of this, Sempronius continued his advance and despite exhaustion from crossing the river his legionaries were eventually able to penetrate the Carthaginian center.

DISASTER FOR ROME

A force of cavalry and light troops, until now concealed in a ravine, attacked the Roman rear. Although Sempronius and his immediate command, perhaps 10,000 legionaries, were able to break through the Carthaginian force and fight clear of the disaster the remainder of the army was cornered and methodically worn down.

In all, perhaps two-thirds of the Roman force was lost, with many killed as they tried to escape back across the river. Most of those who survived the massacre were in small groups that had become detached in the fighting and managed to escape under cover of darkness and foul weather.

THE SITE OF THE BATTLE AT CANNAE TODAY. *Stand on the ridge above the river as Hannibal must have done and let your imagination conjure up the enthusiastic Romans rushing into the trap.*

Cannae 216 B.C.E.

THE DOUBLE ENVELOPMENT IS A DIFFICULT TACTIC TO PERFORM SUCCESSFULLY. ON THIS OCCASION, HOWEVER, HANNIBAL'S PLAN WORKED PERFECTLY AND DELIVERED A CATASTROPHIC DEFEAT TO THE ROMAN ARMY. AS A RESULT THE DOUBLE ENVELOPMENT, OR PINCER ATTACK, IS SOMETIMES REFERRED TO AS THE "CANNAE MANEUVER".

The Second Punic War between Carthage and Rome ran from 219 to 202 B.C.E. and ended in defeat for Carthage, but the early years of the war were a desperate time for Rome. The talented and ruthless Carthaginian general, Hannibal Barca (247–183 B.C.E.), launched a successful invasion of Italy by the unlikely overland route, humiliating the Roman army with several major victories. Hannibal, however, wanted an even more decisive triumph to drive Rome's allies away and to push his campaign forward. Despite the many battles he had already fought, he still commanded a powerful force of 40,000 infantry and 10,000 cavalry, who were experienced and confident. In order to draw out the Romans, Hannibal occupied the supply base at

BATTLE FACTS

Who: A Roman Consular army numbering 80,000 infantry and 7,000 cavalry under Consuls Paulus and Varro, opposed by a Carthaginian army of 40,000 infantry and 10,000 cavalry under Hannibal.

What: Hannibal lured the Romans into attacking his position. His center gave way, drawing the Romans in while they were outflanked and attacked in the rear.

Where: Near Canosa, in the province of Bari.

When: August 2, 216 B.C.E.

Why: During the Second Punic War (218–202 B.C.E.) between Rome and Carthage, Hannibal wanted a decisive victory to further his campaign in Italy.

Outcome: Hannibal's plan was an unqualified success and the Roman army was shattered in defeat.

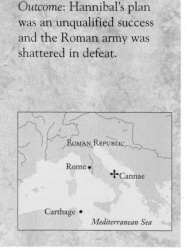

Cannae. When a massive Roman army moved into the area to attempt its recapture, he deployed for battle very close to the Roman camp, daring his enemies to come out and fight. This move was well judged. Two consuls, Varro and Paulus, commanded the Roman army, which numbered 80,000 infantry and 7,000 cavalry. The consuls alternated command each day. Varro was known to be reckless and so Hannibal chose to goad him into giving battle. In this he was successful; Varro ordered his army to deploy for battle on August 2, 216 B.C.E.

ROMAN LINES

The Romans deployed in their standard manner, with lightly equipped *velites* (light infantry) in front, backed by more heavily armored legionaries. Allied Italian infantry flanked the Roman contingent. Roman cavalry held the right wing, allied horsemen held the left. Hannibal deployed his forces behind a screen of light troops, concealing the dispositions of the bulk of his army. His infantry were placed in a crescent formation, bowed out toward the Romans. Light Numidian cavalry were arrayed on the right, with heavy cavalry on the left. Faced with a superior number of better-equipped infantry, Hannibal's center was in grave danger of being driven in. He was not too worried about this.

In fact, he was counting on it. As Hannibal had predicted, the Roman infantry rolled forward, intent on crushing the inferior troops in front of it. The *velites* pulled back, allowing the legionaries to engage. The crescent of Carthaginian swordsmen was flattened out and then driven in, encouraging the Romans to push onward, deeper into the enemy formation. In fact, Hannibal had ordered his swordsmen to give ground, though they had little choice in the face of the enormous Roman steamroller that faced them. As the main line conducted its fighting retreat, the light troops that had made up the screen reformed on the flanks and to the rear.

Meanwhile Hannibal's cavalry advanced and encountered its Roman opposite numbers. The heavy cavalry was successful in driving off the Romans it engaged, and was able to detach a sizeable force to attack the rear of the Romans' allied cavalry. Even as the Roman commanders were sensing victory and committing ever more troops to the center of the line, the light Carthaginian infantry was swinging around to close the flanks while their cavalry attacked the Roman rear.

Surrounded on all sides, the Romans were pushed

HANNIBAL AND HIS ARMY *parade through the streets of a captured Italian town. Roman influences are obvious in the armor and equipment of the Carthaginian troops.*

together so tightly that many could not raise their weapons. Some realized in time that their overconfidence had caused them to march into a death trap and began trying to cut their way free. Some 8,000 men managed to escape the slaughter. The rest were massacred.

Rome committed eight of its own legions and eight of its allies, adding up to approximately 80,000 men. About 55,000 were killed, including the Consul Paulus, 80 senators, and 21 tribunes. Another 10,000 soldiers were captured. Several cities withdrew from alliance with Rome after the battle, and morale in Rome itself fell ever lower.

However, although Hannibal had utterly smashed a Roman army for the loss of fewer than 6,000 men, and achieved a useful political result, he was unable to follow up his victory because he did not have the siege equipment necessary to capture Italy's walled cities. He was thus forced to continue campaigning in Italy. Rome remained undefeated and would eventually return to the ascendant under the generalship of Publius Cornelius Scipio (236–184 B.C.E.).

CARTHAGINIAN INFANTRYMAN

In the early clashes with Rome, Carthaginian spearmen had strong Greek influences, but changes were taking place by the time of Hannibal's campaign into Italy. The spearman shows the influence of contact (and conflict) with Rome. His spear is shorter than it would have been a few years previously, and a large oval shield slung from the left shoulder protects him. By turning to the right, he can place his shield in front of him, though it is not as mobile as a shield carried entirely on the arm. He carries a dagger or short sword as a backup weapon.

27

CANNAE

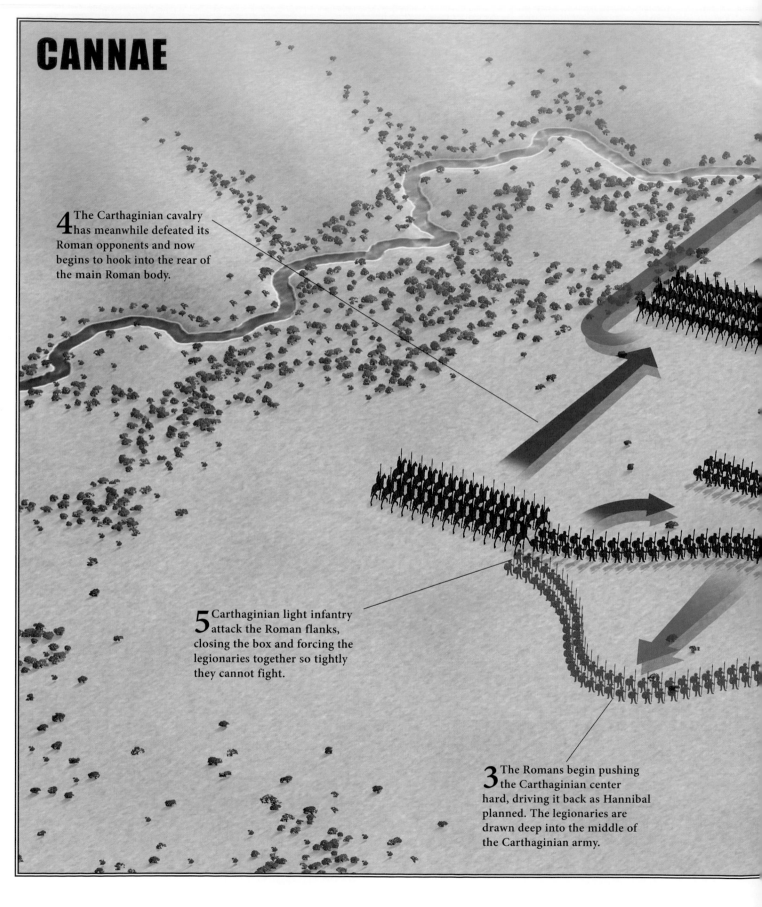

4 The Carthaginian cavalry has meanwhile defeated its Roman opponents and now begins to hook into the rear of the main Roman body.

5 Carthaginian light infantry attack the Roman flanks, closing the box and forcing the legionaries together so tightly they cannot fight.

3 The Romans begin pushing the Carthaginian center hard, driving it back as Hannibal planned. The legionaries are drawn deep into the middle of the Carthaginian army.

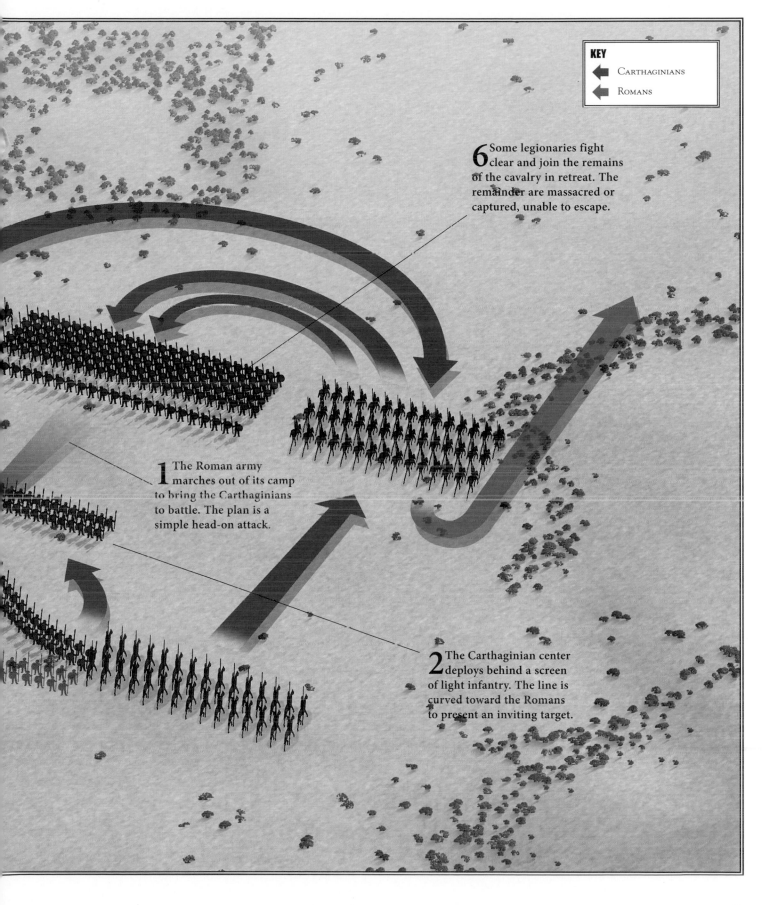

KEY

⬅ CARTHAGINIANS

⬅ ROMANS

6 Some legionaries fight clear and join the remains of the cavalry in retreat. The remainder are massacred or captured, unable to escape.

1 The Roman army marches out of its camp to bring the Carthaginians to battle. The plan is a simple head-on attack.

2 The Carthaginian center deploys behind a screen of light infantry. The line is curved toward the Romans to present an inviting target.

GERMANIC WARRIORS CHARGE *a Roman legion from the cover of a forest. The concentrated warrior charge relied on momentum to be successful. At Aquae Sextiae, Roman discipline proved superior.*

Aquae Sextiae 102 B.C.E.

AT AQUAE SEXTIAE, GAIUS MARIUS EXPLOITED HIS OWN OPPONENTS' AGGRESSIVE FIGHTING STYLE AND HIS LEGIONS' TACTICAL FLEXIBILITY TO WIN A DECISIVE VICTORY.

The Roman military system evolved over time. The early Greek-style hoplite army was replaced by a more flexible system of legions but this, too, was subject to change. The burden of military service had originally fallen on well-off citizens who could afford to arm themselves properly. This worked well enough at first but as Rome's power grew its military commitments did likewise. The absence of Rome's citizen-soldiers from their businesses and estates was financially harmful to the state and to individuals, and service became increasingly unpopular.

Among the reforms implemented by Gaius Marius was a new system whereby any citizen could be recruited and would be armed to the appropriate standard at the expense of the state. He would also be paid from the state's coffers, and subject to a rigorous training regime that not only turned recruits into formidable fighters but also trained soldiers to work as part of a tactical unit.

The new system of recruitment was implemented in 107 B.C.E., unofficially at first. Marius also did away with as

BATTLE FACTS

Who: A Roman consular army and supporting troops of 40,000 men, commanded by Gaius Marius (157–86 B.C.E.), opposed by more than 100,000 Germanic tribesmen.

What: The Germanic warriors were drawn into an uphill attack, which was halted and then successfully counterattacked by the well organized Roman forces.

Where: Aquae Sextiae in what is now southern France.

When: 102 B.C.E.

Why: Marius' army was ordered to prevent the migration of the Germanic Teutones tribe from becoming a threat to Rome.

Outcome: The Teutones were decisively defeated and prevented from migrating into northern Italy.

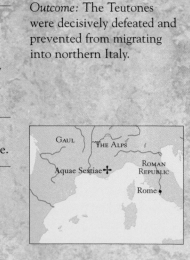

much of the baggage train as possible, improving mobility in the field. This naturally meant that troops had to carry more, earning them the nickname "Marius' Mules."

TRIBAL MIGRATIONS

Marius was given command of an army raised under the new system and sent to protect Rome's frontiers against the threat posed by migrating Germanic tribes. The Teutones, Ambrones, Cimbri, and Scythians were all on the march, with tens of thousands of warriors available to them. Rome had been sacked by Gauls in 390 B.C.E., and Marius was tasked with ensuring it did not happen again.

The threat posed by these tribes was both severe and ambiguous. They moved in groups of varying sizes, and not always predictably. Roman forces were defeated in 107 B.C.E. and 105 B.C.E., implying that the Germanic tribesmen had the ability to cause severe damage if they chose to enter Italy.

MARIUS PREPARES

In 102 B.C.E., the Ambrones and the Teutones began marching directly toward Italy. Marius was ordered to stop them, and took up a blocking position in a fortified camp. There, his force was attacked by the Teutones and repulsed them. This was what Marius wanted; his army was inexperienced and the Germanic tribes were renowned for their ferocity. By engineering a fight on his own terms Marius demonstrated to his troops that they could win against the tribesmen, improving morale for the decisive battle to come. Unable to eliminate Marius' position the Teutones bypassed it and marched onward toward Italy.

THE BATTLE

Marius' force broke camp and pursued their Germanic opponents. The legions' training regime had included long marches, and now this paid off in terms of superior strategic mobility. Marius overtook the Teutones and positioned his force to meet them at Aquae Sextiae.

While the legionaries built their usual fortified camp, troops sent to obtain water became involved in a skirmish with Teutones doing the same. The fighting escalated, with the Romans coming off best. Marius' troops spent the night in their camp and deployed for battle the next day.

Marius knew that his opponents were good fighters but used somewhat basic tactics. He thus drew up his main force at the top of a slope while a detachment was sent on a flank march. Marius himself led from the front rank much like a tribal chieftain, though his force was much more disciplined and his tactics more sophisticated.

The Teutones, true to form, charged up the hill at Marius' waiting legionaries, who hurled their *pila* down to meet them. As the Germanic warriors struggled up the slope they became tired and their advance disjointed, whereas the countercharge led by Marius was as disciplined as it was ferocious.

The Teutones were pushed back down the hill in a close-fought hand-to-hand struggle. Driven back to level ground, they formed a shield wall. The Romans struggled to penetrate the hedge of spearpoints and barricade of interlocked shields until Marius' flanking force arrived in the enemy rear.

ROMAN VICTORY

Once disrupted by the flanking force's charge, the shield wall broke up. This handed the advantage back to the Romans. As the Teutones broke and fled, Marius' men burned their camp and ruthlessly killed large numbers of noncombatants.

The destruction of the Teutones at Aquae Sextiae removed a significant threat to Rome, but other tribes were still advancing toward Italy. Marius fought another action at the plain of Vercellae soon afterward, winning a victory that secured the safety of Rome.

ROMAN HASTATUS

Equipped with pila *(heavy throwing spears) and a* gladius *(a short stabbing sword), the* hastatii *formed the front line of the legion and engaged the enemy first. If necessary, these troops swapped position with the similarly equipped but more experienced second rank of* principes, *resting until the time came to engage again. Thus Roman organization ensured that fresh, supporting troops were always available to shore up the defense or exploit enemy weakness.*

VERCINGETORIX THROWING HIS WEAPONS AT THE FEET OF CAESAR, *Lionel-Noël Royer's (1852–1926) painting offers a romanticized view of the Gallic leader's surrender.*

Alesia   52 B.C.E.

CAESAR'S VICTORY AT ALESIA, WHERE ROMAN SKILL AT MILITARY ENGINEERING ENABLED HIM TO DEFEAT A VAST GALLIC ARMY COMING TO RELIEVE THEIR CHIEFTAIN VERCINGETORIX, BESIEGED IN THE TOWN, SECURED ROMAN RULE IN GAUL. BUT FOR ALL HIS FORTIFICATIONS, CAESAR HAD A HARD FIGHT TO CONTROL THE TERRITORY.

In 59 B.C.E., Gaius Julius Caesar was elected consul in Rome. He used his position and political connections to secure his appointment as the governor of Cisalpine and Transalpine Gaul and Illyricum at the conclusion of his consulship. Over the next five years he waged a number of successful, if sometimes close-run, campaigns in Gaul, forcing many of its tribes to submit to him, at least temporarily. Moreover, Caesar also launched campaigns across the Rhine and twice invaded Britain.

Despite Caesar's success, there was definite unrest in Gaul, which began to manifest itself in late 54 B.C.E. At the beginning of 52 B.C.E., the Gauls then began a coordinated general rebellion aimed at expelling Roman rule. The revolt began early in the year with the massacre of Roman citizens living at Cenabum, city-state of the

BATTLE FACTS

Who: Gaius Julius Caesar (100–44 B.C.E.), with an army of 45,000 men, besieged an army of around 70,000 Gauls under Vercingetorix of the Arverni (d. 46 B.C.E.) and faced a relief force reputed to number 250,000 warriors.

What: Caesar made use of the Roman skill at siege warfare by constructing lines of siege works facing both inward and outward and Roman discipline to defeat threats from both the besieged and relieving forces.

Where: Alesia, some 30 miles (48 km) northwest of modern Dijon in France.

When: Late September/early October 52 B.C.E.

Why: Caesar sought to defeat Vercingetorix's threat to Roman rule once and for all.

Outcome: The defeat of the charismatic Vercingetorix and the sizeable forces mustered for the battle ended the Gauls' ability to resist the Roman empire.

Carnuntes tribe. This signal inspired the Gauls, and a young, charismatic noble of the Arverni, Vercingetorix, to put together a coalition of tribes and place a significant army in the field.

In the subsequent battles, both sides experienced victory and defeat. Caesar moved into the territory of the Bituriges and took their major stronghold, Avaricium, but Vercingetorix defeated a six-legion attempt to take the capital of the Arverni at Gergovia. Yet it became clear to Vercingetorix that his forces could not stand up to Caesar's in open battle, and in September he decided to fall back on the fortified town of Alesia, building a fortified camp nearby. Caesar concluded that Alesia and the Gallic camp were far too strong to be assaulted, and so decided instead to surround and blockade the town, constructing extensive siege works and fortifications both to trap the town and protect against attacks from an expected relief force.

THE BATTLE
The Gallic relief force arrived as predicted and, after having camped within a mile of the Roman lines, made an attack. There was an initial, brutal clash between opposing cavalry on a nearby plain, but the Roman and allied cavalry took the field. The Gauls of the relief force, therefore, spent the following day preparing the materials needed for a major assault, including ladders, grappling hooks, and fascines. At midnight, they quietly advanced and, once near the Roman siege works, gave a shout to let the besieged know they were beginning the assault—Vercingetorix now led out his forces from Alesia at the same time, so that the Romans would be engaged to front and rear. Yet the Gauls were unable to penetrate the Roman lines and, fearing a counterattack, retreated.

The Gauls now held a council of war, and decided to use their main army to threaten the siege works, while a force of 60,000 picked men attacked a Roman camp on the north side of the town. This camp was defended by two legions, but due to the nature of the terrain, it lay outside of the lines of circumvallation.

Meanwhile Vercingetorix would again lead an attack, so the Romans would be forced to defend both the inner and outer defenses against simultaneous assaults. Some 60,000 Gallic warriors from the relief force marched through the night to get into position, resting until noon, at which point they attacked. At the same time Vercingetorix pushed out from the town against the inward-facing fortifications. Caesar was compelled to reinforce the camp after its defenses were broken in places, eventually repulsing the Gauls when he personally led some troops to the breach. He then launched a desperate counterattack, while also ordering his cavalry to sally out and assault the Gallic warriors from behind. Although the Gauls put up a fight, the appearance of cavalry behind them was too much and they were routed. The besieged Gauls were dismayed by this turn of events and retired into Alesia.

With the defeat of their relief army, the Gauls within Alesia were forced to surrender. Vercingetorix was handed over to Caesar. Some of the Gauls were used to help gain the loyalty of their tribes, but many were distributed to the troops as booty and became slaves. The victory at Alesia effectively broke Gallic resistance, although Caesar would spend the next two years consolidating his position. Vercingetorix remained a prisoner for some six years until, after having been paraded in Rome during Caesar's great triumph, he was publicly strangled.

BALLISTA

In the third century B.C.E., the Romans began adopting Greek siege-warfare technology. The ballista was a new version of the stone-throwing lithobolos. The frame and base were now sturdier, the holes through which the rope was inserted and the washers by which it was secured went from being square in earlier models, to an oval shape. This allowed more rope to be used in the springs and these were also twisted tighter. The springs were now exclusively made of sinew, much stronger than the old horsehair versions. All of this gave the machine much greater range and accuracy.

ALESIA

6 The men inside Alesia coordinate their attacks with the relief army, but are defeated by Caesar's Germanic cavalry.

5 A large relief army of about 250,000 men arrives, and makes three serious attempts to lift the siege of the town.

KEY

■ ROMAN FORCES

◄ GALLIC FORCES

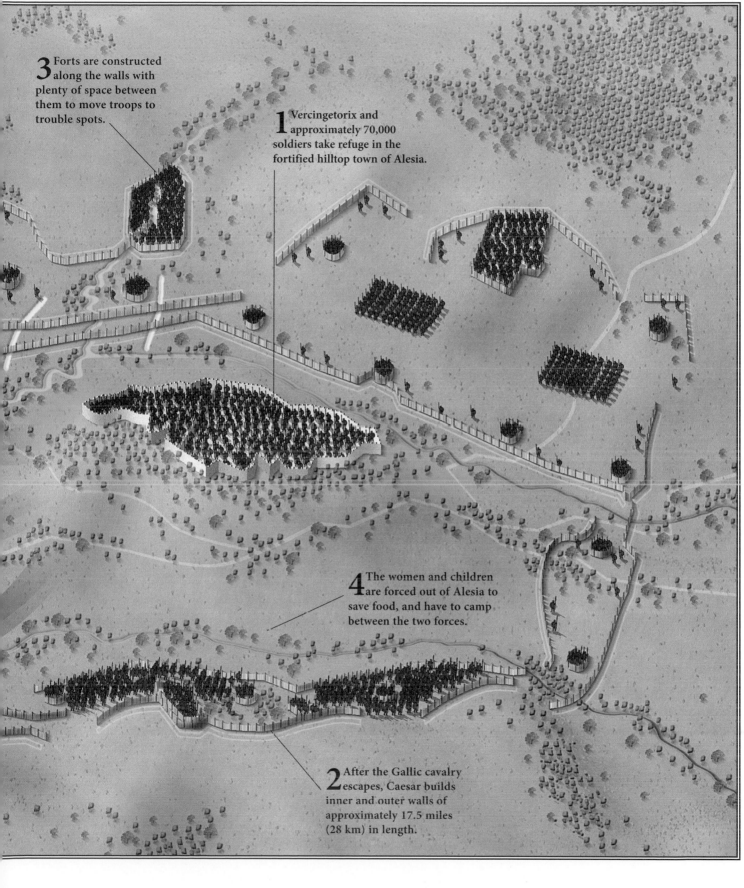

3 Forts are constructed along the walls with plenty of space between them to move troops to trouble spots.

1 Vercingetorix and approximately 70,000 soldiers take refuge in the fortified hilltop town of Alesia.

4 The women and children are forced out of Alesia to save food, and have to camp between the two forces.

2 After the Gallic cavalry escapes, Caesar builds inner and outer walls of approximately 17.5 miles (28 km) in length.

THIS RATHER FANCIFUL *illustration in a classical style shows Crassus and his cohorts losing the Battle of Carrhae to the Parthians. An unmounted Parthian archer attacks the Romans from the left.*

Carrhae 53 B.C.E.

THE DEFEAT OF MARCUS LICINIUS CRASSUS AND SEVEN ROMAN LEGIONS AT THE HANDS OF THE PARTHIANS HASTENED THE END OF THE THIRD TRIUMVIRATE.

When Marcus Licinius Crassus landed in Syria in late 55 B.C.E., his motivation for raising an army and leading it against the Parthians, a powerful people from neighboring Persia, was primarily to gain the prestige of winning a battlefield victory and conquering an apparently invulnerable foe. Although he had accumulated vast personal wealth and a share of power with Julius Caesar (100–44 B.C.E.) and Pompey (106–48 B.C.E.), Crassus had not achieved the fame that accompanied military triumphs.

When Crassus marched against the Parthians, he commanded 35,000 foot soldiers in seven legions and about 8,000 cavalry, some of whom had been provided by Artavasdes, the king of Armenia, who further advised him to advance through the Armenian mountains rather than taking a more direct route across the inhospitable desert of Mesopotamia. Crassus shrugged off the warning and the offer of an additional 16,000 cavalry and 30,000

BATTLE FACTS

Who: Roman legions under the command of Marcus Licinius Crassus (115–53 B.C.E.) against the Parthian army of General Surena (84–52 B.C.E.).

What: The Parthians defended their kingdom against Crassus, who was bent on conquest.

Where: Near the town of Carrhae in what is now eastern Turkey.

When: 53 B.C.E.

Why: Crassus intended to

cross the desert and bring the main Parthian army to battle, winning fame and riches for Rome as he plundered cities along his line of march.

Outcome: The Roman legions were decimated by a Parthian army a quarter of its size as Surena skillfully employed his horse archers and heavy cavalry called *cataphracts*.

infantry, crossed the mighty Euphrates River at Zeugma, and accepted misleading directions from Ariamnes, an Arab who was secretly loyal to the Parthians.

THE "PARTHIAN SHOT"

As Crassus marched into the arid desert, the Parthian king, Orodes II, attacked Armenia with the bulk of his army in retaliation for Artavasdes' support of the Romans. Orodes II detailed a force of 10,000 cavalry under General Surena to delay the legions of Crassus. Surena commanded 9,000 horse archers, expert bowmen who were capable of firing to their rear as well as forward, giving rise to the familiar phrase "Parthian shot," and 1,000 *cataphracts*, heavy cavalrymen armed with lances and well protected by extensive armor.

Ignoring pleas for assistance from the Armenians, Crassus was nevertheless shocked to encounter the small army of Surena in the vicinity of the town of Carrhae. Gaius Cassius Longinus (85–42 B.C.E.), one of his subordinate commanders, advised a traditional deployment with cavalry on the flanks and infantry in the center. Instead, Crassus formed a battle square with ranks as deep as 12 men. Recklessly, he advanced into battle with a tired command that was tightly formed and immobile.

The Parthian horse archers harassed the Roman formation and rained arrows on the densely packed legionaries, whose armor and shields were rather ineffective in stopping the missiles, resulting in scores of wounded and dead. Each time Crassus advanced, the swift horse archers dashed to safety, flinging arrows as they went. Frustrated, Crassus ordered

his troops to join shields, presenting an interlocking front in the *testudo* formation. This maneuver invited repeated charges by the *cataphracts*, who slaughtered the Romans in great numbers. When Crassus abandoned the *testudo*, his soldiers were once again subjected to the withering fire of the Parthian archers.

DISASTER

Crassus found himself surrounded but ordered his son, Publius (82–53 B.C.E.), to charge the enemy archers before the ring was closed. Publius followed the retreating Parthians into a trap, and his force of more than 1,200 was annihilated by the *cataphracts*. Publius was decapitated, his head displayed on the end of a spear. As the fighting ebbed, the beaten Romans were finally able to withdraw to Carrhae.

The following day, Surena invited Crassus to negotiate terms for an end to the battle. Although he offered the surviving Roman troops safe passage back to Syria in exchange for renouncing claims to lands east of the Euphrates, an argument broke out. Crassus and the Roman delegation were killed to a man.

At Carrhae, the worst Roman defeat since Cannae in 216 B.C.E., Crassus lost at least 30,000 soldiers. His own death marked the end of the First Triumvirate and contributed to the outbreak of civil war between Julius Caesar and Pompey. Cassius managed to escape the debacle at Carrhae and was a principal conspirator in the assassination of Julius Caesar in 44 B.C.E. Surena was later executed by the jealous Orodes II.

PARTHIAN HORSE ARCHER

The Parthian horse archer used a recurved bow similar to the Huns. A horse archer typically held arrows in his left hand ready for use because this was quicker than reaching to a quiver. The archer could shoot at any point in the horse's stride, but at the top of the rise in a canter, with all four hooves off the ground, was the optimum moment for accuracy.

Teutoburg Forest 9 C.E.

"QUINCTILIUS VARUS, GIVE ME BACK MY LEGIONS!" WAILED EMPEROR AUGUSTUS CAESAR UPON RECEIVING THE NEWS OF A DISASTROUS MILITARY DEFEAT IN FAR-OFF GERMANIA. IN THE TEUTOBURG FOREST, THREE ROMAN LEGIONS, 25,000 STRONG, HAD BEEN ANNIHILATED. AUGUSTUS FEARED NOT ONLY A THREAT TO THE ROMAN EMPIRE, BUT ALSO THE END OF 40 YEARS OF TERRITORIAL EXPANSION.

T he Roman disaster at the Teutoburg Forest began in the fall of 9 C.E., with a message. Although by this time the Romans appeared to have gained control over Germania's previously unruly tribes, the northern Roman province was monitored carefully by a garrison of three Roman legions, plus around 800 cavalry. Presiding over these forces was Germania's governor, Publius Quinctilius Varus. Two years after his appointment, the governor was encamped with his legions west of the

BATTLE FACTS

Who: Germanic tribes led by Arminius (17 B.C.E.–21 C.E.) versus three Roman legions and support troops under Publius Quinctilius Varus (46 B.C.E.–9 C.E.).

What: A confederation of German tribes ambushed the Roman legions in the dense forest and annihilated them in a series of ambushes over a number of days.

Where: Teutoburg Forest, Lower Saxony, near modern-day Osnabrück, Germany.

When: September 9–11, 9 C.E.

Why: The Germanic tribes intended to avoid domination by the expanding Roman Empire.

Outcome: The Roman legions were destroyed, Varus committed suicide, and Germania remained free from Roman rule thereafter.

Weser River for the summer. In early September, possibly as the legions were relocating to winter quarters near the Rhine, word reached Varus that an insurrection was gaining momentum farther to the west.

Delivering this alarming news was a trusted adviser, Arminius, a member of the Cherusci tribe. In fact, Arminius had secretly turned on his Roman overlords, fostering an alliance with several Germanic tribes to strike a blow against imperial Rome. The plan was simple. The false news of the rebellion would provoke Varus to march out with his forces. Along the route of march, on ground favorable to the tribal coalition, the Germanic soldiers would crush the column in an ambush.

After directing Varus along an unfamiliar route on September 9, Arminius excused himself, telling the governor he intended to recruit friendly men to assist the Roman legions. Yet despite being warned of the deception, Varus chose to press forward. His column, which included women, children, and camp followers, became stretched out on the journey in an undisciplined fashion, eventually entering the dense and hill-studded Teutoburg Forest.

THE TRAP IS SPRUNG

Here, the waiting tribesmen unleashed their ambush, closing with the enemy from out of the forest. Roman casualties were horrific, but miraculously some semblance of order was regained. The Romans camped in a defensive position on a wooded hillside, and the following day they even forced an opening in the Germanic cordon that surrounded them. For a time, the column succeeded in reaching open country, but soon enough they were deep in the forest once again, their cavalry unable to screen a retreat due to the thick vegetation. Casualties on the second day were even higher than those of the first. Attempting to defend themselves, the legionaries found their swords, javelins, and shields so waterlogged by the torrential rains that they could hardly wield them.

Apparently, Arminius had anticipated the next move by Varus. Slogging through the night, the surviving Romans reached the foot of Kalkriese Hill.

OFTEN FIGHTING IN CLOSE RANKS, Roman legionaries relied on their long spears to keep an enemy at bay. Their short swords were put to use during close combat.

Unwittingly, they had marched into a hopeless position. Hemmed in by the heights on one side, an extensive area of marshes on another, and trenches and a large wall of earth thrown up by the tribesmen on a third, the fate of the Romans was sealed. Their tormenters assailed them from the cover of the wall and trenches and from a distance along the flanks. As a desperate attempt to breach the wall ended in failure, the Roman cavalry led by Numonius Vala, second in command to Varus, fled the field, only to be hunted down and slaughtered by Germanic horsemen. Some Roman soldiers suffered the ignominious fate of becoming prisoners. Others, wrote ancient historian Cassius Dio, chose suicide: "Varus, therefore, and all the more prominent officers, fearing that they should either be captured alive or killed by their bitterest foes, for they had already been wounded, made bold to do a thing that was terrible yet unavoidable. They took their own lives."

Arminius' deception had precipitated the Roman debacle in the Teutoburg Forest, but the ineptitude of Varus had compounded it. Three legions had been wiped out, and their numeric designations would never be used again. Roman prisoners were ransomed, sold into slavery, or sacrificed to pagan gods. The Germanic warriors had suffered few casualties.

During the coming months, Arminius put numerous Roman outposts east of the Rhine to the torch. Seven years of conflict followed, but Germania remained free of Roman domination for the next 400 years. In the end, it was the Roman Empire that declined and fell.

Masada   73 C.E.

THE DEFIANT STAND OF FEWER THAN 1,000 JEWS WHO CHOSE SUICIDE RATHER THAN SUBJUGATION BY THE ROMANS REMAINS SOMETHING OF A MYSTERY.

As tensions between the Jews and the Roman occupiers of Palestine erupted into open conflict in approximately 66 C.E., the Sicarii, a faction of Jewish Zealots, took control of Masada, a plateau that rose as high as 820 ft (250 m) above the desert floor near the banks of the Dead Sea, fortified as a potential haven from unrest by King Herod the Great (74–4 B.C.E.) more than a century earlier. Under the leadership of Eleazar ben Ya'ir, the Sicarii, which translates from the Hebrew as "Knife Men," sometimes raided the surrounding countryside but refrained from direct participation with other armed Jews in the defense of Jerusalem, which was under siege for a prolonged period.

THE SIEGE
Following the capture of Jerusalem, Lucius Flavius Silva realized that the Jews holding out at Masada presented the last appreciable resistance to Roman preeminence in Palestine. He marched the X Legion to Masada in 73 C.E.,

THE MIGHTY HILLTOP FORTRESS of Masada as seen from the air today. Daunting though it appears, Roman siege techniques were up to the task of assaulting such a strong, defensible position.

BATTLE FACTS

Who: Jewish Zealots led by Eleazar ben Ya'ir were confronted by the might of the Roman X Legion under Lucius Flavius Silva.

What: After the capture of Jerusalem, the Romans marched to Masada to capture the seemingly impregnable fortress originally built by Herod the Great.

Where: The heights of Masada near the Dead Sea in Palestine.

When: 73–74 C.E.

Why: Flavius sought to crush the last bastion of Jewish resistance to Roman rule in Palestine.

Outcome: The Romans breached the fortifications at Masada and attacked the following day only to find the bodies of nearly 1,000 Jews who had chosen death rather than submit to Roman rule.

determined to capture the imposing heights. It was apparent that his troops could not ascend to the fortifications of Masada along the single narrow path known as the "Snake" that led up from the desert floor. Therefore, the commander initiated a pair of ambitious construction projects.

First, Flavius built a high wall, stretching 3 miles (4.8 km), 6 ft (1.8 m) thick in some places and with watchtowers at intervals of 60–80 ft (18–24 m), to protect his besieging force from attack by the Jews. Then, he employed slave labor to construct a large ramp ascending the northwestern escarpment of Masada. With the completion of the ramp in 74 C.E., the Romans were able to bring up heavy siege equipment to assault the fortifications. The Roman *ballistae* hurled heavy stones at the walls, and their battering rams succeeded in making a breach. The Jews quickly constructed a wooden wall to impede the Romans, who set this second barrier afire.

MASS SUICIDE

Although the interpretations of modern historians differ as to the events that followed, the only account of the Battle of Masada that is contemporary is that of Josephus, a former member of the Jewish resistance who had been captured and managed to save himself by praising the combat prowess of the Romans. Traveling with them at Masada, Josephus recorded what he apparently saw. However, his version of the final hours at Masada is the subject of continuing theory and conjecture.

Josephus asserted that the Romans had destroyed the wooden wall and then rested for the night, certain that their conquest of Masada would be completed in short order the following morning. Meanwhile, Eleazar was reported to have exhorted the Jewish defenders to choose death rather than slavery. He was said to have ordered all possessions to be burned and the men to kill their families. Then, ten men were to be chosen by lot. These men were to kill all the others, with one of the ten then killing the other nine and finally committing suicide. According to Josephus, the Romans attacked the next day as planned but found the lifeless bodies of more than 900 Jews. Josephus was said to have been told this account by two women, who survived the slaughter along with five children by hiding in a cistern.

Although much of Josephus's story has been verified by modern archeologists, including evidence that suggests the burning of the wooden wall and the name of Eleazar himself on a shard, which might have been used when the lots were cast, questions remain as to the authenticity of the whole account. Nevertheless, for many modern Jews Masada has become a symbol of defiant resistance to the enemies of Israel. At Masada, organized Jewish opposition to Roman dominion in Palestine came to an end.

ROMAN SIEGE TOWERS

Roman siege towers were built as large as they needed to be for the task at hand. The one used to storm Masada was 99 ft (30 m) high, though smaller towers were usually sufficient for lesser fortifications. Roman towers mounted a variety of weapons including rams and siege artillery, as well as bridges to reach the wall tops.

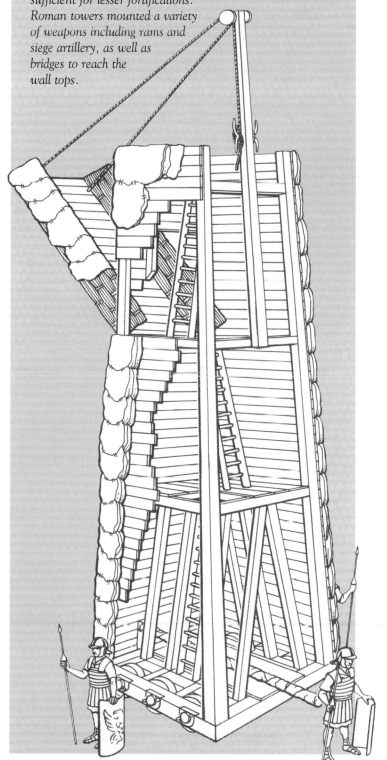

THIS DRAMATIC DETAIL from the Ludovisi Sarcophagus (c.250–260 C.E.), shows Roman troops in a life-or-death struggle with barbarian invaders.

Adrianople   378 C.E.

DESCRIBED BY THE SOLDIER AND HISTORIAN AMMINAUS MARCELLINUS AS THE WORST ROMAN MILITARY DISASTER SINCE THE INFAMOUS DEFEAT AT CANNAE, THE BATTLE OF ADRIANOPLE SAW THE FIELD ARMY OF THE EASTERN ROMAN EMPIRE VIRTUALLY DESTROYED AND THE EMPEROR KILLED. ADRIANOPLE BECAME A LANDMARK GOTHIC VICTORY IN CENTURIES OF WARFARE.

I n 376 C.E., two Visigothic chieftains, Fritigern and Alavivus, made a request to the Eastern Roman Emperor Valens to cross the Danube and settle on the Roman side of that great river. Valens consented, seeing in the Goths a potential source of military manpower and imperial revenue, but relations between the Goths and the Romans irrevocably broke down, and descended into open warfare. In 377 Roman Thrace was devastated in the fighting, and Valens himself marched out with an army, eventually about 30,000 strong, to crush the rebellious Goths. In early August 378 he came upon Fritigern's forces, encamped in a large laager formed from wagons about 10 miles (16 km) from Adrianople (modern-day Edirne, in Turkey).

BATTLE FACTS

Who: The Eastern Roman Emperor Valens (d. 378) with an army of 20,000 men faced a slightly smaller army of Goths under Fritigern.

What: The Goths took advantage of the impetuous advance by the Romans and the serendipitous arrival of the Gothic cavalry (who had been away foraging) to catch the Romans between the Gothic fortified wagon laager and their returning Gothic horsemen.

Where: Near Adrianople in modern-day Edirne, Turkey.

When: August 9, 378 C.E.

Why: The Goths, driven west by the Huns, invaded Thrace to take by force supplies the Romans had promised them but withheld.

Outcome: The battle was a devastating tactical defeat for the Romans, who lost more than 60 percent of the eastern field army.

Even before battle was joined, Valens made some critical mistakes. He refused to wait for Roman reinforcements, already on the march, to join him. He immediately deployed his troops ready for battle—his cavalry on the wings and infantry in the center—but without giving them adequate time for food, water, and rest after the long march. He also became embroiled in negotiations with the enemy, which were actually designed to buy time for Gothic cavalry forces to reinforce Fritigern's foot army. Unbeknown, Valens was sowing the seeds of disaster.

DEVASTATION

At first light on August 9, Valens led his army out, marching in columns. Yet even now events began to slip out of Roman control. Two units of Roman cavalry, including one of archers, which had been skirmishing with the Goths, launched an unexpected and ill-considered attack against the wagon laager. These skirmishers, who may have been formed on the army's right, were probably neither in the proper formation for such an attack nor would they have had the necessary supporting troops. As a result, they were forced to retreat. At that very moment, the Gothic cavalry made their return to the battlefield and charged impetuously into the Roman ranks. It appears that the Gothic horsemen attacked the units of the cavalry on the left flank, who were still strung out while they moved into position. The Roman cavalry were hard-pressed by the Goths, and those who had made their way as far as the Gothic laager found themselves without support from the other Roman troopers, who had not yet reached their assigned positions.

As a result, the Roman cavalry were quickly and decisively defeated. No doubt this played havoc with the Roman infantry, who were still attempting to form themselves into a line of battle. The defeat of the cavalry on their left created a large gap in the Roman line, a gap which the Gothic cavalry were quick to exploit. At this point in the battle, frontline Roman infantry units found themselves engaged with the Gothic infantry, but with the defeat of the skirmishers and the left-wing cavalry, the Roman infantry found themselves attacked not only from the front but also in

A GOLD COIN of Roman emperor Valens (reigned 364–378 C.E.), later converted into a necklace. Valens was one of the last Roman emperors to appear on coins in civilian garb.

the flank by the Gothic horsemen. The fighting was incredibly fierce, but the excellent Roman infantry fought on, even as those in the front found themselves pressed together so tightly that it became difficult to make proper use of their weapons.

The battle went back and forth for a considerable period of time, and the combat was a close-run affair. But after repeated attacks, and exhausted not only by fighting but by the heat, hunger, and the weight of their armor, the Roman lines began to give way. Valens took up position with two legions, the *Lanciarii* and *Mattiarii*, which were still holding out, but then even the Roman reserves began to flee, including the elite Batavian auxiliaries.

All resistance broke and a general rout ensued. The Goths pursued, which led to the destruction of two-thirds of the Roman army. As the army began to disintegrate, Valens was wounded by an arrow. His body was never found and he is assumed to have died on the battlefield. One tradition had him and a small group of bodyguards falling back to a farmhouse with a well-fortified second story.

Valens' Roman guardsmen fiercely defended their wounded emperor, but the Goths eventually burned the place to the ground with the occupants inside, a final act in an unmitigated Roman disaster.

ROMAN AUXILLIARY

By the time of the Battle of Milvian Bridge in 350 C.E. the appearance of the Roman soldier had changed dramatically from when the empire was at its peak. This figure is armed with a long spear and carries a long sword more suitable to the cutting strokes favored by the Germanic auxiliaries in Rome's service than the gladius. His shield is oval, made of wood with a leather or linen covering, and has a metal rim and boss. He wears a simple iron helmet made in two halves and joined in a central ridge, with flexible cheek pieces. He wears no armor, relying on his shield for protection. Instead of the Roman sandal, he wears a hobnailed boot.

THIS DRAMATIC NINETEENTH-CENTURY PAINTING *by Carl von Steuben (1788–1856) depicts Charles Martel leading the Franks in a heroic stand at Tours/Poitiers.*

Tours/Poitiers 732 C.E.

THE BATTLE OF TOURS/POITIERS WAS A TURNING POINT IN WORLD HISTORY, ONE THAT AFFECTED THE CULTURAL DEVELOPMENT OF WESTERN EUROPE. IT WAS HERE THAT THE TIDE OF MUSLIM CONQUEST WAS TURNED BACK, WITH ENORMOUS LONG-TERM IMPLICATIONS FOR THE FUTURE OF EUROPEAN CHRISTENDOM.

From the early seventh century C.E., Muslim Arabs began a seemingly inexorable expansion out from the Middle East and into Asia and Europe. By 713 Spain had fallen to the Arabs, and in 730 the then Arab leader, Abd-ar-Rahman, launched a successful expedition over the Pyrenees into the Duchy of Aquitaine, breaking its power and reducing its strongholds. The kingdom of the Franks further north, effectively ruled by its greatest prince, Charles Martel ("The Hammer"), was now directly threatened. Yet Charles was one of the leading military innovators of his age. Although he did engage in various campaigns between 720 and 732, he was well aware of the threat from the southeast and had begun to create an army to defeat it. This is typical of the man—he did not rush in to fight his foes but instead worked out how they

BATTLE FACTS

Who: A force of Franks under Charles Martel (688–741), versus a seemingly superior army of Muslim Moorish cavalry under Emir Abd-ar-Rahman (d. 732).

What: The Frankish infantry established itself in a defensive position and awaited attack by the Moorish cavalry. After a hard-fought battle the Franks emerged victorious.

Where: Between modern Tours and Poitiers in France.

When: October 10, 732.

Why: Muslim forces had taken Iberia and were spilling over the Pyrenees mountains to conquer more of Europe. They were opposed by the Christian Franks.

Outcome: A decisive victory for the Franks. Charles Martel made his reputation in this battle. The Moorish commander was killed and his army retired to Spain.

could be beaten before offering battle. The core of Charles' strategy against the invaders was the creation of a force of elite heavy infantry, professionals capable of training all year round. (This was not the practice of the time; other than small bodyguards, fighting men were normally raised for a campaign then went home to their farms afterward.) Charles equipped his professionals lavishly and protected them with good armor. He trained them well and allowed them to gain experience in combat, increasing their confidence and steadiness. He did have some mounted troops but cavalry was not much in use in Europe at that time and they lacked stirrups. These mounted soldiers, who were not true cavalry and could not stand against the excellent horsemen of the Moorish Caliphate, were used as a mobile reserve or simply dismounted to fight. Now they would be tested against one of history's most successful conquering armies.

BLOCKING POSITION

As the Arabs pushed on toward the Loire River, winning further victories, Charles marched his force to intercept them. The exact location at which he established his blocking position is unclear, but it lay somewhere between Poitiers and Tours, hence the fact that the battle is known to historians by two names.

The advancing Muslims stumbled upon Charles' force in its blocking position in early October 732, and paused for six days to allow Rahman to gather intelligence. Rahman had under his command between 40,000 and 60,000 victorious cavalry, and had every confidence that he would break the Franks' large defensive square formation, which had reserve units inside.

FRANKISH SHIELD WALL, *mid-eighth century. The troops are mainly spearmen, although some hold axes and swords. The formation depended on the mutual support of the men within it for its strength.*

On October 10, the battle began. The Moorish cavalry made repeated charges, and on several occasions groups of Moorish horsemen fought their way into the Frankish square. Yet reserve forces within the square fell on them— infantry rushed confidently up to attack armored cavalry, something that rarely happened and was even less often successful—and killed them or drove them out. Eventually the assaults abated, and the Frankish square was battered but intact.

Meanwhile, some of Martel's scouts had managed to get into the Moorish camp during the battle, taking advantage of overconfidence on the part of the enemy. There they freed prisoners and generally caused mayhem. This confusion in their rear, coupled with the worry that their hard-won plunder might be stolen back by the Franks, drew many of Rahman's troops back to the camp and severely disrupted the attack on the Franks' square. Rahman tried to stop the rearward movement, but in so doing exposed himself with an inadequate bodyguard—he was killed by Frankish soldiers. The Moors were dismayed and they withdrew from the battlefield in some disorder, the Franks choosing not to pursue, despite still retaining considerable power.

The Battle of Tours/Poitiers has at times been lauded as the only reason Europe is not a Muslim state and a part of the Arab Empire. While this is an exaggeration, it is fair to say that Charles deserved "The Hammer" nickname, which was conferred on him for handing the Muslim expansion such a dramatic defeat. Expeditions over the Pyrenees would continue, and Charles Martel would oppose them for the rest of his life. The Muslim occupation of Iberia also lasted for many centuries, and advantage ebbed and flowed between Muslim and Christian forces in southwestern Europe. The Battle of Tours/Poitiers was, however, the point at which the easy Muslim victories ended.

THE NORMAN ARMY *on the Bayeux Tapestry consists of cavalry and archers. The archers have an exaggerated presence because of their role in the death of King Harold.*

Hastings   1066

NORMAN MOUNTED MEN-AT-ARMS MET THE ANGLO-SAXON SHIELD WALL IN THE LONGEST, HARDEST-FOUGHT, AND MOST DECISIVE BATTLE IN ENGLAND IN THE EARLY MIDDLE AGES. WILLIAM THE CONQUEROR'S VICTORY CHANGED ENGLISH HISTORY FOREVER, AND USHERED IN THE DOMINANCE OF THE MOUNTED KNIGHT THROUGHOUT EUROPEAN WARFARE.

On September 28, 1066, an invasion force of the Norman Duke William, some 7,000 men strong, landed at Pevensey Bay in Sussex, southern England. News that William had landed reached Harold II, England's king, at York on October 1, in the middle of celebrations following a victory over the Vikings at Stamford Bridge. Harold rushed south via London, gathering an army of 6,000–7,000 troops on the way. It was late in the afternoon on October 13 that Harold reached Senlac Ridge near Hastings, a location that he had, during the summer's idleness, chosen as a possible battleground (the Norman invasion had been long expected). Senlac was a gently sloped ridge with a marsh area to the south around the Asten brook, and with its

BATTLE FACTS

Who: William, Duke of Normandy (1028–87), invaded England with an army of 6,000 men to lay claim to the throne of King Harold II Godwinson (1022–66), who faced him with an army of 6,300.

What: Norman cavalry and archers eventually wore down the Saxon shield wall formation.

Where: Senlac Ridge, 7 miles (11 km) north of the town of Hastings, southeast England.

When: October 14, 1066.

Why: William wanted to conquer England and claim himself a kingdom he felt was his right by birth.

Outcome: Harold and most of the Anglo-Saxon nobility were killed in the battle, and William secured the throne of England.

western and eastern flanks protected by deep ravines covered by thick brushwood. An even steeper ridge protected the northern side and would thus prevent the Normans attacking Harold's army in the rear.

William marched out to meet Harold. He divided his army into three divisions, with the Bretons as the vanguard, followed by the Franco-Flemish troops, and then, finally, William leading his own Normans. William had chosen as the assembly point the Blackhorse Hill, on the Hastings to London road, where the Bretons arrived by 7:30 A.M. Here, out of sight of the Saxons, William left his baggage train and ordered his men to put on their mail hauberk armor, which they had slung across the back of their horses. The Norman army then marched north to take up position opposite the Saxons.

BATTLE OF ATTRITION

Sharp trumpet blasts at 9 A.M. on October 14 announced the beginning of the battle, as William's three divisions advanced up the slope of Senlac Ridge. The Bretons were the first to reach Harold's lines, but by 10:30 A.M. they had retreated, being unable to break through. William dispatched a charge of armored knights to assist, cutting down large numbers of Saxon infantry, and saving his army from disaster. He then regrouped and personally led a second attack at 11 A.M. The ground was slippery from the previous attack and littered with dead men and horses, so progress was slow and hesitant.

Waves of attacks were launched against the shield wall for two hours, but again the attacks were beaten off. At 2 P.M. William recalled his men and returned them to his own lines below the ridge, to regroup, rest, and eat. Harold used this respite to shorten his thinning line because Saxon losses, whatever the Normans may have thought, had been considerable and Harold was worried he would run out of men to plug the ever-rising number of holes in the line. But at least his men were more rested than the Normans, who faced an ever more debris-ridden and cluttered slope as they prepared for a renewed attack.

Having lost one-quarter of his army—around 1,800–1,900 men—in five hours of almost continuous fighting, as well as a horrendous number of horses cut down by the axe-

SAXON HUSCARL

The huscarls were an oath-sworn bodyguard of the Anglo-Danish aristocracy, which ruled England prior to the Norman Conquest of 1066. This man wields a long-handled axe, with which he could decapitate a horse. He has slung his kite-shaped shield on his back to allow him a double-handed grip for extra weight in the blow.

wielding Saxons, William saw that many of his men-at-arms were now fighting on foot. He decided that the whole army would attack in a single formation of all arms combined.

FINAL ASSAULT

The third and final attack saw the entire army advance with archers at the back, from around 3 P.M., at a slow pace. It took the Normans an agonizing half-hour to reach the Saxon line, but now the Saxon shield wall began to waver, break in places, and then come apart under the Norman onslaught. Once a hole had been created in the wall the Norman cavalry poured through and, with their lances, swords, and spears, tore at the soft underbelly of the Saxon army. After 4 P.M. the flow through the breach became unstoppable and the fighting degenerated into group actions and hand-to-hand combat.

A large group rallied around Harold's standard as William joined his men on the ridge. Harold led his men with customary tenacity and courage, setting a personal example for his huscarls. But there were not enough of them to fight back the Normans. The final straw for the Saxons was the death of Harold himself. He was cut down by the Normans leading his few remaining huscarls. Both sides had lost more than 2,000 men, the Normans well over one-third of their army. For William, however, it was a triumph against the odds that paved the way for his being crowned king of England on December 25, 1066.

THE MOST FEARSOME MILITARY TACTIC *of the Middle Ages was the cavalry charge, as demonstrated here by Norman horse. At a time when success in battle often depended more on forcing one's enemies to flee the battlefield than on actually killing them, resisting such a charge depended on the discipline of lower-class infantry troops.*

HASTINGS

5 Harold attempts to regroup his infantry into a new shield wall. William launches yet another, more ferocious assault, and Harold is hit in the eye with an arrow and slain. The remaining English retreat from the battlefield, giving the Normans victory.

1 Harold Godwinson orders his troops into a shield wall along the top of Senlac Ridge, with his heavier huscarls positioned in the center.

3 The Breton infantry on the flank retreat and the English troops break their shield wall to chase them from the battlefield. However, under William's command, the Norman cavalry cut down the pursuing Saxon infantry.

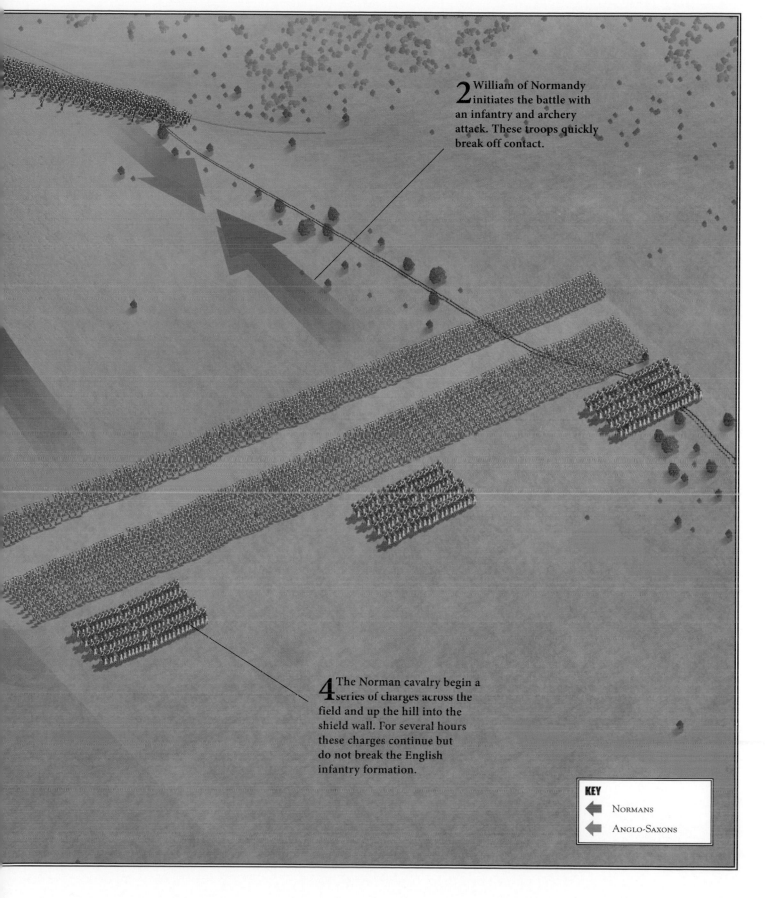

2 William of Normandy initiates the battle with an infantry and archery attack. These troops quickly break off contact.

4 The Norman cavalry begin a series of charges across the field and up the hill into the shield wall. For several hours these charges continue but do not break the English infantry formation.

KEY

← NORMANS

← ANGLO-SAXONS

THE DEFEATED CRUSADERS OFFER THEIR ARMS after the catastrophic defeat at Hattin. The defeat prompted the launch of the Third Crusade, which recaptured Acre in 1191.

Hattin   1187

HATTIN WAS A GREAT VICTORY FOR SALADIN, WHO USED HIS FASTER, LIGHTER FORCES TO IMPRESSIVE EFFECT. HE WAS ASSISTED TO A LARGE EXTENT BY HIS ENEMY, KING GUY, WHO CHOSE TO MARCH HEAVILY ARMORED TROOPS THROUGH A WATERLESS REGION AT THE HOTTEST TIME OF THE YEAR.

I n the 1180s, the divided Frankish leaders in Outremer (a combination of Christian Palestine and Syria) were faced with the expanding threat of the Arab warrior Saladin who, by 1187, had managed to bring Egypt and Syria under his control. On July 1 that year, Saladin then besieged the fortress of Tiberias with about 20,000 men, and the Christians decided to act in concert. A 13,000-strong force was assembled, commanded by Reynald of Chatillon (circa 1125–87), Raymond III of Tripoli (1140–87), and King Guy (of Lusigan) of Jerusalem, and it marched out to face the Muslim army in June 1187.

The opposing armies were of a very different character. The forces of Saladin consisted of light infantry armed with spears, shields, and a formidable type of bow and arrow. The cavalry, armed with bow and lance, were mainly

BATTLE FACTS

Who: Christian forces under King Guy versus the Saracen army of Saladin, Sultan of Egypt (1138–93).

What: The Christian army, harassed by the mobile Saracens and ineptly led by King Guy—(reigned 1186–92)—was defeated.

Where: The Horns of Hattin, near Tiberias, located in present-day Israel.

When: July 4, 1187.

Why: The Christian army marched with intent to relieve the besieged fortress of Tiberias.

Outcome: The army of King Guy suffered terribly and was completely destroyed by the Saracens. Saladin was able to capture the Crusader port of Acre, cutting off the Christian Kingdom of Jerusalem from the sea. In September Saladin laid siege to Jerusalem, and by October 2 had captured the Holy City.

Askari, skilled horsemen from Syria and Egypt. In contrast, the Christian forces consisted of some 1,200 heavily-armored mounted knights, 10,000 infantry armed with spears and slow-firing crossbows, and a small complement of Turcopoles, mounted-archer mercenaries whose services had been financed by King Henry II of England. While the knights themselves were superb shock troops—given the proper circumstances—the Christian force lacked its adversary's speed and mobility.

ADVANCE TO OBLIVION

Rather than attacking the Christians directly, Saladin hoped that by besieging the fortress at Tiberias he would draw Guy out to fight in the open. Raymond, however, urged caution. Reinforcements were expected from Antioch, while water and food were plentiful at Acre. Nevertheless, Guy felt obliged to march to the relief of Tiberias. Failing to grasp the implications of his decision, the king ordered his army forward. On the night of July 2, 1187, the Christian force camped at Sephoria, near a good source of water. While Raymond continued to plead for restraint, others, including Reynald of Chatillon, agitated for a continuing advance.

Guy knew that an army of heavily armored soldiers and their hundreds of horses could not possibly traverse the Plain of Toran, where there was no water, then approach Tiberias directly and take on the Saracens without having their fighting efficiency seriously degraded. Ignoring Raymond, he chose a calculated risk. The army was to proceed to Tiberias across the Wadi Hamman, where a source of water was supposed to be found.

On the morning of July 3, the parched Christian force renewed its advance, playing into Saladin's hands. As the Christians neared the Horns of Hattin, a double-hill formation within sight of the Sea of Galilee, Saladin sent a strong force sweeping behind Guy to seize the vital spring at Turan and cut off Guy's escape route. Rather than fully engaging, the Saracens stood off and rained arrows on their hapless enemy.

As the sun rose on July 4, a panic gripped the Crusader infantry, who broke in a desperate effort to reach the Sea of Galilee. Hemmed in by Saladin's troops, they were forced onto the eastern horn. Those who were not killed

THE BODIES OF DEAD CRUSADERS, pierced repeatedly by Muslim arrows, lie in a heap with a crucifix among them. A dove and circle of stars, depicting the Holy Spirit, hover above.

were taken prisoner. With its infantry screen decimated, the knights had little choice but to attack. If they remained stationary, their horses would be easy marks for Muslim bows.

Raymond gallantly led about 200 knights in a bold charge, hoping to break out of the cordon, but the mobile Saracens merely flexed and allowed the heavy Christian cavalry to shoot its bolt. Wounded three times, Raymond managed to escape with a few of his number. The majority of the knights, however, were trapped on the western horn. Three more desperate charges proved futile, and the dwindling force collapsed around the tent of King Guy.

At last, the exhausted defenders capitulated. Among Saladin's prisoners were several nobles, Reynald, and Guy himself. About 200 Knights Templar and Hospitaller, sworn enemies of the Saracens, were beheaded swiftly. Saladin was said to have executed Reynald personally. Estimates of the Christian casualties are as high as 17,000. King Guy was eventually ransomed and set free. After his decisive victory at Hattin, Saladin quickly captured Acre and several other cities. Jerusalem fell on October 2, and news of these dramatic reversals shocked all of Christendom.

HATTIN

4 The heavy knights' charge fails to overcome the more flexible Arab skirmishing cavalry.

6 King Guy and the remaining knights halt at the western horn, which becomes the focal point of the Crusaders' last stand.

5 A portion of the Crusaders make a break for safety and manage to get back to Acre.

1 Despite being beset by skirmishing cavalry the Crusaders break camp and move off.

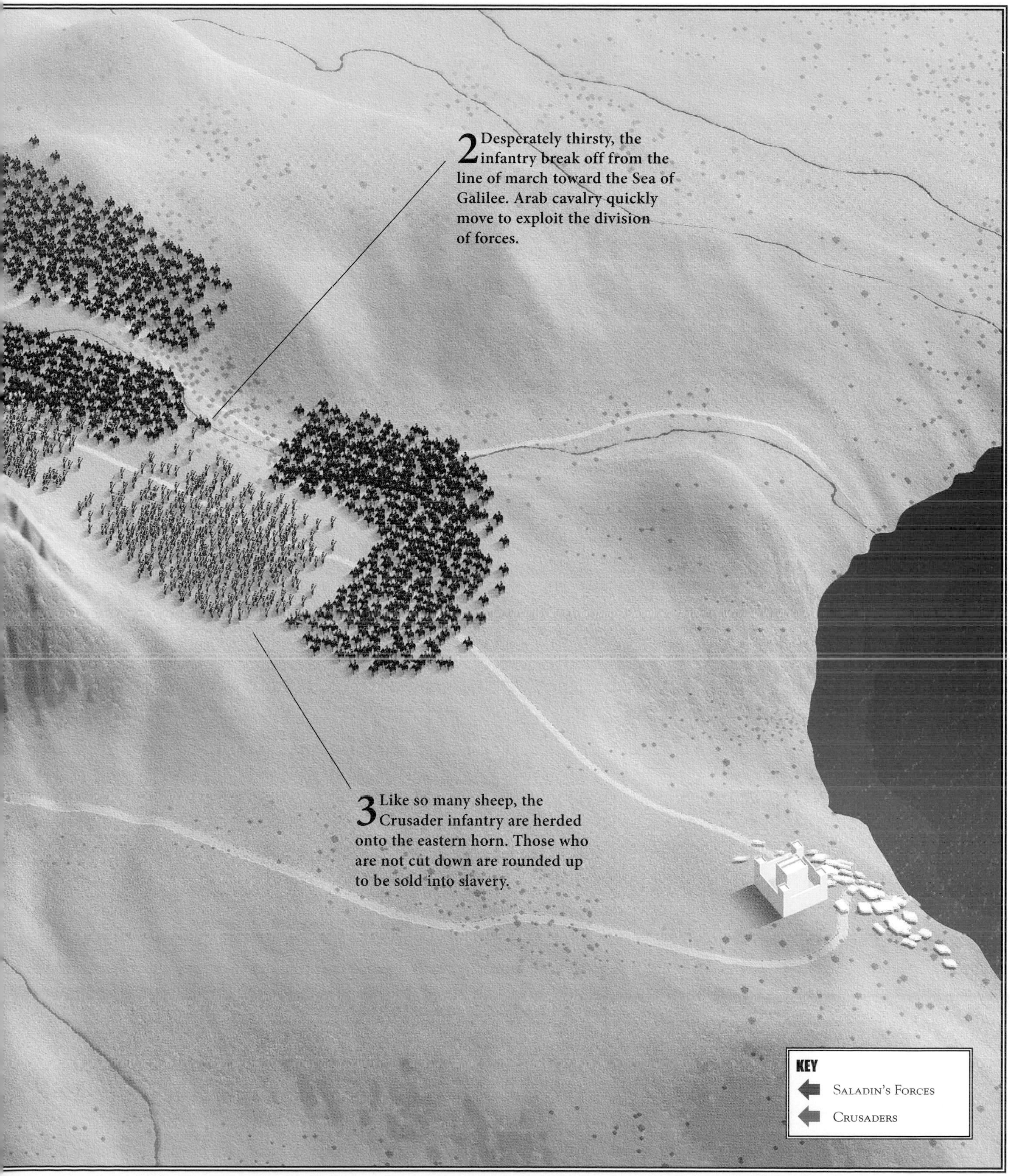

2 Desperately thirsty, the infantry break off from the line of march toward the Sea of Galilee. Arab cavalry quickly move to exploit the division of forces.

3 Like so many sheep, the Crusader infantry are herded onto the eastern horn. Those who are not cut down are rounded up to be sold into slavery.

KEY

◄ SALADIN'S FORCES

◄ CRUSADERS

Liegnitz 1241

A SMALLER MONGOL DIVERSIONARY ARMY INFLICTED A CRUSHING DEFEAT ON A FORCE OF EUROPEAN ALLIES, THREATENING THE KINGDOM OF HUNGARY FROM THE EAST.

When King Bela IV (1206–70) of Hungary refused to turn Cuman refugees over to the Mongols, Subutai (1176–1248), a renowned military strategist, planned the horde's invasion of Eastern Europe. By the spring of 1241, the Mongols had moved forward, their forces split into three armies.

Two of these, led by Subutai and Batu Khan (1207–55), were to attack Hungary directly, while a third, commanded by the trio of Baidar, Kadan, and Orda Khan, advanced into Poland to prevent interference from European armies intent on aiding the Hungarians. Estimates of the strength of the diversionary army vary from 8,000 to more than 20,000. Regardless, the Mongol warriors were superb fighters capably led by outstanding tacticians.

Believing the Mongols intended to advance further westward, Duke Henry II The Pious of Silesia gathered

THIS MEDIEVAL MANUSCRIPT ILLUMINATION *shows the European army of Duke Henry II suffering under a rain of missiles fired by the highly mobile Mongol horse archers. The Mongol composite bow proved decisive on the day.*

an army with an estimated strength of between 2,000 and 25,000. In its ranks were troops from various Polish states, Bavarians, Moravians, and a relatively few Knights Templar and Knights Hospitaller. Unconfirmed accounts include Teutonic Knights as well.

FEIGNED RETREAT

Aware that another European army was approaching, the Mongol diversionary army made contact with Henry on April 9. The Duke divided his forces into four sections and ordered three successive cavalry charges forward. Each of these was turned back by the Mongols, who feigned retreat and utilized a smoke screen to conceal the trap they were to subsequently spring.

The European cavalry and then the knights followed the fleeing Mongol vanguard, separating themselves from the support of their own infantry. Soon they were assailed by heavy Mongol cavalry from the front and swift light cavalry on both flanks. Mounted archers fired tremendous volleys of arrows into the confused Europeans, and the knights in their ponderous armor were slaughtered.

Henry was caught and beheaded during the disorganized European retreat that ensued. The total casualties suffered on each side are unknown, although the Knights Templar were said to have lost 500. After its victory, the diversionary army headed southward to rejoin Subutai, who had defeated the Hungarians at Mohi and then opted to retire eastward.

BATTLE FACTS

Who: The Eastern European army of Duke Henry II The Pious (1207–41) confronted the Mongol army of Baidar, Kadan, and Orda Khan (1204–51).

What: The Mongols sought a decisive battle with Henry's army before a second European force could join the fighting.

Where: Near the town of Liegnitz in Silesia.

When: April 9, 1241.

Why: The diversionary army of Baidar, Kadan, and Orda Khan screened the main

Mongol thrust into Hungary, while Henry attempted to aid the Hungarians and stop the Mongols' movement to the west.

Outcome: The Mongols employed the tactic of the feigned retreat and inflicted a decisive defeat on the Europeans.

Nicopolis 1396

THE FINAL MAJOR CRUSADE OF THE MIDDLE AGES ENDED IN HORRENDOUS DEFEAT FOR THE CHRISTIANS AT THE HANDS OF THE OTTOMAN ARMY IN THE BALKANS.

In the fall of 1396, a coalition army of Hungarian, French, and German knights along with troops from other European kingdoms joined forces at Buda and marched on the city of Nicopolis, occupied by the Ottomans. An Ottoman relief army of about 16,000 under Sultan Bayezid I marched along the Danube River in Bulgaria.

The Crusaders, whose numbers are uncertain but approached 15,000, had not achieved unity of command with the Hungarians under King Sigismund, the French led by Philip of Artois (1358–97), and others under leaders reluctant to relinquish control. On September 12, the Crusaders approached Nicopolis, laying siege to the town while Venetian warships patrolled the Danube.

When word reached the Crusader encampment that Bayezid was approaching, French nobleman Enguerrand de Coucy (1340–97) advanced 700 knights and archers toward the Ottoman vanguard. He ordered a feigned

HUNGARIAN KING SIGISMUND *retreats with his armored knights to boats waiting in the nearby Danube River. Although Sigismund escaped, many of the Christian rearguard were not so fortunate.*

retreat and then attacked from behind, killing or capturing a large number.

Philip subsequently denounced a battle plan formulated by Sigismund, which directed French knights to follow infantry into battle. Philip impetuously led the French ahead of any supporting troops and attacked. Initially successful, the French knights and mounted archers pressed on but encountered obstacles of pointed stakes. The Ottoman infantry retreated behind their cavalry. As the French finally topped a hill, they expected to see a retreating enemy but were confronted by the massed Ottoman horsemen, who rapidly counterattacked. Some French knights stood their ground and were killed or taken prisoner. Among the dead and captured were several noblemen.

CRUSADER DISINTEGRATION

At some distance, Sigismund was entangled with panicked, riderless horses and withdrawing Frenchmen. He fought to prevent an envelopment by the Ottomans advancing on his flanks, but soon his command disintegrated. Sigismund escaped the battlefield. However, Bayezid took up to 3,000 prisoners. Some of these were Frenchmen who had sacked the town of Rachowa and massacred its people en route to Nicopolis. In retribution, the Sultan ordered hundreds of prisoners executed.

With their victory at Nicopolis, the Ottomans prevented the unification of any European opposition for nearly 50 years and strengthened their grip on the Balkans.

BATTLE FACTS

Who: European crusaders led primarily by French noblemen and the Hungarian army under King Sigismund (1368–1437) against the Ottoman army of Sultan Bayezid I (1360–1407).

What: The final major crusade of the Middle Ages attempted to reverse the Ottoman expansion into Europe and relieve pressure on Constantinople.

Where: Near the city of Nicopolis on the Danube in what is now Bulgaria

When: September 25, 1396.

Why: The Europeans were wary of Ottoman military ambitions in Central Europe and were compelled to defend Christianity against the spread of Islam.

Outcome: The Ottoman army won a decisive victory and faced virtually no organized opposition in the Balkans for half a century.

THIS PAINTING BY POLISH ARTIST *Wojciech von Kossak (1824–99) gives a taste of the bloody battle, with the Royal Army in desperate hand-to-hand combat with the Teutons.*

Tannenberg 1410

THE DECISIVE BATTLE OF TANNENBERG, BETWEEN THE ARMY OF THE TEUTONIC KNIGHTS AND THE ROYAL ARMY OF POLAND-LITHUANIA, BROUGHT TO A HALT THE EASTWARD EXPANSION OF THE HITHERTO INVINCIBLE MILITARY ORDER AND SECURED THE INDEPENDENCE OF POLAND-LITHUANIA.

Founded in Acre in 1190 to defend the Holy Land, the Teutonic Order was a military order of warrior-monks which, by the beginning of the fifteenth century, ruled over much of Prussia and the Baltic States. Their power, however, brought them into conflict with their eastern neighbors, particularly the Poles, Lithuanians, and Russians, and in 1410 the Polish king (and former Grand Duke of Lithuania) Ladislas II Jagiello decided to act. He organized a combined Polish and Lithuanian campaign, supplemented by Russian and Tartar troops, and went to war against the Teutonic Knights.

Fighting, let alone defeating the Order, was no easy proposition for Jagiello because the Order's army had been victorious ever since its appearance in the region in 1230. Its heavy cavalry of men-at-arms clad in white

BATTLE FACTS

Who: The army of the Teutonic Order under their Grand Master Ulrich von Jungingen (d. 1410) fought the Royal Army of Poland-Lithuania under King Ladislas II Jagiello (circa 1350–1434).

What: The Royal Army of Poland-Lithuania, annihilated the more experienced and heavily armed Teutonic army.

Where: On a shallow grass plain between the East Prussian villages of Tannenberg and Grünwald.

When: July 15, 1410.

Why: The Royal Army were caught by surprise when the whole Teutonic army bore down on them but the Teutons squandered a great opportunity to secure a victory by not attacking first.

Outcome: The Polish-Lithuanian victory halted the Teutonic Order's eastward expansion and effectively broke its power.

surcoats with black crosses, numbering some 2,000–3,000 men, were probably the best in Europe and formed the superlative core of an outstanding military machine. With the technological progress of the fourteenth century, the Order had to supplement its knights with mercenaries and specialists such as English longbowmen, Genoese crossbowmen, German and Swiss infantry, and French artillery. All in all the army of the Order was a dangerous and formidable foe. By contrast the Poles and Lithuanians were far weaker and had less reason to be confident of a victory if faced with the grim German warrior-monks. The Poles had a conventional European-style medieval army of no particular distinction or reputation as yet. By contrast, the Lithuanian host, commanded by Grand Duke Witold (Jagiello's cousin), was more Asiatic than European in appearance, equipment, and tactics because they had fought for centuries against the Mongol occupiers of Russia. As a result, they placed great reliance upon skirmishing, maneuvering, and mobility with light and medium cavalry forces, rather than a head-on collision with heavy cavalry and massed infantry.

THE CAMPAIGN

Once the various military components had gathered together, the Polish-Lithuanian campaign began in earnest in early July 1410, with the Prussian frontier crossed on July 9. The opposing armies finally drew together on July 14, in a rough triangle of land between three small Prussian villages—Tannenberg, Grünwald, and Ludwigsdorf. The battlefield was shaped like a shallow soup plate measuring 1.9 miles (3 km) in diameter. Jagiello's combined army numbered 10,000–20,000 infantry and as many as 40,000 cavalry (including Tartar auxiliaries), while Ulrich von Jungingen, the Grand Master of the Teutonic Order, had 21,000 cavalry and a mere 6,000 infantry.

Ulrich wanted the enemy to make the first move but they—primarily the cautious and shrewd Jagiello—were reluctant to act. As the morning hours of July 15 wore on and his men grew impatient, Ulrich decided to goad the "cowardly" Poles and Lithuanians into action with diplomatic taunts, and eventually Jagiello gave the order to attack. The Poles advanced in good order on the left while the Lithuanians, Russians, and Tartars could not control themselves and threw themselves at the Germans, who buckled under the onslaught. The Teutonic knights counterattacked, and the Lithuanian army began to falter and retreat as the Tartars (either fleeing or executing a feigned retreat) moved out of range. Only Witold's central regiments held the line and Witold was forced, in person, to beg his cousin to save his flank.

Jagiello sent in his last remaining reserves, who managed to stem the Teutonic advance, but as the dust settled Ulrich noticed how exposed the Polish king was on a small knoll on the battlefield, and sent a force either to kill or capture him. The assassination attempt failed, for some alert Polish knights saw what was happening and moved to intercept the Teutons. Witold used this time to rally his men, who turned around and rode back to the center of the battlefield. It was the Teutons' turn to be caught unawares as Tartar arrows, Russian battleaxes, and Lithuanian swords cut at them. The Poles, having held their line, forced the Order's knights back and surrounded them. Ulrich, stubborn, proud, yet brave, chose like his men to stand and fight where they stood and as a consequence they were cut down. Few remained alive when the battle finally ended, at 7 P.M., at the village of Grünwald. Some 14,000 of the Order's knights and soldiers were taken prisoner while the rest lay dead or dying on the battlefield. The Teutonic Order had been truly humbled.

TEUTONIC KNIGHT

The roots of the Teutonic Order were military-monastic in the simple white garb with its equally simple cross as the only decoration on shield, uniform, and horse. The main strength of the order's military might was its mounted knights, who acted as the foremost offensive arm. They wore scale armor, instead of plated armor, to improve mobility, speed, and striking power in the face of ever better-equipped, better-disciplined, and better-led infantry armies. Tannenberg was a cavalry battle but one in which infantry and support forces played a vital role in the defeat of the hitherto invincible Teutonic Knights.

TANNENBERG

3 The Grand Master believes, with the enemy's right in disarray, that the time has come for a final push and sends a group of his toughest men to capture Jagiello. This lunge fails and with it any hope of a Teutonic victory.

6 The Order's army is completely wiped out with 18,000 dead littering the battlefield and the remaining 14,000 captured.

5 By afternoon the battlefield is a confusing tangle of struggling, dying, and wounded men fighting one another in close combat where no mercy is given or expected. One by one the Teutonic Knights are overwhelmed.

1 After the Teutonic emissaries' taunts at first light, the Polish-Lithuanian army advance across the open fields toward the Teutonic lines. Their left flank attack with abandon but are stemmed by heavy Teutonic Knights.

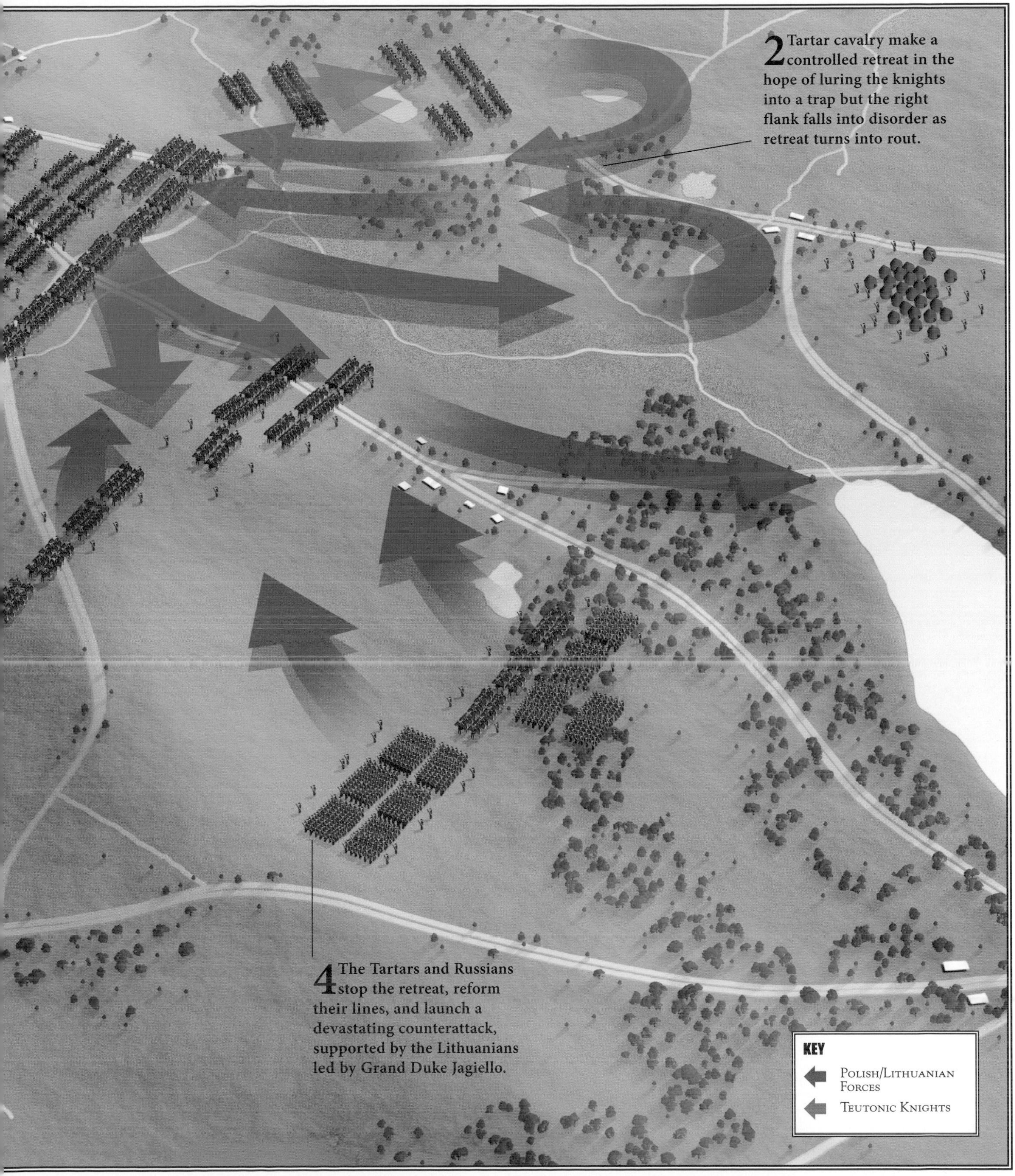

2 Tartar cavalry make a controlled retreat in the hope of luring the knights into a trap but the right flank falls into disorder as retreat turns into rout.

4 The Tartars and Russians stop the retreat, reform their lines, and launch a devastating counterattack, supported by the Lithuanians led by Grand Duke Jagiello.

KEY

POLISH/LITHUANIAN FORCES

TEUTONIC KNIGHTS

AN ENGLISH FOOT SOLDIER TAKES A FRENCH NOBLEMAN CAPTIVE *at the Battle of Agincourt. This image symbolizes the superiority that infantrymen could exercise over their social betters.*

Agincourt   1415

THE VICTORY OF HENRY V'S SMALL, EXHAUSTED, AND STARVING ARMY OVER A VAST FRENCH HOST WAS THE GREATEST TRIUMPH OF THE ENGLISH IN THE HUNDRED YEARS' WAR BETWEEN ENGLAND AND FRANCE. BUT DESPITE THE LEGENDARY LONGBOW ARROW-STORM, THE BATTLE CAME DOWN TO HAND-TO-HAND COMBAT, AND WAS FAR FROM A WALKOVER FOR THE ENGLISH.

T he Battle of Agincourt was the culmination of Henry V's invasion of France, which landed on French shores on August 13, 1415. Harfleur was the first English objective—it fell on September 22 following a long siege—and then Henry pushed northward toward Calais. However, a 20,000-strong French army commanded by the Constable of France, Charles d'Albret and Marshal Jean Bouciquat shadowed Henry's much smaller force, which consisted of about 1,000 knights and men-at-arms and 5,000 archers. This French army, and a flooded Somme River, forced the English soldiers on arduous detours in

BATTLE FACTS

Who: An English army of 6,000 under King Henry V (1388–1422) defeated a French army of 36,000 under the command of Charles d'Albret, Constable of France (1369–1415).

What: Agincourt saw a small, well-disciplined, and entrenched English army defeat a far larger French army through massed archery.

Where: Near the Castle of Agincourt, approximately halfway between Calais and Abbeville in northern France.

When: October 25, 1415.

Why: Henry sought to revive the English claim to the throne of France.

Outcome: Agincourt was the greatest English victory of the Hundred Years' War against France.

appalling weather. Finally, Henry realized he had no choice but to stand and fight, and he did so near the village of Agincourt, northwest of Arras.

Henry decided to extend the English line between the woods and hedges surrounding the villages of Maisoncelle and Tramecourt. Because the ground in front of the English line, fronted by a line of sharp stakes, had turned into a rain-soaked quagmire, the French attack would be slowed down and prove a most welcoming target for his archers. Conditions were ideal and Henry placed the dismounted men-at-arms in the middle of his battle line and the archers on the flanks. A confident French army drew up and readied itself for battle.

ST. CRISPIN'S DAY

After a long, cold night of torrential rain, the fields were even muddier as the sun rose on St. Crispin's Day—Friday October 25, 1415. The English had spent the night in the open, while the French had slept in tents and gorged themselves on wine and plentiful provisions. The French were sure that they would win an easy victory.

It was not to be. The English archers unleashed flights of arrows against the French ranks at extreme bow ranges, and the French responded with a cavalry charge that proved too puny—of 1,200 knights on horse only one-third (420 men) actually attacked. Their noble colleagues on foot were quickly in trouble as their heavy armor pulled them into the mud below. As they floundered and sunk into the mud up to their knees, Sir Thomas Erpingham, the English commander of the archers, gave the signal for an intensified rain of arrows. Thousands of arrows whined through the air like a cloud before hitting the target or plopping into the muddy

ground. Enough steel-tipped, armor-piercing bodkin arrows struck home to break up the French advance. Their effect upon the less-protected horses was terrifying and masterless horses, bleeding and neighing wildly, ran back into the French lines, trampling many dismounted knights into the mud.

The battle now descended into a confused and grim hand-to-hand combat. The English archers, and even camp followers, swarmed forward armed with axes, swords, and stiletto knives, preying on the less mobile armored knights. For three gruesome, bloody hours the slaughter went on as the French dead piled up in heaps in front of the English lines. There was a last-minute flurry among the French as the Duke of Brabant arrived in the afternoon—his presence came to nothing, and he was killed along with his men. Yet alarmed by this attack, and fearing that the scores of French prisoners already taken might return to the fight if there was another attack, Henry took no chances and broke all rules of chivalry by putting them to death where they stood.

There was no French rally. Instead, what remained of the French army fled the field of battle leaving thousands of dead, wounded, and captured to the less-than-tender mercies of the English. The English had lost a mere 112 men, two-thirds of them archers, and had won the most miraculous of victories against all the odds and expectations. The French death toll was as high as 10,000 men.

A month later Henry was back in England, his men were amply paid, and England celebrated that Day of St. Crispin, while the traumatized French simply referred to Agincourt as "that unfortunate day" (*la malheureuse journée*) for generations to come. The Hundred Years' War was nevertheless set to continue for another four decades.

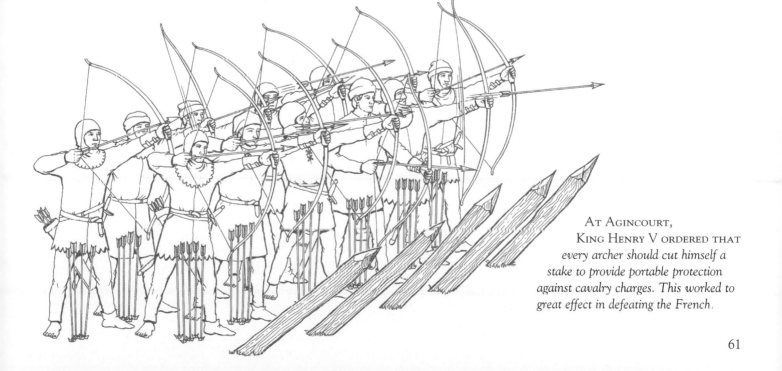

AT AGINCOURT,
KING HENRY V ORDERED THAT
*every archer should cut himself a
stake to provide portable protection
against cavalry charges. This worked to
great effect in defeating the French.*

THIS DETAIL FROM A SIXTEENTH-CENTURY FRESCO *depicts spear-and bow-armed Ottoman horse cavalry during the seven-week siege of Constantinople.*

Constantinople 1453

THE FALL OF CONSTANTINOPLE IN 1453, ITS ONCE-IMPREGNABLE WALLS BREACHED BY OTTOMAN SIEGE GUNS, BROUGHT TO AN END THE BYZANTINE EMPIRE AND ESTABLISHED THE OTTOMAN EMPIRE AS THE MAJOR THREAT TO CHRISTENDOM IN THE MEDITERRANEAN AND EASTERN EUROPE FOR THE NEXT TWO CENTURIES.

From 1396 to the 1450s Constantinople, the center of the Byzantine Empire, had managed to resist no fewer than three sieges by the Ottoman Turks. In 1453, however, Sultan Mehmed II decided to try again, but with a greater utilization of early artillery. The key to a successful siege of Constantinople was the ability to breach the massive 3.5-mile (5.7-km) long Land Wall, with its moats, towers, and triple-layered lines of walls. Mehmed II had found a renegade Christian, Urban of Transylvania, willing to build a monster of a gun measuring 26 ft 8 in (8.1 m) long, with a caliber of 8 in (20.3 cm) and could lob a solid stone cannon ball weighing a ton more than 1 mile (1.6 km). Urban's monster gun was completed and ready for

BATTLE FACTS

Who: Sultan Mehmed II Fatih (1432–81) laid siege to the city with an army of 120,000 men, opposed by a force of 10,000 Christian defenders led by Emperor Constantine XI (1405–53).

What: Turks used, for the first time, massive siege artillery to blow a hole in the walls protecting the city.

Where: Constantinople was the Imperial Byzantine capital located on a peninsula by the Bosporus and facing the Golden Horn in what is now Turkey.

When: April 5–May 29, 1453.

Why: The Ottomans wished to make Constantinople their capital and eliminate the Christian stronghold.

Outcome: The city was taken with great bloodshed, and became the capital of the Ottoman Empire.

Constantinople✝

OTTOMAN EMPIRE

inspection by a most satisfied Mehmed in January 1453. It would take a crew of 700 to transport, load, and handle it but it proved most effective against Constantinople's walls.

Numbers were also on Mehmed's side. Constantinople had no more than 10,000 armed men to defend it. Mehmed's elite guard, the Janissaries, alone numbered 12,000 men and his whole army would be ten times that size (figures vary from 100,000 to 150,000 troops). What was far worse was that Mehmed had managed, through a massive effort, to create a real galley fleet— the first in Ottoman history—built and manned by renegade Balkan Christians. Its commander, the Grand Admiral of the Fleet (Kapudan Pasha) Suleyman Balthoghlu, was a converted Bulgarian. To the consternation of the defenders this fleet entered the southern (Marmara) Sea in early March 1453. Now the Marmara sea wall was threatened as well, requiring a garrison from Constantine's tiny army.

THE SIEGE BEGINS

The first Ottoman troops, the vanguard, appeared beneath the Land Wall on April 1 and, at a signal from Emperor Constantine XI himself, the gates were shut, the wooden bridges across the moat burnt, and the walls manned. Constantinople was now clearly under siege and cut off from the rest of the world. Five days later Mehmed arrived with the main army and set up camp beneath the walls.

Shortly after, the Ottoman artillery began an unrelenting bombardment of the Land Wall that went on for six weeks. Urban's gun fired seven times a day, alongside 70 other smaller cannon, the cannon shot chipping away at the defenses and opening several breaches, although most of the openings were repaired. Indeed, the defenders were proving obdurate. Mehmed launched infantry assaults on April 18 and May 7, 12, and 21, but all were repulsed. Not that the Byzantines were having everything their own way. For example, a heavy iron chain stretched across the mouth of the Golden Horn estuary prevented the Muslim forces from sailing in there, but the resourceful Turks simply carried their ships overland to bypass the defenses.

At 1:30 A.M. on May 29, some 20,000 irregulars (*bashi-bazouks*), screaming and running at top speed, rushed the Land Wall, but after two hours of bloody and merciless fighting the heavily armored defenders had left only heaps of Turkish dead on the ground. The Anatolian army regulars failed equally miserably and assaults against the sea wall were also fiascos. Then, through treason or carelessness on the part of the defenders, some irregulars found that the small Kerkaporta gate between the Blachernae Palace section of the wall and the main Theodosian Wall

had been left slightly ajar. Wasting no time the Turks, hundreds strong, rushed the gate and were through between the first and second walls where the few defenders were simply unable to stem the tide.

The Turks had by this time been able to open the main gate and poured through, where small groups of defenders, including the armor-clad Constantine, were cut down where they stood. The Catalans fought with grim Hispanic fatalism secure in the knowledge that fighting the infidel assured them a speedy passage to heaven.

Some 4,000 defenders lay dead, and it was claimed most of the population was enslaved while churches, monasteries, and houses were burned to the ground or defiled. Mehmed immediately converted Hagia Sophia into a grand mosque. The fall of Constantinople was the end of the Byzantine Empire, and established the Ottoman Turks as a threat to Europe that lasted until their failed siege of Vienna in 1683.

CROSSBOWMAN AND KNIGHT

Crossbowmen were more effective in a siege situation, and some Aragonese and Genoese crossbowmen mercenaries were employed to defend Constantinople. By this time Western plate armor had become so heavy that knights ceased using a shield, freeing them to use heavy two-handed weapons.

CONSTANTINOPLE

1 Mehmed II establishes his camp outside the Land Wall in early April 1453. The city is cut off and the walls receive a constant battering.

4 On the night of May 28–29 the Turks break in over the wall and through a small postern gate.

5 Constantine XI is killed. For three days the city is sacked and looted.

KEY
← Ottoman forces
■ Christian forces

3 Mehmed sends Turkish ships overland round Pera on rollers and into the Golden Horn. Constantinople is now fully blockaded.

2 A small Italian fleet breaks through and is let into the Golden Horn, giving temporary relief.

Golden Horn

Constantinople

CHAPTER TWO

The Gunpowder Revolution

The introduction of barreled gunpowder weaponry in the late medieval period brought the most profound changes in warfare. Over the following centuries, firepower rather than muscle power became a decider of battles.

The advent of firearms and cannon steadily changed the nature of tactical decision-making on the battlefield. Now a commander not only had to chose the right time and place to apply infantry and cavalry, but also how to concentrate his fire to best effect. Firepower transformed the nature of armies themselves, introducing a technological professionalism that would ultimately displace the aristocratic warrior from his primary place in the military hierarchy. Traditional edged weapons, such as sword and pike, persisted alongside firearms for many centuries, but on both land and sea the combination of gunpowder weapons, and the inexorable growth of state armies, meant battles became more destructive than ever.

LEFT: THIS SLIGHTLY ROMANTICIZED PORTRAYAL *of the Charge of the Light Brigade at the Battle of Balaclava (October 25, 1854) shows British lancers and hussars attacking the Russian gunners, the object of their charge.*

MUGHAL PRINCE BABAR'S TROOPS *employ field guns against the elephant-mounted troops of Ibrahim Lodi at Panipat, as depicted in a magazine illustration dating from 1901.*

Panipat 1526

HEAVILY OUTNUMBERED, BABUR, RULER OF KABUL, UTILIZED SUPERIOR TACTICS AND FIELD ARTILLERY TO DEFEAT SULTAN IBRAHIM KHAN LODI AND ESTABLISH THE MUGHAL DYNASTY IN INDIA.

I n late 1525, Zahir ud-din Muhammad Babur, ruler of Kabul and a descendant of the great Mongol warlord Genghis Khan, embarked on his fifth military expedition into Hindustan. Taking control over all of the Punjab, Babur advanced toward a major prize, the city of Delhi. His enemy, Sultan Ibrahim Khan Lodi, had captured Delhi earlier in the year, and by the spring of 1526 had raised an immense army of nearly 130,000 soldiers and 300 war elephants. In contrast, the force under Babur's command numbered no more than 15,000, and their ranks were somewhat diminished during an arduous march and the crossing of the swift Indus River.

Determined to wrest control of northern India from Ibrahim and establish the Mughal Dynasty, Babur conducted a skillful campaign that culminated with a decisive victory at

BATTLE FACTS

Who: The small army of Zahir ud-din Muhammad Babur (1483–1531), ruler of Kabul, faced Sultan Ibrahim Khan Lodi (1489–1526) and his army of more than 100,000 troops and 300 war elephants.

What: Babur's use of innovative tactics, matchlock firearms, archers, and artillery routed the forces of Ibrahim, who was killed during the course of battle.

Where: The village of Panipat in the modern Indian province of Haryana.

When: April 21, 1526.

Why: Babur believed he was the rightful ruler of northern India and sought to capture the cities of Agra and Delhi.

Outcome: With the victory at Panipat, Babur established the Mughal Dynasty in India and ended the Delhi Sultanate.

Panipat on April 21, 1526. In February of that year, during the march toward Delhi, Babur detached a force commanded by his son, Humayun (1508–56), to defeat a small army loyal to Ibrahim at Hisar-Firuza. Moving eastward and then southward, Babur won another victory at Doab on April 2. Meanwhile, Ibrahim advanced from Agra to Delhi and then northward toward a showdown at Panipat.

INNOVATIVE TACTICS

As the distance separating the two armies diminished, Babur realized that he was outnumbered nearly ten to one. However, he was also aware that a well-conceived plan of battle and the skillful use of emerging technology could win the day. An innovative tactician, Babur deployed his troops at Panipat into three large divisions occupying the center of his line and the left and right flanks. He further divided the flank divisions into forward and reserve formations, facilitating rapid maneuver to simultaneously attack Ibrahim from multiple directions.

Babur also ordered his men to gather 700 carts, join them with ropes, and allow enough space between them for several mantlets to provide cover for his soldiers to fire their matchlocks. He placed his archers in advantageous positions and sited 24 pieces of field artillery that could be brought to bear against Ibrahim.

For several days, Babur's men attempted without success to goad Ibrahim into attacking their strong defenses. A night attack against Ibrahim disintegrated into a confusing march and was hastily withdrawn at daybreak. Ibrahim aroused his forces to pursue, but opted instead to remain stationary. Then, on April 21, Ibrahim finally advanced.

THE BATTLE

Some accounts of the battle assert that the thunder of Babur's artillery panicked Ibrahim's war elephants, resulting in a mêlée in which many of his soldiers were killed. Others, including that of Babur himself, mention the artillery only in passing. However, it is known that Babur's battle plan worked effectively and in somewhat similar fashion to a classic double envelopment.

As Ibrahim pressed forward, flank attacks hit his large and ponderous army from left and right while small detachments harassed his concentrated formations from behind. Backed by their artillery, the matchlock-armed soldiers stood firm in Babur's center. His archers rained arrows on the confused mass of Ibrahim's troops, caught in an ever-shrinking pocket and assailed from four directions.

From early morning until midday, the fighting raged. Ibrahim was killed, and his army fled the field in disorder. Babur pursued his beaten enemy toward Agra, capturing the city along with Ibrahim's treasury and sending Humayun forward with a large force in a continuing effort to destroy the remnants of the opposing army. Three days later, Babur triumphantly entered Delhi, where he captured several members of Ibrahim's family and was reported to have treated them with honor and dignity.

In due course, the Mughal Dynasty was established in India as the decisive victory at Panipat ended the reign of Ibrahim and the Delhi Sultanate. Babur's forces suffered only light casualties, while estimates of his enemy's losses range from 15,000 to 40,000. He had won the day and a sizeable addition to his empire at Panipat, one of the earliest battles to employ firearms and artillery in significant numbers.

THIS ILLUMINATION *from the memoirs of Babur-Nama, founder of the Mughal Empire (dating from 1590), shows the heat and confusion of the Battle of Panipat in a dazzling array of colors.*

THE BATTLE OF LEPANTO, (Venetian school of painting). The painting accurately portrays the crowded nature of the battle, where ships' cannon blasted each other from point-blank range.

Lepanto 1571

BEFORE THE EPIC BATTLE OF LEPANTO, THE OTTOMAN TURKISH FLEET SEEMED ALL BUT UNBEATABLE. HOWEVER, DEVELOPMENTS IN ARMAMENT, ALONG WITH THE TACTICS TO GO WITH THEM, PERMITTED THE HOLY LEAGUE TO DEFEAT A SUPERIOR FORCE OF TURKISH GALLEYS.

The Ottoman Turks were immensely powerful in the middle of the sixteenth century, and conflict with European powers was common. Europe at the time was weak and divided by internal struggles, which made it possible for the Turks to push steadily into European territory, at one point besieging Vienna. Meanwhile the powerful Ottoman fleet attacked the ships and holdings of maritime states, such as Venice and Genoa.

Following the Turkish assault on Venetian-ruled Cyprus in 1570, Pope Pius V (1504–72) and Philip II of Spain (1527–98) cooperated to raise a Holy League, and a European battle fleet, to punish the Muslim forces of Selim II (1524–74). Cyprus actually fell to the Turks on August 3, 1571, but by this time the fleet was approaching readiness for battle. Commanded by Don John of Austria, the Holy

BATTLE FACTS

Who: Philip II of Spain and Pope Pius V founded the Holy League to fight the Ottoman Turks under Sultan Selim II. The League's Fleet was commanded by Don John of Austria (1545–76) while the Turks were led by Ali Pasha (d. 1571).

What: Lepanto was the greatest Christian naval victory against the Muslims and the last sea battle fought exclusively with oared galleys.

Where: In the Gulf of Patras on the western coast of Greece, near the port of Lepanto (Naupaktos).

When: October 7, 1571.

Why: The Ottoman Empire posed a deadly threat to Italy and the rest of Europe.

Outcome: Christian gunfire smashed the Ottoman fleet, breaking Turkish naval power in the Mediterranean.

League set sail with 316 ships, 50,000 crew and 30,000 soldiers, a force that included 208 cannon-armed galleys and six larger galleasses, the latter bristling with heavy-caliber guns. The Turkish fleet around Cyprus, commanded by Ali Pasha, consisted of 250 galleys—these tended to be faster than the European vessels, but their armament was lighter, relying more on marine archery and small-caliber cannon. On October 7, the two fleets finally met off Lepanto in southwestern Greece.

Both sides formed up in four bodies consisting of a center, two wings, and a reserve force. The Christians pushed their galleasses out in front of the main body, while the Ottomans advanced confidently, keen to get into bow range and begin winning the battle. The Christian right wing was somewhat out of position at this point, mainly due to having the greatest distance to travel when rounding Point Scropha on the Greek coast.

As the Ottoman force advanced, the galleasses opened fire with their heavy cannon, which came as something of a shock. The galleasses were converted merchant vessels and did not look like conventional warships; they had been mistaken for supply vessels. Two Ottoman galleys were sunk and others damaged, with significant disruption to the battle formation, before the Ottoman force closed to bow range.

The Ottoman galleys were adeptly and boldly handled, advancing in a broad crescent to engage their opposite numbers. Commanders of groups and individual ships seized any opportunities that presented themselves. The commander of the southern division, Uluj Ali, saw the Christian right wing shifting southward to avoid being flanked. This increased an already sizeable gap in the Christian line between the right and center divisions. Uluj Ali therefore switched his force northward, hitting the flank of the main Christian division and creating a local superiority while the 53 galleys of the Christian right wing were out of position.

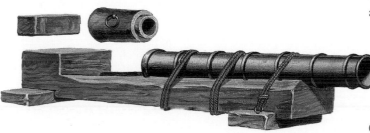

THE EARLIEST BREECH-LOADING NAVAL CANNON *spat fire around the breech, which was potentially disastrous for the gunner. The gunner would place gunpowder in the hollow breech and the ball in the barrel, then use wedges, weights, and prayers to hold the weapon together as it fired.*

THIS OTTOMAN ARCHER CARRIES the dreaded and effective short composite bow, which was made famous in cavalry action but was equally handy and lethal in combat at sea. The Turkish short bow was made of laminated wood and horn, which were held together by a glue that suffered from long exposure to moisture.

TURNING THE BATTLE

The 62 galleys of the Christian center were hard pressed. The force in front of them had a similar number of galleys, plus 32 lighter galliots (small galleys with one or two masts and 20 oars), and the flanking group was also powerful. However, the 30 galleys of the Christian central reserve and the Christian right wing, coming into action at last, stabilized the situation, and a pounding match ensued.

Meanwhile, the Christian left wing, near the shore, was suffering as well. A fast force of Ottoman galleys made a flanking move and for a time the line was threatened. Gradually, however, the situation was brought under control. The cannon of the galleasses were instrumental in this turn of events—they were heavy enough to smash and sink ships, and the weight of fire began to tell.

The Battle of Lepanto had much in common with a land battle in many ways, with enemy units softened up by missile fire and finished off by shock action in the form of boarding parties. Several vessels on either side were boarded and captured, sometimes changing hands more than once.

However, the cannon of the Christian ships proved decisive. Ottoman vessels closing to board had great holes blown in them, killing many men, and often preventing a successful attack. At bow range, cannon could not miss and did far more damage than arrows could. The Ottoman guns—never considered a decisive weapon—were insufficiently supplied and ran out of ammunition.

The cannon tipped the balance, especially where the galleasses could pound other ships into matchwood from a distance. However, there were other elements to the Ottoman defeat. Ali Pasha was hit in the head by a musket ball and his vessel successfully boarded. Displaying his head on a pike and in possession of the Banner of the Caliphs, the Christians demoralized their foes and forced them into retreat.

As the tide turned, most of the Ottoman fleet was captured or sunk. Uluj Ali was able to break off the action and retreat with much of his force, but annihilation was more or less complete for the remainder of the Ottoman fleet.

LEPANTO

1 Don John's squadrons move into the Gulf of Patras toward the Turk's anchorage, protected by towers and shore artillery. The Christian formation becomes a crescent with the horns toward the enemy.

KEY

◀ CHRISTIAN FLEET

◀ OTTOMAN FLEET

2 Ali Pasha is eager to engage. Keeping his fleet clustered around his flagship, he forges forward, directly into the crescent. As the Turks approach, the six galleasses of the special squadron advance under tow ahead of the rest of the crescent.

3 The Turkish fleet divides in passing the galleasses. The six hybrids' powerful broadside armaments inflict heavy damage on the Turks, then the galleasses move slowly toward the Turks' rear.

4 Fighting is the fiercest in the center, while a struggle on the flanks gradually favors the Christian forces, which move to surround the Turks.

5 Some Turks manage to break through the Christian flank, but most are trapped or driven aground. The Christians annihilate almost the entire Turkish fleet.

A TWISTED LINE OF SPANISH GALLEONS and English fighting ships engage at Gravelines. The Great Armada was then forced to sail around the British Isles to reach Spain.

Spanish Armada 1588

KING PHILIP II OF SPAIN, CONFIDENT THAT HE WAS EXECUTING THE WILL OF ALMIGHTY GOD, WENT TO WAR AGAINST ENGLAND IN 1585. A DEVOUT ROMAN CATHOLIC, PHILIP HAD A CLEAR INTENTION. PROTESTANT ENGLAND AND ITS HERETIC QUEEN ELIZABETH I MUST BE RETURNED TO THE PAPAL FOLD WHILE SPANISH SOVEREIGNTY IN FLANDERS MUST BE AFFIRMED.

On May 28, 1588, a Spanish fleet of 130 ships, including 22 prestigious galleons, set sail from Lisbon. Commanded by the Duke of Medina Sidonia, its purpose was to take control of the English Channel, then provide security and transport to bring a 30,000-strong Spanish invasion army across the Channel from the Netherlands to Britain.

The English knew they were coming. In harbor at Plymouth, the English fleet, which ultimately numbered as many as 200 ships (although a relative few were combat vessels), waited for the Armada to appear on the horizon. In overall command of the British naval force was Charles Howard, Lord High Admiral and Earl of Nottingham, who was capably supported by his squadron commanders

BATTLE FACTS

Who: The Spanish Armada (22 galleons and 108 armed merchant vessels) led by Don Alonso Pérez de Guzmán el Bueno, Duke of Medina Sidonia (1550–1619), versus the English Fleet (35 warships and 163 armed merchant vessels) under Charles Howard (1536–1624), Lord High Admiral.

What: The Spanish attempted to defeat the English fleet and launch an invasion of England.

Where: The English Channel and the North Sea off the coast of Flanders.

When: July–August 1588.

Why: Spain's King Philip II sought to restore Roman Catholicism in England and halt English raiding of his treasure galleons.

Outcome: The Spanish Armada was defeated in a series of engagements culminating with the battle off Gravelines and then mauled in severe weather during its return to Spain.

Sir Francis Drake (1540–96), Martin Frobisher (1539–94), and John Hawkins (1532–95). Hampered by bad weather, the Spanish Armada did not arrive off the English coast until the middle of June. On June 19, the enemy ships were sighted off Cornwall, and a warning was flashed to the defending fleet and the court of Elizabeth I in London via a system of beacons. More than 50 English warships weighed anchor to confront the invaders.

Although their vast fleet made an imposing sight, the Spanish would soon discover that their tactics and equipment were outmoded and inferior. Their galleons were large, unwieldy vessels, and the Spanish gun crews were also hardly even taught how to reload, instead focusing on delivering a single broadside and then boarding. In contrast, English warships were crewed by more professional sailors and gunners. The English fighting ships were smaller, of shallower draft, and much faster than the ponderous Spanish galleons. Taking advantage of their more nimble vessels, the English captains intended to stay on the weather gauge of the enemy fleet, keeping a safe distance, and pounding the Spanish with accurate cannon fire.

RUNNING ENGAGEMENTS

For several days, the English probed the fighting capabilities of the Armada during indecisive clashes. On July 31, the Spanish maneuvered into battle formation, two wings, each of 20 or more ships, supporting a main force of about 36 galleons arrayed to protect the transports. In battle lines, Drake and Howard were unable to inflict major damage. Near Eddystone and Portland, the adversaries fought inconclusive actions. Off the Isle of Wight, on August 4, the English prevented Medina Sidonia from safely anchoring and forced him

back to the open sea in order to avoid running aground. (Nevertheless, two galleons did just that.) Eventually, the Spanish anchored in a great crescent off the Flemish coast near Dunkirk, where the invasion army was camped. There was no harbor available large enough to shelter them, and Howard ordered eight fireships, which had been packed with tar, pitch, and gunpowder, loosed against them. Two of these were taken in tow and led away, but one Spanish ship caught fire and several were compelled to cut their cables and sail out of harm's way.

Finally, after sparring for nearly three weeks, the opposing fleets came to blows once again on August 8. Off Gravelines in Spanish-occupied Flanders, the agile English employed disciplined fire, allowed the Spanish to loose their single broadside, and then closed to more favorable range. Estimates of Spanish ships lost in the fight are as high as 11, with at least two run aground and more than 800 men dead. The following day, their ammunition nearly depleted, the English pursued their enemy into the North Sea and away from any hope of assisting an invasion.

Faced with the prospect of running the English gauntlet or sailing a circuitous route around Scotland and Ireland to reach safety, Medina Sidonia chose the latter. Encountering vicious storms, the Armada was chewed like a bone, and many of its galleons were dashed against the rocks of the Irish coast. Thousands more men died when their ships sank.

BATTERED AND BEATEN

Months after undertaking its foray against England, the remnants of the Armada, only 67 battered and beaten ships, reached the safety of Spanish waters. More than 8,000 of its sailors were dead, wounded, or suffering from illness. English casualties had amounted only to about 500 as a result of the fighting. Yet although England had been saved from invasion and the House of Tudor would remain on the throne of Protestant England, the war with Spain dragged on for 18 more years.

NAVAL GUN CARRIAGE

The wheels of this gun carriage allowed the cannon's recoil to expend itself in movement, rather than in damaging a vessel's timbers, while gunners could elevate the weapon by movement of the wooden wedge beneath the breech. Reloading tackles also allowed the cannon to be trained from the side. Carriages of this design enabled the British to achieve a superior rate of fire during the Armada battles.

Sacheon 1592

EMPLOYING THE ART OF DECEPTION, ADMIRAL YI SUN-SIN, KOREA'S GREAT NAVAL HERO, DEFEATED A FORMIDABLE JAPANESE FLEET, COMPELLING THE WITHDRAWAL OF A SUBSTANTIAL ENEMY LAND FORCE.

On May 25, 1592, a powerful Japanese army landed on the Korean peninsula at Pusan. Intent on subjugating the Korean people and facilitating an ongoing war with China, the Japanese determined to consolidate and defend an important base of operations and supply at Sacheon. A flotilla of Japanese warships and supply vessels anchored there, and troops disembarked and began constructing fortifications to guard the occupied town and its harbor.

Fresh from a resounding victory at Okp'o just days earlier, Admiral Yi Sun-sin sailed to Sacheon with 26 Korean warships. Familiar with the area, Admiral Yi was aware that the confines of the harbor and its substantial ebbing tides offered no advantage for his ships in combat. Therefore, he instructed his captains to feign retreat, presenting the Japanese commander, whose name is lost to history, with

THIS JAPANESE PAINTING *from 1876 shows sixteenth-century general Kato Kiyomasa, one of the senior Japanese commanders in the Seven Year War (1592–98) against the Koreans.*

BATTLE FACTS

Who: Korean Admiral Yi Sun-sin (1545–98) and 26 Korean warships against approximately 13 Japanese vessels led by an unknown naval commander.

What: Yi lured the Japanese force into open water by feigning retreat and inflicted a costly defeat on his enemy, forcing them to evacuate a land force and withdraw.

Where: The harbor and open sea near the town of Sacheon in southern Korea.

When: May 29, 1592.

Why: Japan had invaded Korea, and Admiral Yi sought to sever lines of supply and reinforcement.

Outcome: Admiral Yi utilized deception and sent the innovative turtle ship into combat for the first time, resulting in a resounding Korean victory.

an apparent opportunity to rout the Koreans. Once the Japanese had been drawn into open water, Yi intended to turn on the enemy and utilize his freedom of movement to full advantage.

THE TURTLE SHIPS
On May 29, 1592, the Korean vessels appeared on the horizon and executed the planned deception. The Japanese took the bait and in short order fell victim to the sudden Korean onslaught. Admiral Yi did allow a few of the Japanese ships to remain intact, correctly assuming that they would return to Sacheon harbor, evacuate their troops from the town, and abandon their construction effort.

Sacheon marked the combat debut of the turtle ship, a vessel with its entire exterior covered in spikes to prevent hostile boarding, while sailors moved freely along protected internal passageways and served guns from six ports on each side and cannon in the bow and stern. Although only one turtle ship engaged the Japanese at Sacheon, its presence was decisive.

While the Japanese suffered heavy losses in the brief but sharp clash, the Koreans were relatively unscathed. Admiral Yi suffered a minor wound but remained in command. In the coming days, he would crown a string of stunning naval victories with the defeat of a major Japanese force at Hansando.

Sekigahara 1600

THE ARMY OF TOKUGAWA IEYASU, *DAIMYO* OF THE KANTO PLAIN, DEFEATED LOYALIST FORCES UNDER ISHIDA MITSUNARI, ESTABLISHING THE TOKUGAWA SHOGUNATE, WHICH RULED JAPAN UNTIL 1868.

Toyotomi Hideyoshi (1537–98), great *daimyo* of the Sengoku period, had succeeded in unifying Japan near the end of the sixteenth century. However, his untimely death in 1598 triggered a web of intrigue as two former lieutenants vied for dominion over the island nation, one, Tokugawa Ieyasu, to consolidate power in himself, and the other, Ishida Mitsunari, supporting Hideyori, the five-year-old son and heir of the deceased Lord Hideyoshi.

As their rivalry intensified, Ishida determined to attack Ieyasu from the rear while the latter was campaigning from Edo (Tokyo) to secure the borders of his dominion. Ishida marched with 85,000 samurai and foot soldiers in late 1600. At a disadvantage from the outset, he faced a veteran warrior in Ieyasu. Several of Ishida's subordinate *daimyo* had also bargained treacherously to turn on their master and fight with Ieyasu.

TOKUGAWA IEYASU *was one of the great* daimyo, *or lords, of his era. Following his victory at Sekigahara, the Tokugawa Shogunate ruled Japan for the next 250 years.*

Before dawn on October 21, Ishida had reached the narrow, mountainous pass at Sekigahara, where the two armies joined battle about 8 A.M. in driving rain. Although he was at a numerical disadvantage, Ieyasu used the intelligence he had gathered to formulate a plan of attack. He would feign a northward march, then wheel abruptly westward to confront Ishida directly.

TREACHERY

Surprised by the swiftness of Ieyasu's tactical about-face, Ishida chose Sekigahara as a strong defensive position to block the advance of his enemy. Ishida was initially assailed in his center by fierce cavalry known as the Red Devils. While Ishida's center was hard pressed, Ieyasu's troops advanced sluggishly in the north. Ishida's southern flank, however, held firm against Ieyasu's assaults.

At noon, the battle still raged. Ieyasu had waited for the 17-year-old Kobayakawa Hideaki (1577–1602) to betray Ishida and fall on the southern flank of the enemy army. Finally, Ieyasu ordered his harquebusiers to fire a volley in Kobayakawa's direction. Spurred to action, the young commander turned on his former allies, precipitating a rout. Ishida was beheaded at Kyoto.

Following his victory at Sekigahara, Ieyasu consolidated power. In 1603, Emperor Go-Yozei awarded him the title of Shogun. His line, the Tokugawa Shogunate, was destined to rule Japan for more than two centuries.

BATTLE FACTS

Who: Tokugawa Ieyasu (1543–1616), *daimyo* of the Kanto Plain, against Ishida Mitsunari (1560–1600), a Toyotomi loyalist supporting Hideyori, the five-year-old heir of Toyotomi Hideyoshi, preeminent *daimyo* of the Sengoku period.

What: The decisive battle for political control in recently unified Japan took place two years after the death of the unifier, Toyotomi Hideyoshi.

Where: The mountain pass at Sekigahara in southwestern Japan astride the strategic crossroads of the Nakasendo.

When: October 21, 1600.

Why: The loyalist *daimyo* Ishida Mitsunari sought to defeat the Tokugawa while they were already engaged in a campaign to secure their own territory.

Outcome: The victory of Tokugawa Ieyasu's forces at Sekigahara ended the influence of the Toyotomi line and put the Tokugawa Shogunate in power for the next 250 years.

Lützen 1632

Having plunged into the mêlée to shore up a faltering unit, the Swedish king's wounded horse carried him into the enemy ranks where he was surrounded by Imperialist troopers and killed.

IN ONE OF THE GREAT BATTLES OF THE THIRTY YEARS' WAR, THE "LION OF THE NORTH," GUSTAVUS ADOLPHUS OF SWEDEN, FACED A REVIVED IMPERIAL ARMY UNDER WALLENSTEIN AT LÜTZEN. THE SWEDISH KING WAS KILLED, BUT HIS TROOPS RALLIED AND WERE VICTORIOUS AFTER A HARD FIGHT AGAINST OPPONENTS WHO HAD LEARNED FROM THEIR PREVIOUS DEFEATS.

The Battle of Lützen was an epic clash between an army of the Holy Roman Empire, commanded by Count Albrecht von Wallenstein, and Swedish troops led by the innovative and aggressive commander, King Gustavus Adolphus. The battleground was Saxony, through which Gustavus had pursued an invading Imperial army. Wallenstein had 25,000 men—facing 18,000 Allies—with the 8,000 troops of Count Gottfried zu Pappenheim (1594–1632) as reinforcements, and he would form his order of battle in a single line just north of the Leipzig road. His right flank rested on a knoll just north of

BATTLE FACTS

Who: King Gustavus II Adolphus of Sweden (1594–1632), commanding the Swedish Army, against Prince Albrecht von Wallenstein, Prince of Friedland (1583–1634), leading the Imperial Army.

What: In a hard-fought battle, the Imperial forces showed they had learned from their previous defeat at Swedish hands, and Gustavus was killed. However, the Swedish army rallied and was victorious.

When: November 16, 1632.

Where: The fields outside the small town of Lützen near Leipzig in Saxony.

Why: Wallenstein threatened Saxony—an ally of Sweden.

Outcome: The battle saved Saxony but the Thirty Years' War (1618–48) ground on despite this Protestant victory.

W**ITH ITS MORE EFFICIENT MECHANISM,** *cavalrymen who were about to ride into combat preferred the wheel-lock pistol. Not only could such pistols be loaded easily but the user could be reasonably sure of being able to fire when they wanted to without the complicated process of using a match for ignition.*

Lützen—Windmill Hill—while his left was left hanging in the open.

On November 16, 1632, by the early light of a gray dawn, the Swedes and their allied troops took up position opposite the Imperial forces. The fog thickened as the morning progressed, so the planned attack had to be postponed from 8 A.M. to 11 A.M., when the fog lifted temporarily and allowed Gustavus to begin his attack. Thanks to skilled and coordinated Imperial artillery and musket fire, the advance was halted on the left and center. It was only on the right where a breakthrough was achieved, but at a high cost. The Swedish and Yellow Brigades managed to clear the trench of musketeers, cross the road, and seize the batteries to the north of the road.

Then the fighting, as the fog descended on the battlefield yet again, became a murderous stalemate. Just as the Imperial left crumbled, Pappenheim arrived and rescued the Imperial army from being overwhelmed by a Swedish–Finnish onslaught. The Swedish Brigade lost 70 percent of its pikemen and 40 percent of its musketeers in the slaughter that now ensued. The other side was just as badly mauled. Swedish cavalry were reduced to scattered small groups on either side of the raised road, and they began to waver. Only the intervention by the army's chief chaplain, Jacob Fabricius, steadied their nerves and brought them back into battle.

TURNING POINT
A key point in the battle now occurred—Gustavus was killed while rallying his troops. The Swedish and allied troops had heard that the King was dead and feared that all was lost. Bernhard, the Duke of Saxe-Weimar (1604–39), was now in command. He rallied the wavering men for a counterattack and as the Swedes advanced they found their hero King's corpse—mutilated and stripped. Bernhard had calculated that they would now thirst for revenge, and so they did, more than willing to avenge Gustavus' humiliating death. The general Swedish attack had bent the Imperial line into something resembling a crescent, but both sides were now tired and wearying of fighting. They came to a halt as they fired at each other, but could not break the deadlock. Bernhard decided that the only way to bring this dismal battle to an end would be to attack Windmill Hill, knock out Wallenstein's remaining 13 guns and break through between the enemy's center and left.

The Swedish batteries unleashed a storm of shot that silenced the battery atop Windmill Hill and then, at 3 P.M., the Swedes, Finns, and other troops marched swiftly up the slope leading to the hill. They were thrown back by withering fire, but regrouped and attacked again until they had seized the hill and the trenches around. These were filled with dead and dying men. Finally, after two hours of intensive fighting, the Swedish colors were raised—at 5 P.M.—atop the hill. The battle was won.

Wallenstein could have fought on, but his troops were now utterly exhausted and demoralized. Wallenstein's son, Bertold, was one of the casualties and the whole slaughter had cost 7,000 lives—some 4,000 Imperial and the rest Swedish–Allied. Lützen was a Swedish–Allied victory but only just, and it was Bernhard who had led the army to victory. Amazingly the war dragged on until finally, on October 24, 1648, the exhausted combatants finally signed a lasting peace—that of Westphalia.

IMPERIAL CUIRASSIER

Cuirassiers of the Thirty Years War continued to wear plate armor for maximum defense but had discarded the lance in favor of pistols. Their armor was usually of a good quality and could stop both sword cuts and pistol balls. It was also articulated, which means the many layers could slide over each other, allowing a lot of movement. However, it also earned them the nickname of "lobsters."

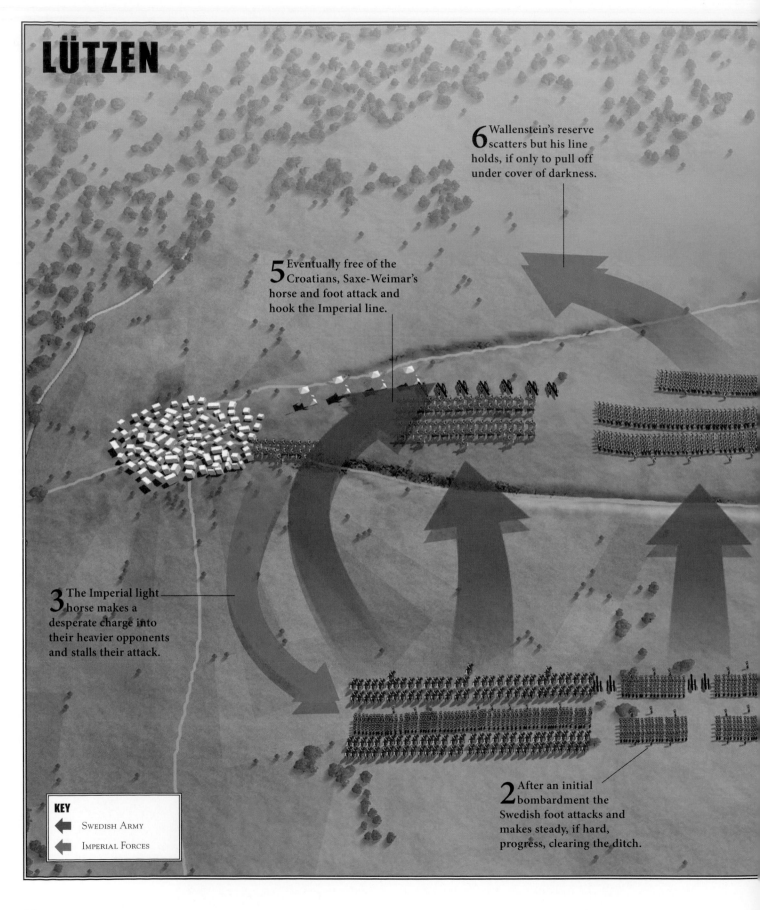

LÜTZEN

6 Wallenstein's reserve scatters but his line holds, if only to pull off under cover of darkness.

5 Eventually free of the Croatians, Saxe-Weimar's horse and foot attack and hook the Imperial line.

3 The Imperial light horse makes a desperate charge into their heavier opponents and stalls their attack.

2 After an initial bombardment the Swedish foot attacks and makes steady, if hard, progress, clearing the ditch.

KEY

← SWEDISH ARMY

← IMPERIAL FORCES

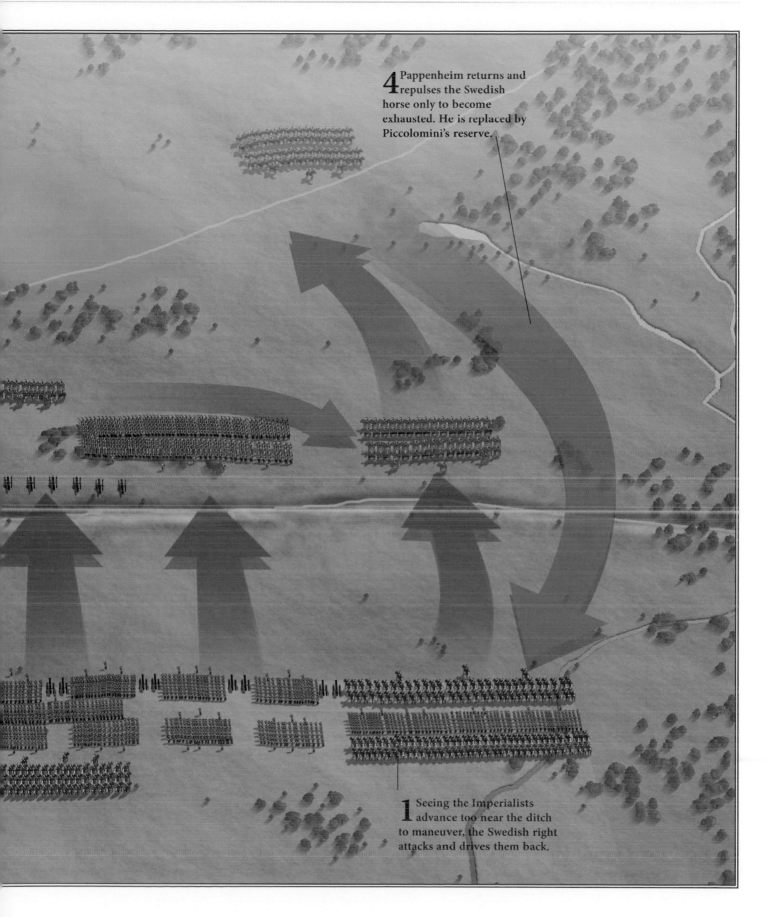

4 Pappenheim returns and repulses the Swedish horse only to become exhausted. He is replaced by Piccolomini's reserve.

1 Seeing the Imperialists advance too near the ditch to maneuver, the Swedish right attacks and drives them back.

A BESIEGED VIENNA IN THE BACKGROUND, *Ottoman and European cavalry fight at close quarters on top of the hill of Kahlenberg in the foreground.*

Kahlenberg 1683

BREAKING A TWO-MONTH SIEGE, THE COALITION ARMY OF JAN SOBIESKI, KING OF POLAND, DEFEATED OTTOMAN FORCES OF KARA MUSTAFA PASHA, HALTING THEIR INCURSION INTO CENTRAL EUROPE.

The arrival of Crimean Tatar forces near Vienna in the summer of 1683 prompted Holy Roman Emperor Leopold I (1640–1705) to flee the city, while Ernst Rudiger Graf von Starhemberg was left to defend it with only 11,000 soldiers. Soon, the Ottoman host would number more than 150,000, and its commander, Grand Vizier Merzifonlu Kara Mustafa Pasha expected to claim the decisive victory in a 300-year struggle between the Muslim forces of the Ottoman Empire and the Holy Roman Empire of Central Europe, dominated by the House of Habsburg.

Kara Mustafa Pasha had persuaded the Ottoman court that he might capture Vienna, succeeding where a previous siege had failed more than a century earlier. However, when war was declared in August 1682, the timing was anything but advantageous. The campaign could not

proceed until the following spring because of weather and logistical concerns.

OTTOMAN THREATS

Nevertheless, the Ottoman Sultan Mehmet IV (1642–93) sent a threatening message to Leopold I. It read, "Primarily we order you to await us in your residence city of Vienna so that we can decapitate you…We will exterminate you and all your followers…Children and adults will be exposed to the most atrocious tortures before they are put to an end in the most ignominious way imaginable."

The Europeans did not waste a 15-month window of opportunity, and Leopold concluded treaties with others threatened by the westward movement of the Ottoman army. Most important among these was an agreement with Jan Sobieski, King John III of Poland. When the Ottoman forces reached Vienna, Sobieski marched to the aid of Starhemberg. His army numbered nearly 40,000 and combined with troops from Austria, Bavaria, Saxony, Swabia, and Franconia. Eventually, more than 80,000 soldiers were assembled.

Meanwhile, Mustafa squandered his advantage, refusing to press his greater numbers against Starhemberg, whose soldiers suffered from shortages of food and other supplies. He instead chose to lay siege to Vienna and discovered to his dismay that the 300 guns he had transported hundreds of miles were ineffective against the strong defenses of the city. From July until the climactic battle in September, Mustafa attempted to tunnel beneath the walls of Vienna and detonate large charges of gunpowder to breach the defenses. None of these efforts were successful, although one massive mine was defused by the defenders in the nick of time.

CAVALRY CHARGE

As Sobieski approached Vienna, Mustafa did little to impede his progress, and the troops of the European confederation reached the high ground at Kahlenberg, or "Bald Hill," early on the morning of September 12. When Mustafa realized that his enemy was deploying for battle, he attacked but encountered stiff opposition from Austrian troops on his left and Germans in his center under the command of Duke Charles of Lorraine (1643–90). Soon, he committed a tactical error, attempting to rush the city itself rather than deal with the military force opposing him. Sobieski committed Polish infantry to the contest and gained high ground on his right.

While their infantry had been engaged for hours, a large contingent of Polish, Austrian, and German cavalry waited among the neighboring hills. At 5 P.M., Sobieski ordered the largest cavalry charge in history forward. At the head of 20,000 horsemen, Sobieski broke the Ottoman lines. His 3,000 heavy lancers, the famous Winged Hussars, put the Ottoman troops to flight. The pursuit resulted in the capture of Ottoman supply trains and camps. When the battle was over, 15,000 Ottoman soldiers were dead or wounded. The European coalition had suffered about 4,500 casualties.

THE TIDE TURNED

Sobieski's victory at Vienna ended Ottoman incursions into Central Europe and hastened the decline of the Eastern dominion. Sobieski has been hailed as a legendary hero, who saved Christendom and preserved Western culture. Mustafa was executed by strangulation in Belgrade on December 25, 1683.

OTTOMAN JANISSARIES

The Janissaries were the elite of the Ottoman Turkish army. They were generally well equipped with flintlock firearms as well as pikes and other handheld weapons and were considered the best disciplined forces in seventeenth-century Europe. By the eighteenth century, however, they had been eclipsed by the standing armies of the major European powers.

THE BATTLE OF BLENHEIM TAPESTRY *is displayed in the Green Writing Room at Blenheim Palace, in England. Here, the Duke of Marlborough sits astride a white horse, in commanding posture.*

Blenheim 1704

DURING THE WAR OF THE SPANISH SUCCESSION, THE DUKE OF MARLBOROUGH LEAD A DARING MARCH ACROSS EUROPE TO DEFEAT A SUPERIOR FRANCO-BAVARIAN FORCE AT BLENHEIM ON THE DANUBE. THIS VICTORY SECURED NOT ONLY THE SAFETY OF THE HABSBURG CAPITAL, BUT ALSO MARLBOROUGH'S REPUTATION AS ONE OF THE GREAT MILITARY COMMANDERS OF HISTORY.

The forces that faced one another at Blenheim were roughly equal, with an Allied army of about 52,000 British, Dutch, and German troops facing some 56,000 men from France and the Electorate of Bavaria. John Churchill, the Duke of Marlborough, led the Allied contingent alongside Prince Eugene of Savoy; the opposing commanders were the Marshals Tallard and Marsin (1656–1706), plus the Elector of Bavaria, Maximilian II Emmanuel (1662–1726). The battle finally began with a massive artillery barrage from the French, at 8:30 A.M. on

BATTLE FACTS

Who: A Franco-Bavarian army under Marshal Tallard (1652–1728) faced an Allied army under the Duke of Marlborough (1650–1722) and Prince Eugene of Savoy (1663–1736).

What: Marlborough's shrewd battlefield tactics coupled with superior infantry firepower and cavalry shock tactics ended French military supremacy in the War of the Spanish Succession.

Where: At the village of Blenheim (Blindheim) on the Danube in Bavaria.

When: August 13, 1704.

Why: The Grand Alliance sought to limit Franco-Bavarian power by decisively defeating their forces.

Outcome: Marlborough defeated the Franco-Bavarian army and thereby saved Austria from invasion.

August 13, 1704, answered by an equally earshattering blast in reply from the British batteries (some 90-cannon strong). Tallard had almost no time to devise a sophisticated battle plan. The Franco-Bavarians would remain on the defensive, but the two armies would fight separately. Marsin would hold the center, the Elector on the left, and Tallard himself around Blenheim down to the Danube.

Marsin and the Elector would take positions right down to the banks of the Nebel, while Tallard's force would hold a position some 1,000 yards (914 m) south of the stream. Tallard hoped that Marlborough would advance across the Nebel, get caught in the crossfire from Oberglau and Blenheim—garrisoned with French troops—and thereby allow Tallard to counterattack and drive the British into the marshlands flanking the Nebel.

Marlborough had noticed that the enemy's right was stronger than its left and it was therefore on the stronger flank he would attack. Marlborough had a hunch about Tallard's ruse and sent Eugene to pin down the Elector, while he advanced to neutralize the French garrisons at Blenheim and Oberglau. The British and French artillery dueled for four hours, while a mixed cavalry and infantry column led General Lord John Cutts' column across the Nebel and created a bridgehead on the southern bank. Marlborough waited impatiently for news that Eugene had attacked and pinned down the Elector's Bavarians before he attacked.

At long last the Savoyard's aide-de-camp arrived with the welcome news, and at 12:30 P.M. Marlborough said to

THE TYPICAL THREE-RANK INFANTRY FORMATION *in use during the eighteenth century was made possible because of the availability of the bayonet. Shown here are infantry prepared to receive cavalry. The front rank kneels to ward off the horsemen with the bayonet while the second and third ranks fire.*

his generals, "Gentlemen, to your posts." Fifteen minutes later Brigadier-General Archibald Rowe's British brigade attacked Blenheim where—quite uselessly—12,000 French troops were bottled up. In the center, Prince Holstein-Beck's Germans attacking Oberglau were in trouble until Marlborough got Austrian cavalry from Eugene to beat back the French cavalry with heavy losses. Holstein-Beck drove the French back to the village and kept them confined there for the rest of the battle.

COLLAPSE

By 3 P.M. the Elector was kept away from joining the French while the villages had been prevented from supporting Tallard's counterattack. Marlborough finally crossed with the rest of his army an hour later and at 4:30 P.M. came the welcome news that Eugene had driven the Elector from the well-fortified position of Lützingen. Tallard finally realized that Marlborough had outmaneuvered him and rushed nine battalions to hold the position near Oberglau. It was "too little, too late."

The battalions fought ferociously to hold their positions but were slaughtered to the last man where they stood, while the much vaunted French cavalry fled into the waters and marshy banks of the Danube. By 5:30 P.M. the battle was over, with Tallard having fallen into British hands and the whole Franco-Bavarian army having ceased to exist as an organized military force. To their lasting honor the French garrisons of Blenheim and Oberglau held out until 9 P.M. when they too had finally had enough of the slaughter.

It had been neither an easy victory nor a bloodless one. A fifth of the Allied army was gone—4,500 killed and 7,500 wounded—but this was nothing to the destruction wrought on the Franco-Bavarians who had lost 15,000 prisoners and 13,600 dead and wounded.

TO PREPARE A CANNON TO FIRE, *the crew would have to go through a number of stages: first, swab the barrel with a wet sponge; then, load powder into the barrel; then, ram in the charge with the ramrod; next, direct the gun using a handspike; and finally, apply a lighted match to fire.*

BLENHEIM

3 Prince Eugene sends his army against the whole of Max Emmanuel's position, preventing him from giving assistance to Tallard.

6 The collapse of Tallard's position compels Max Emmanuel to abandon his ally and withdraw his forces.

5 Tallard's cavalry charges Marlborough's forces as they cross the Nebel stream, but are repulsed with heavy losses, as the weight of the British attack falls upon the outnumbered French cavalry.

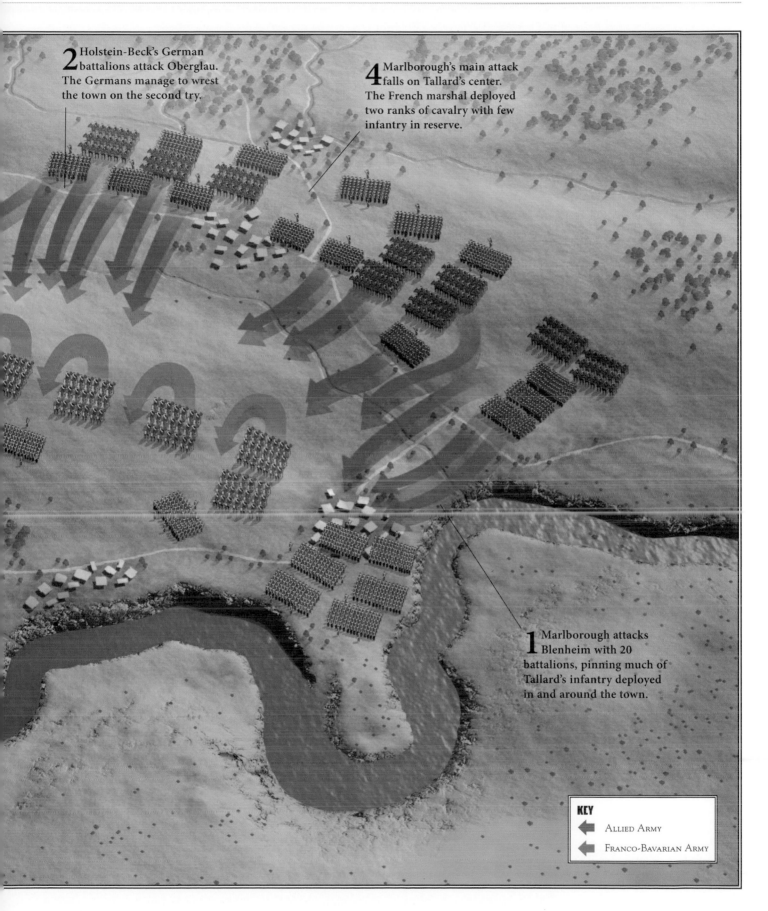

2 Holstein-Beck's German battalions attack Oberglau. The Germans manage to wrest the town on the second try.

4 Marlborough's main attack falls on Tallard's center. The French marshal deployed two ranks of cavalry with few infantry in reserve.

1 Marlborough attacks Blenheim with 20 battalions, pinning much of Tallard's infantry deployed in and around the town.

KEY

◀ ALLIED ARMY

◀ FRANCO-BAVARIAN ARMY

Rossbach 1757

WITH PRUSSIA ASSAILED ON MULTIPLE FRONTS, FREDERICK THE GREAT DEALT A STUNNING BLOW TO THE ARMIES OF AUSTRIA, THE HOLY ROMAN EMPIRE AND FRANCE AT ROSSBACH.

Shortly after the outbreak of the Seven Years' War, the Prussian army of Frederick the Great faced hostile forces from nearly all points of the compass. Fighting France, Austria, the Holy Roman Empire, and Russia, Frederick chose initially to deal with his westernmost enemy.

Marching 170 miles (275 km) in 13 days, Frederick's army of 22,000 reached the vicinity of Rossbach. He was significantly outnumbered, yet was intent on bringing the 42,000-man combined army of France, the Holy Roman Empire, and Austria to battle. On the morning of November 5, 1757, Frederick warily watched as the allied commander, Prince Charles of Soubise, initiated a flanking maneuver. As the two allied columns began an eastward turn, their commander believed he would soon be pursuing the Prussians, in retreat to avoid being flanked. Frederick, however, saw his opportunity and achieved a spectacular victory.

PRUSSIAN KING FREDERICK THE GREAT *is saluted by his troops during the Battle of Rossbach. Frederick's success at Rossbach confirmed him as one of the great generals of the era.*

BATTLE FACTS

Who: The army of Frederick the Great, King of Prussia (1712–86), against the combined armies of France, the Holy Roman Empire, and Austria under Prince Charles of Soubise (1715–87).

What: Frederick the Great marched from Dresden to Rossbach in 13 days to confront an Allied army before Russian forces could reach the Prussian eastern frontier in great numbers.

Where: The town of Rossbach in eastern Germany.

When: November 5, 1757.

Why: Frederick the Great sought to defeat the westernmost of his enemies and prevent an invasion of Prussia.

Outcome: Frederick combined the elements of surprise and rapid movement to achieve a stunning victory with minimal losses.

SEYDLITZ'S CHARGE

Utilizing the cover of nearby hills, Frederick rushed artillery and infantry forward. The Allied movement was complex in its execution, and Frederick expected to strike the exposed enemy flank or the head of the marching formations as they turned. General Friedrich Wilhelm von Seydlitz (1721–73) led a rapid cavalry advance, while 18 Prussian guns opened fire from nearby heights. Simultaneously, Prussian infantry surged down the slope of Janus Hill.

Almost immediately, the Allied columns began to disintegrate, and efforts to form a cohesive resistance proved futile. French infantry vainly launched a few counterattacks that were quickly crushed. The swift assault of the Prussian horsemen caught the Allied cavalry unprepared, separated from Soubise's main troop concentration, and drove them from the field. Seydlitz then reformed his cavalry and fell upon the Allied right flank. Disorganized and defeated, the Allied army quickly withdrew.

Within 90 minutes, Frederick had utilized rapid movement and the element of surprise to defeat an enemy army nearly twice the size of his own, while only a portion of the Prussian army was even engaged in the battle. At Rossbach, more than 5,000 Allied soldiers were killed or wounded and another 5,000 captured. In sharp contrast, the Prussians suffered only 169 dead and 379 wounded.

Quebec 1759

BRITISH FORCES CAPTURED THE FRENCH-CANADIAN CITY OF QUEBEC FOLLOWING A THREE-MONTH SIEGE AND A BRIEF BATTLE ON THE PLAINS OF ABRAHAM OUTSIDE ITS IMPOSING WALLS.

By the spring of 1759, victories in North America had swung the momentum of the Seven Years' War in the Western Hemisphere, where it has come to be known as the French and Indian War, decidedly in favor of the British Crown. The French bastion of Quebec on the St. Lawrence River was vulnerable to attack, and an expedition of approximately 4,800 British regulars and colonial soldiers under General James Wolfe landed slightly downstream from the city on June 28, 1759.

Wolfe was opposed at Quebec by a force of approximately 4,200 French regulars, colonials, militia, and Indians under Louis-Joseph, Marquis de Montcalm, who deployed his forces on the north bank of the St. Lawrence. Montcalm discounted the potential threat of a landing upstream.

MORTALLY WOUNDED, GENERAL WOLFE *is tended by a representative selection of his army, as British forces emerge victorious on the Plains of Abraham.*

BATTLE FACTS

Who: British forces under General James Wolfe (1727–59) against the French army of Louis-Joseph, Marquis de Montcalm (1712–59).

What: The British sought to gain control of the city of Quebec and dominate the St. Lawrence River and the surrounding area.

Where: The Plains of Abraham near Quebec, at the narrowing of the St. Lawrence River in Canada.

When: September 13, 1759.

Why: British and French forces fought for control of the vast colonial areas established in the Western Hemisphere, while the Seven Years' War raged in Europe.

Outcome: In a sharp but brief battle, lasting only about 15 minutes, British troops fired two volleys, breaking the French advance and forcing a retreat.

THE PLAINS OF ABRAHAM

Following the dismal results of an effort to land British troops on the north shore of the river on July 31, however, during which he lost 450 men killed or wounded, Wolfe decided to do just that. Realizing that a landing at L'Anse-au-Foulon above Quebec would force Montcalm to defend his supply route to Montreal, Wolfe undertook the operation on the night of September 12. Approximately 3,300 British soldiers climbed the 174 ft (53 m) escarpment and marched 1 mile (1.6 km) to the Plains of Abraham, open ground stretching up to the city walls.

At dawn on September 13, Montcalm was greeted by elements of nine British regiments formed in a single line. His troops marched out to meet the enemy. As skirmishers engaged, the advancing French fired from too great a distance. The British, lying down to avoid such fire, rose and delivered two shattering volleys, the first at a scant range of 35 yards (32 m). Within 15 minutes, it was over. The French retreated, but both Wolfe and Montcalm had been mortally wounded.

During the short fight, the British lost 60 killed and 600 wounded, while French casualties amounted to 200 dead and 400 wounded. Five days after the battle, Quebec surrendered to the British, who withstood a later siege by the French but never relinquished their hold on the city.

COLONIAL FORCES DEFEND BUNKER HILL against British attack. Although the victors, the British Army suffered more than a thousand casualties, or one-third of their troop strength.

Bunker Hill 1775

A PYRRHIC BRITISH VICTORY DROVE COLONIAL FORCES FROM THE HEIGHTS ON THE CHARLESTOWN PENINSULA BUT DID LITTLE TO RAISE THE SIEGE OF BOSTON.

Following the opening battles of the American Revolution at Lexington and Concord, British forces in Boston found themselves encircled by colonial troops and militia. British strength in the besieged city had grown to approximately 6,000 men by the spring of 1775, and General Thomas Gage, commander of the garrison, determined that the capture of the heights on the Charlestown Peninsula, north of Boston, would strengthen his position.

Through an informant, the colonials became aware of the planned British initiative and on June 16 hastened 1,500 men under the command of Colonel William Prescott and General Israel Putnam to Breed's Hill, placing the city of Boston within range of their artillery. Breed's Hill was closer to Boston than nearby Bunker Hill, and Prescott's soldiers fortified the high ground while taking fire from the 38-gun frigate HMS *Lively*, anchored in Boston harbor. Aware that his flanks were exposed, Prescott ordered the fortifications

BATTLE FACTS

Who: Colonial forces under Colonel William Prescott (1726–95) and General Israel Putnam (1718–90) confronted British troops under Major General William Howe (1729–1814).

What: British troops attempted to gain control of the Charlestown Peninsula to prevent colonial forces from closing their grip on Boston.

Where: Breed's Hill on the Charlestown Peninsula near Boston harbor.

When: June 17, 1775.

Why: General Thomas Gage (1719–87), commander of the Boston garrison, believed control of the Charlestown Peninsula would improve his defense of Boston.

Outcome: British troops captured Bunker Hill, but suffered terrible casualties during the fighting.

extended to the shoreline. The British moved quickly to counter the threat from Breed's Hill and assembled a force of about 1,500 troops under the command of Major General William Howe to attack the colonials the following day. After several hours of preparation and the formation of a plan involving assaults against the colonial center and right flank, British troops were ferried in longboats to Moulton's Point on the southern end of the Charlestown Peninsula. Meanwhile, Prescott called for reinforcements, and some additional colonial troops arrived and took up positions on Bunker Hill. Many of them, however, were reluctant to move forward to the more exposed positions on Breed's Hill.

BRITISH ATTACK

The initial assault by the British was undertaken against the colonial left flank near the shoreline by several companies of light infantry under the direct command of General Howe. This was quickly followed by a general assault on the strong redoubt in the center, which the colonials had constructed during the previous night.

With the British light infantry and grenadiers deployed in long lines and to a depth of up to four men, the first wave of attackers made easy targets for the colonials, a number of whom had taken up firing positions from behind a rail fence and steadied their muskets for better aim. The first assault came to grief, and the British regrouped.

A short time later, a second attack was concentrated on the strong positions of the rail fence and the central redoubt. Scores of British troops fell dead or wounded within moments of exposing themselves to the colonists' fire, and the second attempt to carry Breed's Hill met a similar fate to the first. By this time, however, the colonials

WITH DRUMMERS BEATING THE ADVANCE, *British grenadiers assault Bunker Hill. Officers and flag bearers tended to lead from the front, making them prominent targets for the colonial marksmen.*

THIS BRITISH SOLDIER IS ARMED *with the Long Land Pattern musket, the "Brown Bess," used by British forces from the 1720s until the 1830s. The trained British regular was able to load and fire his musket up to three times a minute.*

were running low on ammunition, and General Putnam was desperately calling for reinforcements from the idle ranks on Bunker Hill. Relatively few responded.

Frustrated, Howe called for reinforcements from the Boston garrison and sent a third assault forward against the depleted colonial center and the formidable redoubt. As the defenders ran out of ammunition, British troops breached the redoubt wall. Hand-to-hand fighting ensued, the British thrusting bayonets and the colonials responding with fists and empty muskets used as clubs. At last, the colonials abandoned the hilltop and began to withdraw from both Breed's Hill and Bunker Hill. Roughly handled and now much depleted, the British did not pursue in large numbers.

PYRRHIC VICTORY

The British held the high ground on the Charlestown Peninsula until their troops were evacuated from Boston in late 1775. Howe and other senior British commanders during the battle have been criticized for landing in front of the colonials' fortifications rather than beyond them on the peninsula, facilitating a flanking operation and then capture of the high ground from the rear. To compound the ineptitude of the British effort, their 6-pounder cannon had been supplied with 12-pounder ammunition, rendering them useless in any effort to bombard the colonial positions. As for the Americans, the embryonic Continental Army did stand against its disciplined, professional foe. However, the refusal of large numbers of soldiers to fight and a pronounced lack of discipline proved problematic for the future.

British casualties were an appalling 226 killed and 828 wounded, roughly one-third of the total troop strength ultimately committed to the battle and the largest toll suffered during the entire American Revolution. Among the British casualties were 19 officers. Colonial losses amounted to 115 dead and 305 wounded. Although the British had succeeded in capturing the Charlestown Peninsula, an assessment of the cost caused General Henry Clinton (1730–95), one of those who had planned the offensive, to comment that the so-called Battle of Bunker Hill was "…a dear bought victory, another such would have ruined us."

ARTIST JOHN TRUMBULL *captured the surrender of General John Burgoyne (left) at Saratoga to the Continental Army under General Horatio Gates (right).*

Saratoga 1777

IN THE FALL OF 1777, THE BRITISH MAJOR-GENERAL JOHN BURGOYNE MOVED HIS ARMY SOUTHWARD THROUGH THE REBELLIOUS COLONY OF NEW YORK, TOWARD ALBANY, IN THE MAIN THRUST OF A THREE-PRONGED OFFENSIVE. RATHER THAN VICTORY, BURGOYNE FOUND FRUSTRATION, HARDSHIP, AND, EVENTUALLY, SURRENDER FOLLOWING A SERIES OF BATTLES THAT ENDED AT SARATOGA.

O n June 13, 1777, Burgoyne set off on his expedition down Lake Champlain with just over 7,000 men. Although there were successes, such as the capture of Fort Ticonderoga on July 6, the going was hard both militarily and physically. A particularly grievous blow was suffered when some 1,000 men were lost attempting to capture the American supply base at Bennington on August 16. Combined with the depredations inflicted by American guerrilla warfare tactics, and the fact that the two other prongs of the New York offensive failed to perform,

BATTLE FACTS

Who: British General John Burgoyne (1722–92) and a force of British regulars, Indians, and German mercenaries numbering 8,000 faced 7,000 Continental soldiers under General Horatio Gates (1727–93).

What: In the climax of his ill-fated campaign, Burgoyne was forced to surrender his army following defeats at the battles of Freeman's Farm and Bemis Heights.

Where: Eastern New York in the valley of the Hudson River north of Albany.

When: October 17, 1777.

Why: The British determined a grand strategy to split New England, the hotbed of revolutionary ardor.

Outcome: The surrender of an entire British army convinced France to enter the war on the side of the Americans.

Burgoyne was in a much-weakened position as he went into the fall. Along with the Battle of Bemis Heights, fought on October 7, the battle at Freeman's Farm on September 19, 1777, was to be the decisive action of the Saratoga campaign. In mid-August, Horatio Gates had replaced General Philip Schuyler as commander of the main American army in the north. Burgoyne had not recovered from the serious casualties sustained at Bennington, while Gates had received reinforcements and was recruiting successfully, volunteers spurred by news of atrocities committed by Indians allied to the British.

Occupying a strong position at Bemis Heights, Gates became aware that Burgoyne had crossed the Hudson and marched southward in September. Gates deployed his forces with three infantry brigades and massed artillery to his right, nearest the river, 2,000 soldiers under Brigadier Ebenezer Learned in the center, and the combined forces of Benedict Arnold (1741–1801) and Daniel Morgan (1736–1802), numbering about 2,000, on his left. One major concern was that the British might skirt the American left flank and occupy nearby high ground, forcing the Americans out of their position with artillery fire.

For this reason, Arnold strongly urged Gates to allow him to attack the British first. Gates, however, waited for Burgoyne to join the battle. When Burgoyne moved three divisions forward around Freeman's Farm on the morning of September 19, Gates ordered Morgan's riflemen, crack shots to a man, forward. As they concentrated their fire on British officers, Morgan's men goaded the redcoats into a charge. Arnold committed his reserve force and pushed the British, under General John Hamilton, to the breaking point. When Arnold requested reinforcements, Gates refused and ordered Arnold to retire to the American lines. Arnold did not respond to the order and continued to attack. Only the arrival of 1,100 fresh troops under the command of the German General Baron von Riedesel managed to drive Arnold back. In the evening gloom, Burgoyne counted his losses at 600, twice that of the Americans, who held the high ground.

BEMIS HEIGHTS

When Burgoyne took stock of his situation after the fight at Freeman's Farm, the tally was disconcerting. Supplies were inadequate, and his strength had been reduced through combat, desertion, and disease. No help was forthcoming from other British units. Still, one decisive blow against Gates might save the campaign for the British. From their positions around Freeman's Farm, the British advanced, 1,500 strong under the command of Simon Fraser, to probe the American positions around Bemis Heights. Fraser's movement was discovered, and Gates again sent Morgan forward to exact a

COLONIAL INFANTRYMEN

Infantrymen of the fledgling Continental Army, inexperienced and often badly equipped, demonstrated a remarkable resolve when under capable leadership. Enduring tremendous hardship, their eventual victory was bolstered by militia, irregular units, and the intervention of the French military.

toll on the British. Morgan hit Fraser's right at the edge of a wheat field, while Enoch Poor's 800-man brigade hit the left. Both flanks collapsed and exposed Riedesel's Germans in the center to attack by Learned's brigade.

A growing animosity between Gates and Arnold had erupted into open contempt, and Gates replaced his unruly subordinate with General Benjamin Lincoln (1733–1810). During the Battle of Bemis Heights, Arnold was officially without a command. He did not, however, stay out of the fight. Arnold galloped to the sound of the guns and shouted to Learned's attacking troops to follow him. Riedesel's veterans broke, and Fraser was shot dead trying to patch together a second line of defense. With Fraser's reconnaissance force shattered, Arnold exhorted his men to attack a pair of British fortifications at Freeman's Farm. The first, Balcarre's redoubt, was flanked and captured as its German defenders threw down their arms. A short time later, Breymann's redoubt also fell to the Americans.

When the fighting ended, the British had lost another 600 men. In comparison, American casualties were relatively light at 150. Leaving casualties behind, the British tramped toward the high ground around the village of Saratoga the following day. At first, the commander agreed with his officers that a fighting retreat to Fort Edward might be accomplished. He later reconsidered and opened negotiations for surrender. On October 17, 1777, the surrender of Burgoyne at Saratoga altered the course of the American war for independence.

SARATOGA

5 His situation desperate, General John Burgoyne orders the remaining British forces to withdraw northward along the river road toward the village of Saratoga.

2 Daniel Morgan's frontier riflemen spearhead a devastating assault on the British left, while 800 more Colonials assail their exposed right flank.

3 Without orders, General Benedict Arnold reaches the field and directs the Colonials in pursuit of the routed British and Hessian mercenaries.

4 Initially repulsed, the Americans eventually capture a pair of British redoubts. While directing the effort, Arnold is seriously wounded in the leg by a musket ball.

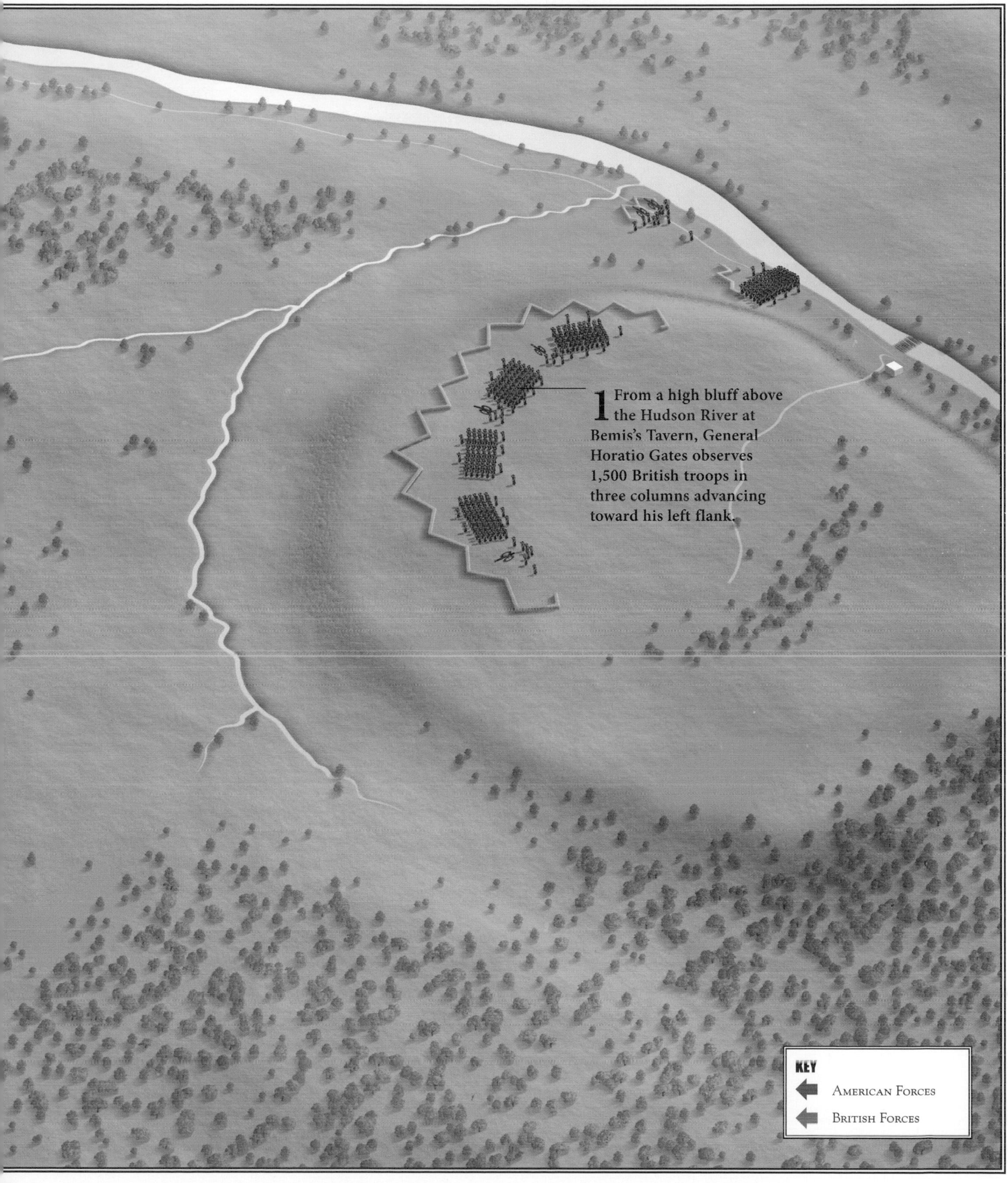

1 From a high bluff above the Hudson River at Bemis's Tavern, General Horatio Gates observes 1,500 British troops in three columns advancing toward his left flank.

KEY

AMERICAN FORCES

BRITISH FORCES

THE AMERICAN COMMANDER-IN-CHIEF *and future president George Washington stands at the center surrounded by French engineers in Louis Couder's painting entitled* SIEGE OF YORKTOWN.

Yorktown 1781

THE CLIMACTIC BATTLE OF THE AMERICAN REVOLUTION RESULTED IN THE CAPTURE OF MORE THAN 7,000 BRITISH TROOPS BY WASHINGTON'S CONTINENTAL ARMY AND ITS FRENCH ALLIES.

When the British army of General Charles Lord Cornwallis turned northward from the Carolinas in the summer of 1781, it proved to be a fatal mistake. Cornwallis had determined that he would continue his campaign in Virginia but was instead instructed to fortify a port with access to Chesapeake Bay and beyond to the open Atlantic.

Cornwallis undertook the task at Yorktown, Virginia, situated on a peninsula between the James and York rivers. At the same time, a combined force of Continental troops under General George Washington and the Comte de Rochambeau had assembled in New York and begun moving southward in conjunction with a substantial French naval force under Admiral François Joseph Paul de Grasse (1722–88), which was maintaining a blockade

BATTLE FACTS

Who: Continental and French forces under General George Washington (1732–99) and the Comte de Rochambeau (1725–1807) confronted the British army of General Charles Lord Cornwallis (1738–1805).

What: The allied armies besieged Cornwallis' troops at Yorktown, Virginia.

Where: Yorktown, Virginia, on a peninsula between the James and York rivers.

When: September 28 to October 19, 1781.

Why: Washington and Rochambeau sought a decisive victory over British forces in America.

Outcome: The allied armies forced the British to surrender, resulting in the decisive victory of the American Revolution.

ATTACKS BY AMERICAN AND FRENCH *troops on the British redoubts did not breach the perimeter but served notice that the position was untenable and so induced Cornwallis to open negotiations for surrender.*

of the Chesapeake. In conjunction with de Grasse, whose ships defeated a British naval squadron under the command of Admiral Thomas Graves (1725–1802) during the Battle of the Capes on September 5, 1781, Washington and Rochambeau arrived at Yorktown in late September and began to dig siege lines, trapping Cornwallis and his assembled army of approximately 9,000 British regulars and Hessian mercenaries.

THE SIEGE

Cornwallis had expected reinforcements from General Henry Clinton (1730–95) in New York and chose to remain in Yorktown, where these reinforcements might easily disembark, rather than moving once again southward into the Carolinas or northward toward Clinton's base of operations in New York. However, the defeat of Graves ultimately prevented reinforcement from the sea, and it quickly became apparent that Cornwallis had waited too long to make good his escape from Yorktown.

By early October, Washington had gathered enough forces to begin a bombardment of Yorktown itself. Continental and French troops had occupied fortifications the British had abandoned earlier and extended a semicircular siege line called the "first parallel". Washington himself was said to have fired the initial cannon shot of the siege of Yorktown.

On the night of October 14, a contingent of 400 French troops seized Redoubt No. 9, while 400 Continental soldiers stormed Redoubt No. 10 along the banks of the York River. The fighting was intense and often hand-to-hand. Cornwallis had lost the most vital strongpoints

in his defensive line. Washington was able to extend his second siege parallel and bombard Yorktown simultaneously from three sides.

Two nights later, Cornwallis attempted to ferry some of his troops across the York River to Gloucester, possibly to establish an avenue of escape into the Virginia countryside. While the operation was under way, an intense storm buffeted the British boats and thwarted the attempt. As the allied cannon fire intensified by the hour, Cornwallis knew that the British army at Yorktown was doomed.

"THE WORLD TURN'D UPSIDE DOWN"

Early on October 17, a British officer accompanied by a drummer boy appeared on top of their earthworks and were taken into the allied lines. Surrender negotiations began the following day and were concluded on October 19. The British marched into captivity as their fife-and-drum contingent played a popular tune of the day, "The World Turn'd Upside Down." Cornwallis, stating that he was ill, did not attend the surrender ceremony, sending General Charles O'Hara (1740–1802) instead. O'Hara initially attempted to hand Cornwallis's sword to Rochambeau, who declined and pointed to Washington. In turn, Washington instructed O'Hara to surrender to his own subordinate, General Benjamin Lincoln (1733–1810). British and Hessian casualties included about 300 dead, 600 wounded, and more than 7,000 taken prisoner. Combined Continental and French losses were 88 killed and 300 wounded. The victory of the Continental and French armies at Yorktown proved to be the decisive battle of the American Revolution.

NAVAL SIEGE CANNON

By the eighteenth century, cannon tubes were comparatively inexpensive items of equipment, and a single warship could carry far more guns than the average army could transport or maintain. This naval gun was used in the siege of Yorktown. The British Royal Navy was not only called upon to provide artillery for besieging fortresses. At Yorktown, General Cornwallis had ships' guns like this one landed to assist in the defense.

Karánsebes 1788

FOR A BATTLE TO TAKE PLACE, THERE NORMALLY HAVE TO BE TWO OR MORE OPPOSING FORCES PRESENT. THIS WAS NOT THE CASE AT THE "BATTLE" OF KARÁNSEBES, WHICH WAS SIMPLY AN ESCALATING SELF-INFLICTED DISASTER OF UNBELIEVABLE PROPORTIONS.

When fighting broke out between Imperial Russia and Turkey in 1787, Austria dutifully declared war on Turkey in support of her ally and assembled an army for campaign. Joseph II (1741–90), the Holy Roman Emperor, led the army, but even though he had greatly admired the brilliant Prussian king, Frederick the Great (1712–86), Joseph was entirely incapable of emulating his prowess on the battlefield.

The Austrian army advanced with the intention of intercepting a Turkish advance on the fortress of Vidin, located on the southern bank of the Danube River in north-western Bulgaria. As usual, scouts were pushed out ahead of the army to search for the enemy. For this purpose, the Austrian army used hussar light cavalry. As the Austrian army reached the Timis River, a party of hussars was

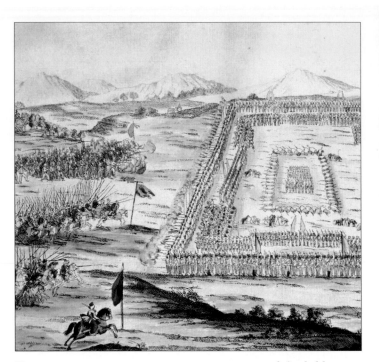

TURKISH CAVALRY CHARGE AN AUSTRIAN CAMP *defended by infantry drawn up in square. The Austrians had good cause to fear the Turkish cavalry.*

BATTLE FACTS

Who: The Austrian Army against itself.

What: A trivial incident sparked panic, with units firing on one another in the confusion. Up to 10,000 Austrian troops were killed or wounded.

Where: Near the town of Karánsebes in modern-day Romania.

When: September 17, 1788.

Why: Random misfortune compounded by linguistic difficulties led to Austrian units firing on each other in the mistaken belief that

they were fighting Ottoman Turkish forces.

Outcome: The Austrian Army fled in disarray as the Turkish army arrived two days later and took the city unopposed.

sent across the bridge at Karánsebes to search for the enemy. They did not find any evidence of the Ottoman army, which was still two days' march away, but they did encounter a group of Wallachian gypsies, who offered to sell them schnapps. Naturally the hussars accepted the offer and quickly became drunk.

CHAOS AT KARÁNSEBES

As the hussars were making merry with their new gypsy friends, they clashed with a group of Austrian infantry, who wanted to share the drink. Shots were fired. Other infantrymen came up with a clever ruse to scare off the cavalry by pretending that either they were Turks or that the Turks were approaching. This did not work exactly as planned—the situation quickly dissolved into a mass exercise in "friendly fire" and moral collapse. Individuals, small groups, and artillery batteries fled or tried to make a stand, firing at anyone who approached them. In the darkness it was impossible to tell that what seemed to be a charging enemy was actually a terrified friend, nor that other groups trying to protect themselves from imaginary attack fired the bullets that tore across the camp. The Austrian army arrived at Karánsebes 100,000 strong. It lost one-tenth of its manpower during one night, taking into account dead, wounded, and missing soldiers, some of whom simply melted away into the countryside. The camp was mostly destroyed and large quantities of supplies were lost.

Nile 1798

A BRITISH NAVAL SQUADRON UNDER ADMIRAL HORATIO NELSON DEFEATED NAPOLEON'S FLEET DECISIVELY AND ASSURED CONTROL OF THE MEDITERRANEAN SEA BY THE ROYAL NAVY.

The territorial ambitions of Napoleon Bonaparte (1769–1821) nearly came to premature ruin as his fleet headed for Egypt was relentlessly pursued across the Mediterranean Sea in the summer of 1798. Once Napoleon's French army was ashore near the great Nile River, however, his fleet awaited its pursuer, Rear Admiral Horatio Nelson and 13 ships of the line of the British Royal Navy, at Aboukir Bay.

ATTACKED FROM TWO SIDES
The French fleet, under Vice Admiral Francois-Paul Brueys d'Aigalliers, included 13 ships of the line and four smaller frigates. D'Aigalliers' flagship was the massive 118-gun *L'Orient*, and the French commander arrayed his fleet along the edge of a treacherous shoal, placing his ships in line with *L'Orient* in its strong center. Nelson's fleet sighted the

THE BATTLE OF THE NILE *featured the biggest explosion of the Napoleonic Wars, when the magazine on the French warship* L'Orient *spectacularly combusted.*

BATTLE FACTS

Who: The British fleet under Rear Admiral Horatio Nelson (1758–1805) against the French Fleet commanded by Vice Admiral François-Paul Brueys d'Aigalliers (1753–98).

What: The British pursued Napoleon's French invasion fleet across the Mediterranean to Egypt and brought it to battle.

Where: Aboukir Bay, near the mouth of the Nile in Egypt and the Eastern Mediterranean.

When: August 1–3, 1798.

Why: Napoleon mounted a military campaign in the Middle East with the ultimate goal of conquering British India.

Outcome: The British Royal Navy won a decisive victory, and Napoleon's land campaign failed in part because of his loss of control of the Mediterranean.

French on the afternoon of August 1, 1798, and the British commander aboard the 74-gun HMS *Vanguard* ordered his captains to prepare for battle.

At 6:20 P.M., the French ships *Guerrier* and *Conquerant* opened fire; however, Captain Thomas Foley (1757–1833) aboard HMS *Goliath*, exploited a gap between *Guerrier* and the shoal. *Goliath* was followed by HMS *Zealous*, and soon the French were under attack from two sides. In the center, *Vanguard* engaged the French on the starboard side. Fighting raged for more than three hours. A fire was spotted aboard the French flagship shortly after 9 P.M., and an hour later the huge vessel's magazines exploded.

The battle continued on August 2, and by afternoon the British were boarding prize ships while a few French vessels escaped to the open sea. Eleven French ships of the line had been blown up or captured. Among the British vessels, *Vanguard*, *Bellerophon,* and *Majestic* sustained hull damage, *Majestic* and *Bellerophon* also losing masts. Nelson was wounded, and d'Aigalliers was killed. British casualties totaled 218 dead and 677 wounded, while estimates of French losses are as high as 5,000.

With the victory at the Battle of the Nile, also known as the Battle of Aboukir Bay, the Royal Navy was preeminent in the Mediterranean, blockading French ports, neutralizing the French garrison on the island of Malta, and cutting supply lines to Napoleon in Egypt.

Trafalgar   1805

NELSON'S VICTORY AT TRAFALGAR FINALLY ENDED THE THREAT OF FRENCH INVASION OF THE BRITISH ISLES AND SECURED THE ROYAL NAVY'S DOMINANCE OF THE SEAS FOR THE NEXT 100 YEARS. BUT AT THE MOMENT OF HIS GREATEST TRIUMPH, BRITAIN'S FOREMOST NAVAL HERO WAS KILLED ON THE DECK OF HIS FLAGSHIP HMS *VICTORY*.

A t 11 A.M. on October 21, 1805, in the middle of the Napoleonic Wars, Vice Admiral Lord Nelson hoisted a morale-boosting signal to his fleet of 27 warships off Cape Trafalgar, southwestern Spain. It read "England expects that every man will do his duty." There was an almighty roar of approval from officers and men across the British fleet as the signal was read and understood.

The British fleet was facing an opposing force of 18 French and 15 Spanish vessels, which had sailed out of Cádiz on October 19, commanded by Admiral Pierre de Villeneuve. The Franco-Spanish column had been spotted,

BATTLE FACTS

Who: A Franco-Spanish fleet of 33 ships under Admiral Pierre de Villeneuve (1763–1806) versus a British fleet of 27 ships under Vice Admiral Lord Horatio Nelson (1758–1805).

What: Nelson's head-on attack on the Franco-Spanish line broke their formation and allowed superior British gunnery to destroy the enemy.

Where: At the entrance to the Straits of Gibraltar off Cape Trafalgar, Spain.

When: October 21, 1805.

Why: Nelson, having chased the Franco-Spanish Fleet, caught up with it in the Straits of Gibraltar and de Villeneuve chose to fight rather than flee.

Outcome: The Combined Fleet was smashed and Britain had removed the threat of a French invasion.

and, as the British aggressively approached, de Villeneuve turned his ships north in a single column, ready to deliver crushing broadsides.

Forty-five minutes after Nelson hoisted his signal, the first hesitant firing began as de Villeneuve, on his flagship *Bucentaure* (80 guns), gingerly hoisted his pennant. Nelson, by contrast was on the poop deck of the *Victory*, as he made—at 11:50 A.M.—his last signal for the fleet to "Engage the enemy more closely." By 12:04 P.M. *Victory's* massive oak sides were being showered with shot from *Bucentaure*, *Redoutable*, *Héros*, and the Spanish behemoth—the 136-gun *Santissíma Trinidad*, the flagship of Admiral Baltazar de Cisneros.

While these ships fired broadsides against *Victory*, the French and Spanish sharpshooters on the decks and in the masts swept *Victory's* decks with musket fire. Yet *Victory* finally passed under the stern of the *Bucentaure*, and unleashed a devastating double-shotted raking broadside through her stern galleries, dismounting 20 guns and killing dozens of her crew. The rest of the fleet followed, breaking the Franco-Spanish line just as Nelson had planned and the battle became a mêlée of individual ship-to-ship actions, in which superior British gunnery would dominate.

By 1:10 P.M. *Victory* was entangled with the French *Redoutable* commanded by Captain Jean-Jacques Lucas—a firebrand Provençal—who inspired his crew to fight ferociously against their British enemy. In a matter of minutes the accurate and deadly French fire had killed 40 Marines. A sharpshooter aboard the *Redoutable* hit Nelson with a shot that penetrated the admiral's shoulder and lung, and pierced his spine.

HEAVY GUNFIRE

Now and for the next two hours the battle was at its fiercest. The *Redoutable* was under fire from both sides as the 98-gun HMS *Téméraire* joined the fight. At 1:40 P.M. the *Téméraire* raked the *Redoutable*—by now a wreck—with repeated broadsides, but Lucas and his brave crew refused to strike their colors until *Téméraire* was in as equally miserable shape as their own vessel. Finally Lucas and his men surrendered. The *Redoutable* had lost 487 killed and 81 wounded, including Lucas.

By 2:30 P.M. the *Santissíma Trinidad* too was a complete wreck, but when a British boarding party stepped onto the deck a Spanish officer told them that the proud flagship had not capitulated despite being unable to fire a single gun. It would be hours until she was finally seized by the British. *Bucentaure* was also, by 4:15 P.M., out of commission with 450 casualties, hardly a crew member still standing after the prolonged and brutal firefight.

De Villeneuve, who had been standing completely still during the whole ordeal, hoping with all his heart to be killed, did not have a scratch on him when his crippled flagship finally surrendered to Captain Israel Pellew of the *Conqueror*. Fifteen minutes later, at 4:30 P.M., Nelson died knowing that his beloved fleet had won a great victory. By this time Admiral Collingwood (1750–1810) had smashed most of the Spanish squadron under Admiral Gravina (1757–1806), well to the southwest of the main battle area. The Spanish, like the French, had put up a ferocious defense of their ships, but were in the end defeated by the more experienced British.

The news of Nelson's victory reached England on November 6, where rejoicing at the defeat of the enemy fleet and the end of the invasion threat was tempered by grief at the loss of the nation's greatest hero. The Battle of Trafalgar, one of the most decisive victories in naval history, was the beginning of a century of almost unrivaled dominance for the Royal Navy.

GUN DECK

Three-tiered gundecks marked the "First Rate" capital ships of the Age of Fighting Sail. On the top deck the loaded cannon is run out on its truck through the open gun port, ready to fire on the approaching enemy. The middle deck depicts a fired cannon rolling back into the ship from the recoil of its shot, where it will be cleaned and reloaded by the gun crew. The lowest deck shows a gun secured against the closed gun port for sea worthiness. A "loose cannon" was more than metaphorically dangerous in a ship rolling and pitching in heavy weather.

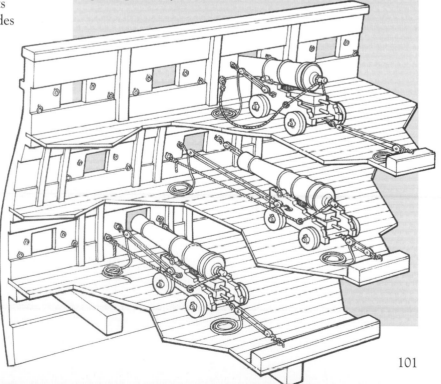

TRAFALGAR

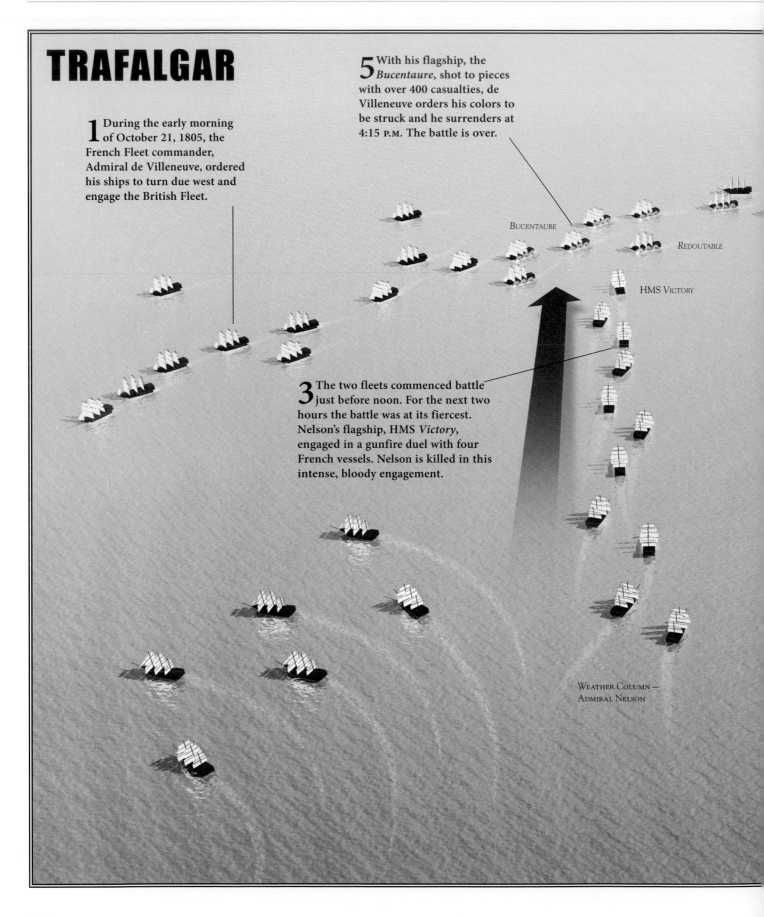

1 During the early morning of October 21, 1805, the French Fleet commander, Admiral de Villeneuve, ordered his ships to turn due west and engage the British Fleet.

5 With his flagship, the *Bucentaure*, shot to pieces with over 400 casualties, de Villeneuve orders his colors to be struck and he surrenders at 4:15 P.M. The battle is over.

3 The two fleets commenced battle just before noon. For the next two hours the battle was at its fiercest. Nelson's flagship, HMS *Victory*, engaged in a gunfire duel with four French vessels. Nelson is killed in this intense, bloody engagement.

BUCENTAURE

REDOUTABLE

HMS VICTORY

WEATHER COLUMN—
ADMIRAL NELSON

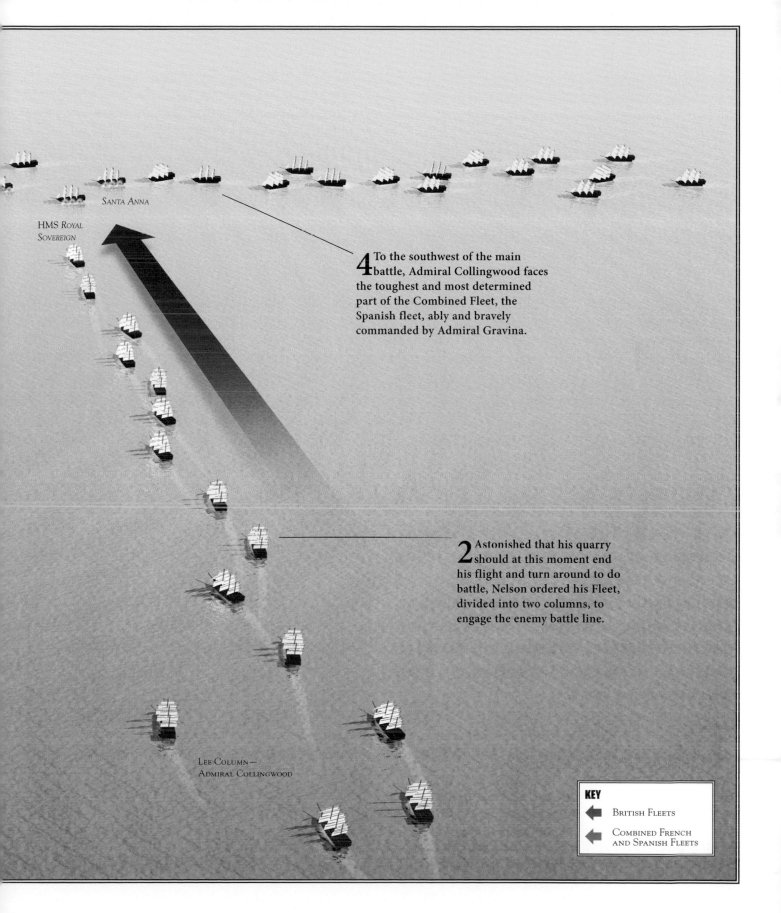

SANTA ANNA

HMS ROYAL
SOVEREIGN

4 To the southwest of the main
battle, Admiral Collingwood faces
the toughest and most determined
part of the Combined Fleet, the
Spanish fleet, ably and bravely
commanded by Admiral Gravina.

2 Astonished that his quarry
should at this moment end
his flight and turn around to do
battle, Nelson ordered his Fleet,
divided into two columns, to
engage the enemy battle line.

LEE COLUMN—
ADMIRAL COLLINGWOOD

KEY

⬅ BRITISH FLEETS

⬅ COMBINED FRENCH
AND SPANISH FLEETS

IN THIS OIL PAINTING NAPOLEON is seen encouraging his troops in their bivouacs during the night prior to the battle on December 2, 1805 (by Baron Louis Albert Bacler d'Albe [1761–1848]).

Austerlitz   1805

A YEAR AFTER HIS CORONATION AS EMPEROR, IN THE CULMINATION OF THE GREATEST CAMPAIGN OF HIS CAREER, NAPOLEON DEFEATED THE COMBINED ARMIES OF RUSSIA AND AUSTRIA AT AUSTERLITZ, WHERE HE, HIS GENERALS, AND SUPERBLY TRAINED TROOPS DISPLAYED THEIR PROWESS ON THE BATTLEFIELD. BUT FOR ALL ITS GENIUS, NAPOLEON'S VICTORY AT AUSTERLITZ DID NOT IMMEDIATELY BRING PEACE.

The Battle of Austerlitz, fought on December 2, 1805, as part of Napoleon Bonaparte's Danube campaign, shows the French emperor and commander at his tactical best. He stopped, with 70,000 troops, near the village of Austerlitz, Moravia, in the second half of November, hoping to tempt an 86,000-strong combined Russo-Austrian army into battle. A key feature of the battlefield was the elevated Prätzen Heights. This area of high ground dominated the battlefield, but Napoleon deliberately withdrew his forces from the feature, drawing

BATTLE FACTS

Who: The Emperor Napoleon (1769–1821) with 73,000 men defeat the combined armies of Imperial Russia, led by Czar Alexander I (1777–1825), and Austria lead by Emperor Francis II (1768–1835) with 85,000 troops.

What: Napoleon provoked the Allies into launching an attack, then occupied the Prätzen Heights in the center of the battlefield, dividing the enemy and defeating them.

Where: Near the village of Austerlitz in Bohemia, 70 miles (113 km) north of Vienna.

When: December 2, 1805.

Why: The new revolutionary state in France threatened the established monarchies of Europe.

Outcome: The Allied army was shattered. The French had dealt a major blow to the Third Coalition.

the Allied army up onto the heights instead. At 5 A.M. on December 2, when he held his council of war, Napoleon left General Legrand and Marshal Davout with 18,600 men to hold the right while he concentrated the bulk of his army, 65,000 men, on his left.

Over breakfast, Czar Alexander I of Russia reprimanded the nominal commander of the combined army, General Mikhail Kutuzov (1745–1813), for not getting his troops to advance more quickly. Kutuzov replied that he needed all the units to be in line before he could advance—which they finally did by 6 A.M. At the village of Telnitz the Austrian advance guard ran into heavy fire from the elite Corsican Legion. For an hour a fierce battle was fought around the small village until the French retreated.

Some 13,600 Russians, led by General Doctorov, could have fulfilled the Allied plan had he pressed on and hit Napoleon's vulnerable and open flank. But delay and confusion allowed the French to reform, and during the morning hours 10,000 French troops held up the advance of 50,000 Russians and Austrians.

THE PRÄTZEN HEIGHTS

Napoleon had set up his field HQ on the nearby Zarlan Heights and at 8:45 A.M. he observed through his telescope how the Allies marched south, abandoning the crucial Prätzen Heights. Napoleon asked how long it would take for Marshal Soult's men—concealed at the bottom of the hill—to march up and seize the heights. Soult replied that it would take only 20 minutes. So Napoleon waited until the very last Allied troops had left Prätzen before he ordered Soult to advance.

Despite the French observing almost complete silence as they carefully advanced up the slope, their movement was observed and reported by a Russian officer to Kutuzov. The general ordered his firebrand deputy Miloradovich to retake the heights but it was too late, although the Russians made valiant efforts to dislodge

Soult's force from the village of Prätzen. By 11 A.M. the heights were held by Soult, despite several failed attempts by the Russians to take it back. Both Kutuzov and the Czar were nearly killed by the heavy French artillery fire.

Growing ever more desperate the Czar sent his brother, Grand Duke Constantine, and his 8,500 Imperial Guards—which had been kept in reserve—into the fray. These tall, handpicked troops advanced on the Prätzen Heights and broke through the first French line, but the heavy musket and artillery fire proved too much, and they were driven from the heights. Now Soult's men wheeled around to attack the flank and rear of the Russian-Austrian assault on the French right, threatening the Allies with encirclement.

By 2 P.M., however, there was nothing left of the Russian army's central position and the Allies now began to flee the battlefield. In the streets of the village of Zokolnitz (in the south of the battle) and around its venerable old castle, dead, dying, and wounded lay in heaps. Davout, in an order that sullied his good reputation, gave orders for his troops to spare no Allied prisoners or wounded. However, large numbers of Allied troops escaped the French onslaught unscathed across the frozen ground and marshes.

As it began to snow the battle came to an end, with the French too exhausted to pursue the fleeing Allied troops. Napoleon had dealt a massive and fatal blow to the Third Coalition that left Austria crushed, Russia humiliated, and Britain shorn of its continental allies. The French had lost 9,000 men—a mere 12 percent of their numbers—while the Allies had lost almost one-third of their army—some 27,000 troops.

AUSTRIAN DRAGOON

To match Napoleon's Cuirassiers, the Austrians had the elite dragoon, who were similarly attired and equipped as their feared French enemy. However, the Austrian dragoons lacked the fearsome reputation of their opponents and proved much less effective in combat. Heavy cavalry of this type were used as shock troops on the battlefield—either to force the issue through a massed frontal assault, or by turning a battle by quickly exploiting weaknesses or gaps in the enemy's lines.

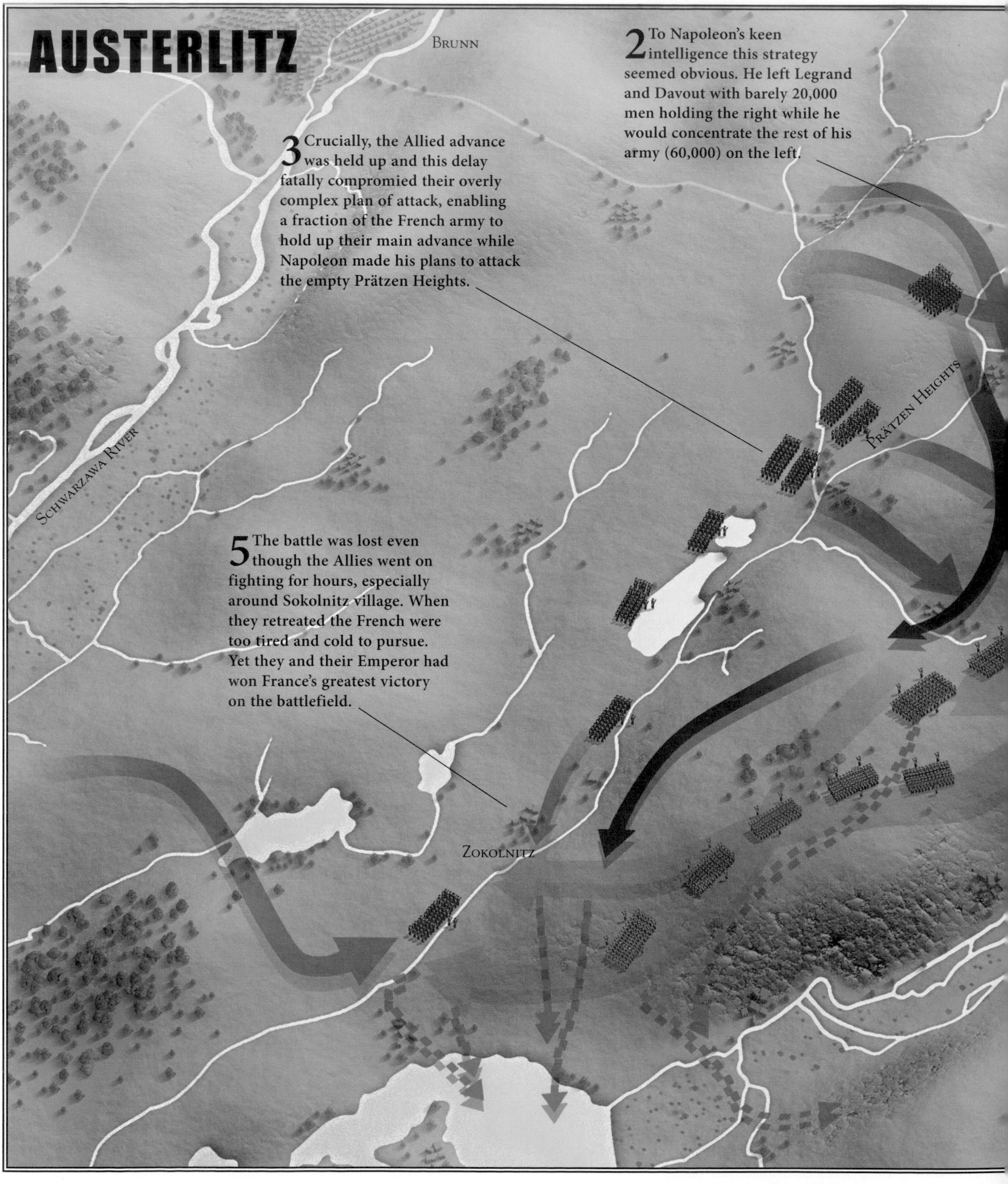

AUSTERLITZ

BRUNN

2 To Napoleon's keen intelligence this strategy seemed obvious. He left Legrand and Davout with barely 20,000 men holding the right while he would concentrate the rest of his army (60,000) on the left.

3 Crucially, the Allied advance was held up and this delay fatally compromised their overly complex plan of attack, enabling a fraction of the French army to hold up their main advance while Napoleon made his plans to attack the empty Prätzen Heights.

5 The battle was lost even though the Allies went on fighting for hours, especially around Sokolnitz village. When they retreated the French were too tired and cold to pursue. Yet they and their Emperor had won France's greatest victory on the battlefield.

SCHWARZAWA RIVER

PRÄTZEN HEIGHTS

ZOKOLNITZ

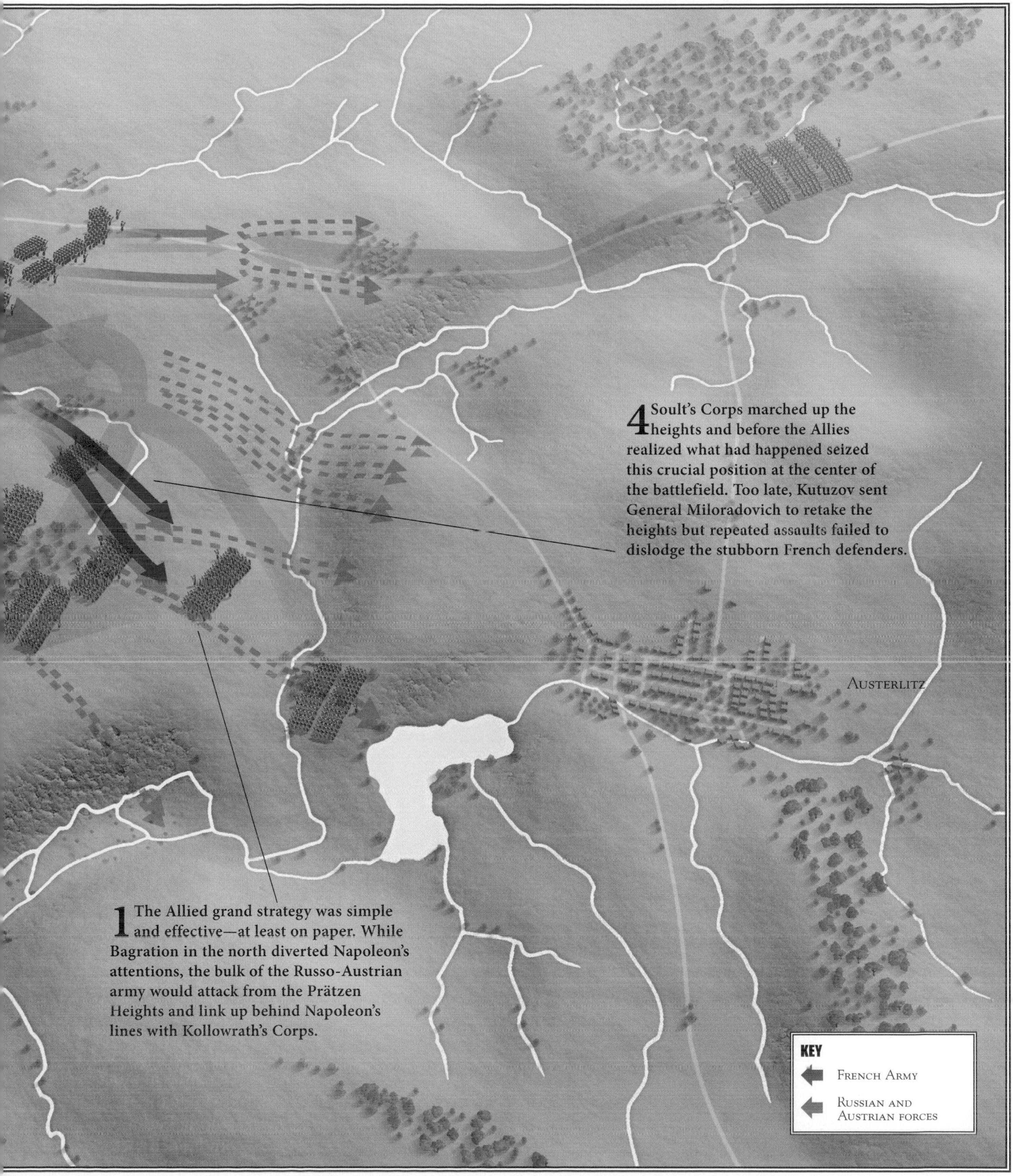

4 Soult's Corps marched up the heights and before the Allies realized what had happened seized this crucial position at the center of the battlefield. Too late, Kutuzov sent General Miloradovich to retake the heights but repeated assaults failed to dislodge the stubborn French defenders.

AUSTERLITZ

1 The Allied grand strategy was simple and effective—at least on paper. While Bagration in the north diverted Napoleon's attentions, the bulk of the Russo-Austrian army would attack from the Prätzen Heights and link up behind Napoleon's lines with Kollowrath's Corps.

KEY

FRENCH ARMY

RUSSIAN AND AUSTRIAN FORCES

Jena-Auerstädt 1806

TWIN VICTORIES SKILLFULLY FOUGHT BY NAPOLEON BONAPARTE AND HIS ABLE CORPS COMMANDERS RESULTED IN THE EVENTUAL CAPTURE OF BERLIN, THE PRUSSIAN CAPITAL.

With 180,000 veteran troops, Napoleon Bonaparte marched northward through the Thuringian Forest in October 1806 and found himself east of a substantial Prussian army, numbering up to 145,000. The Prussians, under the Duke of Brunswick, Prince Friedrich Ludwig Hohenlohe, and General Ernst Friedrich von Ruchel (1754–1823), believed that Napoleon was to their front and were slow to react to the discovery of their enemy.

After brushing aside a small Prussian force at Saalfeld on October 10, Napoleon mistakenly assumed that he had found the main enemy army at Jena near the Saale River three days later. Ordering four corps, roughly 96,000 troops, to attack this Prussian contingent of slightly more than 50,000, Napoleon routed the enemy on October 14 and inflicted 26,000 casualties. French losses totaled 5,000.

BATTLE FACTS

Who: The French Army of Napoleon Bonaparte (1769–1821) against the Prussian Army led primarily by the Duke of Brunswick (1735–1806) and Prince Friedrich Ludwig Hohenlohe (1746–1815).

What: During one of his most successful campaigns, Napoleon employed the tactic of distributed maneuver with independent but mutually supporting corps.

Where: The vicinity of Jena and Auerstädt in central Germany near the Thuringian Forest.

When: October 14, 1806.

Why: Napoleon intended to defeat his Prussian enemy and then deal with a threat from Russia to the east.

Outcome: Although he initially mistook a smaller Prussian Army for the main enemy force, Napoleon and his lieutenants achieved resounding victories.

TROOPS MOVE IN NEAT COLUMNS *at the Battle of Jena, as imagined by an artist. Actual battles of the period were far more confused, not least because of the gun smoke that would cover the entire battlefield.*

TWIN VICTORIES

At Jena, Napoleon displayed his genius for maneuver, advancing with independent corps on the same general route but capable of supporting one another as needed. During the fighting, he narrowly averted disaster when the corps of Marshal Michel Ney (1769–1815) attacked without orders, became overextended and took Prussian artillery fire. Napoleon ordered Marshal Jean Lannes (1769–1809), who had already displayed his command skills at Saalfeld, to move from the French center in support of Ney. He then placed his Imperial Guard in the center. The movement was successfully executed, and Ney was saved.

Once the Prussians were located, Napoleon had ordered Marshals Louis-Nicholas Davout (1770–1823) and Jean-Baptiste Bernadotte (1763–1844) to the north and east in an attempt to flank the Prussians as they were engaged with the main French army along the Saale River. At Auerstädt, Davout's 27,000-man III Corps was outnumbered nearly three to one by Prussian troops under the Duke of Brunswick, who was killed in the fighting.

The audacious Davout outmaneuvered the Prussians, who committed their strength piecemeal, and soundly defeated them. Bernadotte marched and countermarched, participating in neither battle, and was later reprimanded by Napoleon. The French lost 10,000 casualties at Auerstädt, the Prussians 13,000. Following the twin victories, Napoleon pursued the Prussians, capturing Berlin on October 24. The campaign ended with French victories that virtually extinguished organized Prussian resistance.

Wagram 1809

IN THE FINAL BATTLE OF THE WAR OF THE FIFTH COALITION, NAPOLEON DEPLOYED LARGER NUMBERS OF TROOPS AND HEAVY GUNS TO DEFEAT THE AUSTRIANS.

On the heels of a tactical setback at Aspern-Essling in May 1806, during which his forces sustained more than 25,000 casualties, Napoleon Bonaparte withdrew his Grande Armée of French, Italian, and German troops south of the Danube River. The opposing Austrian army under Archduke Charles failed to seize the initiative.

In turn, Napoleon regrouped and crossed the Danube a second time on the night of June 4. His concentrated army numbered nearly 180,000, outnumbering the 130,000 Austrians opposing him. The lethargic Austrians reacted slowly to Napoleon's offensive move and took positions astride the town of Wagram on the Marchfield, a plain northeast of Vienna.

HARD FIGHTING

On the evening of July 5, Napoleon, hoping to win a victory before 30,000 Austrian reinforcements under

EMPEROR NAPOLEON OBSERVES ENEMY *troop movements at Wagram, in a painting by Horace Vernet, from the Musée National du Château at Versailles, in France.*

Charles's brother Archduke John (1782–1859) could arrive, attacked his enemy's left and made nominal gains. An attack against the Austrian center was repulsed when Charles himself led a counterattack and pushed the French back to their original position.

Charles realized his center remained vulnerable and ordered his troops forward all along Napoleon's line on the morning of July 6. The French left flank was hard pressed, and Napoleon ordered the corps of Marshal André Massena (1758–1817) to march 5 miles (8 km), smash into the flank of the advancing Austrians, and stabilize the situation. In the center, massed artillery and cavalry attacks stopped the Austrian advance.

Napoleon then hurled 8,000 men under General Jacques MacDonald (1765–1840) against the Austrian center. Although this attack failed to penetrate the Austrian line, it prevented Charles from bolstering his own heavily engaged left flank. The Austrians began to buckle, and the order was given to withdraw. Napoleon did not pursue with vigor, although the Austrians were compelled to seek peace soon enough.

Each side suffered heavily at Wagram, the Austrians losing more than 40,000 casualties and the French nearly 38,000. Napoleon had been denied a clear-cut victory and had lost more than 60,000 troops since mid-May. Clearly, the quality of his opponents was improving, while that of his own forces appeared to be in decline.

BATTLE FACTS

Who: The Grande Armée of Napoleon Bonaparte (1769–1821) against the Austrians under Archduke Charles (1771–1847).

What: Napoleon renewed his campaign against the Austrians after a temporary reversal at Aspern-Essling.

Where: The town of Wagram on the Marchfield, 10 miles (16 km) north of Vienna.

When: July 5–6, 1809.

Why: Napoleon sought to defeat the Austrians during the War of the Fifth Coalition, thus preventing

the forces of other nations from joining Austria and Great Britain.

Outcome: Although victorious, Napoleon failed to achieve a decisive triumph and sustained heavy casualties. The Austrians later asked for peace terms and signed the Treaty of Vienna on October 14, 1809.

NAPOLEON'S ARMY ATTACKS *the heavily fortified Russian defenses at Borodino. Napoleon dispensed with maneuver in favor of head-on attacks, an approach that was to prove very costly.*

Borodino 1812

ALTHOUGH NAPOLEON CLAIMED VICTORY 70 MILES (110 KM) FROM MOSCOW, HE FAILED TO DESTROY THE RUSSIAN ARMY AND WAS EVENTUALLY UNDONE.

When the Grande Armée of Napoleon invaded Russia in the spring of 1812, he audaciously pursued the army of Michael Andreas Barclay de Tolly (1761–1818) across the vastness of the country. Disputes among his own commanders caused Barclay to avoid a pitched battle with Napoleon's force, which initially numbered 286,000 troops, raising the ire of government officials in the Russian capital at Moscow. However, the strategy actually worked to Russian advantage, stretching French supply lines perilously thin and subjecting them to flank attacks.

By August 29, Barclay had been removed from command and replaced with 67-year-old Prince Mikhail Kutuzov. Kutuzov continued the strategy of retreat, with Napoleon following and losing soldiers to disease, fatigue, and desertion. By September 3, the Russian commander turned to stand at the village of Borodino, a scant 70 miles

BATTLE FACTS

Who: Le Grande Armée of Napoleon I (1769–1821) against a Russian army under Prince Mikhail Kutuzov (1745–1813).

What: The bloodiest single day of fighting during the Napoleonic Wars occurred after a Russian withdrawal to their country's interior.

Where: Near the town of Borodino, 70 miles (110 km) west of Moscow.

When: September 7, 1812.

Why: Napoleon sought to

augment his empire in the vastness of Russia.

Outcome: Borodino was a pyrrhic victory for the French. When the Russian army withdrew, Napoleon entered Moscow. Eventually, he was forced to begin the disastrous winter retreat from the Russian capital.

(110 km) from the gates of Moscow. He ordered the erection of formidable earthworks. One of these was at Shevardino, astride the route of Napoleon's advance. The center of the Russian line was dominated by earthworks known as the Raevsky redoubt, and three arrow-shaped strongpoints on the left, which were called the Bagration Flèches, after one of Kutuzov's subordinates, Prince Peter Bagration (1765–1812).

FRONTAL ASSAULTS

When the Grande Armée arrived in the vicinity of Borodino early in September, it had been reduced to about 160,000 French and allied troops, while Russian strength was slightly less at 130,000. On September 5, the French assaulted the Shevardino redoubt, catching the Russians realigning the forces on their left. Cavalry clashes preceded a full-scale attack the following day, and the position fell in savage fighting that cost the attackers 5,000 killed and wounded. The Russians suffered 6,000 casualties.

Reports of Kutuzov's conduct during the unfolding battle have been contradictory, some asserting that most high-level command decisions were left to subordinates. Kutuzov was well schooled in defensive fighting, and Borodino did in fact develop into a defensive struggle for the Russians. However, the fall of Shevardino weakened the left flank of the army, and despite pleas for reinforcements there, Kutuzov was unmoved. Further, over half the Russian artillery, 300 guns, remained idle with many of his troops along the right wing, which was never attacked. Bagration gave his life defending the left.

As for Napoleon, Borodino was far from his finest hour in command. He brushed aside the counsel of his marshals and ordered a direct assault against the Bagration Flèches rather than a flanking movement. From dawn until nearly their capture at noon, control of the three Flèches changed hands. French casualties were appalling, but Russian reinforcements were shredded by concentrated artillery fire.

NAPOLEON'S POLISH LANCERS *charge General Duka's 2nd Cuirassier Division in front of the Great Redoubt in this panoramic painting by artist Franz Roubard (1856–1928).*

PYRRHIC VICTORY

Toward the center, the Raevsky redoubt fell to the French and was then recaptured in vicious hand-to-hand fighting. At 2 p.m., the decisive assault of Napoleon's army carried the redoubt, with Polish and Saxon cavalry supporting yet another frontal assault. On the extreme Russian left at Utitsa, fighting raged in the morning, and troops under the command of Prince Jozef Poniatowski (1763–1813), a Pole who became a Marshal of France, fought Russian infantry and grenadiers for control of the village. The French entered Utitsa but were ejected before a final push drove the Russians out of the burning town.

Napoleon had been ill and remained some distance from the battlefield. Despite the urging of his commanders and the general sentiment that the Russians were ready to break, leaving the road to Moscow open, Napoleon refused to commit 30,000 reserve troops, two-thirds of which were his vaunted Imperial Guard, the elite of the Grande Armée. His reluctance to exploit the hard-won gains of September 7, the largest and bloodiest day's action of the Napoleonic Wars, resulted in a Pyrrhic victory. The Russian army was defeated but not destroyed, and a golden opportunity to bring Czar Alexander I (1777–1825) to the negotiating table was lost.

At Borodino, Russian casualties topped 45,000, while the French lost more than 28,000. A week later, Napoleon entered Moscow. He waited at length for a Russian surrender that never materialized and then was compelled to begin the long, disastrous trek westward, which decimated his once-proud army.

PROTECTED BY AN ARMORED CUIRASS *(breastplate) and helmet, and armed with a straight thrusting sword, the French cuirassier was a potent force on the battlefield.*

ON THE RETREAT FROM MOSCOW as painted by artist Laslett John Pott (1837–98), shows the suffering of Napoleon's troops as they trudge through the bitter Russian winter to safety.

Retreat from Moscow 1812

EMPEROR NAPOLEON IS SOMETIMES KNOWN AS THE "GREAT GAMBLER." MANY OF THE RISKS HE TOOK PAID OFF HANDSOMELY, BUT THE INVASION OF RUSSIA IN 1812 WAS AN UNMITIGATED DISASTER. THE FRENCH GRANDE ARMÉE WAS DESTROYED BY COLD, HUNGER, AND ATTRITION RATHER THAN A DECISIVE BATTLE.

After the Battle of Friedland in 1807, Russia and France entered into an alliance, which many Russians considered to be one-sided. By 1810 Czar Alexander I (1777–1825) had begun to ignore some of the terms of the Treaty of Tilsit, which defined the alliance. In 1812 Napoleon (1769–1821) decided that the arrangement no longer suited his purposes and launched a massive invasion of Russia.

Napoleon's strategy for dealing with international crises was straightforward. He would march into the target

BATTLE FACTS

Who: The French Grande Armée, numbering 600,000 under Emperor Napoleon, opposed by three Russian armies and a large number of partisan and irregular forces, totaling 900,000.

What: Having captured Moscow, the French were forced to retreat in the depths of winter.

Where: The French advance was via Vilna (modern-day Vilnius, Lithuania) and Smolensk to Moscow. The retreat followed a similar route.

When: June–December 1812.

Why: Napoleon hoped to force a treaty on the Russians by taking Moscow.

Outcome: The Grande Armée was ruined. Military losses amounted to 300,000 French and 260,000 allied troops. Russian losses were similar.

EMPEROR NAPOLEON IN MILITARY UNIFORM. By 1812 he was past his best and willing to buy victory at the cost of heavy casualties.

country and try to bring about a decisive battle in order to destroy the country's military capability. This might be enough to force a treaty favorable to France on the defeated nation. If not, Napoleon would advance on the enemy capital and dictate terms from there.

Napoleon was aware of the military power of Russia and the considerable distance he would have to advance through hostile territory. His nearest bases were in Poland, and it was from there that the Grande Armée—more than 600,000 men—invaded Russia on June 23, with unstable logistical arrangements.

Although Imperial Russia could muster large numbers of troops, these were not concentrated and the individual forces could not halt the French. Attempts to concentrate and establish a good position were defeated by the speed of the French advance, forcing the Russians to fall back.

The French did not have it all their own way, of course. Harassment by Cossacks and regular cavalry was a serious nuisance, and the forage was very poor. By the time the French reached Vilna (modern-day Vilnius, capital of Lithuania) the supply situation was becoming dire, largely because of a "scorched-earth" policy implemented by the retreating Russians. Men had to be detached to guard the line of supply while the logistics troops did their best to bring up food and supplies from the magazines far away in Poland. The Grand Armée was losing men at an alarming rate despite not fighting a major battle. The Russians attempted a stand at Smolensk and then fell back again. At the village of Borodino, some 75 miles (120 km) from Moscow, they assembled sufficient troops in a good enough position and offered battle. Napoleon settled on the unimaginative plan of a frontal assault, and on September 7 the Battle of Borodino, bloodiest clash of the Napoleonic Wars, began. Although possession of the battlefield is a traditional measure of victory, the battle had an indecisive quality to it. Both sides lost 30,000–40,000 men, which the Russians were better able to replace. However, the Russian army retreated and Napoleon was able to lead his army on to Moscow without much further opposition.

DISAPPOINTMENT IN MOSCOW

Napoleon expected the Czar to surrender when he took Moscow, but instead he found that most of the population had fled, taking with them anything edible. Not only was the capture of the city an anticlimax, it created new problems. Winter was closing in and French troops were forced to forage for whatever they could find in the city. Fires broke out, whether deliberately or otherwise, and without strong civil authorities in place to handle the crisis, they soon got out of control. As much as 80 percent of the city was destroyed.

Bereft of victory, food, and shelter, Napoleon made the decision to retreat. He had intended to follow a different route to that he had approached Moscow along, marching through lands not stripped of forage by his army and the Russian scorched-earth policy. However, the vanguard was unable to break through Russian forces, which were holding blocking positions, and the army was channeled back along its former route.

Forced to retreat through a barren area, the French army gradually disintegrated as cold, hunger, and attacks by irregular forces took their toll. Men who had deserted or straggled from the army during its advance now contested the few sources of food available to them. Formations shrank or broke up entirely, though some retained their cohesion right to the end. Similarly, some commanders rallied what men they could find and formed a scratch rearguard that helped protect the others.

There were few major actions, though a Russian attack as the army tried to cross the Berezina River caused major casualties. In truth there was no need to fight another battle; the French were losing massive numbers of men every day. About 30,000–40,000 troops reached French territory in some semblance of military order, and roughly the same number came out of Russia as stragglers. The Grande Armée had essentially ceased to exist.

FRENCH INFANTRYMAN

This "French" soldier's thick greatcoat also serves as a blanket. A cover to reduce damage on campaign protects his hat. Other equipment is minimal, enabling the French army to march quickly, so long as it is possible to forage for supplies along the way. Although an asset in most campaigns, reliance on living off the land led to disaster in Russia.

THE BATTLE OF LEIPZIG, OCTOBER 16–18, 1813 (*oil on canvas*),
*by Alexander Ivanovich Sauerweid (1783–1844), attempts to
portray the huge army employed by the Sixth Coalition at Leipzig.*

Leipzig   1813

**DEFEATED BY THE CONCENTRATED ARMIES OF THE SIXTH
COALITION, NAPOLEON LOST CONTROL OF HIS EMPIRE
EAST OF THE GREAT RHINE RIVER.**

Despite the disastrous Russian campaign, the horrific retreat that followed during the winter of 1812, and a deteriorating military situation on the Iberian Peninsula, Napoleon I, legendary military commander and Emperor of France, regrouped and marched eastward the following spring with nearly 200,000 men to stabilize his hold on his German possessions. Although the number of soldiers under his command appeared impressive, the fighting capabilities of some of the formations were suspect. Many veteran troops and scores of senior officers had perished in recent months.

By October 1813, he had strung together victories in the East at Lützen, Bautzen, and Dresden but had failed to capture Berlin. Perhaps heeding an expensive lesson learned in Russia, he withdrew across the Elbe River to protect his lines of supply and communication and marshaled

BATTLE FACTS

Who: The outnumbered French army under the Emperor Napoleon (1769–1821) against the Allied armies of the Sixth Coalition.

What: A decisive battle at Leipzig also came to be known as the "Battle of the Nations."

Where: The city of Leipzig and its environs in the region of the modern free state of Saxony.

When: October 16–18, 1813.

Why: Napoleon sought to reassert control over previously conquered German provinces.

Outcome: A decisive Allied victory forced Napoleon to abandon his empire east of the Rhine, leading to the invasion of France and the Emperor's abdication in 1814.

his command around the city of Leipzig. While they had previously avoided direct confrontations with Napoleon, the commanders of the various armies that made up the Sixth Coalition then realized the moment of truth had arrived.

From several directions the armies of Prussia, Russia, Sweden, and Austria converged on Leipzig with an aggregate of more than 425,000 soldiers under the command of Austrian Karl Philipp, Prince of Schwarzenberg (1771–1820), Russian Field Marshal Michael Andreas Barclay de Tolly (1761–1818), Prussian General Gebhard von Blücher (1742–1819), and Crown Prince Charles John of Sweden (1763–1844), formerly one of Napoleon's Marshals.

INITIAL CLASHES

The Battle of Leipzig, also known as the "Battle of the Nations," opened on October 16 when separate Allied attacks mounted with inadequate numbers were repulsed by the French on their northern and southern flanks. For one of the few times in his military career, however, Napoleon's force was inherently too weak to exploit the potential gains with a breakthrough of the Allied lines. Other rather isolated clashes occurred at Dölitz, where Austrian troops effectively utilized heavy artillery to wrest control of the town from Polish soldiers fighting with Napoleon under Prince Jozef Poniatowski (1763–1813), and Markkleeberg, where Polish and French troops put up stubborn resistance before retreating.

Also on October 16, Russian troops were roughly handled at Wachau and failed to hold the town against French artillery fire and repeated infantry counterattacks through the village streets. The town of Liebertwolkwitz changed hands twice. A force of 10,000 French cavalry moved forward in large columns only to be smashed by Russian artillery, while more than 100 French guns massed on a nearby hill ravaged the Russian infantry. Elite members of Napoleon's Imperial Guard surged forward, retook both Wachau and Liebertwolkwitz, and were stopped only when elite Russian and Austrian grenadiers formed squares and poured murderous fire into them. To the north, Russian infantry captured two small villages.

More fighting raged at Möckern, where the French defenders used buildings and walls as cover against two corps of attacking Russian and Prussian troops. Blücher handled his command skillfully, inflicted heavy casualties on the French, and was promoted to field marshal on the spot. The French Marshal Auguste de Marmont (1774–1852) ordered a cavalry charge, but his subordinate refused to obey. Soon enough, a charge by Russian hussars inflicted a heavy toll on the French, who lost 9,000 soldiers killed, wounded, or captured. Allied losses were about the same.

THIS FRENCH FOOT ARTILLERYMAN is dressed in the new 1812 regulation uniform. Clothed in the usual dark blue, French artillerymen were considered elite troops and received good pay in recognition. They were chosen for intelligence and strength, and were the best artillery arm of the period.

DECISIVE VICTORY

Blücher's hard-fought victory set the stage for the decisive combat at Leipzig two days later following a lull on October 17, which saw only two clashes, the Russian capture of the town of Gohlis, and another stroke by Blücher, which decimated a contingent of French cavalry.

The arrival of nearly 150,000 additional Russian and Swedish troops spelled the end for Napoleon at Leipzig. On October 18, the French were assailed all along their front, and the fighting wore on for nearly ten hours. Austrian troops retook Wachau and the neighboring village of Lossnig in attacks superbly coordinated by cavalry and infantry. As the battle engulfed Leipzig itself, a contingent of more than 5,000 Saxon infantry defected from Napoleon's army and joined the Allies.

Control of events was rapidly slipping from Napoleon's grasp, and as night fell he ordered a general withdrawal across the Elster River. Early the next day, the Allies' scouting parties realized what was happening but their attacks were blunted by a competent rearguard action executed by Marshal Nicolas Oudinot (1767–1848). When the order was given to blow up the sole bridge across the Elster, an unfortunate corporal carried it out prematurely. Thousands of French troops were either killed or trapped in Leipzig. Poniatowski drowned while attempting to cross the Elster.

Casualties sustained during the three days of fighting at Leipzig amounted to 74,000 French and Polish troops and about 54,000 Allied soldiers. Napoleon was compelled to remain west of the Rhine. In early 1814, the Allies invaded France, and soon Napoleon abdicated. Within weeks, he had been exiled to the island of Elba in the Mediterranean.

BAYONETS FIXED, SCOTTISH INFANTRY STAND FIRM *as elite French cuirassiers charge the interlocking squares. The solid Allied infantry proved their worth at Waterloo.*

Waterloo 1815

THE FINAL BATTLE OF THE NAPOLEONIC WARS SAW THE FRENCH EMPEROR'S AMBITIONS CRUSHED ONCE AND FOR ALL. DESPITE FLASHES OF HIS FORMER BRILLIANCE, NAPOLEON WAS UNABLE TO BREAK UP THE ALLIED ARMIES, AND HIS FATE WAS SEALED BY THE PRUSSIANS MARCHING TO WELLINGTON'S AID ON JUNE 18 RATHER THAN FALLING BACK AFTER THEIR REVERSE AT LIGNY.

The Battle of Waterloo was the climax of the Napoleonic wars. Faced with opposition from multiple Allied armies, Napoleon seized the initiative and went on the offensive against the Duke of Wellington's Anglo-Dutch army (95,000 men) and Gebhard von Blücher's Prussian army (124,000 men) in Belgium. On June 16, Napoleon fought both Allied armies at Ligny and Quatre Bras. He succeeded in putting the Prussians into retreat from Ligny to Wavre, and began an ineffective pursuit, while Wellington eventually pulled 68,000 men to positions near Waterloo, again with French forces hot on his heels.

BATTLE FACTS

Who: The Emperor Napoleon (1769–1821) with 72,000 men attacked an Anglo-Dutch army of 60,000 men under the Duke of Wellington (1769–1852), who was joined by Prince Gebhard von Blücher's (1742–1819) Prussian army that evening.

What: Wellington's army was able to hold off Napoleon's disjointed attacks until the Prussian army arrived.

Where: The ridge of Mont St. Jean, near the village of Waterloo, 10 miles (16 km) south of Brussels in Belgium.

When: June 18, 1815.

Why: Napoleon's restoration of the Empire could not be tolerated by the Allies, who sought to crush this threat to European peace.

Outcome: Defeat at Waterloo forced Napoleon's second abdication and exile.

Napoleon had prepared to attack the Anglo-Dutch army at 10:30 A.M. on June 18 with a force of 72,000 men, but there had been a downpour overnight that made the ground too soft for cavalry and artillery. The main assault was postponed, with fatal consequences, until 1 P.M., although the French began a preliminary artillery bombardment at 10:50 A.M. against the chateau of Hougoumont on Wellington's right, held by the tough Hanoverian troops of the King's German Legion (KGL) and a detachment of Nassau troops.

To distract Wellington's attention from his left flank—where Napoleon's main attack would be launched—Napoleon gave orders that his brother Prince Jérôme was to attack Hougoumont to draw off Wellington's reserves. This action, although bloody, achieved little but tie up French troops. Near 1 P.M., furthermore, as Napoleon prepared to attack, came unwelcome news for the French. General Bülow's Prussian Corps (30,000 men) was now approaching from the direction of Wavre. Napoleon hoped that the Prussians would be held off by a force under Marshal Grouchy, but clearly time was not on his side.

FULL-SCALE ATTACK

It was not until 2 P.M. that Napoleon unleashed Marshal d'Erlon's I Corps. D'Erlon, hoping to break through the Allied lines by sheer weight of numbers, formed his divisions into three massive columns of battalions deployed one behind the other. Although very vulnerable to Allied artillery and musket fire in this formation, the avalanche of blue-clad infantry proved almost irresistible once I Corps' assault got underway, sweeping van Biljandt's exposed 1st Netherland (Dutch-Belgian) Brigade aside. Wellington's left-center position buckled under this huge wave of attacking infantry, forcing him to commit all the units he could spare, and at enormous cost. The French attack ground to

IN THEIR CHARACTERISTIC *bearskin caps, florid whisjers and sideburns, the veterans of the Old Guard was Napoleon's last reserve—one that he threw away at Waterloo.*

a halt. They began to retreat, finally fleeing, leaving some 3,000 prisoners for the British to pick up. An hour later (by 3 P.M.) the British had defeated the first French assault.

At 3:30 P.M. Napoleon ordered his artillery to pound La Haie Sainte and for Marshal Ney (1769–1815) to prepare for a new attack that he would lead in person. The attack, when it came, was botched and launched without Napoleon's express command. Lacking infantry or artillery support, Ney's cavalry stormed with great bravado up the slope to be met by a hail of artillery and massed musket fire at point blank range. Eventually, and despite additional cavalry units being fed into the assault, the attack petered out, Ney being forced to walk back to his own lines on foot. Hundreds of cavalrymen met their deaths with extreme courage, while the British infantry squares repelled wave after wave of the cuirassiers, dragoons, and lancers. The Prussians had also begun to appear at the edge of the battlefield (the Bois de Paris) by 4 P.M. and an hour later Napoleon was forced to shore up Georges Mouton's VI Corps—now reduced to only 7,000 men—by sending 4,000 men of the Young Guard. In a last attempt to break through Wellington's center Napoleon ordered the Old Guard—his final reserve and troops who had never been beaten—to attack. British troops concealed behind a ridge were able to surprise the columns before they could deploy into line and shattered them with close-range musketry. As the Old Guard fell back, the French army's morale finally cracked and they broke and fled. Napoleon took flight in a coach.

The French had lost some 30,000 men, while Wellington had lost 15,000 and the Prussians 6,700. On June 22, Napoleon abdicated for a second time and fled Paris. He boarded HMS *Bellerophon* at Plymouth on July 15 and exactly four months later stepped ashore on the island of St. Helena—his "home" until his death in 1821.

95TH RIFLES

In the British Army and the British expeditionary army in Belgium of 1815, the 95th Rifles stood out for two glaringly simple reasons. First, its infantrymen were equipped with rifles, rather than the rest of the Army's trusted Brown Bess muskets. Second, when the rest of the army, irrespective of arm, wore the King's vivid scarlet uniforms, the 95th were clothed, for reason of camouflage, in dark-hued green. They were formed during the Peninsular War (1808–14) for a dual purpose—to fight as regular infantry and also as skirmishers and snipers ahead of the main army.

WATERLOO

3 At 2 P.M. Napoleon sends d'Erlon's 1st Corps against Wellington's left-center position. Despite massive artillery support and dashing élan the combination of General Picton's Anglo-Hanoverian infantry and the British cavalry halted the onslaught.

5 The first Prussians begin to arrive at the battlefield. Led by General von Bülow and von Zeithen, they distract Napoleon from the main battle and force him to detach more troops to stop their advance.

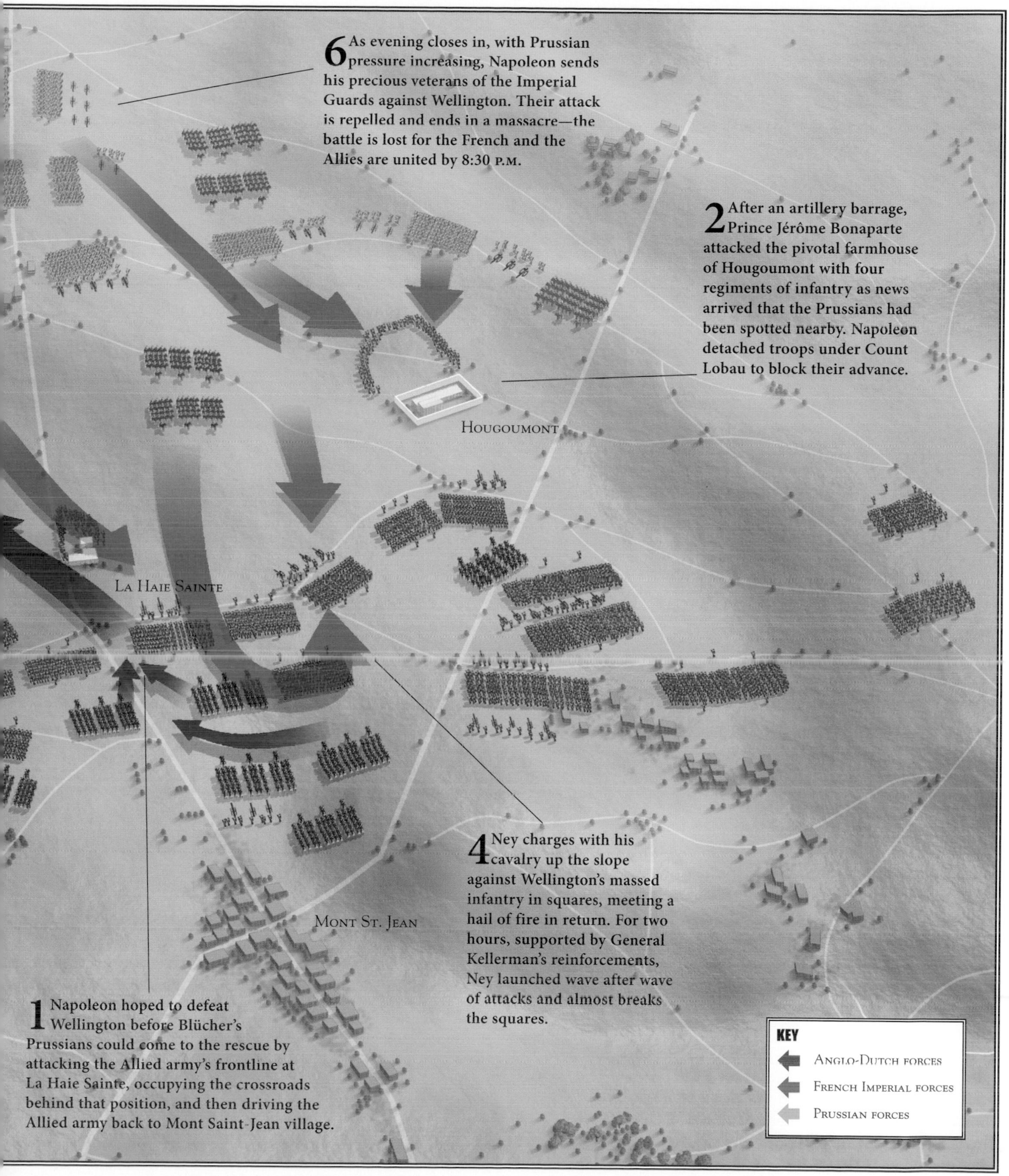

6 As evening closes in, with Prussian pressure increasing, Napoleon sends his precious veterans of the Imperial Guards against Wellington. Their attack is repelled and ends in a massacre—the battle is lost for the French and the Allies are united by 8:30 P.M.

2 After an artillery barrage, Prince Jérôme Bonaparte attacked the pivotal farmhouse of Hougoumont with four regiments of infantry as news arrived that the Prussians had been spotted nearby. Napoleon detached troops under Count Lobau to block their advance.

HOUGOUMONT

LA HAIE SAINTE

4 Ney charges with his cavalry up the slope against Wellington's massed infantry in squares, meeting a hail of fire in return. For two hours, supported by General Kellerman's reinforcements, Ney launched wave after wave of attacks and almost breaks the squares.

MONT ST. JEAN

1 Napoleon hoped to defeat Wellington before Blücher's Prussians could come to the rescue by attacking the Allied army's frontline at La Haie Sainte, occupying the crossroads behind that position, and then driving the Allied army back to Mont Saint-Jean village.

KEY
ANGLO-DUTCH FORCES
FRENCH IMPERIAL FORCES
PRUSSIAN FORCES

LED BY DAVY CROCKETT, WITH MUSKET RAISED, *the Texan defenders of the Alamo attempt to hold back the Mexican infantry as they break into the compound.*

Alamo 1836

A HANDFUL OF TEXANS STOOD FOR 13 DAYS AGAINST THE MIGHT OF THE MEXICAN ARMY UNDER THE COMMAND OF GENERAL ANTONIO LÓPEZ DE SANTA ANNA.

In late 1835, the fomenting Texan war of independence from Mexico had erupted into open hostilities. American settlers and adventurers in Texas, accustomed to little government interference in their lives, resented the dictatorial authority of Mexican President Antonio López de Santa Anna, who also commanded the country's army.

After Mexican troops had been expelled from Texas, Santa Anna was determined to bring the rebellious Texans to heel. Raising an army that eventually numbered more than 6,000 men, he began the long march to San Antonio de Bexar, where the Texans had fortified a former Spanish mission and its outbuildings, collectively known as the Alamo.

Initially about 100 Texans occupied the Alamo, positioning a few artillery pieces along its walls. The commander of the Texan force, Colonel William Barrett Travis, pleaded for more troops and wrangled with famed adventurer James Bowie for command within the Alamo

BATTLE FACTS

Who: The Mexican army under General Antonio López de Santa Anna (1794–1876) against a small band of Texans led by Colonel William Barrett Travis (1809–36) and James Bowie (1796–1836).

What: The Texans fortified the old Spanish mission known as the Alamo, and Santa Anna intended to crush their rebellion.

Where: The Alamo, near San Antonio, Texas.

When: February 23 to March 4, 1836.

Why: The Texans had rebelled against the rule of Santa Anna.

Outcome: The defenders of the Alamo were wiped out. However, a Texas army decisively defeated the Mexicans at San Jacinto on April 21, 1836, driving Santa Anna from Texas.

until Bowie fell ill and was bedridden. Few reinforcements reached the Alamo, and the number of defenders never exceeded 260. Among these was the renowned Indian fighter, frontiersman and former Congressman Davy Crockett (1786–1836). Women and children were also present.

THE LINE IN THE SAND

On February 23, 1836, Santa Anna and about 1,500 Mexican soldiers were discovered some distance from the Alamo. The Mexican leader dismissed overtures from the Texans for an honorable surrender, believing that victory in battle was necessary following the long march. He ordered artillery to bombard the Alamo, and subsequently the besieging cannon were moved closer to the old mission's walls.

For several days, a series of skirmishes took place around San Antonio de Bexar, and temperatures plunged, requiring both sides to forage for firewood. For the Texans, supplies began to run low. Travis wrote an impassioned letter on February 24. Addressed "To the People of Texas & All Americans in the World," it foreshadowed the sacrifice the defenders of the Alamo would make for freedom. Another 900 Mexican troops arrived at the Alamo on March 3, and Santa Anna ordered preparations for an all-out assault.

Travis realized that there was little doubt as to the outcome of the looming battle with the Mexicans. Reportedly, he assembled the defenders inside the walls on March 5 and drew a line in the sand, asking all those who were willing to die for Texas to step across. Legend has it that only one man did not.

NO PRISONERS

Mexican guns bombarded the Alamo that day, continuing after dark and finally ceasing around 10 P.M. Within hours, Santa Anna's troops were massed for the attack, and just before dawn they advanced in four sections. One column was to attack the north wall, while a second would hit the east wall, the third the northwest perimeter, and the fourth the principal objective of the chapel, whose façade is now the most recognized symbol of the struggle. About 1,400 Mexican soldiers, some carrying ladders to scale the walls and axes to batter doorways, took part in the direct assault. About 400 reserves were under the direct command of Santa Anna.

Sharpshooting Texans and their artillery, firing from parapets, took their toll on the advancing Mexicans, many of whom were recent recruits. Some Mexican soldiers reached the walls and mounted ladders but

THE FAÇADE OF THE CHAPEL OF THE ALAMO MISSION *has been preserved as a national monument. It is known to Texan patriots as the "Shrine of Texas Liberty."*

were shot or thrown back. Quickly, the attackers regrouped and came forward once more. The second assault was repulsed in a matter of minutes. Under steady fire from the Texans, the Mexican formations strayed from their initial lines of approach and became crowded together.

As numerous Texans fell, Santa Anna committed his reserves. Soldiers climbed the north wall and opened the gate, allowing their comrades to rush in. Soon, the Texans had been killed almost to a man. Approximately 600 Mexican soldiers were killed or wounded. Women and children were spared, but no quarter was given to those of the defenders who may have surrendered. Accounts differ as to the death of Crockett; however, an eyewitness reported that his lifeless body was found outside the wall of the church, surrounded by 16 dead Mexican soldiers. Travis had fallen early, while leaning across a parapet to fire his shotgun.

The story of the siege of the Alamo has become shrouded in myth, legend, and conjecture. However, it is known with certainty that the fight inspired the Texans. Led by Sam Houston (1793–1863), they fought Santa Anna at San Jacinto six weeks later, routed the Mexican army, and won their independence.

TEXAN OFFICER

Based on a contemporary account, this American officer wears a sealskin hunting cap and gray denim working clothes very similar to the uniform later adopted by the Confederate Army in the Civil War. He is armed with a flintlock pistol and a long cavalry style sword.

MEXICAN SOLDIERS FLEE IN PANIC *before the onslaught of the Texans at San Jacinto in this painting by Henry A. McArdle completed in 1898.*

San Jacinto 1836

CONSIDERING THE SIZE OF THE OPPOSING FORCES, THE BATTLE OF SAN JACINTO MIGHT, AT FIRST GLANCE, APPEAR TO HAVE BEEN NO MORE THAN A SKIRMISH. ONLY ABOUT 2,300 SOLDIERS, BOTH MEXICAN AND TEXAN, WERE INVOLVED, AND ITS DURATION OF LESS THAN 20 MINUTES WAS REMARKABLY BRIEF. WHEN IT WAS OVER, HOWEVER, PERHAPS NO OTHER BATTLE IN HISTORY HAD INVOLVED SO FEW AND PRODUCED SUCH FAR-REACHING CONSEQUENCES.

General Antonio López de Santa Anna, the self-proclaimed "Napoleon of the West," controlled the government of Mexico in the years following its independence from Spain. During the same period, settlers from the territory of the neighboring United States relocated in large numbers to the northern Mexican province of Coahuila y Tejas. The government of Santa Anna steadily became more autocratic, suspending the

BATTLE FACTS

Who: The army of Texas with 900 men commanded by Sam Houston (1793–1863) versus the Mexican army with 700 men under General Antonio López de Santa Anna (1794–1876).

What: Houston seized the initiative, and his charging soldiers virtually wiped out the Mexican force.

Where: Harris County, Texas, near the site of modern-day Houston.

When: April 21, 1836.

Why: Santa Anna hoped for a decisive victory over the rebellious Texans.

Outcome: Santa Anna agreed to withdraw Mexican troops from Texas, which remained independent until annexed by the United States.

country's constitution, levying high taxes, and eventually prohibiting further settlement by non-Mexicans in Texas. Amid the perceived oppression of Santa Anna, a national identity began to stir among the Texans, and open rebellion broke out in the fall of 1835. In March of the following year, delegates gathered at Washington-on-the-Brazos drafted a declaration of independence, and elected David G. Burnet (1788–1870) President of the Republic of Texas. While the convention was underway, Santa Anna and his powerful army had already moved northward against the rebellion.

Santa Anna's campaign struck fear into the hearts of many Texans, as news of atrocities spread like wildfire. The grim highpoints of this early campaign were the infamous siege and eventual massacre at the Alamo on February 23–March 6, 1836, and the murder of Texan soldiers at Goliad on March 27. A small Texan-American army had been raised under General Sam Houston, but as the hour of the decisive battle of San Jacinto approached, Houston counted just over 900 soldiers in his army's ranks. Few in number and relatively untrained, the Texan army needed one thing more than any other—time. As long as Houston's army lived, so did the fledgling independent Texas.

DAY OF RECKONING
After weeks on the march, Santa Anna and 700 footsore soldiers finally made contact with Houston on April 19 at Lynch's Ferry near the banks of the San Jacinto River and ringed by marshy wetlands. There, he was reinforced by more than 500 troops commanded by General Martín Perfecto de Cos, and the Mexican numbers neared 1,400. When he learned of the arrival of Cos, Houston ordered Vince's Bridge, 8 miles (13 km) to his rear and the only avenue of approach or retreat for either army by land, destroyed. Meanwhile, Santa Anna believed Houston was trapped and could be annihilated at leisure. Rather than attacking immediately, he ordered his position fortified with a barricade of crates and baggage.

Faced with yet another command decision, Houston held a council of war on the morning of April 21. Against

THE DEFEATED SANTA ANNA *stands before an injured Sam Houston on April 22, 1836, the day after a small force of Texans defeated the Mexican Army at San Jacinto.*

the advice of his officers, he opted to assume the offensive. At 3:30 P.M., the Texas infantry stepped off, quietly closing on the Mexican line while about 60 cavalrymen skirted the enemy's left flank. Inexplicably, Santa Anna had failed to post sentries or skirmishers, and as the Texans approached, many Mexican soldiers napped during the afternoon siesta.

Within yards of the Mexican line, the Texans charged, shouting, "Remember the Alamo!" and "Remember Goliad!" Santa Anna's startled soldiers were thrown into confusion. With no time to form ranks, many of them fled in terror without firing a shot. Others fought hand-to-hand with the Texans and were routed. Vigorously pursued, many of them were shot dead or slashed by cavalry sabers as they wallowed in the marshes. General Don Juan Almonte attempted to organize a defense, but soon realized the futility of further resistance and surrendered with 400 men. Santa Anna managed to slip away from the debacle on horseback, wearing the coat of a common soldier. Spurring his men forward, Houston was wounded in the foot by a Mexican bullet.

The frenzied Texans exacted revenge for those murdered at the Alamo and Goliad. In 18 minutes, it was over. The Mexican army had suffered 630 dead, 208 wounded, and 730 captured, while only nine Texans were killed and 30 wounded.

The day after his catastrophic defeat at San Jacinto, Santa Anna was captured and brought before Sam Houston, who spared his life in exchange for a pledge that Santa Anna's army would leave Texas. Victory at San Jacinto ensured, at least for a time, the survival of the Republic of Texas, which was later annexed by the U.S. government. In time, vast western lands once belonging to Mexico would constitute all or part of ten of the United States.

Balaclava 1854

WITH THE OUTBREAK OF THE CRIMEAN WAR, THE COMBINED FORCES OF GREAT BRITAIN, FRANCE, AND TURKEY LAID SIEGE TO THE PORT OF SEVASTOPOL AT THE TIP OF THE CRIMEAN PENINSULA. THE SIEGE WAS TO LAST A GRUELING 11 MONTHS, AND THE RUSSIAN ARMY MOUNTED TWO UNSUCCESSFUL EFFORTS TO BREAK IT. THE FIRST OF THESE, THE BATTLE OF BALACLAVA, OCCURRED ON OCTOBER 25, 1854.

The terrain at Balaclava proved to be a contributing factor to the outcome of the battle. British forces, under the command of Fitzroy Somerset, First Lord Raglan, were positioned in two parallel valleys, each dominated by ridges along their flanks. To the left rose the Fedioukine Hills, while in the center stood the ridgeline called Causeway Heights and to the right were a number of broken hills, ridges, and ravines. The difficulty of tactical control lay in the fact that commanders were often limited in their ability to see the battlefield.

AT THE HEIGHT OF THEIR EPIC CHARGE AT BALACLAVA, *cavalrymen of the Light Brigade lash out with sabers at Russian hussars and artillerymen.*

BATTLE FACTS

Who: A combined Anglo-French force of 4,500 men and 26 cannon under the command of Lord Raglan (1788–1855) and Marshal Canrobert (1809–95) against a Russian force of 25,000 troops and 70 guns commanded by General Pavel Liprandi (1796–1864).

What: A series of battles over the strategic Causeway Heights led to the ill-fated Charge of the Light Brigade.

Where: Near the port city of Balaclava in the Crimea.

When: October 25, 1854.

Why: The Russians wanted to capture the Anglo-French supply base at Balaclava, thereby disrupting the siege of Sevastapol.

Outcome: The Light Brigade suffered 40 percent casualties.

IMPERIAL RUSSIA

Sevastapol ✚ Balaclava

• Constantinople

TURKEY

On the morning of October 25, 1854, 25,000 Russian troops attacked Turkish positions in the southern valley and along Causeway Heights, routing more than 30,000 Turkish soldiers from their trenches and capturing a number of artillery pieces. Soon, Russian cavalry advanced to exploit the breakthrough.

The Russian cavalry split into two columns, the first heading straight for Balaclava, but was stopped by the 93rd Highland Regiment. Within minutes, one of the British cavalry units, the Heavy Brigade, had charged headlong into the second Russian mounted column. The Russians were compelled to fall back to the protection of strong artillery positions along the nearby Causeway Heights.

CAVALRY CONFUSION

Surveying the scene from the high ground above the battlefield, Lord Raglan observed that the Russians were attempting to haul away a number of Turkish guns they had seized during the morning action. Therefore, he issued a controversial order. The cavalry commander, George Charles Bingham, Third Earl of Lucan (1880–85), received the following order: "Lord Raglan wishes the cavalry to advance rapidly to the front, follow the enemy, and try to prevent the enemy carrying away the guns. Horse artillery may accompany. French cavalry is on your left. Immediate." Captain Lewis E. Nolan had delivered the order, and when Lucan requested clarification as to which guns were referred to, a heated exchange may have taken place. Nolan was seen making a sweeping gesture with his arm toward Russian guns—more than 50 cannon, with Russian infantry on all sides—occupying high ground at the opposite end of the northern valley about a mile away, not the Turkish guns on the Causeway Heights. Such actions could indicate that Nolan himself was confused as to the direction of the assault.

An order was an order. Numbering about 670, the cavalry's Light Brigade moved into the valley, its commander, James Brudenell, Seventh Earl of Cardigan (1797–1868), riding at its head. Captain Nolan joined the charge, accompanying the 17th Lancers. Moments later, Nolan rode directly across the brigade's front as if to indicate that the charge was headed in the wrong direction. If so, it was too late.

For his trouble, a shell fragment killed Nolan, one of the first to fall. Artillery fire rained down from the high ground.

MOUNTED ON HIS CHARGER AND PREPARING TO RIDE *into combat with his unit, a British dragoon accepts his sword from an attendant during the Crimean War.*

Riderless horses, horribly wounded, shrieked as they stumbled through blinding smoke. The dead and wounded lay everywhere. In spite of the horrific losses, Cardigan and the remnants of the Light Brigade ran the Russian gauntlet, actually reaching the guns at the end of the valley. Apparently, he had been unaware of the carnage occurring behind him and was seething with rage at Nolan, whom he assumed had been trying to take over command of the charge.

Many of the Russian gunners were sabered, but the shattered Light Brigade still faced overwhelming odds, and was forced to retreat. When the battle was over, at least 118 of the brigade were dead and 127 wounded, a casualty rate of nearly 40 percent. The Battle of Balaclava ended with the opposing forces occupying essentially the same ground they had previously held.

A CAVALRYMAN OF THE 17TH LANCERS *charges forward as a pennon attached to his lance flies in the breeze. The pennon was originally intended to frighten opposing cavalry horses but later became a parade item.*

GENERAL ULYSSES S. GRANT *directs Union artillery fire from the edge of a wood at the Battle of Shiloh as Confederate troops attempt to close.*

Shiloh 1862

AT THE BATTLE OF SHILOH, A CONFEDERATE ARMY ATTEMPTED TO DEFEAT UNION FORCES BEFORE FEDERAL REINFORCEMENTS COULD ARRIVE. HOWEVER, A NARROW DEFEAT LED TO THE LOSS OF CORINTH.

The railroad between Richmond and Memphis was one of very few routes that allowed the Confederacy to rapidly move troops and supplies. This made its junction at Corinth a vital objective for the Union; capturing it would severely impede the enemy war effort in the western theater of war. Thus Union General Ulysses S. Grant was given orders to advance on Corinth as soon as his Army of the Tennessee was reinforced by the Army of the Ohio under Brigadier-General Don Carlos Buell (1818–98).

Confederate General Albert Sidney Johnston, responsible for defending Corinth, decided that his best chance was to attack and remove the threat posed by Grant's army before it was reinforced. Although outnumbered, he reasoned that the odds were better than allowing the Union forces to concentrate against him.

BATTLE FACTS

Who: The Confederate Army of the Mississippi, 44,000 men under General Albert Sidney Johnston (1803–62), were opposed by the Union Army of the Tennessee and the Union Army of the Ohio; 62,000 men under the command of Major-General Ulysses S. Grant (1822–85).

What: The Confederates attacked on April 6, achieving significant gains.

Where: Shiloh, on the Tennessee River, 25 miles (40 km) north of Corinth, Mississippi.

When: April 6–7, 1862.

Why: Confederate commanders hoped to prevent an advance on Corinth by the combined Union forces.

Outcome: Confederate defeat, leading to the evacuation of the city of Corinth.

UNION INFANTRYMAN

Generally, Federal troops were better and more uniformly equipped than their Confederate counterparts. However, everybody empowered to raise troops was permitted to equip them as it saw fit. Uniforms and even armament varied considerably according to fashion, availability, and opinion as to what was best. Many soldiers privately obtained extra equipment, such as revolvers, hand weapons, and extra clothing. Most of this extraneous gear was discarded early in the unit's first march. Experienced troops carried only what they needed—rifle, ammunition, and bayonet, plus a basic mess kit, blanket, and a few personal items.

Johnston was able to approach the forces commanded by Grant's subordinate General William T. Sherman (1820–91) undetected, and made camp on the night of April 5 within striking distance of his target. He dismissed subordinates' fears that the Union army had been alerted and resolved to fight even if he found a million men ready and waiting for him.

THE CONFEDERATE ATTACK

In fact, the complacent Union army was totally unaware that there were hostile troops closer than Corinth, some 25 miles (40 km) away. This illusion was shattered when Union pickets were fired on, and soon afterward the Confederate brigades began to roll over the Union forward units. Many were caught totally unprepared and offered little resistance. Others put up a stiff fight but were disorganized and easily overwhelmed.

Surprise was near total. The Union army had not fortified its camps as there seemed to be no need. Command and control was nonexistent; even when units were able to scramble into fighting order there were no orders. Higher commanders as yet had no clear picture of the situation.

With no alternative, the Union troops fought where they stood and rallied alongside any friendly troops they encountered as they fell back. The Confederate advance was slowed and in some areas a semiorganized defense began to materialize. The fighting was especially fierce around Shiloh Church on the Confederate left while on the right a cobbled-together Union force was defending a sunken road with such ferocity that it became known as the "Hornet's Nest."

NEAR-DEFEAT FOR THE UNION

The Union army narrowly managed to avoid total defeat through a day of desperate and disorganized fighting. Ordered to hold the Hornet's Nest at any cost, the Union force managed to do so through six bloody hours, until at last Johnston was able to break the line. The Confederate general assembled a Grand Battery of 62 cannon, the largest concentration of guns in the entire war, and

under cover of its fire he led the decisive attack in person. Although Johnston was mortally wounded the attack succeeded.

As the day ended, the Confederates were close to victory. Grant's army had been pushed into a small area around Pittsburg Landing on the banks of the Tennessee River, and was in total chaos. A final concentrated push might have brought victory, but with Johnston dead and his army both exhausted and disorganized, it was not possible. Supported by gunboats on the river, the Union army held off a Confederate assault and managed to cling to its last positions.

UNION COUNTERATTACK

By the following morning, reinforcements from Buell's Army of the Ohio had reached Grant across the river and additional Union troops had approached overland. Grant resolved to attack, and this time the Confederates were caught unprepared as they rested in the very camps they had captured from their opponents.

Instead of delivering the killing blow, the Confederates found themselves on the defensive. The new Union arrivals gave Grant a huge numerical advantage, and in addition they were fresh whereas the survivors of the previous day's fighting were still very tired. Despite hard fighting the Confederates were forced to retreat.

Failure to win at Shiloh ultimately led to the loss of Corinth. Faced with a greatly numerically superior opponent and deprived of a general of Johnston's caliber, the Confederate army in the west could no longer do more than stave off defeat. Corinth had to be abandoned, and the loss of its railroad hub contributed directly to defeat at Vicksburg a year later.

UNION AND CONFEDERATE TROOPS *are locked in combat along the banks of Antietam Creek in western Maryland. In the background, their banner unfurled, Union soldiers charge across the Lower Bridge.*

Antietam Creek 1862

IN THE COUNTRYSIDE OF WESTERN MARYLAND, THE BLOODIEST SINGLE DAY OF WARFARE IN AMERICAN HISTORY ENDED WITH A TACTICAL DRAW BUT A STRATEGIC VICTORY FOR THE UNION ARMY AS THE CONFEDERATE INVASION OF THE NORTH WAS THWARTED. ISSUED AFTER THE BATTLE, THE EMANCIPATION PROCLAMATION TRANSFORMED THE AMERICAN CIVIL WAR INTO A CRUSADE FOR HUMAN RIGHTS.

The Battle of Antietam was the culmination of a struggle between General Robert E. Lee's Confederate Army of Northern Virginia, and General George B. McClellan's Army of the Potomac. Lee had invaded the North in early September 1862, leading to escalating clashes between the two armies in Maryland, and the humiliating Union defeat at Harper's Ferry on September 14–15. Expecting the full force of the Army of the Potomac to descend on him, however, Lee placed his army in defensive positions along Antietam Creek, with

BATTLE FACTS

Who: The 36,000-man Confederate Army of Northern Virginia, under General Robert E. Lee (1807–70), confronted General George B. McClellan (1826–85) and the Union Army of the Potomac of 75,000 men.

What: The two sides fought to a tactical draw in a three-phase battle.

Where: Western Maryland near the town of Sharpsburg and along Antietam Creek.

When: September 17, 1862.

Why: The Confederate Army of Northern Virginia invaded Maryland, carrying the war into Federal territory.

Outcome: Lee was forced to abandon the offensive. President Abraham Lincoln issued the Emancipation Proclamation, changing the character of the war.

Antietam ✚ • Washington
Richmond •

the Potomac covering his rear. By the evening of the 16th, Lee's force stood at about 36,000 men. At midday on the 15th, by contrast, McClellan had assembled 75,000 troops east of the Antietam. Both sides had placed artillery on the surrounding high ground, and sporadic firing occurred on September 16, while McClellan refined his plan of attack. Two army corps, under Generals Joseph Hooker and Joseph K. F. Mansfield, were placed on the Union right and ordered to make the initial assault, with the corps of Generals William B. Franklin and Edwin V. Sumner available to exploit any significant gains. General Fitz-John Porter's corps took up positions in the Union center along the Boonsborough Pike, and the corps of General Ambrose Burnside was positioned on the left near the lower bridge.

McClellan's plan was simple. If Hooker and Mansfield made significant gains, Burnside would attack the Confederate right flank and perhaps push on into the town of Sharpsburg. Finally, Porter's troops would assault the Confederate center in support of either flank attack. In typical fashion, McClellan had squandered opportunities to attack the much smaller Confederate army on the afternoon of the 15th and again on the 16th. When battle was finally joined on the 17th, Lee was able to utilize his interior lines. Shuffling reinforcements to areas of heavy fighting, he stymied several Union breakthroughs. McClellan failed to coordinate his attacks and committed reserves in a piecemeal manner, negating his numerical superiority.

THE BATTLE

The Union assault began in ferocious fashion at first light, Hooker and, soon after, Mansfield driving their troops in repeated attacks against a weakening Confederate left flank. In areas, Confederate bodies were heaped two and three deep, and by late morning the Union Army appeared to stand on the brink of a decisive victory. Yet a patchwork defense slowed the Union tide. One more push with fresh troops from his ample reserves might have won the day for McClellan, but the commander hesitated and then ordered his troops to hold their positions.

From morning until mid-afternoon, Union troops farther south had been attempting to take the lower bridge across Antietam Creek. While some of his troops found places where the stream could easily be forded, the corps commander, General Ambrose Burnside, was determined to take the bridge that would eventually bear his name. It was defended by only 400 Confederate riflemen from Georgia and South Carolina. After four hours of fruitless attempts to capture the bridge, Federal troops from New York and Pennsylvania charged across and gained the west bank.

Throughout the morning, Lee had stripped his right of troops to support those hard-pressed areas on his left and center. Now, in spite of his slow progress, Burnside was in position to sweep the woefully inadequate Confederate defenders aside, capture Sharpsburg, and cut off the entire rebel army's avenue of retreat. He waited, however, for two precious hours, consolidating his hold on the west side of the creek. When Burnside finally got moving around 3 P.M., he made sluggish progress. The charge of the recently arrived Confederate Light Division then stopped his advance cold, and he retired back toward the creek.

By 6 P.M., the Battle of Antietam was over, both sides too exhausted to prosecute the fighting any further. The casualties from America's bloodiest day were appalling. The Army of the Potomac counted 12,410 dead, wounded, or missing, while the Army of Northern Virginia had lost 10,700. Throughout the day on September 18, Lee stood his ground. McClellan declined to renew the fight and did not pursue the Confederate columns when they withdrew across the Potomac.

In the wake of the Battle of Antietam, President Lincoln became convinced that the outcome was enough of a victory to issue the Emancipation Proclamation, which freed the slaves in territory then in rebellion against the United States. The document transformed the war from an effort to save the Union to one of liberation and the perpetuation of freedom. European governments, which had abolished slavery themselves, were dissuaded from supporting the Confederate cause.

UNION INFANTRY

Ranks of well equipped Union infantrymen march toward the sound of the guns. Although the Union Army of the Potomac consisted of some units from the standing United States Army, a large number of the soldiers were volunteers or had been drafted in. Many of these were farmers and woodsmen from the primarily agricultural areas of the North and Midwest or European immigrants, predominantly Irish and German, from the crowded urban areas of major Northern cities.

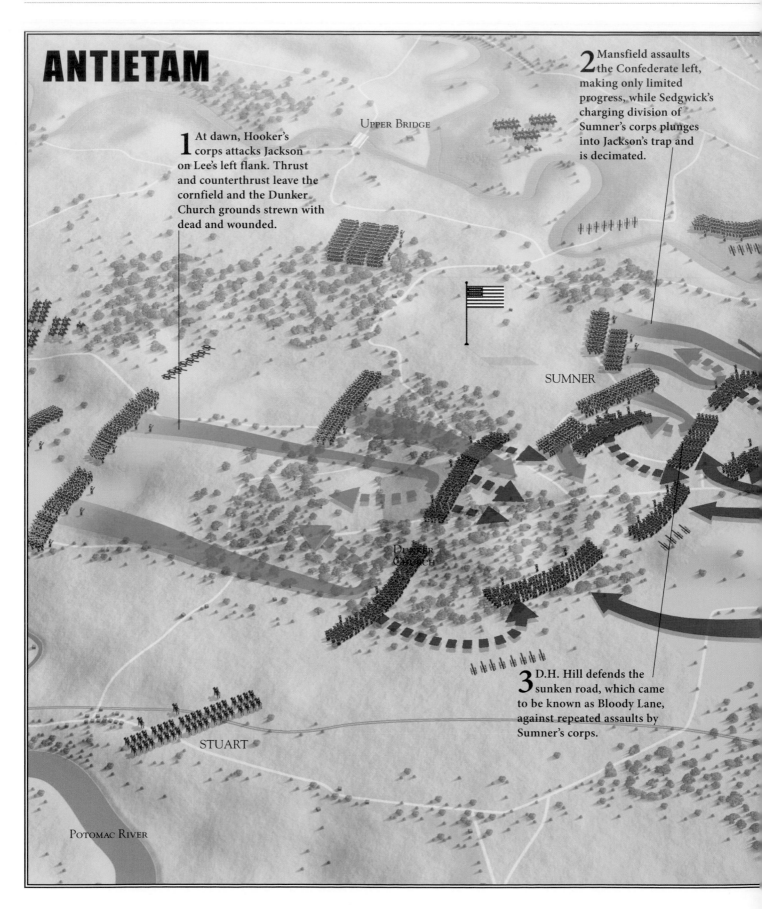

ANTIETAM

1 At dawn, Hooker's corps attacks Jackson on Lee's left flank. Thrust and counterthrust leave the cornfield and the Dunker Church grounds strewn with dead and wounded.

2 Mansfield assaults the Confederate left, making only limited progress, while Sedgwick's charging division of Sumner's corps plunges into Jackson's trap and is decimated.

UPPER BRIDGE

SUMNER

DUNKER CHURCH

3 D.H. Hill defends the sunken road, which came to be known as Bloody Lane, against repeated assaults by Sumner's corps.

STUART

POTOMAC RIVER

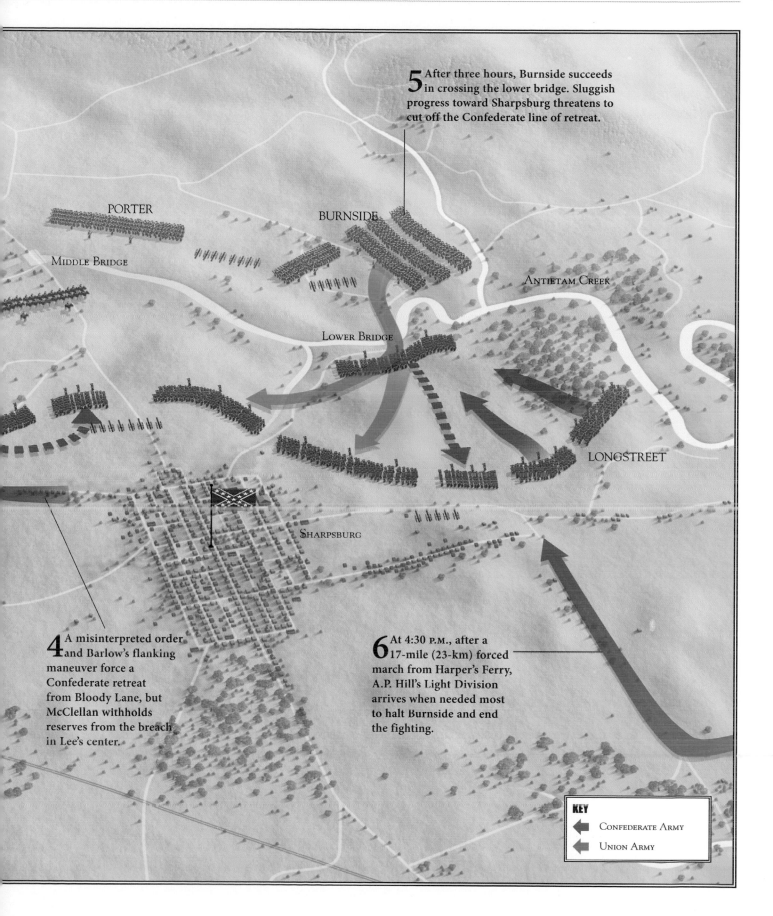

5 After three hours, Burnside succeeds in crossing the lower bridge. Sluggish progress toward Sharpsburg threatens to cut off the Confederate line of retreat.

PORTER

BURNSIDE

MIDDLE BRIDGE

ANTIETAM CREEK

LOWER BRIDGE

LONGSTREET

SHARPSBURG

4 A misinterpreted order and Barlow's flanking maneuver force a Confederate retreat from Bloody Lane, but McClellan withholds reserves from the breach in Lee's center.

6 At 4:30 P.M., after a 17-mile (23-km) forced march from Harper's Ferry, A.P. Hill's Light Division arrives when needed most to halt Burnside and end the fighting.

KEY

CONFEDERATE ARMY

UNION ARMY

UNION INFANTRY STAND FIRM *against the Confederates as Pickett's charge is pressed home. The charge was a bloodbath for the Confederates, with Pickett's division suffering 2,655 casualties.*

Gettysburg 1863

AT APPROXIMATELY 3 P.M. ON JULY 3, 1863, NEARLY 13,000 CONFEDERATE SOLDIERS BEGAN MOVING ACROSS MORE THAN 1 MILE (1.6 KM) OF OPEN GROUND, HEAVILY DEFENDED BY UNION ARTILLERY AND INFANTRY, THEIR OBJECTIVE AN ISOLATED COPSE OF TREES ALONG THE SHALLOW CREST OF CEMETERY RIDGE. THE FOLLOWING THREE DAYS OF THE BATTLE OF GETTYSBURG WERE, COLLECTIVELY, THE BLOODIEST ENGAGEMENT EVER IN THE WESTERN HEMISPHERE.

I n the summer of 1863, General Robert E. Lee and the Army of Northern Virginia embarked on the second Confederate invasion of the North in less than a year. His army of 75,000 men advanced into Pennsylvania, carrying the war from beleaguered Virginia and threatening the cities of Baltimore, Philadelphia, and even Washington, D.C. As he had done in the past, Lee divided up his army, and powerful Confederate forces raided far ahead of the main body. Within three weeks, the bold rebels had

BATTLE FACTS

Who: The Confederate Army of Northern Virginia (75,000 men) commanded by General Robert E. Lee (1807–70), versus the Union Army of the Potomac (97,000 men) under General George G. Meade (1815–77).

What: The second invasion of the North by the Confederates was turned back, punctuated by the disastrous Pickett's Charge.

Where: The vicinity of Gettysburg in southern Pennsylvania.

When: July 1–3, 1863.

Why: Following a victory at Chancellorsville, the Confederates hoped to win a major battle on Union soil and threaten northern cities.

Outcome: At the height of its power, the Confederate Army was defeated, and the strategic initiative passed irretrievably to the Union.

occupied York and Carlisle and were in the vicinity of Pennsylvania's capital city, Harrisburg. The nearby town of Gettysburg had no real strategic value. However, one local commodity—shoes—was of great interest to the Confederates, and a detachment was sent to locate them at Gettysburg. Instead, the Confederates found Union cavalry, and what began as a skirmish quickly escalated, as both sides fed fresh troops into a widening engagement. Neither Lee nor Major General George C. Meade, the new commander of the Army of the Potomac, was yet present on the field.

BLOODY BUT INDECISIVE

Throughout July 1, fighting raged across the hills and fields north and east of Gettysburg. By afternoon, the hard-pressed Union troops had been pushed through the streets of the town and assumed defensive positions on high ground at Culp's Hill and Cemetery Hill. As Union forces arrived, their defensive line was extended southward across Cemetery Ridge to the vicinity of Little Round Top.

The following day, the Battle of Gettysburg increased in scale and ferocity. The fighting resumed on the Union left flank at the Peach Orchard, the Wheatfield, and a craggy jumble of boulders known locally as "Devil's Den." The Army of the Potomac averted disaster by rushing reinforcements to the summit of Little Round Top moments ahead of advancing Confederate troops. Meade held a council of war during the night (the opposing commanders were now present), and the consensus was to await a renewed attack from Lee.

By July 3, Lee remained resolute. Meade had skillfully defended the high ground and utilized the advantage of interior lines, but Lee concluded that the Union force had sapped the strength of the center. To take advantage of this perceived weakness, Lee decided to commit his only reserve, Pickett's division, to assault the Union center along Cemetery Ridge, with two other depleted divisions in support. The attack was to take place in concert with a feint by Confederate General Richard Ewell at Culp's Hill, following preparatory bombardment by nearly 150 massed rebel cannon.

At approximately 1 P.M., the thunder of Confederate cannon shattered the eerie silence that had descended on the battlefield. Their flags unfurled, the Confederate cavalry stepped out of the woods along Seminary Ridge, and advanced toward the copse of trees more than 1 mile (1.6 km) distant. Quickly, they came under artillery fire from Union batteries on Culp's Hill, Little Round Top, and along Cemetery Ridge. Shells tore great gaps in the ranks, and on the left flank one advancing brigade was taken under fire and routed. Musket fire added further slaughter. Although the Union line was breached at one point, no Confederate reinforcements were available to exploit the breakthrough. In the span of 20 minutes, nearly 6,500 men had been lost in the disastrous charge, and the high tide of Confederate arms had begun to recede. Union dead and wounded totaled about 1,500. Witnessing the carnage, a despondent Lee rode out to meet his returning soldiers. "It is all my fault," he said. Pickett and his gallant men had lost their fight, but gained everlasting fame.

The following day, Lee's army began its forlorn trek southward across the Potomac and into Virginia. From Gettysburg to surrender at Appomattox nearly two years later, the Confederacy was obliged to fight a defensive war. Coupled with a crushing defeat in the West at Vicksburg, the decisive battle at Gettysburg sealed the fate of the Confederacy.

UNION ZOUAVES DISPLAY THEIR MUSKETS, *complete with fixed bayonets. The Zouaves' dress was based on French uniforms, and were popular because of the loose-fitting, comfortable pants.*

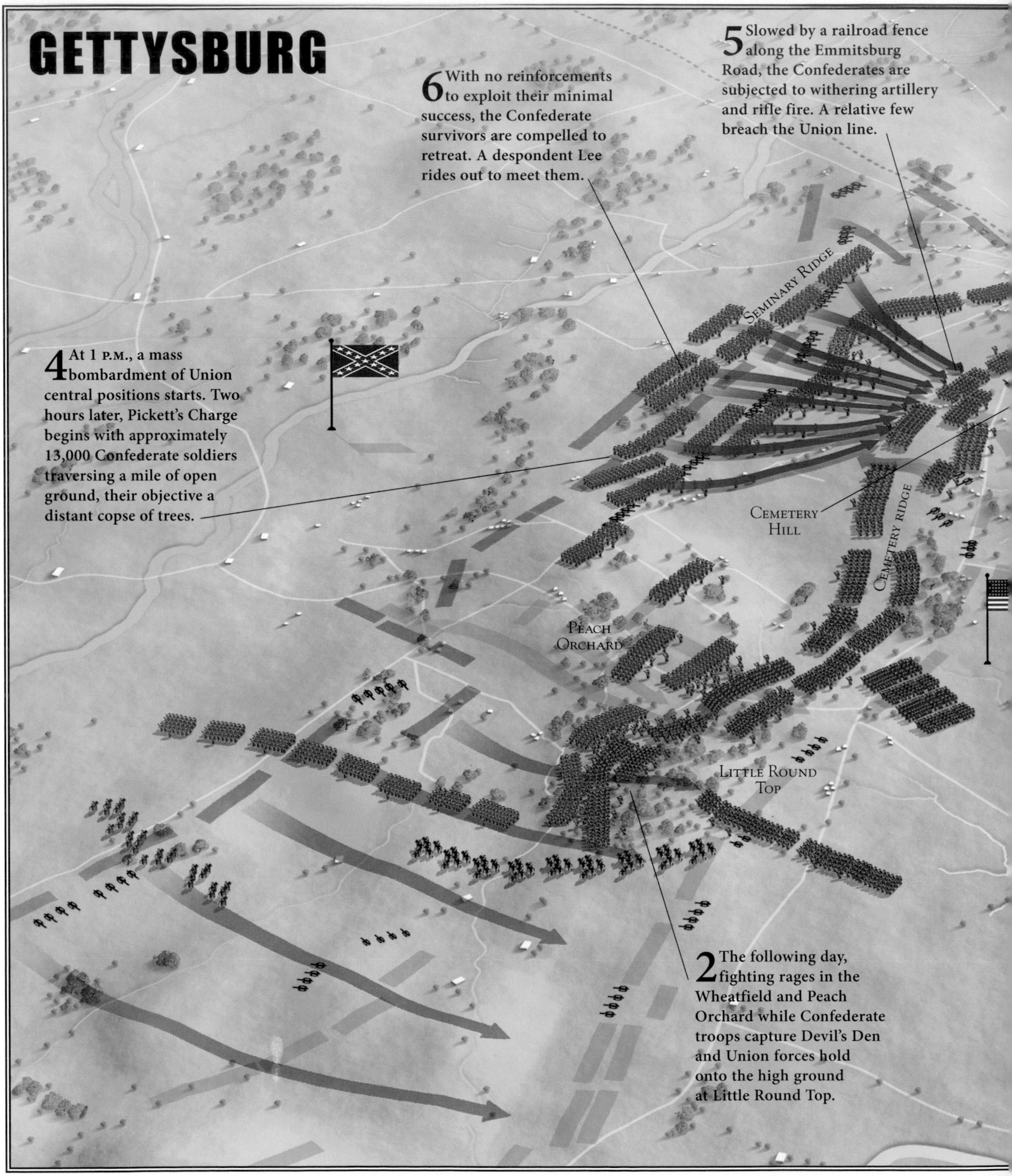

GETTYSBURG

6 With no reinforcements to exploit their minimal success, the Confederate survivors are compelled to retreat. A despondent Lee rides out to meet them.

5 Slowed by a railroad fence along the Emmitsburg Road, the Confederates are subjected to withering artillery and rifle fire. A relative few breach the Union line.

4 At 1 P.M., a mass bombardment of Union central positions starts. Two hours later, Pickett's Charge begins with approximately 13,000 Confederate soldiers traversing a mile of open ground, their objective a distant copse of trees.

SEMINARY RIDGE

CEMETERY HILL

CEMETERY RIDGE

PEACH ORCHARD

LITTLE ROUND TOP

2 The following day, fighting rages in the Wheatfield and Peach Orchard while Confederate troops capture Devil's Den and Union forces hold onto the high ground at Little Round Top.

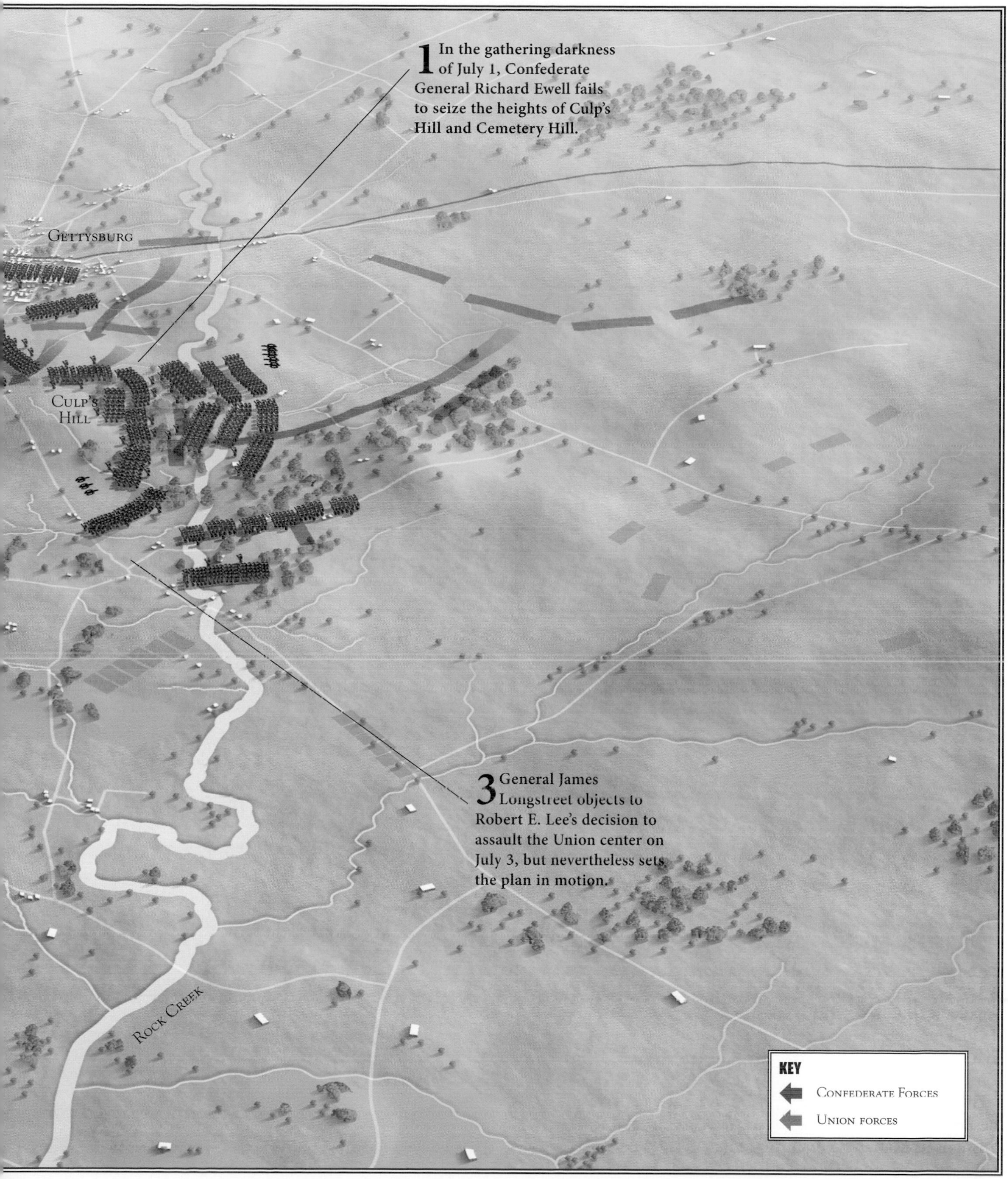

1 In the gathering darkness of July 1, Confederate General Richard Ewell fails to seize the heights of Culp's Hill and Cemetery Hill.

GETTYSBURG

CULP'S HILL

3 General James Longstreet objects to Robert E. Lee's decision to assault the Union center on July 3, but nevertheless sets the plan in motion.

ROCK CREEK

KEY

CONFEDERATE FORCES

UNION FORCES

PRUSSIAN INFANTRY ADVANCE *against French North African Zouaves at Sedan on September 1, 1870. The battle ended in disaster for France, and Emperor Napoleon III was captured.*

Sedan 1870

WITHIN WEEKS OF DECLARING WAR ON PRUSSIA AND ITS ALLIED GERMAN STATES, EMPEROR NAPOLEON III AND FRANCE WERE IN DIRE STRAITS. A SUCCESSION OF PRUSSIAN VICTORIES HAD THWARTED NAPOLEON'S PLAN TO INVADE GERMANY, AND ACHIEVE THROUGH FORCE TERRITORIAL AND POLITICAL CONCESSIONS THAT FRANCE COULD NOT GAIN THROUGH DIPLOMACY.

The Battle of Sedan was the culmination of weeks of clashes and building tension. From August 19, 1870, some 170,000 French troops were besieged by the Prussians in the French fortress of Metz. In response Napoleon III (1808–73) led the 120,000-strong French Army of Châlons, commanded by Marshal Patrice MacMahon, out on a relief operation, one that the Prussian general Helmuth von Moltke aimed to stop with a blocking force.

The Army of Châlons marched northeastward toward the Belgian frontier, intending to pivot south against the Prussians at Metz. The circuitous maneuver, conducted in atrocious weather, served only to degrade the fitness of

BATTLE FACTS

Who: The 120,000-man French Army of Châlons, under General Patrice de MacMahon (1808–93), versus the 250,000 soldiers of the armies of Prussia and allied German states, under General Helmuth von Moltke (1800–91).

What: Initially marching to raise the siege of Metz, French forces were encircled and defeated.

Where: The fortress city of Sedan in the valley of the Meuse River.

When: September 1, 1870.

Why: After their defeat at Beaumont, the French retreated, allowing Moltke to encircle them.

Outcome: German victory in the Franco-Prussian War became a certainty. With the fall of the French Second Empire, the Third Republic was established.

MacMahon's command while leaving both French flanks exposed to constant harassment. Von Moltke recognized an opportunity to squeeze the French in a giant vice. While the First and Second Prussian armies held French forces in check at Metz, the Prussian Third Army and the Army of the Meuse hurried to counter MacMahon.

On August 30, XII Corps of the Army of the Meuse surprised the French V Corps at Beaumont. Another French defeat, the Battle of Beaumont, cost the Army of Châlons more than 7,000 killed and wounded, along with 42 cannon lost. Battered and weary, the French fell back near the fortified town of Sedan in the valley of the Meuse River. MacMahon hoped to halt briefly, replenish ammunition, and rest his troops. Moltke, however, allowed no respite, and closed a ring of steel around the French army.

FRENCH DEFEAT

Just after 4 A.M. on September 1, 1870, the decisive battle of the Franco-Prussian War began, as Bavarian troops fought the French in the soon-blazing village of Baizelles. Riding forward to assess the situation, MacMahon was wounded by a shell fragment, so command passed to General Auguste-Alexandre Ducrot. Two hours later, fighting erupted at La Moncelle on the German right flank, where 72 modern, breech-loading artillery pieces rained destruction on exposed French positions.

Ducrot realized the gravity of the situation, ordering an attempt to break out of what became a German encirclement and make a northward retreat. However, General Emmanuel Félix de Wimpffen arrived and asserted overall command of the French forces. Ducrot's order to withdraw was wholly logical, but the inept Wimpffen immediately countermanded the directive and ordered futile counterattacks at Baizelles and La Moncelle. Exhibiting more bravado than command sense, Wimpffen snorted, "We need a victory, not a retreat!" The French got neither.

Sometime after 2 P.M., Ducrot, on his own initiative, summoned General Jean Auguste Margueritte and ordered the cavalry commander to ready his *Chausseurs d'Afrique* for a desperate charge against the Prussians at Floing. If the charge was successful, a gap could be opened and what was left of the French infantry might follow to the west. Margueritte rode ahead to survey the ground, but was mortally wounded when a bullet shattered his jaw. The gallant cavalry sallied forth, only to be decimated by concentrated fire from Prussian rifles. King Wilhelm I (1797–1888) watched from a distance and could not help but admire the courage of the French. "Ah, the brave fellows," he remarked wistfully.

Napoleon III rode through heavy fire during most of the day, ignoring the peril even when one of his entourage was cut in half by a Prussian shell. With his entire army near

GENERAL HELMUTH VON MOLTKE, *chief of staff to Kaiser Wilhelm, was the principal architect of Prussian victory in the Franco-Prussian War.*

collapse, the French Emperor accepted the counsel of several beseeching generals and authorized them to request surrender terms. Tightening their grip, the Prussians continued attacking from the east and northwest, while the Bavarians advanced from the southwest. The remnants of the Army of Châlons were herded toward the Bois de la Garenne and Sedan itself. A defiant though incompetent Wimpffen would not accept defeat, and led a futile counterattack against the surprised Bavarians at Balan. Temporarily seizing the village, the French could not hold it, and the attack petered out. As Wimpffen withdrew, the white flag of surrender fluttered from the top of the fortress of Sedan.

Napoleon III became a prisoner of war and was later consoled by Bismarck when the two met after the battle. German casualties were relatively light at Sedan, only 2,320 killed and 5,980 wounded.

The French had lost 3,000 dead, 14,000 wounded, and 21,000 captured during the fight. As news of the catastrophic defeat at Sedan reached Paris, the Second Empire was doomed. When the Treaty of Frankfurt ended the Franco-Prussian War on May 10, 1871, France was stripped of Alsace and Lorraine, required to pay a financial indemnity, and forced to endure three years of occupation by the Germans.

THIS ROMANTICIZED DEPICTION of "Custer's Last Stand" shows the controversial commander in the center of his surrounded command, firing his revolver defiantly.

Little Big Horn 1876

FEW CHARACTERS IN AMERICAN MILITARY HISTORY HAVE BEEN AS ROMANTICIZED AS LIEUTENANT-COLONEL GEORGE ARMSTRONG CUSTER. DURING THE AMERICAN CIVIL WAR, HE EARNED A REPUTATION AS A BOLD, AGGRESSIVE COMMANDER. OFTEN CONSIDERED IMPETUOUS AND VAINGLORIOUS, CUSTER APPARENTLY DID NOT SHUN THE LIMELIGHT. NOR DID HE FAIL TO TAKE ADVANTAGE OF AN OPPORTUNITY TO ACHIEVE LASTING FAME.

On the morning of June 25, 1876, Lieutenant Colonel George A. Custer, commander of the U.S. 7th Cavalry, received reports that a massive Indian encampment was located roughly 15 miles (24 km) away, on the Little Big Horn River, Montana. U.S. troops had been pursuing a combined Sioux, Cheyenne, and Arapaho force since February, fighting several major engagements but with a decisive victory proving elusive. Custer was now intent on forcing the issue, and on defeating the great

BATTLE FACTS

Who: The U.S. 7th Cavalry Regiment commanded by Lieutenant-Colonel George Armstrong Custer (1839–76), versus Cheyenne, Sioux, and Arapaho warriors led by Sitting Bull (1834–90), and Crazy Horse (1849–77).

What: The battle was the largest action of the Great Sioux War of 1876–77, and was a great victory for the Cheyenne tribes.

Where: The valley of the Little Big Horn River, Montana Territory.

When: June 25–26, 1876.

Why: The battle took place during an effort by the U.S. Government and Army to move renegade Indians to a reservation.

Outcome: Custer and elements of his command were slaughtered in fighting popularly known as Custer's Last Stand.

Lakota leader, Crazy Horse, in battle. Although Custer initially intended to attack on June 26, a subsequent report that approximately 40 Indians had been seen nearby raised concerns that the element of surprise had been lost. Custer, therefore, decided to act immediately.

Just after midday, he divided his force into four detachments. The first, led by Custer, counted just over 200 soldiers. The second included 115 soldiers commanded by Captain Frederick Benteen, while the third, totaling 142 soldiers and about 35 scouts, was led by Major Marcus Reno. The fourth detachment consisted of the regimental train escorted by about 135 soldiers.

Custer and Reno were to ride down the divide between the Rosebud River and the Little Big Horn. When the Indian village was sighted, Reno would attack directly. Benteen was to proceed to the left, toward the upper valley of the Little Big Horn, searching for the Indian village and cutting off the most likely escape route. Shortly after 2 P.M., a scout spotted several Indians heading toward the Little Big Horn. When Custer received word, his adjutant delivered his only order of the day to Reno: "Custer says to move at as rapid a gait as you think prudent and to charge afterward, and you will be supported by the whole outfit."

FATAL FLAWS

Custer has been criticized not only for his risk-taking at Little Big Horn, but also for impetuous command decisions. He declined additional cavalry support and the use of some Gatling guns, and divided his force of more than 600 cavalrymen into weaker units, although he was not certain of the enemy strength. In the event, his command faced a hostile Indian force estimated at more than three to four times its number.

At about 3 P.M., Reno crossed a small creek, which now bears his name, and attacked the southern end of the Indian village. Quickly, it became apparent that he was confronted by a large contingent of Indian warriors. Fighting dismounted, the troopers soon gave ground. Although some accused him of faltering under fire, Reno appears to have held his troopers together as well as could be expected. As Reno fell back, Custer committed his two detachments in an assault on the other end of the

village. While many of the Cheyenne and Sioux warriors took on this second threat, Crazy Horse led a large force downstream, then doubling back against Custer in a classic envelopment. The hard-pressed cavalrymen were pushed northward to the slope of a long ridge.

Meanwhile, Benteen had advanced 10 miles (16 km) up the valley and found nothing. A scribbled message from Custer hurried him toward the sounds of gunfire. Benteen joined Reno, and following a second day of fighting the remnants of these commands were able to withdraw safely.

Custer, however, had come to grief. His force had been trapped nearly 3 miles (5 km) from Reno's position and killed to the last man. Modern archeological investigations reveal that the slaughter, which came to be known as "Custer's Last Stand," may have been a running battle rather than that commonly depicted—a prominent Custer and his embattled troopers dying in an evertightening ring of Indian warriors.

Custer's furious fight for survival may have been short, possibly no more than half an hour in duration. Yet more than 260 soldiers and civilians were dead, and 55 wounded, while casualties among the Indians are estimated at 130 killed and 160 wounded. Custer's impetuous nature had led to disaster.

SIOUX WARRIOR

This Sioux warrior, mounted on a blanket of buffalo hide on a sturdy horse, is typical of the Plains Indians who fought to maintain their tribal lands against the inexorable westward advance of white settlers. Expert horsemen and deadly with the bow and arrow, Sioux and Cheyenne warriors overwhelmed the U.S. 7th Cavalry at Little Big Horn. This warrior carries his bow and a small shield.

CHAPTER THREE

The Modern Era

During the nineteenth and early twentieth centuries, much traditionalism still persisted in warfare. As the twentieth century progressed, however, battles became matters of crushing firepower and fast maneuver, rather than linear formations fighting in head-to-head combat.

The transformation in warfare from the Napoleonic era to the present day is profound. At the beginning of this period, armies still clashed with musket and smoothbore cannon, and often fought from regular formations such as line and column. From the American Civil War onward advances in firepower (particularly the shift to rifled, breech-loading firearms and cannon) meant such formations became suicidal. During the twentieth century, therefore, the tenets of maneuver warfare, plus the need for cover and concealment, took hold. New combat weapons—including combat aircraft, armored vehicles, guided missiles, and machine guns—plus critical advances in battlefield communications, have meant that applying technology has become far more central to victory or defeat, although the need for courage remains as strong as ever.

LEFT: U.S. SOLDIERS IN VIETNAM *prepare to fire at North Vietnamese Army forces somewhere near Hue, 1967. The soldiers are armed with M14 carbines and an M60 squad machine gun.*

Adowa 1898

POSSESSION OF ADVANCED FIREARMS ALLOWED THE EUROPEAN COLONIAL POWERS TO CONQUER LARGE AREAS IN LESS-DEVELOPED REGIONS. HOWEVER, THE ADVANTAGE COULD NOT LAST FOREVER. AS THE ITALIANS FOUND OUT AT ADOWA, MOTIVATED LOCAL TROOPS WERE CAPABLE OF BEATING COLONIAL REGULARS WHEN BEARING THE EQUIVALENT WEAPONRY.

I n 1895, war flared up in Italy's troubled new protectorate of Ethiopia, as the Ethiopian emperor, Menelik II, attempted to shrug off European rule. The Italian government launched a punitive, and initially successful, military expedition commanded by General Oreste Baratieri, and in late February 1896 the two armies faced each other at Adowa, 80 miles (129 km) south of Asmara, Eritrea. Baratieri had a command of 20,000 men, and had captured Adowa once before, but he preferred to wait for the 80,000-strong Ethiopian army to fragment through food shortages and desertion. Yet the Italian Premier, Francesco Crispi, stepped in and ordered Baratieri

NINETEENTH-CENTURY COLONIAL WARFARE *often pitted European soldiers against large numbers of tribal irregulars. At Adowa, the irregulars were as well armed as the Europeans.*

to do battle for his country's honor. Baratieri hoped to advance and occupy the high ground around Adowa before taking the city a second time. To this end, he divided his outnumbered force into four brigades, each using a different route. The Italian force became badly confused, with brigades becoming intermingled, strung out, and downright lost during the march.

CONFUSION

It was in this state of total confusion that the Ethiopians intercepted the Italian expedition on March 1. In most previous "colonial" battles, the Europeans had always enjoyed a massive superiority in firepower. At Adowa, however, there were five Abyssinian riflemen to each Italian. Worse, Menelik had positioned his artillery on high ground and the guns began pounding the Italians as they tried to reform their scattered brigades. Although the Abyssinians possessed modern firearms, theirs was not a trained European army but a vast horde of armed men led by charismatic leaders. The result was a series of uncoordinated, disorganized rushes against the Italians. Even so, there was never any real chance that the dispersed Italians might win the battle. The Abyssinians were brave, persistent, and numerous, and if their rifle fire was inexpert and undisciplined, there was nonetheless a huge amount of it. The Italians were not capable of concerted action, and after the lead brigade had been surrounded and destroyed, the other brigades were defeated in detail. Eventually, the surviving Italian units were able to retreat, leaving about 5,000 men dead on the field of battle. Large numbers of men—wounded and otherwise—were captured. What had meant to be a moment of Italian triumph, had turned into the country's shame.

BATTLE FACTS

Who: Italian regular forces including 17,700 infantry and 56 artillery pieces under General Baratieri (1841–1901) opposed by Abyssinian irregulars numbering up to 100,000 men armed with modern rifles and 28 artillery pieces loyal to Emperor Menelik (1844–1913).

What: Dispersed Italian forces were defeated piecemeal by a determined Abyssinian force.

Where: Near the border of Abyssinia (modern-day Ethiopia) and Eritrea.

When: March 1, 1896.

Why: Italy sought greater colonial possessions by expanding their empire in East Africa.

Outcome: Decisive defeat forced the Italian government to recognize Abyssinian independence.

Spion Kop 1900

AT SPION KOP, POOR COMMAND AND CONTROL ON THE BRITISH SIDE ALLOWED A GREATLY OUTNUMBERED BOER FORCE TO WIN A DEFENSIVE VICTORY.

Three months after the outbreak of the Second Boer War, with 10,000 British troops besieged in Ladysmith and others trapped in Mafeking and Kimberley, it was imperative that a relief expedition break through to them. Their surrender would be an appalling political blow, so the British under Sir Redvers Buller were unable to operate freely. Instead they were forced to advance against Boer forces dug in at the Tugela River.

After a drive up the rail line to Ladysmith was defeated at Colenso on December 15, 1899, Buller made another attempt near the Rangeworthy Hills on January 19, 1900. Spion Kop was thought to be the key to this position, so a column was sent to take it. This enterprise was entirely successful. The small Boer party on the hill was driven off and the British began to entrench themselves.

However, Spion Kop turned out to be overlooked by other summits, and the British came under accurate rifle

A BOER PICKET POSE FOR THE CAMERA *at Spion Kop. Armed with rifles, including the latest German Mauser Gewehr 98, the Boer marksmen proved deadly accurate in the fighting for the high ground.*

BATTLE FACTS

Who: British troops under General Sir Redvers Buller (1839–1908) totaling 24,000 infantry, 2,600 cavalry, and artillery, opposed by Boer forces numbering 6,000–8,000 with little artillery, under General Louis Botha (1862–1919).

What: Attempting to fight past the Boer positions, the British tried to turn the Boer flank but were repelled and forced to retire.

Where: A hill on the north bank of the Tugela River in Natal Province.

When: January 19–24, 1900.

Why: British troops were attempting to break the Boers' siege of Ladysmith.

Outcome: Defeat for the British delayed the relief of Ladysmith, but later victories allowed the advance to continue.

and artillery fire. Heavy casualties were taken on both sides as parties of Boers tried to retake the hilltop, with British reinforcements fed in as diversionary attacks were directed at Boer positions on other nearby hills.

BATTLE FOR SPION KOP

Poor command and control at higher levels, combined with officer casualties, severely impeded the British defense of the hill. Matters were scarcely any better on the Boer side, with few volunteers to join the close-range firefight on top of Spion Kop. Eventually the Boers decided they could not capture or hold Spion Kop and withdrew.

The British came to the same conclusion at roughly the same time. Rather than exploit the victory they were not aware they had just won, British troops withdrew from Spion Kop, allowing the Boers to reoccupy it and retain their blocking position north of the Tugela.

Spion Kop was a disaster for both sides. In Britain, the government was almost brought down while among the Boers there was a feeling that the war was more or less won. Their forces were all volunteers, and many decided it was time to go home. This reduction in manpower, as much as anything else, made the eventual relief of Ladysmith possible.

GEYSERS FROM JAPANESE SHELLFIRE *bracket the vanguard of the Russian Baltic Fleet in Tsushima Strait. The Russians held the upper hand briefly before Japanese guns were brought to bear.*

Tsushima Strait 1905

AT APPROXIMATELY 2:45 A.M. ON THE FOG-SHROUDED MORNING OF MAY 27, 1905, THE JAPANESE MERCHANT SHIP *SHINANO MARU* WAS PATROLLING 150 MILES (240 KM) SOUTH OF THE ENTRANCE TO THE KOREAN STRAITS. THE SHIP'S CREW CAUGHT A GLIMPSE OF SHADOWY SHIPS IN THE DISTANCE AND KNEW A DESPERATE HOUR HAD ARRIVED. THE SHIP'S CAPTAIN DASHED OFF A WIRELESS MESSAGE: "ENEMY FLEET IN SIGHT IN SQUARE 203. APPARENTLY MAKING FOR THE EASTERN CHANNEL."

By May 1905, Japan had been at war with imperial Russia for more than a year. In January, Russia's Far East bastion at Port Arthur had capitulated following a protracted siege, and from the surrounding heights Japanese heavy guns had pounded the warships of the Tsar's Pacific Squadron in the harbor below into useless hulks. Before the fall of Port Arthur, Russia had renamed its Baltic Fleet the Second Pacific Squadron, which was sent

BATTLE FACTS

Who: The Japanese fleet with 31 ships under Admiral Togo Heihachiro (1848–1934) versus the Russian Baltic Fleet with 37 ships under Admiral Zinovy Rozhestvensky (1848–1909).

What: The Baltic Fleet was attempting to reach a safe anchorage at Vladivostok.

Where: Tsushima Strait between the Japanese home island of Kyushu and the Korean peninsula.

When: May 27–28, 1905.

Why: The Japanese were determined to maintain naval preeminence in the Pacific and hoped to strike a blow against Russian prestige.

Outcome: Togo employed the classic naval maneuver of crossing the enemy's "T" to concentrate fire. The Russian fleet was annihilated.

18,000 nautical miles (33,336 km) in an attempt to join what remained of its navy in the East and fight the Japanese in their home waters.

The Baltic Fleet—eight battleships, eight cruisers, nine destroyers plus several other vessels—sailed on October 15, 1904, commanded by Admiral Zinovy P. Rozhestvensky, who crucially had no combat experience. While anchored at Madagascar, Rozhestvensky received the disheartening news of Port Arthur's surrender. His original destination in Japanese hands, his only option was to sail for the port of Vladivostok, via the Tsushima Strait between Korea and Japan. Here the Russians would face the highly motivated, well-trained fleet of Admiral Togo Heihachiro—four battleships, eight cruisers, 21 destroyers, and 60 torpedo boats.

CROSSING THE "T"
Togo weighed anchor from Masan, Korea, just before 6 A.M. on May 27. Sometime after 1 P.M., in two ragged lines, Rozhestvensky's ships appeared in the Tsushima Strait. Togo then took a tremendous gamble. His ships were to turn to port in succession, each executing the turn at the same position. The maneuver was dangerous because the Japanese would be exposed to Russian fire at a point when many of their own guns could not reply. Yet once the maneuver was completed, the Japanese would be crossing the Russian "T," firing their heavy broadsides at the enemy against only a few of the Russians' forward guns. The Japanese sailors executed the turn with precision, but for several minutes a rain of Russian shells inflicted serious damage on several key vessels.

When the Japanese ships came out of their turn, however, they were completely across the Russian "T" at a range of 5,000 yards (4,572 m). Concentrated fire set the Russian flagship *Suvorov* ablaze. A shell struck the flagship's bridge, wounding Rozhestvensky, who fell unconscious and was evacuated to a destroyer. *Suvorov's* helm jammed, and the doomed battleship began turning in circles. Simultaneously, the battleship *Oslyabya*, at the head of the second Russian line, capsized and sank. Following *Suvorov*, the new battleship *Alexander III* began to turn in a circle with the flagship. Third in line, the battleship *Borodino* was burning furiously. During the same exchange, which reduced the *Suvorov* to a smoking ruin, *Alexander III* drifted out of control.

RELENTLESS ADMIRAL TOGO
Less than two hours later, Togo regained contact with what was left of the main Russian fleet. *Alexander III* had assumed the lead of the Russian column, but rolled over and sank in a hail of Japanese fire. As *Suvorov* slipped beneath the waves, the Japanese concentrated their fire on *Borodino* and the nearby battleship *Orel*, which was set ablaze.

Daylight faded, and Togo ordered his ships to disengage. Just before firing ceased, *Fuji* loosed the day's last salvo of 12 in (30 cm) shells at the stricken *Borodino*. At least one of these penetrated the battleship's magazines, and it disappeared in a catastrophic explosion.

Command of the shattered Russian fleet devolved to Admiral Nikolai Nebogatov aboard *Nikolai I*. In a vain attempt to resume a course for Vladivostok, Nebogatov ordered his fleet to take a northerly course. In the darkness, Japanese torpedo boats and destroyers attacked. The elderly battleship *Sisoi Veliky* took a torpedo aft and sank about dawn, while four torpedoes smashed into the battleship *Navarin*, which went down at 10 P.M.

The Russian cruisers that accompanied the main body were also destroyed, and on the morning of May 28, Nebogatov found he was hemmed in on three sides by Japanese cruisers with Togo's main force again moving across the Russian "T." The Japanese stood out of range of the most powerful remaining Russian guns and began shelling the survivors from 12,000 yards (11,000 m). Nebogatov ordered his flag lowered to half-mast and sought surrender terms. Only the cruiser *Izumrud* and two destroyers reached Vladivostok.

Tsushima had been a debacle for the Russians. They had lost 34 ships, 4,830 dead, and 5,917 wounded and captured. The Japanese lost only three torpedo boats. Japan's victory over a traditional European power stunned the world.

BATTLE OF THE PRE-DREADNOUGHTS

At Tsushima, the elderly Japanese battleship Fuji *(top) employed its 12-in (30-cm) guns against the Russian Baltic fleet. In the final action of the first day, a salvo from* Fuji *struck the magazine of the crippled Russian battleship* Borodino, *which exploded and sank. The 15,000-ton Russian battleship* Suvorov *(bottom) was set ablaze from stem to stern during the battle.*

TSUSHIMA STRAIT

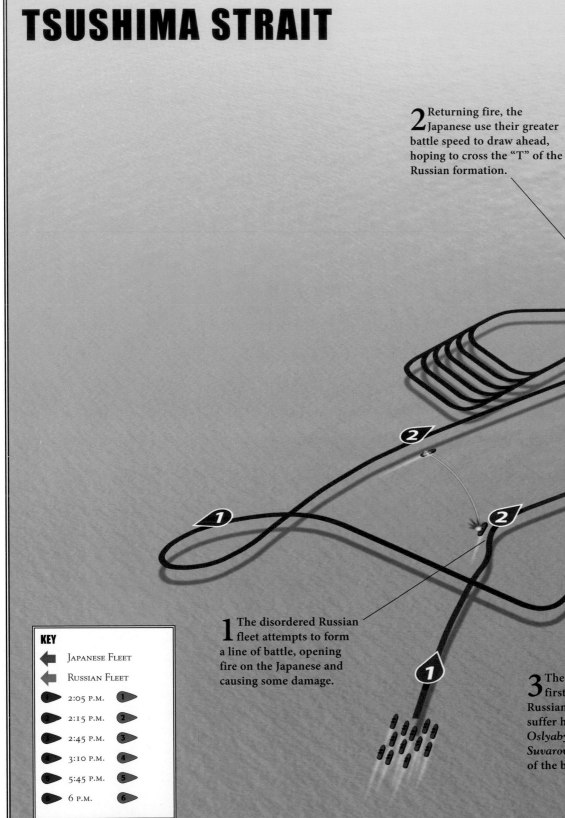

2 Returning fire, the Japanese use their greater battle speed to draw ahead, hoping to cross the "T" of the Russian formation.

1 The disordered Russian fleet attempts to form a line of battle, opening fire on the Japanese and causing some damage.

3 The flagships of the first and second Russian divisions both suffer heavy damage. *Oslyabya* sinks; *Suvarov* is driven out of the battle line.

KEY

←	JAPANESE FLEET
←	RUSSIAN FLEET
1	2:05 P.M.	1
2	2:15 P.M.	2
3	2:45 P.M.	3
4	3:10 P.M.	4
5	5:45 P.M.	5
6	6 P.M.	6

6 The stragglers of the Russian fleet are either scattered or finished off by torpedo attacks from torpedo boats and destroyers. Only a handful of ships survive.

5 At 6 P.M., after a series of isolated exchanges, the two fleets reengage en masse. By 7:03 P.M. the *Alexander III* has also been sunk.

4 After a lull in the action, *Alexander III* leads the Russian fleet in a renewed attack. Most of the Russian battleships are crippled or sunk as the Japanese fleet crosses the "T" again.

ANZAC SOLDIERS MILL AROUND ON THE LANDING BEACHES
*at Gallipoli as supplies are unloaded. The Allied assault against
Ottoman Turkey proved a colossal failure.*

Gallipoli   1915

"HE CAME, HE SAW, HE CAPITULATED," GROANED
WINSTON CHURCHILL, WHO HAD RECENTLY RESIGNED
AS FIRST LORD OF THE ADMIRALTY, IN ASSESSING
THE DECISION OF GENERAL SIR CHARLES MONRO TO
SWIFTLY EVACUATE THE SOLDIERS OF THE BRITISH
COMMONWEALTH AND FRANCE LANGUISHING ON THE
PENINSULA OF GALLIPOLI.

A s the Western Front descended into stalemate in
late 1914, military planners on both sides searched
for an alternative that might lead to ultimate
victory. Responding to a plea from their Russian allies,
the British and French settled on an attempt to seize the
Dardanelles, a narrow waterway connecting the Black Sea
to the Mediterranean. Control of this strait would establish
a supply line to Russia, relieve pressure on the Czar's Eastern
Front armies, and possibly compel Turkey to sue for peace.
It was soon discovered that land forces would have to secure
the heights that commanded either side of the Dardanelles,

BATTLE FACTS

Who: More than 400,000
Allied troops commanded
by General Sir Ian Hamilton
(1853–1947), and later
General Sir Charles Monro
(1860–1929), versus 500,000
Turkish troops under General
Otto Liman von Sanders
(1855–1929).

What: A bloody stalemate
prompted the Allies to
evacuate.

Where: Gallipoli peninsula
and the Dardanelles in
modern-day Turkey.

When: April 25, 1915 to
January 9, 1916.

Why: The Allies hoped to
establish a supply link to
Russia and compel Ottoman
Turkey to sue for peace.

Outcome: The Turkish
victory produced hundreds of
thousands of casualties and
a crisis in confidence among
Allied leaders.

in order for shipping to transit the waterway unscathed. On February 19, 1915, a flotilla of 42 Allied warships pounded Turkish fortifications in the Dardanelles, but achieved limited results. A month later, a fleet of 18 battleships attempted to run the gauntlet of Turkish defenses, but was roughly handled by coastal guns and mines. When it quickly became apparent that naval power alone could not secure the Dardanelles, a plan was devised to land Commonwealth and French troops on the Gallipoli peninsula, with the intent that they advance rapidly overland and capture the Turkish fortifications. Eventually, the Allies committed more than 400,000 soldiers to the land expedition, against Turkish forces numbering about half a million.

HELLES AND ANZAC COVE

The Allied force consisted of the British 29th Division, the Royal Naval Division, the Australian and New Zealand Army Corps (ANZAC) and the French Oriental Expeditionary Corps, and was commanded by General Sir Ian Hamilton. On April 25, British and French troops came ashore at Helles, on the southern end of the Gallipoli peninsula, while ANZAC troops disembarked near Gaba Tepe on the coast of the Aegean Sea. The operation continually suffered from inadequate planning and tactical execution—amphibious landings under fire from hostile forces, which occupied surrounding high ground, had rarely been practiced.

At Helles, the old collier *River Clyde*, converted to a troop transport, was run aground to land its soldiers. The men of the Royal Hampshires and the Royal Munster Fusiliers stepped down narrow gangways into a hail of machine-gun fire. Only 21 of the initial 200 men off the ship managed to reach the shore unscathed. The Lancashire Fusiliers lost 600 of their 1,000 men in the first hours of battle. ANZAC forces also sustained heavy casualties north of Gaba Tepe,

LORD HERBERT KITCHENER, *British Secretary of State for War, visits the front lines at Gallipoli. The costly stalemate damaged Kitchener's reputation.*

and their confined landing area has come to be known as ANZAC Cove.

Throughout the spring of 1915, attempts to penetrate the Turkish cordon and capture the town of Krithia failed. Turkish forces, commanded by the German General Otto Liman von Sanders, were too weak to push the invaders into the sea. While the thinly stretched Turkish lines staved off appreciable Allied gains, counterattacks were fruitless.

HEAVY CASUALTIES

Illustrative of the high casualties suffered was the ANZAC assault on May 2–3 against Baby 700, the smaller of two hills that dominated their exposed positions at ANZAC Cove, and the Turkish offensive against ANZAC Cove on May 19. Within hours of attacking, ANZAC troops were forced to retreat, having suffered hundreds of casualties traversing gullies and ravines against murderous fire. When more than 40,000 Turkish soldiers hit an ANZAC force less than half their size, the attackers lost 10,000 casualties.

On August 6, Allied troops landed at Suvla Bay, intending to link up with forces at ANZAC Cove. Within a week, primarily due to the ineptitude of field commanders, the attack lost momentum. Thus, a third Allied lodgment was effectively bottled up.

After months of fighting, the lines at Gallipoli began to resemble those of the Western Front. Snipers picked off soldiers who raised their heads above the parapets of their trenches. Unburied corpses bloated in the stifling heat of summer, and clouds of flies compounded the misery. Fall and winter brought rain, snow, and freezing temperatures. Turkish artillery dominated Allied positions, and the troops were subjected to constant shelling. When Hamilton requested nearly 100,000 additional soldiers for Gallipoli at the end of August, he received only one-quarter of that number.

With their hopes for a decisive victory in the Dardanelles dashed, discord was rife among Allied leaders. By October, confidence in Hamilton's leadership had evaporated. At long last, on December 7, more than 100,000 men were evacuated from ANZAC Cove. The withdrawal of 35,000 soldiers from Helles did not occur until January 9, 1916.

In ironic retrospect, the withdrawal of Allied troops from Gallipoli during the winter of 1915–16 may be considered the most successful component of the ill-fated expedition against Ottoman Turkey. During more than eight months of bitter fighting, Allied losses reached a staggering 220,000, or 59 percent, while the Turkish defenders suffered approximately 300,000 dead and wounded, or 60 percent of those engaged. Responsibility for the disaster at Gallipoli lies chiefly in the disregard of Allied commanders for the difficulty of the task assigned to their troops—a task that heroism alone could not successfully complete.

BRITISH BATTLECRUISER HMS *LION (left) is shelled by German warships as HMS* Queen Mary *(right) explodes in a mass of smoke during the Battle of Jutland, May 31, 1916.*

Jutland   1916

JUTLAND WAS THE ONLY MAJOR FLEET BATTLE OF WORLD WAR I AND ONE OF THE LARGEST NAVAL ACTIONS OF ALL TIME.

Sea power played an enormous part in the Great War. With the Grand Fleet intact, Britain could maintain a blockade of German ports that would eventually force a surrender. Thus the German High Seas Fleet had to defeat its greatly superior opponent, while the British had only to avoid decisive defeat.

German naval strategy was to try to draw out part of the Grand Fleet, ambushing it with overwhelming force. If the British could be weakened enough a decisive battle might be possible. To this end a series of battlecruiser raids were launched against the east coast of England. Meanwhile, the British were trying to bring the High Seas Fleet to action and actively sought an engagement. On May 31, 1916, both fleets were at sea. Each hoped to catch a part of the other and inflict a mauling, not realizing that the whole opposing force was in the offing.

BATTLE FACTS

Who: The British Grand Fleet, commanded by Admiral Sir John Jellicoe (1859–1935) and comprising 37 battleships plus 34 cruisers and 78 destroyers, opposed by German High Seas Fleet of 27 battleships plus 11 cruisers and 61 destroyers under Admiral Reinhard Scheer (1863–1928).

What: An encounter battle developed into a major fleet action before the High Seas Fleet broke off.

Where: The North Sea, near the mouth of the Skagerrak.

When: May 31–June 1, 1916.

Why: Both fleets sought to draw the other into an engagement on its own terms, leading to a major battle.

Outcome: Although the British suffered heavier losses, the strategic situation remained in their favor.

THE BATTLE OPENS

Light forces from both sides spotted a neutral merchant ship at about the same time. Turning to investigate, they sighted one another and opened fire. This drew in more light forces, including several light cruisers, and the German battlecruiser force was sent to chase down the British cruisers as they retired. This brought the German battlecruisers into range of their British counterparts. Turning away, the Germans endeavored to do what they had been briefed for—get the British battlecruisers to chase them onto the guns of the High Seas Fleet's battleships.

As the German battlecruisers ran southward, exchanging fire with pursuing British battlecruisers and fast battleships, German gunnery was significantly better. Coupled with serious defects in the design of British battlecruisers, this caused two ships to explode and sink, and others were damaged. However, the Germans were also taking hits as they neared their supports.

Almost at the last possible moment, British Vice-Admiral David Beatty (1871–1936), commanding the battlecruisers, realized he was about to run straight into the entire German fleet. His ships executed a hard turn and began to flee northward toward the Grand Fleet with the German fleet in pursuit.

As Beatty's ships made their escape, the destroyer forces on both sides attempted to attack one another and the heavy ships they protected. A savage gun and torpedo engagement broke out as the German fleet pursued northward. So far, it appeared that things were going according to the German plan; a portion of the Grand Fleet had been drawn out and engaged by vastly superior gunpower. However, exactly the same thing was now about to happen to the High Seas Fleet.

THE FLEETS CLASH

Hearing that the High Seas Fleet was approaching from the south, Admiral Jellicoe ordered the Grand Fleet to deploy from columns to line of battle. This allowed the entire fleet to fire on the enemy force with their full broadsides from the classic "across the T" position, while the German ships could return fire only with their forward armament.

Outgunned and in a bad position, the High Seas Fleet came about and began to run southward once more. A gunnery duel took place, with several ships badly hit. Jellicoe, worried about torpedo attacks, turned away for a time before resuming his pursuit. His intent was to force the German fleet to fight by placing his force between the High Seas Fleet and its home port.

For his part, Admiral Scheer wanted to disengage his fleet and escape. An attempt to get across the British rear resulted in another heavy gun action. Abandoning this attempt, Scheer ordered his heavy ships to break off. The disengagement was covered by an attack by destroyers and battlecruisers.

The fall of darkness caused the fleets to lose sight of each other, though they were close together and on parallel courses. Scheer eventually decided that his best chance of escape was to turn for home and hope to slip by the British. He was resolved to crash right through the British fleet if necessary.

The result was a series of chaotic, close-range encounters, but the High Seas Fleet was eventually able to escape and return to port. Although it had inflicted significant losses on the British, this was not enough to affect the strategic situation. The blockade would continue, contributing greatly to the eventual Allied victory.

GERMAN NAVAL OFFICER

The typical dress of a German naval officer in World War I was a blue tunic with matching pants, a white shirt with a wing collar worn with a black tie, black shoes, and the naval peaked cap. The cap was blue in color and had a black mohair surround and leather brim. It also featured Imperial cockade surrounded by oak leaves and surmounted by a crown. The rank (Lieutenant Captain) of this officer is indicated by the rings on the sleeve capped by the Imperial crown, though naval officers during this period often had rank displayed through shoulder boards and shoulder straps.

THE GERMAN BATTLECRUISER DERFLINGER *carried eight powerful 8 in (30 cm) guns and was more heavily armored than her Royal Navy counterparts.*

Verdun 1916

VERDUN EPITOMIZES THE ATTRITIONAL STRUGGLE THAT BECAME CHARACTERISTIC OF WORLD WAR I ON THE WESTERN FRONT. INTENDED TO DESTROY THE FRENCH RESERVES, THE BATTLE DREW IN MASSIVE NUMBERS OF GERMAN TROOPS AS WELL, AND ENDED WITHOUT ANY DECISIVE RESULT.

B y 1916, victory in the Great War had at a strategic level largely become a matter of exhausting the other side, of making the cost of continuing so high that peace became essential. The key here was reserves. As long as the opposition had sufficient manpower available to feed into the combat zone, the war could go on. The German High Command therefore came up with a plan to destroy the French reserves by drawing them into a "meatgrinder" battle. The German plan was to attack something that the French had to defend, and to destroy their army with artillery and infantry attacks. The chosen objective was the fortified city of Verdun. Verdun was an ideal target in many ways. Lying in a loop of the

BATTLE FACTS

Who: French Second Army under General Henri-Philippe Pétain (1856–1951), later replaced by General Robert Nivelle (1856–1924), versus the German Fifth Army under Crown Prince Wilhelm (1882–1951).

What: The fortified city of Verdun was besieged and the attackers slowly ground their way in while artillery inflicted horrendous casualties. A counteroffensive eventually regained the lost ground.

Where: The city of Verdun on the Meuse River, France.

When: February 21 to December 18, 1916.

Why: The Germans wanted to destroy the French reserves, forcing France to make peace.

Outcome: After a hideous attritional struggle all that was achieved was massive casualties on both sides.

Meuse River, the city had poor communications. Only one road ran in and out of the city. The logistical problems of the attack were eased by the fact that there was a major German railroad junction just 12 miles (19 km) away, allowing quick transportation of ammunition, supplies, and reinforcements as the attack developed. Verdun lay in a relatively quiet sector of the front, and many of the heavy guns of its forts had been sent to other sectors where they seemed to be more badly needed. It was garrisoned by three French divisions, which represented fairly light defenses.

German offensive plans included the assembly of ten divisions to make the actual attack, supported by huge quantities of heavy guns. The offensive was codenamed Operation "*Gericht*" ("Judgment"). Its aim was to force the French into a battle of attrition on unequal terms. If they failed to meet the challenge, Verdun would fall. If they stood and fought, their army would be bled white and they would ultimately be forced to sue for peace.

OPENING BARRAGE

As February 21, 1916, dawned, the frigid air around Verdun was shattered by the scream of artillery fire. More than two million shells fell on the forward French positions in the next 12 hours, after which the infantry began their attack. For the first two days the German forces made relatively little headway, but on the 24th they broke through the main defensive line, taking 10,000 prisoners and capturing 65 artillery pieces. The whole Verdun defense was collapsing.

For the French, something had to be done, and fast. Verdun was supposed to be invincible, yet on February 25 Fort Douaumont, a key component of the city's defenses, fell to a German assault. At the same time that Fort Douaumont was being captured, General Henri-Philippe Pétain was arriving to take charge of the French units. He found a desperate situation, with the only supply route into the city along a single road and a narrow-gauge railroad alongside it. This road, dubbed La Voie Sacrée, was Verdun's inadequate lifeline, and Pétain's first task was to improve it. Thousands of men worked to widen the road, allowing a less-restricted flow of supplies into the city. By the time they had finished, something like 6,000 trucks could use the road every day. Of further encouragement to the French was the fact that German troops were also suffering horrific casualties by this time, plus problems with large numbers of artillery pieces being worn out or destroyed by counterbattery fire.

ON THE OFFENSIVE

In May, Pétain was relieved by the offensively minded General Robert Nivelle, and the French began to recover their spirit. At first Nivelle could do no more than Pétain;

German attacks were still making gains, and on June 7 the critical Fort Vaux also fell. Nevertheless, the balance was shifting. Nivelle was an artillery officer, and under his command the French guns became more effective. Nivelle's position was also improved by the Anglo-French Somme offensive farther north, launched on July 1 partly to reduce the pressure on Verdun. As the pressure eased, Nivelle launched counterattacks to drive the Germans out and retake the lost forts. By the end of November, Fort Douaumont and Fort Vaux were back in French hands, and in mid-December the German Army retreated from Verdun, leaving what was left of it in French hands.

By the end of the Verdun offensive, the Germans had indeed managed to cause vast French casualties—550,000 of them in fact. The original German plan was reasonably sound—to attack something the enemy had to defend and drain his resources by artillery bombardment followed by infantry occupation of the devastated territory, but the German Army fell victim to "mission creep," and at some point the capture of Verdun became the objective of the operation. This was not the plan originally—the idea was to destroy the French Army, not to seize a city—and Verdun was not worth the 450,000 casualties it cost the Germans.

FRENCH INFANTRY SERGEANT

There were no great differences between the equipment used by troops on both sides in World War I; this French sergeant's equipment is similar to that used by his German foes. A metal helmet offers some protection against overhead shell bursts and he is armed with a rifle and a bayonet. He may have a grenade or two available. Although heavy artillery hurled tons of shells across the trench lines and specialist weapons gradually emerged, including aircraft and armored vehicles, most of the great battles of the war were decided by infantrymen who doggedly clung to their positions or struggled to prize one another out of them.

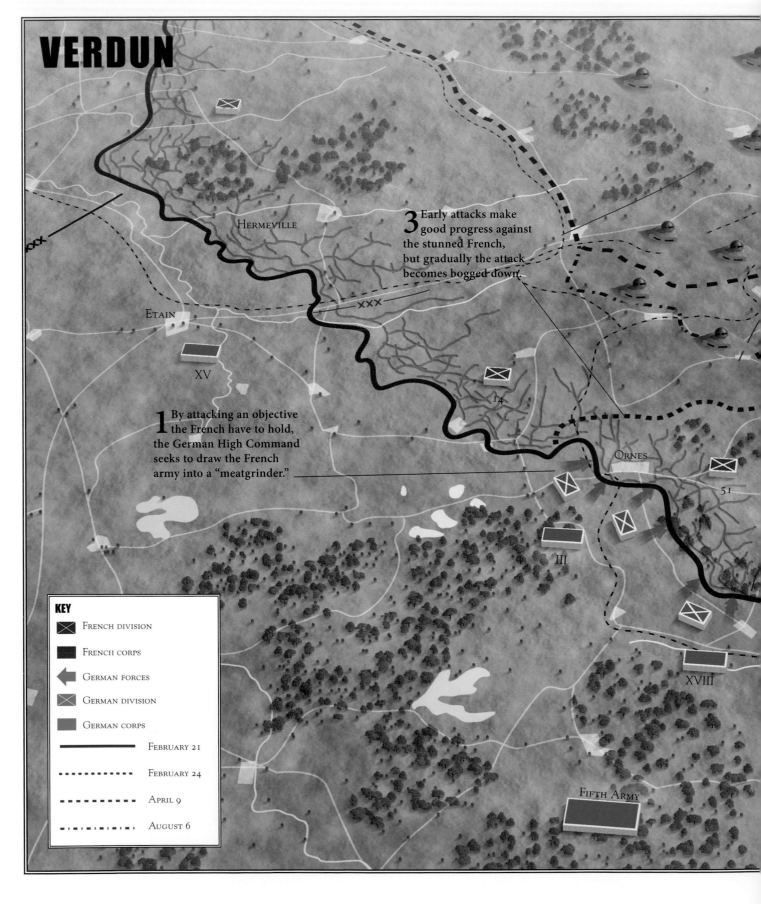

VERDUN

HERMEVILLE

3 Early attacks make
good progress against
the stunned French,
but gradually the attack
becomes bogged down.

ETAIN

XV

1 By attacking an objective
the French have to hold,
the German High Command
seeks to draw the French
army into a "meatgrinder."

14

ORNES

51

III

XVIII

FIFTH ARMY

KEY

French division

French corps

German forces

German division

German corps

————————— February 21

• • • • • • • • • February 24

▬ ▬ ▬ ▬ ▬ April 9

▬ · ▬ · ▬ · ▬ August 6

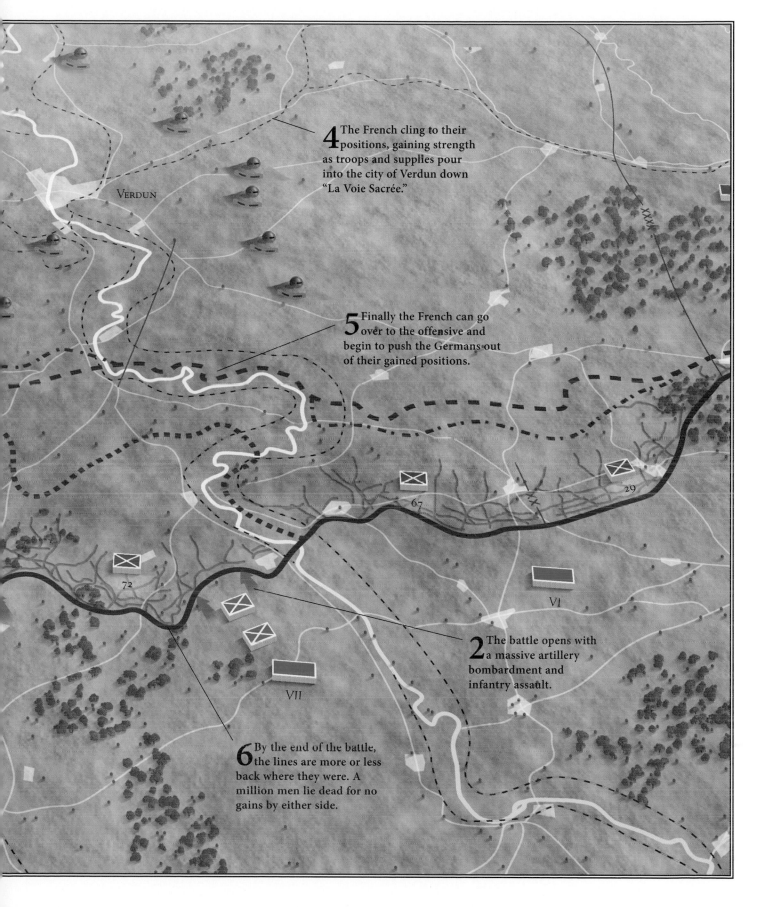

4 The French cling to their positions, gaining strength as troops and supplies pour into the city of Verdun down "La Voie Sacrée."

5 Finally the French can go over to the offensive and begin to push the Germans out of their gained positions.

VERDUN

67

29

72

VI

VII

2 The battle opens with a massive artillery bombardment and infantry assault.

6 By the end of the battle, the lines are more or less back where they were. A million men lie dead for no gains by either side.

GOING OVER THE TOP: *a platoon of British or Commonwealth infantry move along a communication trench in preparation for an attack, somewhere in the Somme sector.*

Somme 1916

THE BATTLE OF THE SOMME IS TODAY SYNONYMOUS WITH MILITARY FOLLY AND POINTLESS BLOODSHED, BUT IN TRUTH THERE WERE GOOD REASONS TO ATTEMPT THE MASSIVE ASSAULT. THE MILITARY BALANCE AT THE TIME FAVORED THE DEFENDER, BUT THERE SEEMED TO BE NO OTHER WAY TO BREAK THE DEADLOCK.

The Somme offensive was conceived by General Sir Douglas Haig (1861–1928), commander in chief of the British Expeditionary Force (BEF), and French Army commander General Joseph Joffre (1852–1931) as a combined Anglo-French push through the German frontline on the Western Front, and also as a pressure-release valve for the French fighting at Verdun. While Third Army under General Sir Edmund Allenby (1861–1936) made a diversionary assault around Gommecourt in the north of the Somme sector, the main thrust would be launched by the British Fourth and French Sixth Armies across a broad front, hopefully smashing through and beyond German defenses stunned by artillery fire.

BATTLE FACTS

Who: British Fourth Army with support from British Third Army and French Sixth Army, attacking German Second Army.

What: After massive artillery preparation the British and French forces attacked well defended German positions and gradually ground their way in, forcing costly counter-attacks to regain lost ground.

Where: Between the Somme and Ancre rivers on the Western Front in France.

When: July 1 to November 18, 1916.

Why: With the war deadlocked, the Allies wanted to regain the initiative and relieve pressure on Russia and the French at Verdun.

Outcome: After massive casualties, little was gained. However, the German army lost much of its best manpower and later withdrew to the Hindenburg Line.

The infantry attack phase of the battle began at 7:30 A.M. on July 1, after 1.7 million artillery shells had been pumped into the German lines during the preceding week. Yet as history now knows, the massive preparatory bombardment had not destroyed the German barbed wire defenses nor completely suppressed the enemy riflemen and machine gunners. All along the line, the attacking units went "over the top," and the defenders emerged from their bunkers, set up machine guns, and began firing at them. Over the unfolding minutes, British troops were cut down in their thousands, often just beyond their trenches or in gaps in the wire that were becoming choked with bodies. The first day alone of the Somme offensive resulted in some 57,470 British casualties, of whom almost 20,000 were killed. This horrific slaughter was made worse by the ponderous linear formation used by attacking units, although with such inexperienced troops there may have been no alternative. The British had attacked with 200 battalions in 17 divisions of about 100,000 men. Of these, only five divisions got any men into the enemy positions at all. The rest were halted in no-man's-land.

ATTRITIONAL STRUGGLE

Despite the fact that fully 20 percent of the initial attacking force had been killed, the Allies kept on going. At first the slaughter was very much one-sided—the Allies threw in new assaults that were chewed up by the machine guns and artillery, or stalled on the wire. For a fortnight, little was achieved. Then, on July 14 a force of French and British troops managed to make some gains along the flanks of the Somme River. Further minor gains followed, but the cost was immense, and fresh troops were fed into the battle on a regular basis as shattered formations had to be pulled out. Through July and August the slaughter went on, though now it was less one-sided. Forty-two German divisions were deployed to the Somme sector in those two months, and the necessity of counterattacking Allied gains resulted in heavy casualties. At the end of July, casualties reached 200,000 for the Allies and 160,000 among German troops. The Allies had advanced 3 miles (4.8 km), and little had changed by the end of August.

It was time to try something new. Thirty-six "tanks"— boxy metal monsters seeing combat for the first time in history—were deployed for a

A BATTERY OF BRITISH 4.7-IN (11.75-CM) *breech-loading guns fire a salvo. In the American Civil War, just 50 years earlier, most artillery guns were short-range smoothbore cannon.*

renewed assault on September 15, despite the fact that their crews were not fully trained. Only 18 went into action as the rest had broken down, but their appearance shocked the defenders into a panic. The Allies gained 3,500 yards (3,200 m) for relatively slight cost, easily the biggest success of the offensive to date. However, it was not possible to exploit the breakthrough and several tanks were lost to artillery fire. The rest broke down or became stuck in the mud.

As the weather worsened through October and November, the Allies attacked again and again, battering at the German positions until November 18, when the Somme finally ceased in the face of exhaustion and winter. At that point the Allies had advanced no more than 7 miles (11.2 km) along a 20-mile (32.2-km) front. In mid-November, the casualty figures came to 419,654 for the British and 194,541 for the French, and this while the slaughter at Verdun was on-going. These immense losses—just short of 615,000—were sustained in failing to break through the Somme positions. However, the German Army also took 650,000 casualties in repelling the assault, and this had serious repercussions. The German Army in 1914 was a splendid military instrument built on Prussian military traditions and victories in France and Austria. As 1917 began it was a tired and dispirited force, whose best men had fallen in the struggles on the Somme. The battle is remembered as the worst slaughter in British military history, but in some ways it achieved its aims. The German Army was badly battered and perhaps dismayed at the doggedness of the attackers. Whatever the reason, it fell back to the more easily defended Hindenburg Line in February 1917.

THE GERMAN MAXIM 08 *could spit death at a rate of 450 rounds per minute at a range of 6,560 ft (2,000 m). Its effectiveness as a defensive weapon was amply demonstrated at the Somme, when just a few guns were able to mow down entire British battalions in a matter of minutes.*

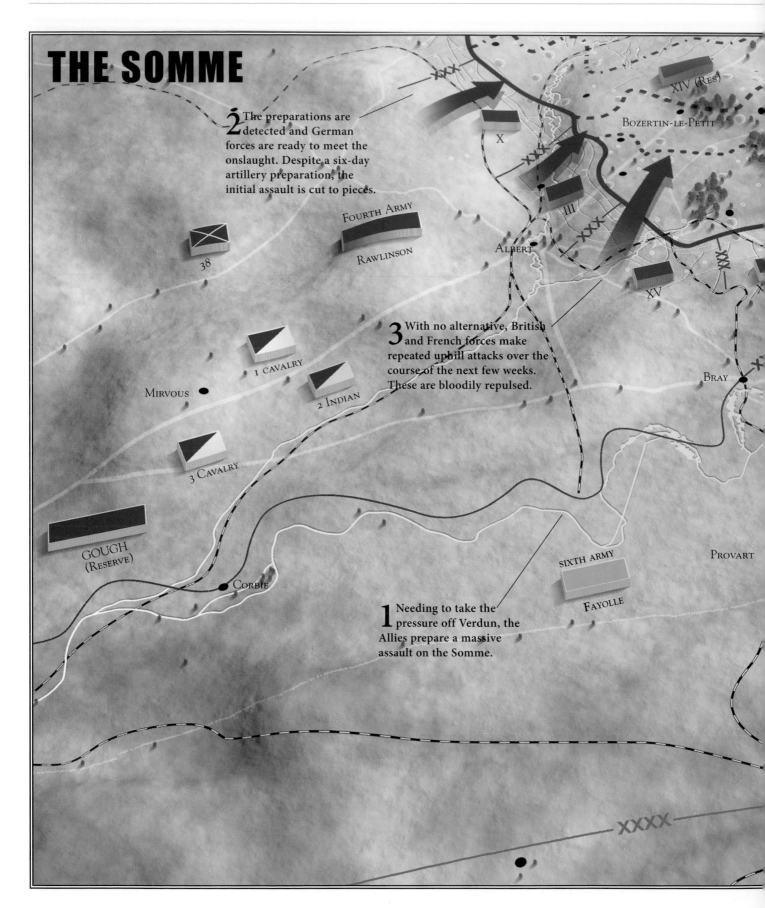

THE SOMME

2 The preparations are detected and German forces are ready to meet the onslaught. Despite a six-day artillery preparation, the initial assault is cut to pieces.

XIV (Res)

BOZERTIN-LE-PETIT

X

38

FOURTH ARMY

RAWLINSON

III

ALBERT

XV

3 With no alternative, British and French forces make repeated uphill attacks over the course of the next few weeks. These are bloodily repulsed.

BRAY

1 CAVALRY

MIRVOUS

2 INDIAN

3 CAVALRY

GOUGH
(RESERVE)

PROVART

SIXTH ARMY

CORBIE

1 Needing to take the pressure off Verdun, the Allies prepare a massive assault on the Somme.

FAYOLLE

XXXX

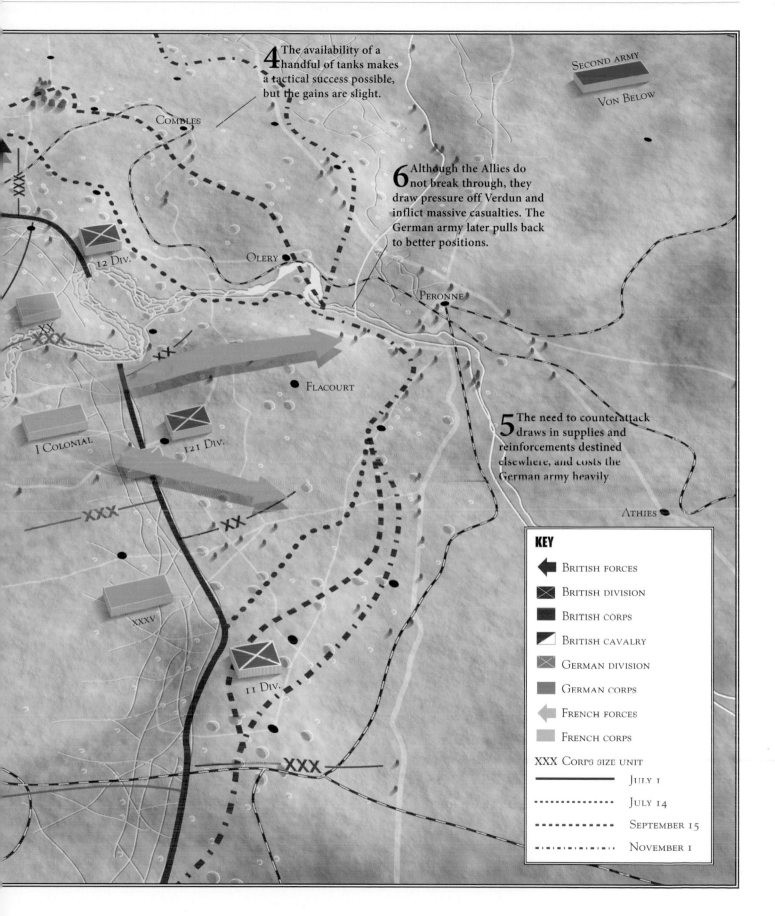

4 The availability of a handful of tanks makes a tactical success possible, but the gains are slight.

SECOND ARMY
VON BELOW

COMBLES

6 Although the Allies do not break through, they draw pressure off Verdun and inflict massive casualties. The German army later pulls back to better positions.

OLERY

PERONNE

12 DIV.

XXX

XX
XXX

XX

FLACOURT

I COLONIAL

121 DIV.

5 The need to counterattack draws in supplies and reinforcements destined elsewhere, and costs the German army heavily

ATHIES

XXX

XX

XXXV

11 DIV.

XXX

KEY

◀	BRITISH FORCES
▨	BRITISH DIVISION
▬	BRITISH CORPS
◨	BRITISH CAVALRY
▨	GERMAN DIVISION
▬	GERMAN CORPS
◀	FRENCH FORCES
▬	FRENCH CORPS
XXX	CORPS SIZE UNIT
————	JULY 1
··············	JULY 14
– – – – –	SEPTEMBER 15
·–··–··–·	NOVEMBER 1

WEARING THEIR WINTER GREATCOATS, *Italian troops retreat in disorder along the Udine-Codroisto road following the decisive defeat at Caporetto, November 1917.*

Caporetto 1917

DURING WORLD WAR I, THE HORROR OF TRENCH WARFARE ON THE WESTERN FRONT WAS LIKE NOTHING THAT SENIOR COMMANDERS OF EITHER THE ALLIED OR CENTRAL POWERS COULD HAVE IMAGINED. THE STATIC LINES OF OPPOSING ARMIES STRETCHED FROM THE NORTH SEA TO THE SWISS FRONTIER, CHANGING LITTLE AS OFFENSIVE OPERATIONS EBBED AND FLOWED.

Stalemate, however, was not only to be found in the West. To the south, where the Italian Army faced the forces of Austria-Hungary on a 400-mile (644-km) front, neither side could gain the upper hand in the only logical area for offensive operations, the Isonzo River Valley. Italy had entered the war on May 23, 1915, and its war planners had long conceived of a bold move into Austria-Hungary through the Isonzo Valley. Perhaps, should it meet with success, the Italian Army could drive northward—even to the gates of Vienna. The advantage, however, obviously lay with the defenders. For more than 60 miles (96 km), the Isonzo flowed through Austria-Hungary

BATTLE FACTS

Who: General Luigi Cadorna (1850–1928) and an Italian army of 41 divisions versus a combined German and Austro-Hungarian army of 35 divisions under General Otto von Below (1857–1944).

What: German and Austro-Hungarian forces conducted a deftly executed offensive against poorly prepared Italian defenses.

Where: Near Caporetto in modern-day Slovenia.

When: October 24 to November 9, 1917.

Why: The Central Powers assumed the offensive to relieve pressure on the forces of Austria-Hungary.

Outcome: Italian forces were routed in a defeat of epic proportions. Italian losses were enormous: 11,000 were killed, 20,000 wounded, and 265,000 were taken prisoner.

parallel to the Italian border. On either side rose high mountains, stretching from Alpine passes to the Adriatic Sea, and the river was prone to flooding during heavy rains. The challenge for Italian General Luigi Cadorna was formidable. To transit the valley, enemy troops defending the mountains on either flank must be dislodged.

For two years, the Italians attempted to wrest control of the Isonzo Valley from the Austro-Hungarians. Cadorna assaulted the enemy defenses no fewer than 11 times, but each side was being bled white in the process, for little gain and hundreds of thousands of casualties. Yet from time to time, Central Powers' military planners also reached the conclusion that the most effective defensive posture lay in assuming the offensive. Such was the case at Caporetto in the fall of 1917.

Boldly conceived, the fall offensive was to be a coordinated effort. Two Austrian armies, commanded by General Svetozar Borojevic (1856–1920), were to assault Italian positions on the east side of the salient they occupied on the hard-won Bainsizza Plateau. The newly constituted Fourteenth Army, which included six fresh German divisions and nine Austrian divisions led by the German General Otto von Below, was to strike the northeastern shoulder of the salient from the nearby Alps. In the center of the two-pronged thrust lay the village of Caporetto.

OUT OF THE MIST

At 2 A.M. on October 24, 1917, the predawn stillness was shattered by the thunder of German and Austro-Hungarian artillery. The morning mist and smoke from the artillery fire shrouded the battlefield as the main German and Austro-Hungarian assaults stepped off about 6:30 A.M. Those Italian troops still manning forward positions spotted the silhouettes, but were unable to identify immediately the soldiers coming toward them. Numerous Italian frontline positions were quickly overrun, the Germans also utilizing relatively small numbers of "stormtroopers," soldiers specially trained in fast trench-assault tactics.

Chaos reigned as Italian soldiers were shot down in their trenches, raised their hands in surrender, or threw their weapons to the ground and fled. On the first day, the Germans and Austro-Hungarians penetrated 14 miles (22 km). Within the week, they had occupied Udine, where Cadorna had previously had his headquarters. By the end of the month, they had reached the Tagliamonte River, halting only when they had advanced an astonishing 70 miles (113 km), their supply lines stretched and mobility hindered by heavy rain and a lack of motorized transportation. Cadorna's center collapsed, and he withdrew rapidly, finally halting in early November along the banks of the Piave River, less than 20 miles (32 km) from Venice. Great Britain and France both diverted troops from other fronts to shore up the Italians.

The offensive had exceeded the grandest expectations of its commanders. Italian losses were at least 11,000 killed, 20,000 wounded, and 275,000 captured, although some estimates of the number taken prisoner exceed a staggering 500,000. German losses totaled about 20,000 dead and wounded. Cadorna was sacked and replaced by General Armando Diaz (1861–1928), who was given the task of rebuilding a shattered army. During the fighting, Erwin Rommel (1891–1944), a young lieutenant commanding a company of mountain troops, earned the *Pour le Mérite*, one of Germany's highest military decorations, for his part in the capture of Monte Matajur and 3,000 Italian soldiers. Twenty-five years later during World War II, Rommel gained fame as the "Desert Fox," commanding the vaunted *Afrika Korps*.

While the victory of the Central Powers at Caporetto was nothing short of spectacular, one major development did benefit the Allied cause. The disaster led to the Rapallo Conference, establishing the Supreme War Council to facilitate unity of command and cooperation between the Allied armies.

SKODA 3 IN (75 MM) MOUNTAIN GUN M1915

The Skoda 3 in (75 mm) Mountain Gun M1915 resulted from a concerted effort by the Czech arms manufacturer to develop artillery that could be disassembled rapidly, transported by mules into the mountains, and placed in action. The weapon proved successful and became a mainstay of the Austro-Hungarian forces during World War I. The gun was widely used during the fighting around Caporetto.

FOLLOWING AN AERIAL ATTACK, smoke bellows from the Polish outpost of Westerplatte. In the foreground is the German battleship Schleswig-Holstein, which provided supporting fire for the assault.

Westerplatte 1939

GDANSK'S WESTERPLATTE PENINSULA WAS THE SITE OF THE OFFICIAL START OF WORLD WAR II. A SMALL FORESTED ISLAND SEPARATED FROM DANZIG (GDANSK) BY THE HARBOR CHANNEL, WESTERPLATTE WAS ESTABLISHED AS A POLISH MILITARY OUTPOST DURING THE YEARS BETWEEN THE WORLD WARS.

The Poles at Westerplatte were equipped with one 2.95 in (75 mm) field gun, two 1.45 in (37 mm) antitank guns, four mortars, and several medium machine guns, but lacked any true fortifications. By the fall of 1939, the Polish garrison there comprised 182 men, who were expected to withstand any attack for 12 hours. The Versailles treaty made the city of Danzig (Gdansk) a free city state under the protection of the League of Nations, where Poland had a post office, special harbor, rights and, from 1924, the right to have a "protected" depot. The site of the railroad depot was the small, flat sandy peninsula of Westerplatte, which covered about one-fifth of a square mile (0.5 square km) of land, and featured several defensive

BATTLE FACTS

Who: Major Henryk Sucharski (1898–1946) led the small Polish garrison's resistance during a week of fighting against superior German naval and military police forces under the respective commands of Rear-Admiral Gustav Kleikamp (1896–1952) and Police General Friedrich Eberhardt (1892–1964) .

What: The attack on the morning of September 1 began World War II.

Where: At the mouth of the Vistula River north of Danzig (today's Gdansk).

When: September 1–7, 1939.

Why: Hitler was determined, despite the existence of a nonaggression pact from 1934, to destroy Poland.

Outcome: Fierce Polish resistance delayed the German occupation of the narrow Polish coastline.

THE SCHLESWIG-HOLSTEIN

Built between 1905 and 1908, the old battleship was retained in service after 1919, when most of the German Navy was sunk, and modernized in 1925–26, 1930–31, and 1936. She was used as a cadet training ship and a floating battery. Her displacement was 14,830 tons (13,454 tonnes), her dimensions 413 ft (126 m) long and 73 ft (22.2 m) broad, while her draft (the depth of water needed in order to float) was 27 ft (8.25 m). The Schleswig-Holstein was armed with four 11-in (280-mm), ten 6-in (150-mm), and four 3.46-in (88-mm) naval guns, as well as four 8-in (200-mm) AA guns. Her crew was reinforced with 225 Marines and 60 AA artillery troops when facing the indomitable Poles of Westerplatte. The ordinary crew numbered 907 men, but with all the troops this had grown to a total of 1,197 by August 25, 1939.

bunkers. The commandant was Henryk Sucharski, alongside his deputy Captain Dabrowski. On the German side, the fighting would be done by the SS-Heimwehr force of 1,500 men led by Police General Friedrich Eberhardt. He had some 225 crack German Marines, under Lieutenant Henningsen, to spearhead any attack on the depot. Overall command would rest with Rear-Admiral Gustav Kleikamp whose flagship *Schleswig-Holstein*, built in 1908, was officially on a courtesy visit in Danzig. It had anchored on the southern embankment of the harbor canal at Neufahrwasser during the morning of August 25—only 164 yards (150 m) away from the target.

ATTACK BEGINS

At 4:48 A.M. on Friday September 1, the massive guns of the *Schleswig-Holstein* fired eight shells at the southeastern sector of Westerplatte. World War II had erupted and Sucharski radioed to Hel Peninsula, "SOS: I'm under fire." Eight minutes later, Henningsen's marines attacked in a three-platoon formation, while his pioneers managed to blow up the railroad gate in the perimeter fence cutting across the land bridge. But then things went wrong for the Germans. The Poles counterattacked, and over several hours of fighting they took or held ground while inflicting heavy losses on the enemy. By noon, the fighting had cost the Germans 82 lives and Westerplatte was still holding out. The only consolation for the Germans was that they had massacred the Polish defenders of the post office in Danzig city. The German strike against Westerplatte had been an utter fiasco.

In the ensuing days, the Germans claimed they were not making any serious moves on the armed depot, while to the tired, hungry, and harassed defenders there seemed to

be no end to the German attacks. Eberhardt convinced the German commander, General Fedor von Bock (1885–1945), that a land attack was not possible. Bock agreed, having witnessed the fiasco of September 1. The following day, therefore, the *Luftwaffe* attacked the garrison with 60 bombers; Westerplatte had no antiaircraft defenses at all, and vital food stores were destroyed in the raids. On September 5, Sucharski called a council of war in which he urged that Westerplatte should surrender. An angered Dabrowski adamantly opposed such defeatism and stormed out. Sucharski ordered his men to fight on in the same brave and dogged fashion as before.

The battle went on. At 3 A.M. on September 6, the Germans sent a fire-train against the land-bridge, but it was decoupled too early by the terrified engine driver and failed to reach the oil cistern inside the Polish perimeter. If it had succeeded, it would have set the forest alight and destroyed its valuable cover for the defenders. A second fire-train attack came in the afternoon, but it failed too.

On September 7, Sucharski held a second council of war in the evening, and he had by then made up his mind not to continue fighting. After all, the German Army was now outside Warsaw and the first cases of gangrene had appeared among the wounded. At 4:30 A.M., the Germans opened intense fire upon Westerplatte, which continued until 7 A.M., when there was a final rolling barrage followed by German attacks. The Poles repelled the assault, but their defenses were finally collapsing. At 9:45 A.M. the white flag appeared, and the German troops paraded in full order when the haggard and exhausted Polish garrison marched out of Westerplatte at 11:33 A.M. The White Eagle of Poland had surrendered at last, but not without a truly heroic struggle.

A VILLAGE ON THE SHORE OF THE NARVIK FJORD *is swept up in fighting as it burns after an Allied naval bombardment during May 1940.*

Narvik 1940

IN EARLY APRIL 1940, THE RACE WAS ON TO SEE WHICH OF THE WARRING POWERS—BRITAIN OR GERMANY—WOULD BE FIRST TO SEIZE THE STRATEGICALLY VITAL PORT OF NARVIK IN NORTHERN NORWAY. GENERAL EDUARD DIETL, THE COMMANDER OF THE GERMAN EXPEDITIONARY FORCE OF 2,000 MOUNTAIN TROOPS, MADE AN UNOPPOSED LANDING AT NARVIK ON APRIL 9.

The British response to the German landing and easy occupation of Narvik was swift and powerful. Royal Navy assaults destroyed much of the German shipping around the port (including eight destroyers in one attack). Dietl's force was now completely cut off and Hitler wanted to pull him back. Dietl instead built a powerful defensive perimeter around Narvik and along the Ofoten railroad into Sweden. The "neutral" Swedes were to keep him generously supplied and informed.

On April 16, the lackluster British commander, General Pierse Mackesy, wired London telling the Cabinet that he could not advance on Narvik. The following day,

BATTLE FACTS

Who: German and Austrian mountain troops led by Eduard Dietl (1890–1944) faced a larger Allied force commanded first by General Pierse Mackesy (1883–1956) and then General Claude Auchinleck (1884–1981).

What: Narvik was recaptured on May 28 by the Allies.

Where: The iron-ore port of Narvik in the semi-Arctic north of Norway.

When: April 9 to June 7, 1940.

Why: Hitler wanted Norway's strategically valuable coastline, ports, and airfields.

Outcome: The belated Allied recapture of Narvik could not change the outcome of the battle for Norway or the catastrophic fortunes of the Allies on the continent after Hitler's invasion of France.

Hitler canceled the order to evacuate Dietl, and the Allies concentrated on holding southern Norway instead of throwing out Dietl's isolated garrison. By late April, however, the Allied Expeditionary Force (AEF) under Admiral Lord Cork numbered 30,000 men, including four battalions of *Chasseurs Alpins* and Polish mountain troops and two battalions of Foreign Legionnaires, and via a series of localized attacks they turned up the pressure on Dietl's men.

During May, the British General Claude Auchinleck and Antoine Béthouart (1889–1982), French commander of the 1st Division of *Chasseurs*, agreed to take Narvik in a four-pronged attack on the Germans. At 11:45 P.M. on May 27, the offshore Allied fleet opened up a withering bombardment on the landing beaches. Shells plastered Narvik town, Ankenes, Fagernes, and the entire shoreline, until wooden houses along the shore were burning like torches and the coastline was enveloped in thick smoke.

At 12:15 A.M., French Legionnaires landed right into the lap of Naval Artillery Company Nöller, numbering 50 troops, and engaged them in savage hand-to-hand fighting. The heavily outnumbered sailors retreated to the railroad embankment, closely followed up the slope by the Legionnaires, who took control of the railroad area despite fierce resistance. A German gun was firing out of the nearby tunnel. The Legionnaires pulled a French gun up by hand and fired at the mouth of the tunnel until the German battery was silenced for good.

STRONG RESISTANCE

Meanwhile, a Norwegian battalion landed at Orneset, and linked up with the legionnaires to attack Hill 457, where German *Gebirgsjäger* (mountain troops) and sailors had entrenched themselves. They offered strong resistance, and the advancing Allied troops suffered heavy casualties. By 4 A.M., the Poles were also under heavy German fire at Ankenes while the Legion's 2nd Battalion had not landed across Rombaksfjord.

Half an hour later, German bombers attacked the Allied fleet, forcing it away and denying the AEF its supporting fire. Two German companies immediately attacked down the slope of Hill 457, forcing the faltering Allies back and putting their precarious bridgehead in peril. At Ankenes, the Polish left flank was under threat, and at sea Béthouart's chief of staff was killed by German fire while two landing craft were sunk. Things were not looking good.

At 6 A.M., British Hurricanes flew over the battlefield, chasing away the *Luftwaffe* while the 2nd Battalion finally landed at Taraldsvik. The legionnaires and the Norwegians drove back the enemy. They gained the upper hand at Hill 457, which was now pockmarked with craters and littered with corpses. Meanwhile the 2nd Battalion and the

Norwegians pushed back the Germans along the Ofoten railroad, while on the northern side of Rombaksfjord the *Chasseurs Alpins* and Norwegians drove back the Germans toward Hundal. The 2nd Polish Battalion took Nybord, from where it could fire on Ankenes.

At Narvik itself, Major Häussel and his mixed force of 400 sailors and mountain troops had no reserves, were running low on ammunition, and had no communications with Dietl's HQ. Häussel decided to evacuate Narvik, taking his force along the still open Beisfjord road. That left small pockets of Germans still fighting at Hill 457 and Fagernes. By the afternoon, the Allied troops led by Béthouart made a triumphant entry into the newly liberated Narvik.

It did not last. On June 7, the Allies sailed out of Narvik, taking the Norwegian king and government to Britain in exile. By 1941, Narvik's port was supplying the Germans with 674,615 tons (612,000 tonnes) of iron ore. It had all been in vain.

THE NORWEGIAN ARMED FORCES

On paper, the mobilized Norwegian army was to number 100,000 men organized in six territorial divisions, one of which was to be under the command of General Carl Fleischer (1883–1942) at Harstad. The troops were equipped with green uniforms dating from 1912 and armed with 1894 Krag-Jorgensen rifles.

However, the army had no tanks, a handful of armored cars, few heavy machine guns, and no real professional core. The tiny Norwegian airforce numbered 76 planes (mostly Gloucester Gladiators) and 940 men—it was knocked out on April 9. The Navy had 113 vessels including two armored cruisers, Eidsvold and Norge.

GLUM NORWEGIAN SOLDIERS *surrender to the Germans knowing a harsh occupation awaits their country.*

MAY 1940: A GERMAN ARMORED COLUMN *of Panzer II tanks passes French antitank barriers in Sedan, following the evacuation of the town by the French Army.*

Invasion of France—Sedan 1940

THE CONQUEST OF FRANCE AND THE NETHERLANDS DURING THE SUMMER OF 1940 WAS A CONSPICUOUS TRIUMPH FOR GERMANY'S ARMY AND AIR FORCE, LEADING TO THE DEFEAT OF THE FRENCH, DUTCH, AND BELGIAN ARMIES. AFTER THE SUCCESSFUL POLISH CAMPAIGN THE PREVIOUS SEPTEMBER, HITLER RELISHED THE TRIUMPH OF *FALL GELB* ("CASE YELLOW"), WITH ITS EMPHASIS ON MOBILITY AND FLUIDITY.

Hitler's campaign in the West broke on May 10, 1940, in spectacular style. An airborne assault seized the Belgian fortress of Eben Emael, while seven Panzer divisions totaling 2,270 armored vehicles drove unopposed through Luxembourg and into the lightly defended Belgian Ardennes, bypassing France's supposedly impregnable Maginot Line defenses on the Franco-German border.

BATTLE FACTS

Who: German generals Gerd von Rundstedt (1875–1953), Erich von Manstein (1887–1973), and Heinz Guderian (1888–1954) versus General Maurice Gamelin (1872–1958), French Commander in Chief, and his successor Maxime Weygand (1867–1965).

What: The tactics of *Blitzkrieg*—panzers working in close coordination with artillery and dive-bombers—achieved conspicuous successes.

Where: From the French Maginot Line in the east to the English Channel.

When: May 10–28, 1940.

Why: Hitler wished to knock out France and Britain and turn his attentions to a decisive assault on the USSR.

Outcome: French forces in the Allied line's vital center were shattered.

ERICH VON MANSTEIN

Erich von Manstein (1887–1973), the architect of Blitzkreig, achieved promotion to general field marshal on July 19, 1940, after France fell. In 1941–42, he conducted Eleventh Army's conquest of the Crimea, while his Caucasian counteroffensive saved Army Group Don from destruction after Germany's devastating defeat at Stalingrad at the end of 1942. He clashed increasingly with Hitler as the military situation on the Eastern Front declined. This served to fuel Hitler's distrust—probably influenced by Manstein's Jewish origins. Hitler sacked him in 1944, but he proved a tough survivor despite a flirtation with the anti-Nazi resistance movement. In 1948, he was arraigned as a war criminal, imprisoned, and then released in 1953. He was subsequently consultant to the West German government on military matters, dying near Munich on June 1, 1973, aged 85.

In the early hours of the operation, the tanks of General Erwin Rommel (1891–1944), the recently appointed commander of 7th Panzer Division, crossed the southern end of the Belgian frontier, heading for the Meuse at Dinant 65 miles (105 km) away. Simultaneously Hitler's Panzers rolled over the Luxembourg frontier. General Heinz Guderian, the commander of the spearhead XIX Corps, had spelled out to his men the prime objective—the English Channel. The plan was to scythe through the Allied front's center to the English Channel, trapping the British Expeditionary Force (BEF) and the French First and Seventh Armies against the sea.

PANZER THRUST

On May 12, Guderian's corps had captured Bouillon in the western part of the Belgian province of Luxembourg, crossing the French frontier just north of Sedan. Keen to press his advantage, Guderian unleashed his three Panzer divisions across the Meuse near Sedan without waiting for rearguard infantry support. *Luftwaffe* fighters fended off enemy assaults, while to the south Guderian's forces deepened their bridgehead, which by the evening of May 14 was 30 miles (48 km) wide. A gap was opened between Second and Ninth French armies; Guderian's Panzer Corps drove through the breach, heading directly to the English Channel.

Further German advances revealed insufficient coordination between French tanks and infantry. Nevertheless, the 6th and 8th Panzer Divisions had to contend with ripostes of machine-gun fire, which also hampered the work of engineers building pontoons across the river at the village of Monthermé, within some of the most rugged territory in the Ardennes. Regrouped German armor secured the position after a fierce engagement.

Further north, Rommel's 7th Panzer Division had reached the Meuse below the city of Dinant, but encountered French heavy artillery and small-arms fire from troops on the left bank. The German commander's attention fastened on the plight of his motorized infantry, who were attempting to cross the river in inflatable boats. To screen the crossings, he ordered buildings on the German side to be set alight. The resulting smoke drifted across the river, screening the assault troops, who were now able to establish a bridgehead. French reservists were too stunned to fight back.

ROAD TO PARIS

On May 14, Allied forces also had their first encounter with the Germans sweeping through Belgium. Guderian's rapid advance caused anxiety in Berlin that, deprived of infantry, he could be cut off by any counterattack. But, in fact, the Allies were in danger of being outflanked. The British Prime Minister Winston Churchill next day received a despairing telephone call from the French premier Paul Reynaud, who declared, "We are beaten … The road to Paris is open." With forces hastily assembled near the town of Montcornet, north of Paris, Colonel Charles de Gaulle (1890–1970) launched three offensive actions, all but reaching Guderian's advanced headquarters, only to be repulsed. A shaky defensive perimeter, behind which the British and French could retreat, was assembled around Dunkirk.

The situation in Europe deteriorated still further. The concern was how British and French forces could escape annihilation on the French coast. Nevertheless, on May 21, four battalions clashed with the 7th Panzer and Waffen-SS *Totenkopf* Division near Arras, costing the Germans 700 casualties and the loss of 20 tanks. But by this time the German armored divisions had penetrated to the coast. The BEF was cut off, communications severed and ammunition short. To make matters worse, on May 28 the Belgian Army capitulated. From May 27 to June 4, the British conducted their epic naval evacuation from the beaches of Dunkirk, aided by a temporary stop order imposed by Hitler and Field Marshal Gerd von Rundstedt (the overall commander of the offensive) on the armored advance. Many reasons have been cited for Hitler's order. It might have been advice that the boggy terrain near the coast was unsuitable for tanks, or maybe it was the setback at Arras, or perhaps von Rundstedt's wish to regroup forces for the assault on Paris. Nevertheless, with the BEF gone and French resistance collapsing, on June 14 the *Wehrmacht* entered the undefended French capital.

BREAKTHROUGH AT SEDAN

CHARLEVILLE

2 The *Luftwaffe* plays a vital role with Stuka dive-bombers serving as mobile artillery while fighters cut down Allied aircraft. Dorniers and Heinkel bombers blast vulnerable rear areas.

3 German penetration south of Sedan is deep enough for sappers on the Meuse to open their bridges to IX Panzer Corps' heavy vehicles.

FRENCH X CORPS

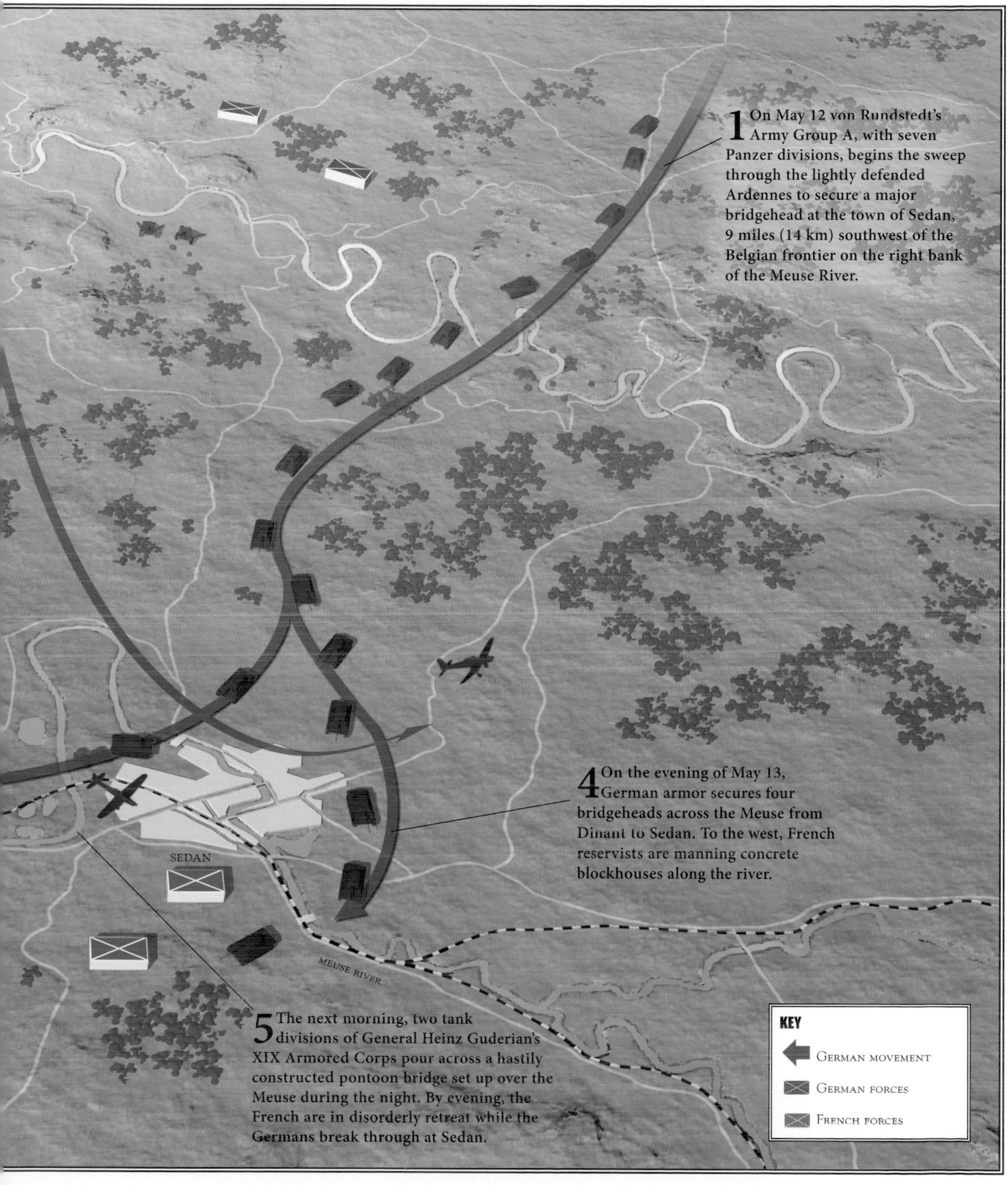

1 On May 12 von Rundstedt's Army Group A, with seven Panzer divisions, begins the sweep through the lightly defended Ardennes to secure a major bridgehead at the town of Sedan, 9 miles (14 km) southwest of the Belgian frontier on the right bank of the Meuse River.

4 On the evening of May 13, German armor secures four bridgeheads across the Meuse from Dinant to Sedan. To the west, French reservists are manning concrete blockhouses along the river.

SEDAN

MEUSE RIVER

5 The next morning, two tank divisions of General Heinz Guderian's XIX Armored Corps pour across a hastily constructed pontoon bridge set up over the Meuse during the night. By evening, the French are in disorderly retreat while the Germans break through at Sedan.

KEY

← GERMAN MOVEMENT

⊠ GERMAN FORCES

⊠ FRENCH FORCES

COURAGEOUS MEMBERS OF THE LONDON FIRE BRIGADE *wrestle a hose into position to combat a fire ignited by* Luftwaffe *incendiary bombs, September 1940.*

Battle of Britain   1940

THE GERMAN CONQUEST OF FRANCE AND THE LOW COUNTRIES HAD BEEN ACCOMPLISHED WITH ASTONISHING SPEED. DURING THE OPENING MONTHS OF WORLD WAR II IN EUROPE, NAZI GERMANY HAD EMERGED VICTORIOUS ACROSS THE CONTINENT. AS GERMAN TROOPS PARADED DOWN THE CHAMPS ELYSÉES, ADOLF HITLER AND HIS GENERALS PLANNED FOR THE INVASION OF GREAT BRITAIN.

E ven as the Germans consolidated their hold over continental Western Europe, the *Wehrmacht* high command was crafting Operation "*Seelöwe*" ("Sea Lion"), the planned invasion of Great Britain. Control of the air was a prerequisite to any successful invasion, so less than three weeks after the Fall of France, *Reichsmarschall* Hermann Göring and his *Luftwaffe* began the effort to wrest

BATTLE FACTS

Who: The German *Luftwaffe* under *Reichsmarschall* Hermann Göring (1893–1946) versus Royal Air Force Fighter Command under Air Chief Marshal Hugh Dowding (1882–1970).

What: The *Luftwaffe* attempted to destroy the Royal Air Force and later to raze British cities.

Where: The skies above Britain and the English Channel.

When: July 10, 1940, to May 10, 1941.

Why: Initially, the Germans needed control of the skies to cover Operation "*Seelöwe*" ("Sea Lion"), the invasion of Britain. Later, the "Blitz" raids were primarily terror attacks.

Outcome: The *Luftwaffe* failed to subdue the RAF and break the will of the British people. Operation "Sea Lion" was canceled.

SUPERMARINE SPITFIRE

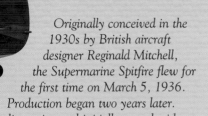

Originally conceived in the 1930s by British aircraft designer Reginald Mitchell, the Supermarine Spitfire flew for the first time on March 5, 1936. Production began two years later. Powered by the Rolls-Royce Merlin engine and initially armed with a pair of 0.78 in (20 mm) cannon and four .303 Browning machine guns, the Spitfire represented the leading edge of technology deployed by the Royal Air Force during the Battle of Britain. The superior performance of the Spitfire made it a worthy adversary of the German Messerschmitt Me-109. However, it was available in limited numbers compared to the older Hawker Hurricane. Therefore, the RAF instructed Spitfire squadrons to engage the German fighters, while the Hurricanes attacked the slower bomber formations. The aircraft depicted is a Spitfire Mk 1 of No. 66 Squadron.

control of Britain's skies from the RAF. Hitler had initially set the date for the invasion as August 15, and the German planes' first objective was to pound British harbors and shipping, in what they knew as the *Kanalkampf* ("Channel Battle"). Göring had gathered more than 750 fighters, 1,300 bombers, and 300 of the infamous Junkers Ju 87 Stuka dive-bombers for his campaign. Air Chief Marshal Hugh Dowding, head of Royal Air Force Fighter Command, could muster few more than 700 frontline Supermarine Spitfire and Hawker Hurricane fighters and other obsolescent types in defense. During the ensuing four weeks, dogfights raged daily. A number of merchant ships were sunk by the marauding Germans and the Royal Navy relocated most of its ships and personnel to Portsmouth from Dover. The *Luftwaffe* failed, however, to dominate the RAF sufficiently, which operated with the advantages of radar and flying over home territory.

DER ADLERTAG AND THE BLITZ

Still confident of victory, Göring nevertheless scheduled *Adlertag*, or "Eagle Day," for August 13, 1940. The second phase of the Battle of Britain was intended to bring the RAF directly to its knees, through the systematic bombing of its airfields and radar installations, and through shooting down its aircraft. On "Eagle Day" itself, the Germans lost 46 planes and the RAF 13, but a week of nearly continuous daylight aerial combat followed. Citizens below could see the swirling vapor trails of the dogfighting planes. Occasionally they saw the puff of an exploding aircraft, or the long, black trail of a burning machine as it hurtled toward the ground.

In concert with daylight raids, Göring also instructed his pilots to fly nocturnal bombing missions against military targets in Britain. Major cities, particularly London, had

not been targeted because of the probability of retaliation by RAF bombers against German cities. However, on the night of August 24, 1940, a few *Luftwaffe* bombers strayed off course and dropped their ordnance on London. The next night RAF bombers hit Berlin. Enraged, the *Führer* vowed to lay waste to British cities.

On September 7, 1940, Hitler authorized a change in strategy. The *Luftwaffe* was to bomb London into submission. A week later, however, he postponed Operation "*Seelöwe*" indefinitely. On the first night of the "Blitz," more than 2,000 Londoners were killed or wounded. Yet the sacrifices of the civilian population proved to be the salvation of Fighter Command, which was given time to rest and refit. London was not the only city ravaged by German bombs in the months to come. On the night of November 14, 1940, Coventry was assailed by more than 400 *Luftwaffe* bombers, killing 568 civilians and injuring more than 1,200 others. Birmingham, Liverpool, and Manchester were hit. But the turning point had come with the change in German strategy and the refusal of the British people to buckle. The last *Luftwaffe* raids of the "Blitz" struck London on the night of May 10, 1941.

Hitler's frustration with Göring's failure to destroy the RAF was tempered by his preoccupation with preparations for Operation "*Barbarossa*," the invasion of the Soviet Union, which was scheduled for June 22, 1941. At any rate, as early as the fall of 1940 Hitler had concluded that the Battle of Britain could not be won. Prime Minister Winston Churchill hailed the spirit of the British people and called the time of peril and suffering "their finest hour." On August 20, 1940, Churchill rose to address the House of Commons, praising the courage of the intrepid RAF pilots. "Never in the field of human conflict," he declared, "has so much been owed by so many to so few."

Battle for Crete 1941

GERMAN PARATROOPERS MOVE FORWARD PAST THE BODIES *of Allied soldiers after their successful air invasion of Crete. The invasion proved a costly success for the Germans.*

THE GERMAN AIRBORNE ASSAULT ON CRETE, ALTHOUGH SUCCESSFUL IN TERMS OF CONQUEST, CAME AT A TERRIFIC COST IN LIVES, AND LED TO THE SHARP DECLINE OF THE *LUFTWAFFE'S* PARACHUTE ARM AS AN AIRBORNE-CAPABLE WEAPON. GERMAN PARATROOPERS WERE NEVER AGAIN TO LAUNCH AN OPERATION ON THIS SCALE.

Crete, a mountainous Aegean island 160 miles (260 km) long, was by late April 1941 the sole piece of Greek territory left in Allied hands. The island being a valuable naval and aviation base for the Allies, Hitler ordered its invasion for April 25, to be designated Operation "*Merkur*" ("Mercury"). However, because of logistical problems, the date was postponed to May 20.

Unlike any other battle in history, the invasion was to be conducted almost exclusively by airborne forces, commanded by General Kurt Student. Opposing Commonwealth forces in Crete were, in May 1941, organized in five, widely separated defensive areas along the north coast—around the three airfields at Heraklion,

BATTLE FACTS

Who: Commander of the 'Creforce' garrison, Major-General Bernard Freyberg VC (1889–1963) versus General Kurt Student (1890–1978), Commander of XI *Fliegerkorps*.

What: The Germans landed in Crete and in ten days of fierce fighting drove out the bulk of Allied troops.

Where: The island of Crete.

When: May 20–June 1, 1941.

Why: The Germans urgently sought a free gateway to the eastern Mediterranean and

Crete posed a threat to their operations in North Africa.

Outcome: German forces occupied Crete until the end of 1944 when, along with Greece and Albania, the island was abandoned and Hitler ordered a major retreat from the Balkans.

Rethymnon, and Maleme, as well as at Suda Bay and the port of Khania. Leading more than 40,000 defenders—ANZAC and British troops, Greek and Cretan irregulars—was Major-General Bernard Freyberg. He faced serious problems: tired and demoralized troops; battered tanks from North Africa; no air cover; and paucity of communications. But Freyberg was receiving intelligence from deciphered German codes alerting him to Student's intentions. He also had the support of a fiercely loyal local population.

The German assault was to be launched in two waves—the first against Maleme and Khania to the west, the second against Rethymnon and Heraklion, further to the east. In total, 22,750 parachute and glider-deployed troops would make the attack.

BRIDGEHEADS ESTABLISHED

Dawn on May 20, 1941, over Crete broke with a ferocious Stuka bombardment followed by vast clouds of German *Fallschirmjäger* (paratroopers) spilling out on the island's rocky landscape. Many of the German paras presented easy targets as they drifted down over Allied positions, while dozens of slow-moving gliders were shot to pieces even as they made their approach. Yet enough Germans survived to regroup and fight fiercely. A severe blow for the Allies on the first day was the loss of a small hill known to the military as Hill 107, with a commanding view of the Maleme airfield from the south. There was a significant buildup of German forces, with paratrooper battalions forming up to the southeast of the airfield. After fierce fighting, including a localized Allied counterattack, the airfield fell into German hands.

Student, more determined than ever to consolidate the Maleme bridgehead, flew in over the next two days a total of 3,200 mountain troops and paras. He encountered fierce local resistance, but the Germans fought with determination and skill to gain the upper hand. On May 25, the New Zealanders under Colonel Howard Kippenberger had some success with a counterattack near Galatas, lying to the southwest of Khania. But this simply delayed the German advance, and Kippenberger had no resources to recover.

The remainder of the Maleme position had to be yielded in the face of the presence of 2,000 additional German mountain troops. The defenders retreated to Khania, which then fell on May 27. Resistance to the overwhelming air and eventually land power of the Germans became impossible, not least through a lack of ammunition, which severely weakened the Allied divisions. With the Allies being squeezed into the south of the island, all was now set for a general evacuation.

Withdrawal from Suda Bay was covered by air-deployed British commandos, while between May 28 and June 1 Britain's Mediterranean Fleet removed around 17,000 men

GENERAL KURT STUDENT

General Kurt Student (1890–1978, pictured right) was a World War I fighter pilot, chosen by Göring in 1938 to form a parachute infantry force, which later expanded to around 4,500 men. After the evacuation from Crete, Student's troops fought mainly as infantry. Student received no decoration for his services. Though he claimed little interest in Nazism, he was brought before an Allied military tribunal in 1947 on eight charges of war crimes in Crete, including sanctioning the execution of British prisoners of war. He was acquitted on certain counts but sentenced to five years in prison. The Greeks requested his extradition from Germany for war crimes but he was never handed over, and died at the age of 88.

EVERY SURVIVING MEMBER OF STUDENT'S FORCES *received an Iron Cross, but after such losses, he said, "Crete was the grave of the German paratroops."*

from Sphakia on the island's south coast, mostly from open beaches during the few short hours of darkness. Nine ships were sunk by the *Luftwaffe*. After an epic battle in their early history, the German airborne forces had taken Crete.

The post-battle balance sheet, however, was not entirely stacked in the Germans' favor. The Germans suffered 7,000 casualties, including more than 4,000 dead and missing. The British and Commonwealth forces lost 23,000 men, the vast majority of those prisoners. For the Allies, the debacle of Crete was complete, but such were the German losses that never again would Hitler's *Fallschirmjäger* be used for major airborne operations, instead spending the rest of the war largely as elite infantry.

FAIREY SWORDFISH TORPEDO PLANES, *the flying anachronisms that slowed the German battleship* Bismarck, *are lashed to the flight deck of the aircraft carrier HMS Victorious amid an angry sea.*

Hunt for the
Bismarck   1941

BY THE SUMMER OF 1941, THE BATTLE OF THE ATLANTIC HAD BECOME A STRUGGLE FOR THE SURVIVAL OF GREAT BRITAIN. NOT ONLY WERE NAZI U-BOATS RAVAGING CONVOYS AND SINKING MERCHANT VESSELS LADEN WITH PRECIOUS CARGOES, BUT SURFACE RAIDERS OF THE *KRIEGSMARINE* (GERMAN NAVY) ALSO POSED A SIGNIFICANT THREAT.

From January to April, more than 672,410 tons (610,000 tonnes) of Allied shipping were lost. Then in May the worst fears of the British Admiralty were realized. The massive 47,200-ton (42,800-tonne) battleship *Bismarck* weighed anchor and sailed out toward the Atlantic. In company with the heavy cruiser *Prinz Eugen*, the great battleship might wreak havoc on Allied merchant shipping with its eight 15in (380 mm) guns. Recognizing the imminent danger, Admiral John Tovey, commander of

BATTLE FACTS

Who: Elements of the British Royal Navy under Admiral John Tovey (1885–1971) versus the German battleship *Bismarck* and cruiser *Prinz Eugen*, under Admiral Günther Lütjens (1889–1941).

What: The *Bismarck* and *Prinz Eugen* tried to attack Allied shipping but were confronted by the Royal Navy in a series of battles.

Where: The North Atlantic near Allied convoy routes.

When: May 18–27, 1941.

Why: The Germans hoped to inflict substantial losses on Allied merchant shipping, thereby strangling the supply line to Great Britain.

Outcome: The Royal Navy sank the *Bismarck*. The German navy mounted no more serious surface threats to Allied shipping in the Atlantic.

the British Home Fleet at Scapa Flow, began to marshal his scattered surface assets to find and sink the *Bismarck*. Meanwhile Admiral Günther Lütjens, at sea aboard the German behemoth, knew that his movements during daylight hours had been observed by the Swedish cruiser *Götland* and patrol planes from the neutral country. On May 21, the battleship was also photographed by a British reconnaissance aircraft.

Lütjens was determined to break out into the open sea and chose the Denmark Strait, one of three options, as his avenue of approach. Shadowed by a pair of British cruisers (*Suffolk* and *Norfolk*), the *Bismarck* and *Prinz Eugen* were engaged in the predawn darkness of May 24 by the brand-new battleship HMS *Prince of Wales* and the venerable battlecruiser HMS *Hood*. Launched in 1918, the *Hood* was equal in firepower to the *Bismarck*, but she was vulnerable to the enemy's heavy guns, her designers having sacrificed armor protection for speed more than 20 years earlier. Seconds into the fight, a German shell from *Bismarck* penetrated the *Hood's* thin armor and detonated an ammunition magazine. A gigantic explosion enveloped the warship and the pride of the Royal Navy was gone.

RETRIBUTION

Devastated by the loss of the *Hood*, the British nevertheless continued their pursuit of the *Bismarck*, which had been damaged by *Prince of Wales*, now separated from *Prinz Eugen* and was making for safe port at Brest on the French coast. On the morning of May 26, however, a Consolidated PBY Catalina flying boat spotted the *Bismarck* less than 800 miles (1,300 km) from the French coast. Several of the Royal Navy warships initially engaged in the chase were obliged to turn home because fuel ran low. The battleship HMS *King George V*, with Tovey aboard, plowed ahead. Detached from convoy duty, the battleship HMS

Rodney joined the pursuit, as did the Gibraltar-based Force H, under Admiral James Somerville (1882–1949). The British had lost critical time and distance, though. The *Bismarck* might still escape.

Tovey had one more card to play. Fifteen antiquated-looking Swordfish biplane torpedo aircraft took off from the aircraft carrier HMS *Ark Royal* on the afternoon of May 26. During an attack through hails of antiaircraft fire and gale-force winds, they managed to jam the *Bismarck's* rudder, putting the great ship in a large turning circle from which she could not escape. Every man aboard the *Bismarck* now knew that the fate of their ship was sealed.

At 8:47 A.M. on May 27, the 16 in (406 mm) guns of the *Rodney* fired at the *Bismarck* from a range of 12 miles (19 km). The *King George V* joined in. The crew of the *Bismarck* fought valiantly, but repeated hits seriously damaged its fire-control system and disabled its main armament. The British battleships closed to less than 2 miles (3.2 km) and bodies of dead and wounded sailors littered the *Bismarck's* decks. By 11 A.M., the ship was still afloat, but blazing from bow to stern and unable to fight back. Shortly afterward, the battleship rolled to port and sank stern first. Three torpedo hits from the cruiser HMS *Dorsetshire* have long been credited with administering the coup de grâce. However, survivors of the *Bismarck* have insisted that they opened the vessel's seacocks and scuttled the ship. Exploration of the wreckage tends to support their claim, but remains inconclusive.

Only 110 of the *Bismarck's* complement of more than 2,000 men were pulled alive from the chilly waters of the Atlantic. In a practical sense, the loss of the great warship effectively ended the threat of the *Kriegsmarine* surface fleet to Allied merchant shipping in the Atlantic. Hitler simply became unwilling to risk his few capital ships in such an endeavor.

THE BISMARCK

Named in honor of the Iron Chancellor of a unified Germany, the battleship Bismarck undertook Operation Rhine Exercise on May 18, 1941. Displacing nearly 47,400 tons (43,000 tonnes), the warship posed a major threat to Allied shipping in the Atlantic. The Bismarck's main armament consisted of eight 15 in (380 mm) guns.

Capable of achieving speed in excess of 30 knots, the Bismarck was relentlessly pursued by heavy units of the Royal Navy. It was disabled by Swordfish torpedo planes and was eventually sunk on May 27. However, the battleship and her consort, the heavy cruiser Prinz Eugen, had previously achieved a great success: the sinking of the battlecruiser HMS Hood, the pride of the Royal Navy.

A CZECH-BUILT 35(T) TANK PASSES A BURNING MANOR HOUSE *in White Russia in early June 1941 as the Nazi* blitzkrieg *rips through Soviet territory.*

Operation "*Barbarossa*" 1941

A MASSIVE GERMAN ARMY OF 3.3 MILLION MEN SUPPORTED BY MORE THAN 3,000 TANKS AND ALMOST AS MANY AIRCRAFT INVADED THE SOVIET UNION ON JUNE 22, 1941. THE HUGE INVASION FORCE AIMED TO CAPTURE MOSCOW, THE UKRAINE, AND LENINGRAD AND DESTROY THE RED ARMY IN THE PROCESS.

The largest military operation of all time, codenamed "*Barbarossa*" ("Red Beard"), was under way, and was based around the advances of three enormous army groups—North, Center, and South. Hitler had placed a particular emphasis in his plans for the capture of Leningrad—the USSR's second city and primary naval base—and the clearing of the Baltic States. Yet he allocated the least number of troops, some 26 divisions, to Army Group North under Field Marshal von Leeb. In consequence, Leeb's advance was slow and it was not until

BATTLE FACTS

Who: Three German Army Groups led respectively by Marshals Ritter von Leeb (1876–1956), Fedor von Bock (1880–1945), and Gerd von Rundstedt (1875–1953) were charged to destroy the Red Army in two months.

What: "*Barbarossa*" was a decisive turning point. If the USSR survived the German onslaught, Hitler's *Reich* would face a two-front war.

Where: The Eastern Front, stretching from Arctic Finland to the Black Sea.

When: June 22, 1941.

Why: Hitler gambled that the *Wehrmacht* could knock out the Red Army before the United States joined the war against Germany.

Outcome: Although making substantial gains, the Germans failed to capture Moscow or destroy the Soviet Red Army.

September that his exhausted troops managed to cut off Leningrad from the rest of the USSR, imposing a long, destructive siege. Meanwhile, Field Marshal Gerd von Rundstedt's Army Group South—41 divisions strong—was entrusted with taking the Ukraine. Unfortunately for Rundstedt, the Southwestern Front, the strongest of the Soviet army groups, offered fierce resistance. As a result, Army Group South was able to advance only slowly and deliberately. Nevertheless, the Panzer forces of Army Group Center intervened, converging on September 10 with those of Rundstedt's Panzers east of Kiev. Three massive Soviet armies were now trapped in and around Kiev, and a staggering 665,000 Soviet troops were captured. More Soviet disasters were to come. By October 6, the 1st Panzer Group had trapped much of the Soviet Southern Front in a large pocket in southeastern Ukraine. Two armies were destroyed, yielding another 100,000 prisoners.

The German advance continued toward Rostov-on-Don, which was captured on November 20. However, the Soviet High Command (Stavka) launched a vigorous counterattack with three armies against the by now over-extended German forces. By November 29, this strategically located city was back in Soviet hands and the Germans had narrowly escaped an early version of Stalingrad.

ADVANCE OF ARMY GROUP CENTER

Hitler's generals—especially Fedor von Bock, the commander of Army Group Center—believed the Soviet Union would collapse if Moscow was captured. In the center of the offensive, as in the south, the Germans scored some major successes. A string of armies were trapped inside the Bialystok salient and in a vast pocket west of Minsk, yielding 300,000 prisoners. The Red Army continued to suffer catastrophic reverses. Smolensk, the gateway to Moscow, fell on July 16, and a series of counterattacks cost Stalin another 300,000 men and 3,000 tanks.

Hitler now diverted most of Army Group Center's Panzer divisions to take part in the battle for Kiev. For more than a month, the Central Front of 496 miles (800 km) remained unchanged, giving the Red Army invaluable time to prepare its defenses. General Andrei Yeremenko (1892–1970) had three armies (30 divisions) at Bryansk, and Marshal Semyon Timoshenko (1895–1972) had six armies with 55 divisions at Vyazma. Incredibly, all these forces had been either wiped out or captured by October.

The march on Moscow, codenamed Operation "Taifun" ("Typhoon"), was unleashed early in the morning of October 2 in brilliant sunshine. Army Group Center numbered a million men in 77 divisions with 1,700 tanks and almost a thousand planes. More huge encirclements were achieved, most notably at Vyazma and Bryansk, destroying entire Soviet armies. Despite torrential rains that

THE "LIBERATOR" SOON TURNED TO SAVAGE OPPRESSOR: *a German* landser (infantryman) *with a burning Russian cottage in the background.*

turned the roads into quagmires, the Germans had covered two-thirds of the distance to Moscow by the middle of the month. In early November, furthermore, the weather turned colder, enabling the Germans to advance again across frozen and hard roads. But soon winter set in in earnest, with temperatures of -6°F (-21°C), and a new commander had appeared on the Soviet side, General Georgi Zhukov (1896–1974), who had already saved Leningrad and was now planning a counterattack against the exhausted Germans. By November 18, Zhukov had 21 rested, fully equipped, and battle-hardened Siberian divisions ready to be unleashed against Von Bock's army.

On November 27, the 2nd Panzer Division was just 14 miles (22 km) from the capital, and could see the spires of the Kremlin palaces through the haze. Yet Von Bock's army group now held a front almost 600 miles (1,000 km) long with a mere 60 divisions. The crawling offensive then came to a halt on December 5, when temperatures plunged to a bone-chilling -31°F (-35°C), immobilizing vehicles and men alike. That same day Zhukov ordered Kalinin Front, commanded by General Ivan Konev (1897–1973), to attack, and the following day his own Western Front unleashed his Moscow counteroffensive. The attack took the Germans completely by surprise, and stopped "Taifun" permanently in its tracks. Moscow, and the Soviet Union, would fight on. Two days after Zhukov began his offensive, the United States entered the war, and Hitler's defeat was now only a question of time.

OPERATION "BARBAROSSA"

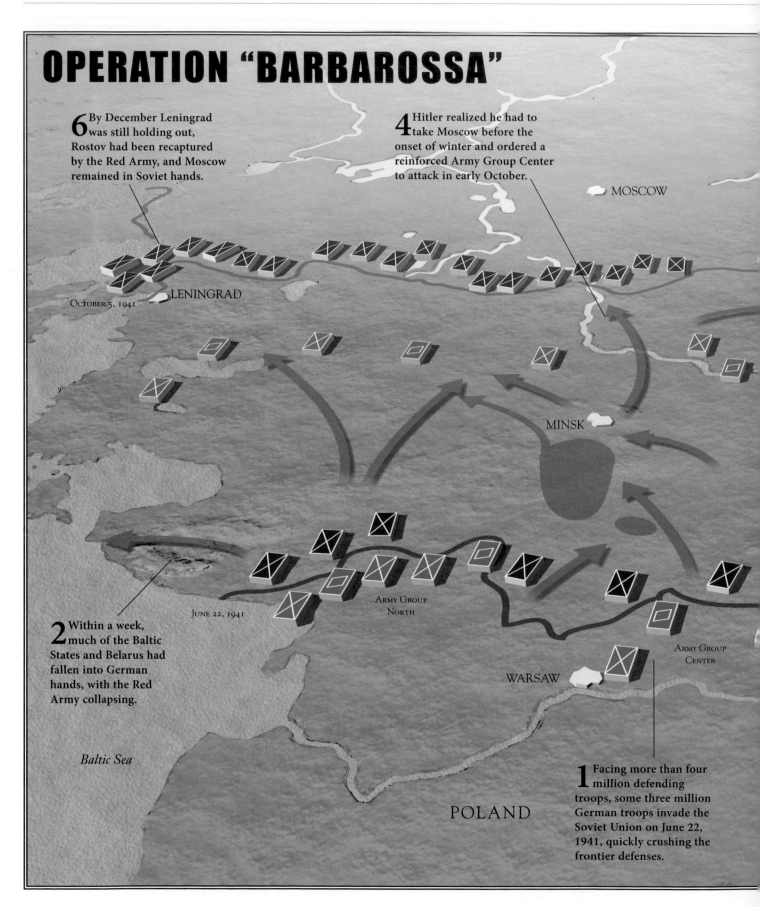

6 By December Leningrad was still holding out, Rostov had been recaptured by the Red Army, and Moscow remained in Soviet hands.

4 Hitler realized he had to take Moscow before the onset of winter and ordered a reinforced Army Group Center to attack in early October.

MOSCOW

OCTOBER 5, 1941

LENINGRAD

MINSK

JUNE 22, 1941

ARMY GROUP NORTH

2 Within a week, much of the Baltic States and Belarus had fallen into German hands, with the Red Army collapsing.

ARMY GROUP CENTER

WARSAW

Baltic Sea

POLAND

1 Facing more than four million defending troops, some three million German troops invade the Soviet Union on June 22, 1941, quickly crushing the frontier defenses.

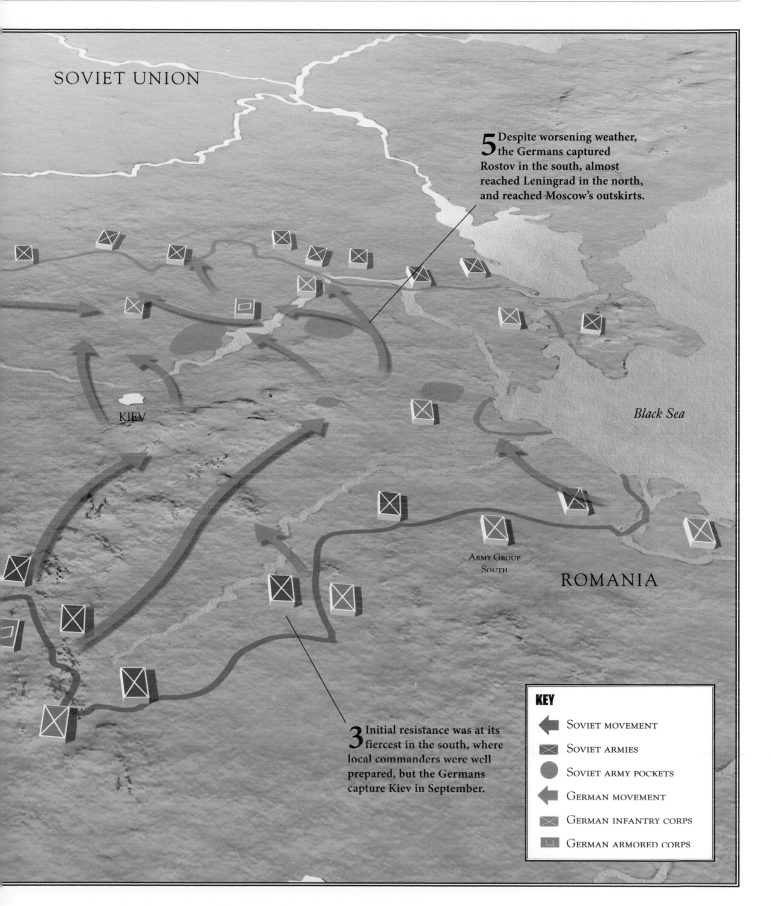

SOVIET UNION

5 Despite worsening weather, the Germans captured Rostov in the south, almost reached Leningrad in the north, and reached Moscow's outskirts.

KIEV

Black Sea

ARMY GROUP
SOUTH

ROMANIA

3 Initial resistance was at its fiercest in the south, where local commanders were well prepared, but the Germans capture Kiev in September.

KEY

←	SOVIET MOVEMENT
⊠	SOVIET ARMIES
●	SOVIET ARMY POCKETS
←	GERMAN MOVEMENT
⊠	GERMAN INFANTRY CORPS
▭	GERMAN ARMORED CORPS

THE LIFELINE—A TRUCK CONVOY *moves across a frozen Lake Ladoga. Under such conditions, up to 400 trucks a day were able to make the journey.*

Siege of Leningrad 1941–44

THE SIEGE OF LENINGRAD WAS A GHASTLY EPIC OF ENDURANCE THAT COST THE LIVES OF UP TO 1.5 MILLION PEOPLE, BOTH SOLDIERS AND CIVILIANS. IN TOTAL, IT RAN FOR NEARLY 900 DAYS.

On June 22, 1941, German forces surged across the Soviet border in Operation *Barbarossa*. Army Group North under the command of Field Marshal Wilhelm von Leeb (1878–1956), had Leningrad as its goal, a large urban zone of a million souls located on the Gulf of Finland. Von Leeb's forces, as with the other elements of *Barbarossa*, seemed destined to succeed, pushing on through the Baltic States and breaking across the Luga River just 75 miles (120 km) south of Leningrad on August 9. By September 15, when Schlisselburg on Lake Ladoga fell, the city was entirely cut off from overland resupply. Yet on September 6, Hitler switched the priority of *Barbarossa* to objectives farther south and

BATTLE FACTS

Who: German Army Group North under several commanders versus the Soviet Volkhov and Leningrad Fronts, commanded by General Kirill Meretskov (1897–1968) and Marshal Leonid Govorov (1897–1955), respectively.

What: A partial blockade of Leningrad reduced the city to starvation, the blockade being broken only by a series of Soviet offensives.

Where: Leningrad (now St. Petersburg), on the Gulf of Finland.

When: September 1941 to January 1944.

Why: Leningrad was an early target of Hitler's Operation *Barbarossa*.

Outcome: A million civilians died from starvation, bombing, and shelling.

A Red Army unit makes a characteristic attack *in the Leningrad sector, winter 1943—a simple charge backed by heavy machine-gun support.*

drew off much of Von Leeb's Panzer strength to support the offensive. Therefore Leningrad would have to be defeated by siege and bombardment.

STARVATION AND RESISTANCE

As the German and Soviet armies outside Leningrad battled for dominance, a horrifying battle against starvation was under way within the city itself. In an especially bitter winter, the citizens of Leningrad were beginning to starve in their thousands, their predicament worsened by a collapse in fuel supplies.

By the end of November, people were trying to survive on a daily ration of less than 9 oz (250 g) of bread. Bodies littered every street people would literally die on their feet or curled up in doorways. On one day alone, 13,500 deaths occurred. Against this horrifying backdrop was the constant German air and artillery bombardment.

The main lifeline to the city was Lake Ladoga, though it was hardly adequate. Small boats of every military and civilian variety sailed the waters in the nonwinter months, frequently under heavy German air assault, to dock in Osinovets, northeast of Leningrad. When Lake Ladoga froze over, up to 400 trucks a day shuttled supplies straight across the ice and took back refugees on the return journey. Conditions for the supply convoys were grim, and many truck crews, ship crews, and refugees found their graves at

the bottom of the lake. However, in the spring of 1942 fuel and electricity pipelines were laid across the river, bringing power for cooking and heating. Yet although circumstances had improved by the end of 1942, blockade conditions existed for nearly 900 days, during which time about one million people died.

BREAKING THE SIEGE

In 1942, the Soviets looked to make further gains. In January, a large offensive by the Volkhov Front between Novgorod and Spasskaya Polist made a 37-mile (60-km) salient in the German frontline, but the offensive had stalled by March, leaving the Germans to nip out of the salient and completely destroy the Soviet Second Shock Army. Nevertheless, the Soviet attack had alarmed Hitler enough for him to replace von Leeb with Field Marshal Georg von Küchler (1881–1958). Küchler himself would go in August 1942, and Field Marshal Erich von Manstein (1887–1973) then took what was proving to be a poisoned chalice for German commanders.

The critical change in fortunes came in January 1943. The Soviet Leningrad Front under Marshal Leonid Govorov launched a combined offensive with the Volkhov Front against the German forces in the Leningrad bottleneck. The sheer weight of men and armor was irresistible, and Schlisselburg was back in Soviet hands by January 19. By early February, the Soviets were running direct train journeys into Leningrad, albeit ones under constant German bombardment because the corridor secured by the Red Army was only 6.2 miles (10 km) wide.

The worst of the siege was now over, but the partial blockade continued until January 1944. On January 14, 1944, an overwhelming Soviet offensive by both Red Army fronts flooded over the German defenses and put the *Wehrmacht* troops on the retreat. On January 27, with the recapture of the Leningrad–Moscow railroad, Stalin officially declared the siege of Leningrad over.

A well equipped Red Army *infantryman, seen here in the season of fall in 1941, armed with the Tokarev SVT-40, an early Soviet semiautomatic rifle.*

STRUCK BY SEVERAL JAPANESE TORPEDOES, the battleship USS West Virginia burns and settles to the shallow bottom of Pearl Harbor. In the foreground, sailors pull a survivor from the water.

Pearl Harbor   1941

WHEN JAPANESE WARPLANES SWEPT IN TO ATTACK THE U.S. NAVAL BASE AT PEARL HARBOR AND OTHER INSTALLATIONS ON THE HAWAIIAN ISLAND OF OAHU ON DECEMBER 7, 1941, THE ACT WAS THE CULMINATION OF YEARS OF GROWING TENSION BETWEEN THE TWO COUNTRIES. JAPAN, SEEKING PREEMINENCE IN ASIA AND THE PACIFIC, REQUIRED LAND AND OTHER NATURAL RESOURCES TO SUSTAIN ITS GROWING POPULATION AND FUEL ITS FORMIDABLE MILITARY MACHINE.

Admiral Yamamoto Isoroku, commander in chief of the Japanese Combined Fleet, was reluctant to go to war with the United States. Nevertheless, he became the architect of what was conceived as a crippling blow to American military power in the Pacific, a preemptive strike by carrier-based aircraft against the U.S. Pacific Fleet anchored at Pearl Harbor. On November 26, 1941, a powerful armada sailed from Hittokapu Bay in the Kurile Islands. Two battleships, three cruisers, nine destroyers, and

BATTLE FACTS

Who: The Japanese Combined Fleet under Admiral Yamamoto Isoroku (1884–1943) and Vice-Admiral Chuichi Nagumo (1887–1944) versus the U.S. Pacific Fleet under Admiral Husband Kimmel (1882–1968).

What: Six Japanese fleet carriers launched an air attack on the U.S. Pacific Fleet base of Pearl Harbor 3,400 miles (5,472 km) away.

Where: Pearl Harbor on the Hawaiian island of Oahu.

When: December 7, 1941.

Why: Japan needed to neutralize U.S. naval power in the Pacific in order to seize British and Dutch resources in the region, especially oil.

Outcome: Japan caused considerable damage at little cost to itself, but made an enemy of the United States.

three submarines escorted the heart of the strike force—six aircraft carriers, *Akagi, Kaga, Soryu, Hiryu, Shokaku,* and *Zuikaku*. In the predawn hours of December 7, the Japanese strike force had reached its appointed station 230 miles (370 km) north of the island of Oahu. At 3:30 A.M. Pacific time, U.S. cryptanalysts in Washington, D.C., intercepted the last of a 14-part message from Tokyo to its emissaries there. The message seemed to indicate the opening of hostilities by Japan within a matter of hours.

At 3:45 A.M., the minesweeper USS *Condor*, on routine patrol, sighted what appeared to be a submarine periscope in a restricted area near the entrance to Pearl Harbor. The sighting was probably one of five Japanese midget submarines tasked with entering the harbor and firing torpedoes at American warships. Although the submarines failed in their assigned task, their two-man crews were lionized as heroes in Japan.

As streaks of daylight brightened the eastern sky, 183 Japanese planes of the first attack wave were being launched from the decks of the carriers. At 6:40 A.M., the destroyer USS *Ward*, patrolling the entrance to Pearl Harbor sighted, attacked, and sank one of the midget submarines, yet the *Ward's* message concerning hostile contact was dismissed as another phantom sighting. Just 20 minutes later, the U.S. Army's Opana radar station at Point Kahuku on Oahu picked up and reported an unidentified formation of aircraft. This warning was also discounted. By 7:30 A.M., the 170 planes of the Japanese second wave were airborne.

"TORA! TORA! TORA!"

Unmolested by U.S. fighters or antiaircraft defenses, the aircraft of Lieutenant-Commander Fuchida Mitsuo (1902–76) cleared the mountains west of Pearl Harbor. When it was apparent that the attackers had achieved complete surprise, Fuchida transmitted the message, *"Tora! Tora! Tora!"* ("Tiger! Tiger! Tiger!"—the code word for the surprise attack) to the Japanese fleet. The first bombs fell on Ford Island at 7:55 A.M.; Kaneohe Naval Air Station, Wheeler Field, Bellows Field, Hickam Field, and Ewa Marine Corps Air Station came under attack from bombers and strafing fighters, destroying most American aircraft on the ground.

Moored along "Battleship Row" southeast of Ford Island, the pride of the U.S. Fleet lay at anchor. Seven battleships—*Nevada, Arizona, West Virginia, Tennessee, Oklahoma, Maryland,* and *California*—represented easy targets for screeching dive-bombers and torpedo planes. The flagship of the fleet, the battleship USS *Pennsylvania*, lay in a nearby dry-dock.

Within minutes, Pearl Harbor was ablaze. Four battleships were sunk. The *West Virginia* was hit by seven torpedoes and two bombs. The *California* took two torpedoes and a bomb. The *Oklahoma* was hit by at least five torpedoes and capsized, trapping many sailors below decks. A bomb fashioned from a modified heavy shell originally intended for a naval gun penetrated the deck of the *Arizona* and ignited a catastrophic explosion that shattered the ship and took the lives of 1,177 men. The *Pennsylvania, Maryland, Nevada,* and *Tennessee* were heavily damaged. The cruisers *Helena, Raleigh,* and *Honolulu,* the destroyers *Cassin, Downes,* and *Shaw,* the seaplane tender *Curtiss* and the repair ship *Vestal* were damaged, and the target ship *Utah* and minelayer *Oglala* were sunk.

In little more than two hours, Japan altered the balance of power in the Pacific. The bold attack had taken the lives of 2,403 Americans. Eighteen of 96 vessels at Pearl Harbor were sunk or damaged heavily. A total of 165 U.S. aircraft were destroyed and 128 others damaged. In exchange, the Japanese lost 29 aircraft, five midget submarines, one fleet submarine, and 185 dead.

Although they had achieved a great victory, the Japanese failed to achieve two major goals. The U.S. aircraft carriers, their primary objective, were at sea and thus spared the attack. The marauding planes had also neglected nearly 5 million gallons (23 million liters) of fuel oil stored in tanks around Pearl Harbor, and had barely touched the repair facilities. The day after the attack, President Roosevelt asked a joint session of Congress for a declaration of war and called December 7, 1941 "a date which will live in infamy."

THE VERSATILE "VAL"

Designed in 1935 as the Dive-Bomber Type 99 Model 11, the Aichi D3A1 was the primary dive-bomber of the Imperial Japanese Navy until 1942. Designated the "Val" by the Allies, this aircraft was utilized in large numbers during the attack on Pearl Harbor, December 7, 1941. In the hands of a skilled pilot, the Val proved a highly accurate platform for the delivery of ordnance, achieving a success rate of greater than 80 percent at its peak. However, following severe losses of veteran airmen, particularly at the battles of the Coral Sea and Midway and during the prolonged actions in the vicinity of the Solomons, the combat efficiency of the Val suffered.

PEARL HARBOR

3 At 7:55 A.M., "Kate" torpedo bombers target ships to the northwest of Ford Island. This was where the missing carriers were normally berthed.

6 The USS *Nevada* attempted to make for the safety of open water, but was attacked by wave after wave of torpedo and dive-bombers.

MIDDLE LOCH

FORD ISLAND
NAVAL AIR STATION

USS *California*

U.S.
NAVY YARD

5 Attacked by both the first and second waves, Hickam Field suffers the heaviest damage of Oahu's airbases.

SOUTHEAST LOCH

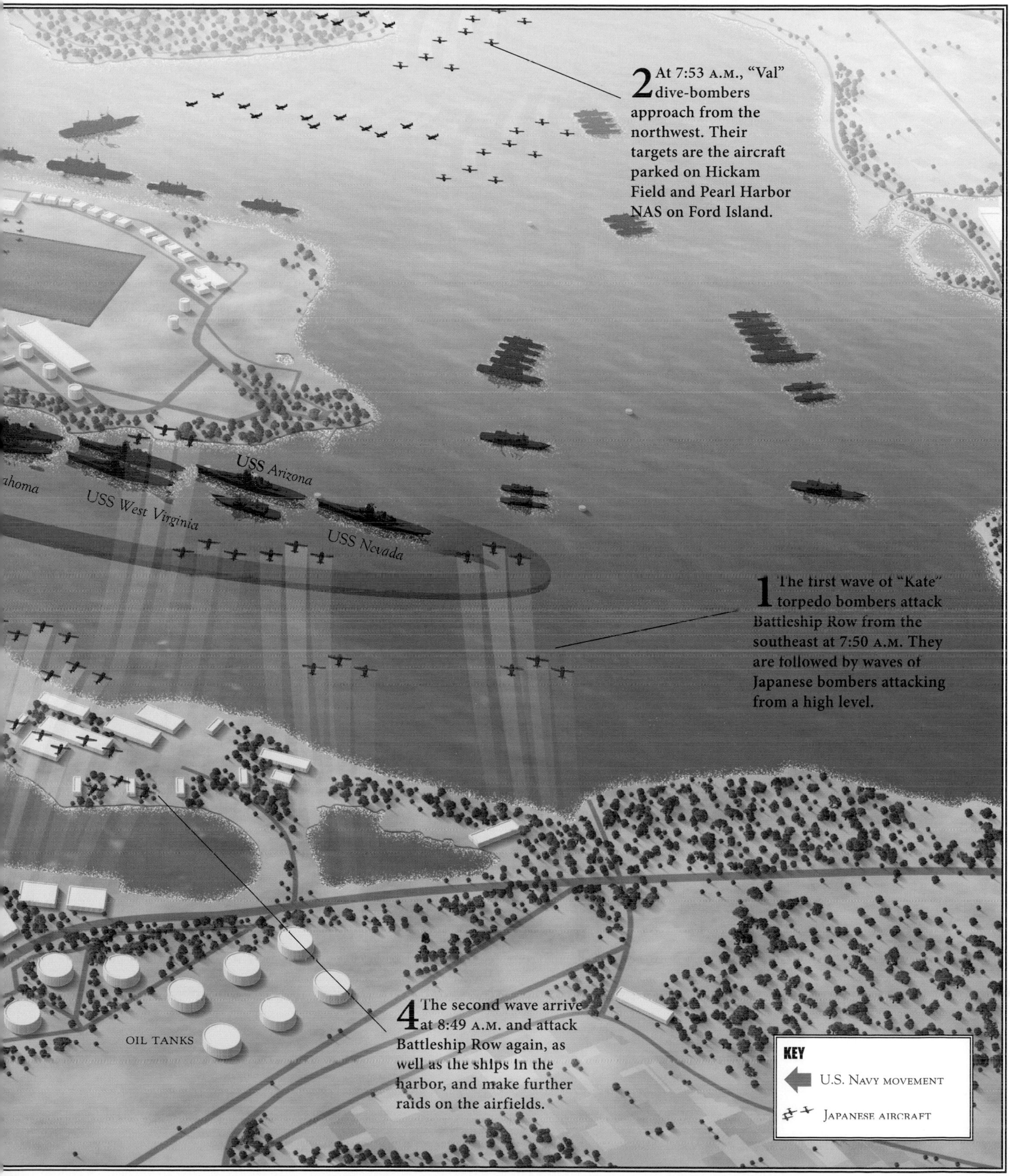

2 At 7:53 A.M., "Val" dive-bombers approach from the northwest. Their targets are the aircraft parked on Hickam Field and Pearl Harbor NAS on Ford Island.

USS Arizona

ahoma

USS West Virginia

USS Nevada

1 The first wave of "Kate" torpedo bombers attack Battleship Row from the southeast at 7:50 A.M. They are followed by waves of Japanese bombers attacking from a high level.

4 The second wave arrive at 8:49 A.M. and attack Battleship Row again, as well as the ships in the harbor, and make further raids on the airfields.

OIL TANKS

KEY

⬅ U.S. NAVY MOVEMENT

✈✈ JAPANESE AIRCRAFT

U.S. NAVY DOUGLAS SBD DAUNTLESS FIGHTER-BOMBERS *were responsible for the damage inflicted on the Japanese carrier fleet during the Battle of Midway.*

Midway   1942

RELUCTANT TO GO TO WAR IN THE FIRST PLACE, ADMIRAL YAMAMOTO ISOROKU, COMMANDER-IN-CHIEF OF THE JAPANESE COMBINED FLEET, HAD WARNED HIS SUPERIORS PRIOR TO THE ATTACK ON PEARL HARBOR, "FOR SIX MONTHS, I WILL RUN WILD IN THE PACIFIC. AFTER THAT, I MAKE NO GUARANTEES."

Although the Pearl Harbor attack in 1941 had been a success, the American aircraft carriers had been at sea and were not destroyed. Yamamoto realized that he had unfinished business. In the first week of June 1942, he forged ahead with plans for the capture of Midway, a tiny atoll less than 1,200 miles (1,930 km) west of Hawaii. With Midway in Japanese hands, the defensive perimeter of the empire would be extended considerably, and Hawaii itself might be open to invasion. In the process, Yamamoto would annihilate what remained of the U.S. Pacific Fleet.

Crucially, Yamamoto was unaware that U.S. Navy cryptanalysts based at Pearl Harbor had cracked the Japanese naval code, JN 25, and that Admiral Chester

BATTLE FACTS

Who: Japanese naval forces under Admiral Yamamoto (1884–1943) and Admiral Nagumo (1887–1944) versus the U.S. Pacific Fleet under Admirals C. Nimitz (1885–1966), F.J. Fletcher, (1885–1973), and R. Spruance (1886–1969).

What: A Japanese fleet of four aircraft carriers carrying 256 aircraft and 11 battleships opposed an American force that included three aircraft carriers and 234 carrier- and land-based airplanes.

Where: The central Pacific west of Hawaii.

When: June 4–7, 1942.

Why: The Japanese wanted to capture Midway atoll.

Outcome: A turning point in the Pacific War, the battle was a devastating defeat for Japan. Four aircraft carriers were sunk and the invasion of Midway was canceled.

Nimitz, commander in chief of the U.S. Pacific Fleet, was planning to counter the Midway operation. Nimitz ordered the aircraft carriers USS *Enterprise* and USS *Hornet* and their escorts to join the USS *Yorktown*—seriously damaged at the Battle of the Coral Sea but returned to service following a Herculean 72-hour repair effort at Pearl Harbor—northeast of Midway, to lie in wait for the Japanese.

Yamamoto, meanwhile, stuck to his penchant for complex operations and formulated a plan that would initially involve a feint against the islands of Attu and Kiska in the Aleutian Islands far to the north. He further divided his forces into a powerful surface fleet formed around the superbattleship *Yamato*, an invasion force transporting 500 soldiers to capture Midway, and a carrier force consisting of four aircraft carriers—*Akagi, Kaga, Soryu*, and *Hiryu*, which together carried 234 combat aircraft. Yamamoto himself sailed aboard the *Yamato*, while Admiral Nagumo Chuichi commanded the carrier force.

BATTLE JOINED

On June 4, 1942, Nagumo launched more than 100 planes to strike Midway in an effort to render its airstrip unusable and soften up the atoll's defenses. The attack was only partially effective and Nagumo faced a dilemma. A portion of his aircraft had been retained and armed with torpedoes to hit the American carriers if and when they were sighted. A second attack on Midway would require that these planes have their torpedoes exchanged for bombs, a hazardous and time-consuming process. The need for a second attack on Midway was confirmed by the appearance of American land-based bombers overhead. Although they scored no hits, Nagumo ordered planes not returning from the first Midway raid to be rearmed with bombs. Sightings of U.S. warships, including a carrier, then complicated the decision. Nagumo considered ordering the planes already rearmed with bombs to take off against Midway, while those still carrying torpedoes attacked the American ships.

To muddy the waters further, the planes returning from the first Midway attack, and the Zero fighters flying protective combat air patrol above his ships, were low on fuel and needed to land. Finally, Nagumo decided to recover planes that were airborne, and to equip with torpedoes the bombers that had been withheld. In their haste to land and refuel aircraft while rearming others, Japanese crewmen stretched fuel lines across the carrier decks and stacked bombs carelessly.

At this point, Fletcher and Spruance swung into action when a search plane located the enemy carrier force at about 5:30 A.M. on June 4. Near the limits of their range, more than 150 dive-bombers, torpedo-bombers, and fighters took off from the *Hornet, Enterprise,* and *Yorktown*. Some of the formations drifted off course and the opportunity for a coordinated attack was lost. In a twist of fate, however, this worked to the advantage of the Americans. The slow, obsolete torpedo bombers found the Japanese first, but were decimated by antiaircraft fire and the covering Zeros.

Shortly after 10 A.M., the Japanese carriers began the launch of their own planes. As the first aircraft roared down the flight decks, lookouts shouted the warning. Unmolested by the fighters, which were off chasing the last of the torpedo planes, 50 American dive-bombers pressed home their attacks. In a flash, the course of the Pacific War was changed. Bombs exploded among aircraft waiting to take off and amid the ordnance stacked below decks. *Akagi, Kaga,* and *Soryu,* engulfed in flames, were doomed.

The lone surviving Japanese carrier, the *Hiryu*, had been steaming in a rain squall some distance away and managed to launch a strike against *Yorktown*, seriously damaging the vessel. Although damage-control parties worked to save the ship, *Yorktown* was then spotted by a Japanese submarine and sunk along with the destroyer USS *Hammann* on June 7. U.S. dive-bombers, however, scored four hits on *Hiryu* on the afternoon of June 4, turning the last Japanese carrier into a blazing hulk.

The action in the waters around Midway on June 4, 1942, turned the tide of World War II in the Pacific. In contrast, the U.S. lost one carrier, a destroyer, 137 planes, and 307 men. The loss of four aircraft carriers, a cruiser, 332 aircraft, and more than 2,000 men was a crippling blow from which the Japanese never recovered.

AIRCRAFT CARRIERS

The Soryu was designed and laid down in 1937, the first in a new series of fleet carriers that became the mainstay of the Japanese navy during the first years of the war. With an excellent power-to-weight ratio and able to accommodate more than 60 aircraft, the Soryu was fast and agile. However, her light armor made her vulnerable to air attack.

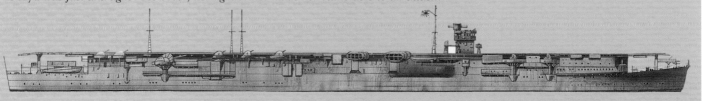

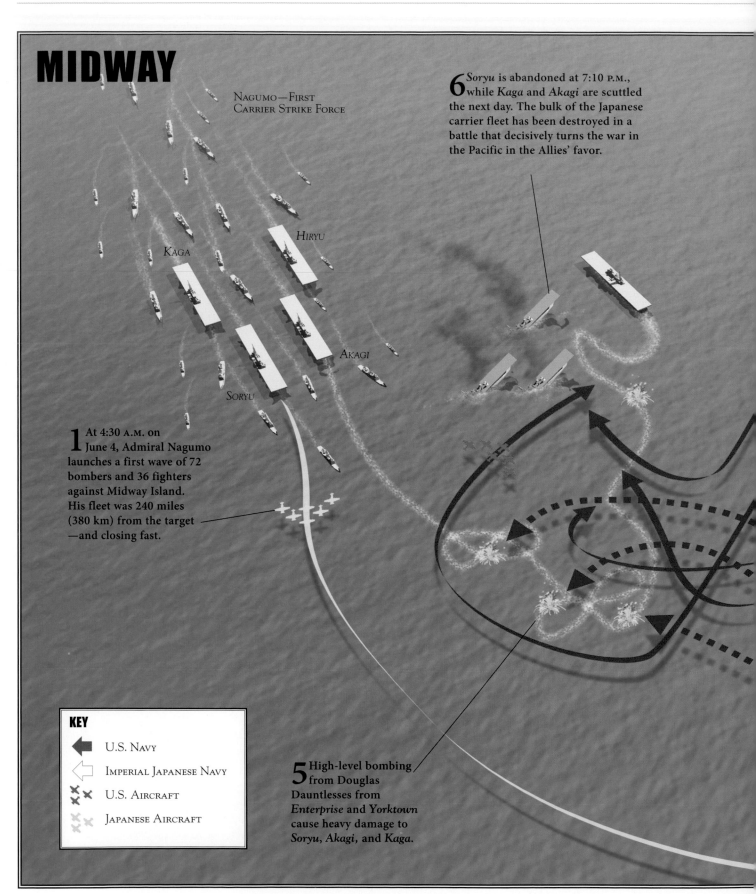

MIDWAY

Nagumo—First
Carrier Strike Force

Hiryu

Kaga

Akagi

Soryu

6 *Soryu* is abandoned at 7:10 P.M., while *Kaga* and *Akagi* are scuttled the next day. The bulk of the Japanese carrier fleet has been destroyed in a battle that decisively turns the war in the Pacific in the Allies' favor.

1 At 4:30 A.M. on June 4, Admiral Nagumo launches a first wave of 72 bombers and 36 fighters against Midway Island. His fleet was 240 miles (380 km) from the target —and closing fast.

KEY

U.S. Navy

Imperial Japanese Navy

U.S. Aircraft

Japanese Aircraft

5 High-level bombing from Douglas Dauntlesses from *Enterprise* and *Yorktown* cause heavy damage to *Soryu*, *Akagi*, and *Kaga*.

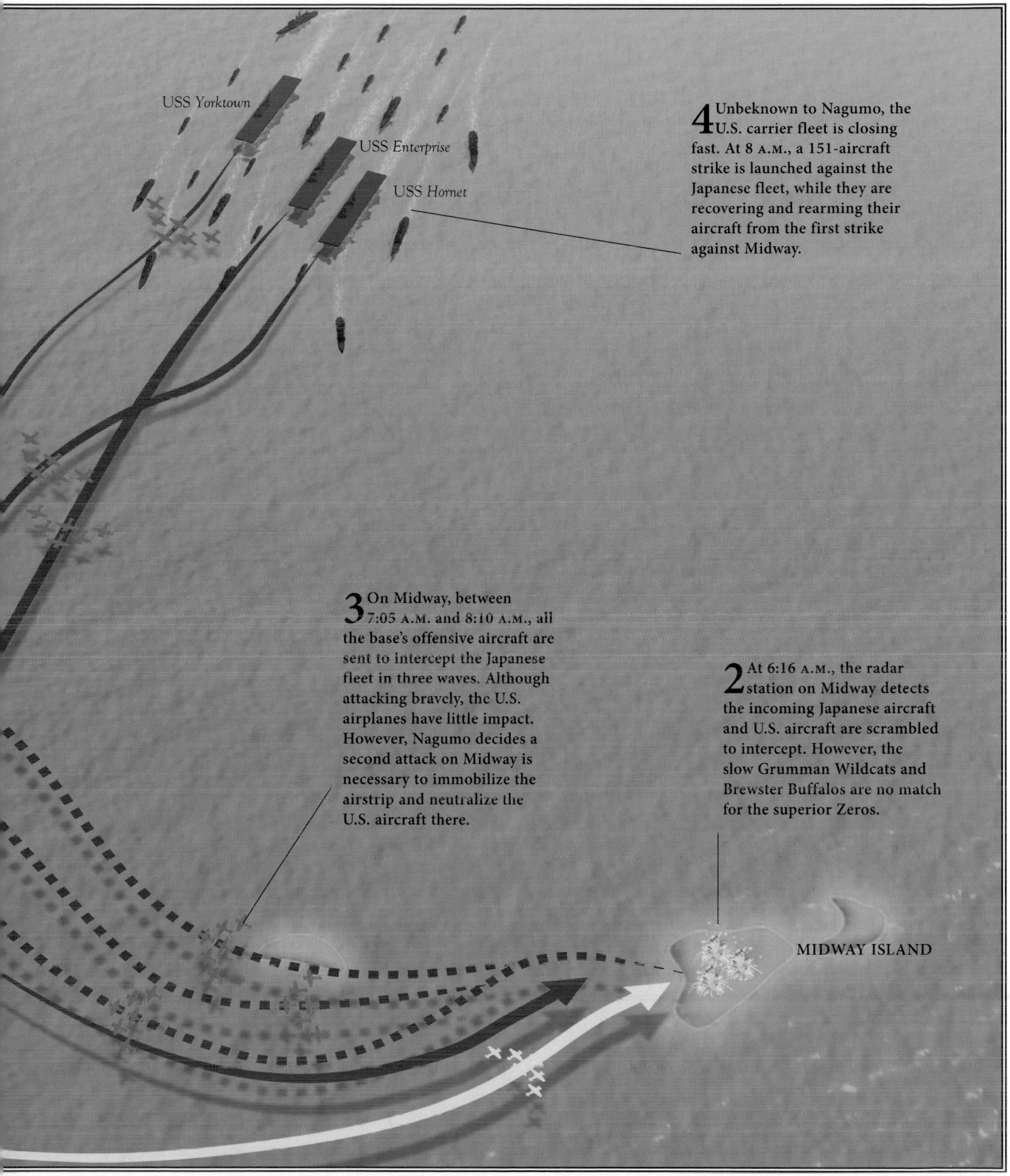

USS *Yorktown*

USS *Enterprise*

USS *Hornet*

4 Unbeknown to Nagumo, the U.S. carrier fleet is closing fast. At 8 A.M., a 151-aircraft strike is launched against the Japanese fleet, while they are recovering and rearming their aircraft from the first strike against Midway.

3 On Midway, between 7:05 A.M. and 8:10 A.M., all the base's offensive aircraft are sent to intercept the Japanese fleet in three waves. Although attacking bravely, the U.S. airplanes have little impact. However, Nagumo decides a second attack on Midway is necessary to immobilize the airstrip and neutralize the U.S. aircraft there.

2 At 6:16 A.M., the radar station on Midway detects the incoming Japanese aircraft and U.S. aircraft are scrambled to intercept. However, the slow Grumman Wildcats and Brewster Buffalos are no match for the superior Zeros.

MIDWAY ISLAND

DEPTH CHARGES EXPLODE IN THE ARCTIC TWILIGHT. *Whether or not the submarine was destroyed, aggressive depth-charging could prevent it from making a successful attack while the convoy escaped.*

Convoy PQ-17 1942

THE BATTLE OF CONVOY PQ-17 WAS IN SOME WAYS A TRIUMPH FOR THE GERMAN HEAVY SURFACE RAIDERS, EVEN THOUGH THEY PLAYED NO PART IN THE ACTUAL ATTACKS. THE THREAT THAT A BATTLESHIP WAS AT LARGE WAS ENOUGH TO FORCE THE CONVOY TO SCATTER, AT WHICH POINT ITS FATE WAS SEALED.

The German attack on Russia in 1941 brought the Soviet Union into the war on the side of the Allies and ultimately doomed the Axis to defeat. There was a time, however, when the situation in Russia was desperate and the British and Americans needed to send support. The only practical way of doing so was to ship vast quantities of tanks, vehicles, artillery, aircraft, and other war material into Russian ports, and the only available route was through the Arctic Ocean, contested by ice, atrocious weather, and German surface vessels and U-boats.

Convoys were given a code name and number that indicated, to those who knew the system, their route and sometimes composition or speed. "Fast" convoys received a

BATTLE FACTS

Who: An Allied convoy of 33 ships with an escort of four cruisers, three destroyers, and two Royal Navy submarines sailing to the Soviet Union, versus ten submarines, aircraft based on the Norwegian mainland and the threat of surface attack.

What: A gradual massacre of the merchant ships and their escorts.

Where: North of Norway in the Arctic Sea, close to the island of Spitzbergen.

When: June–July 1942.

Why: The convoy scattered in response to a supposed surface threat.

Outcome: Massive casualties among the Allied merchant ships, with only 11 ships arriving at their destination. Shortly afterward, the Allies suspended Arctic convoys because of the heavy losses.

different designation to those that could make a relatively low average speed. Each route had its own pair of code letters. Arctic convoys to Russia were designated PQ, with returning convoys labeled QP.

PQ convoys began with PQ-1, which assembled in Iceland and set sail on September 29, 1941. Only one ship was lost among the 103 that set out before the spring of 1941, but the sinking of a destroyer by a U-boat on January 1942 warned of things to come. Losses mounted, with increasing pressure from air and submarine units. PQ-16, for example, lost five of its 30 merchant ships in May 1942, four others arriving damaged.

It was with the expectation of a tough passage that PQ-17 formed up. It was the largest convoy thus far, with 36 merchant vessels. The close escort consisted of four destroyers, ten lighter craft (mostly armed trawlers), and two antiaircraft ships. Distant cover was provided by four cruisers and four destroyers. A heavy force containing two battleships, two cruisers, and an aircraft carrier was available for the first part of the route, but could not be risked past the North Cape.

SETTING SAIL

The convoy sailed on June 27, 1942. It took a very northerly route to keep as much distance between it and the enemy's northern bases as possible. All seemed well until the beginning of July, intermittent air attacks led to two ships being sunk on the 4th. Yet something much more serious happened that day. The Allies received word that the battleship *Tirpitz* was out.

Tirpitz was the most modern and powerful battleship in the German fleet—if she got into range of the convoy, there would be a massacre. Worse, she was reported as sailing in company with two heavy cruisers and several destroyers. The only chance to save any of the convoy was to scatter it and to hope that the heavy raiders found only some of the ships. The British intelligence service was subsequently able to establish that this was not a sortie against PQ-17,

but merely a redeployment. The damage had been done, though. The order to scatter was sent and the covering force was pulled back. The merchant ships struggled on, under intensifying air and U-boat attacks. On July 5, the convoy came under a heavy onslaught from aircraft and lost six ships, while submarines accounted for six more. The remaining close escorts did what they could for nearby vessels, but without an organized convoy the merchants were desperately vulnerable, especially to submarines. With no destroyer force to counter them, U-boats could make their attacks at leisure and consequently were horribly effective. Similarly, the *Luftwaffe* was able to press home its attacks with great precision, because there was little antiaircraft fire. As a result, nine more ships were sunk over the following five days.

The survivors began to arrive in Russia on July 10. Eleven ships straggled in over the next week. More than half the convoy had been destroyed by aircraft and submarines. Some of the ships would have been sunk whether or not the full escort had been available. However, the circumstances leading to the destruction of PQ-17 were brought about just by the threat of surface attack. The very existence of the German "fleet in being" brought ruin on the convoy.

A ROYAL NAVY OFFICER *dressed for Arctic convoy service. The cold was a deadly enemy; men keeping watch or venturing above decks risked hypothermia, and falling overboard meant certain death.*

TYPE VIIC U-BOAT

Coming into service in 1941, just as the "happy time" for U-boats was ending, the Type VIIC was smaller than the Type IX and had a shorter range as well as a smaller torpedo load. It was the mainstay of the German U-boat service for the remainder of the war and several hundred were built.

Although the tide was slowly turning against the U-boats, the Type VIIC was highly successful in combat. Many received Schnorkels starting in 1944, increasing their underwater endurance. Others were modified into flak boats to counter air attacks near the U-boat bases in the Bay of Biscay.

A PHOTOGRAPH, PROBABLY STAGED, OF TROOPS *of the 51st Highland Division running past a knocked-out German Panzer Mark III at El Alamein.*

El Alamein   1942

THE BATTLE OF EL ALAMEIN, OCTOBER 23–NOVEMBER 4, 1942, TAKING ITS NAME FROM AN EGYPTIAN RAILROAD HALT WEST OF ALEXANDRIA, MARKED A TURNING-POINT IN THE WAR IN NORTH AFRICA. THE BRITISH PRIME MINISTER WINSTON CHURCHILL CLAIMED THAT, "BEFORE ALAMEIN WE NEVER HAD A VICTORY. AFTER ALAMEIN WE NEVER HAD A DEFEAT."

The war in the Western Desert had swung back and forth over the course of nearly two years. By the summer of 1942, Field Marshal Erwin Rommel's German-Italian Panzer Army Africa had driven the British back past the Egyptian border, where it was stopped by the Eighth Army under General Claude Auchinleck (1884–1981) between July 1 and 4, 1942, at the first battle of El Alamein. By the time Rommel was ready to try again, Auchinleck had been replaced by Lieutenant-General Bernard Law Montgomery. Montgomery was a meticulous planner and superb trainer of men, who set out to rebuild the Eighth Army. Hence when Rommel attacked in

BATTLE FACTS

Who: The Commonwealth Eighth Army led by Lieutenant-General Bernard Montgomery (1887–1976) faced Field Marshal Erwin Rommel's (1891–1944) German-Italian Panzer Army.

What: Operation Lightfoot was a carefully planned set-piece offensive launched by Montgomery on the over-extended Axis forces.

Where: El Alamein, 60 miles (95 km) west of Alexandria.

When: October 23 to November 4, 1942.

Why: Growing British material strength allowed Montgomery to move to the offensive against Rommel's overextended forces.

Outcome: El Alamein marked a clear turning point in the Western Desert Campaign with the initiative shifting decisively to the Allies.

September at Alam Halfa, the British were well prepared and he was soundly defeated.

Montgomery refused to be pushed by Churchill into going on the offensive against Rommel before he believed his forces were ready. Unlike so many previous desert battles, therefore, Alamein would be a set-piece affair, with both flanks soundly anchored by the Mediterranean to the north and the impassable Qattara Depression to the south. Montgomery could muster 195,000 men to Rommel's 105,000 (of whom 53,000 were German), 1,000 tanks to the enemy's 500, and roughly double the amount of aircraft. The Commonwealth forces, broadly speaking, held a two-to-one advantage in most weapon systems.

Montgomery's plan was that four infantry divisions of XXX Corps would clear a path through the German positions in the north, to allow the two armored divisions of X Corps to push through and take defensive positions in the west. Then the infantry would break up the German line to the north and south—"crumbling" as Montgomery called it. XIII Corps would make strong demonstrations to the south.

SET-PIECE BATTLE

Operation "Lightfoot," a codename in somewhat poor taste given the 445,000 German mines emplaced across the front, opened with a massive barrage on the evening of October 23. The battle started well, but resistance began to stiffen quickly. Rommel concentrated what armor he could muster after the attritional fighting of the previous few days to counterattack a salient created by British 1st Armored Division on the slight rise of Kidney Ridge about 10 miles (16 km) inland from the coast, but both 21st Panzer and 90th Light Divisions were stopped dead by well served antitank guns, artillery, and air power. Meanwhile, Montgomery's forces gradually reduced the Axis positions, although progress was much slower than expected. The failure to make much headway forced Montgomery to come

up with another plan. Operation "Supercharge" shifted the weight of the offensive away from the north to the Kidney Ridge area on the night of November 1. Led by Lieutenant-General Bernard Freyberg's New Zealanders, bolstered by three British brigades, "Supercharge" penetrated deep into the Axis position and convinced Rommel that the battle was lost. On November 3, he began to pull back his armored forces and ordered the rest of his men to disengage. The New Zealanders and 1st Armored Division, then 7th Armored Division threatened to cut off the escape, which was in itself hampered by Hitler ordering Rommel to stand fast. Rommel managed to extricate large numbers of his forces, although 30,000—about one-third of them German—were taken prisoner.

The Battle of El Alamein was over and had cost the Allies 13,560 casualties, Major-General Douglas Wimberley's inexperienced 51st Highland Division taking the brunt, with the other infantry divisions also suffering heavily. Montgomery was hesitant in the pursuit and Rommel was able to retreat westward about 620 miles (1,000 km) before turning to make a serious stand in January 1943. By then, the strategic situation had worsened even further for the Axis, as on November 8, 1942, U.S. and British forces landed in French North Africa, seriously threatening Rommel's rear. The remorseless logic of a two-front campaign doomed the Axis presence in Africa.

El Alamein was the climax of the campaign in the Western Desert and the turning point in the war in North Africa. Montgomery had approached the battle with determination and a hard-headed will to succeed. He had also proved flexible enough—although he would never admit it—to change his plan midway through the battle. More importantly, he had proved that he was a general capable of defeating the Germans. This success was vital for the morale of the Eighth Army, vital for Churchill, who was under political pressure at home, and vital for the British nation as a whole during dark days.

GENERAL BERNARD MONTGOMERY

Bernard Montgomery combined undeniable charisma and flair for showmanship with a single-minded dedication to the profession of arms. He proved to be a superb trainer of men and meticulous planner, who did much to banish the myth of German invincibility. He was seriously wounded in World War I, but by the outbreak of World War II he commanded 3rd Division, which he led with distinction through the French campaign of 1940.

Corps and Area commands in Britain followed. Then, in August 1942, the death of Lieutenant-General William Gott, Churchill's first choice as commander for the Eighth Army, gave Montgomery his opportunity.

U.S. MARINES GO ASHORE IN AUGUST 1942. *There was little opposition to the initial landings on Guadalcanal, though later the island was bitterly contested.*

Guadalcanal 1942–43

AFTER DEFEATING THE IMPERIAL JAPANESE NAVY AT THE BATTLE OF MIDWAY IN JUNE 1942, THE ALLIES SET OUT TO CLEAR JAPANESE BASES FROM THE SOLOMON ISLANDS. THIS REQUIRED AMPHIBIOUS OPERATIONS AGAINST SEVERAL ISLANDS—INCLUDING TULAGI, WHERE A SEAPLANE BASE NEEDED REMOVING, AND GUADALCANAL, WHERE A MAJOR AIRBASE WAS BEING CONSTRUCTED.

The Allies assembled an invasion force at Fiji under U.S. Vice-Admiral Frank Fletcher (1885–1973), with ground forces led by Major-General Alexander Vandegrift (1887–1973), commander of the U.S. 1st Marine Division, which provided most of the ground forces. The assault force went ashore on the Solomons on August 7, 1942. On Guadalcanal itself, things initially went very well. Some 11,000 Marines consolidated their positions on the island, and took the critical airfield—nicknamed "Henderson Field" by the U.S. troops. Japanese naval power

BATTLE FACTS

Who: Allied forces from the United States, Australia, and New Zealand versus Japanese ground, air, and naval forces.

What: The Battle of Guadalcanal was a drawn-out fight lasting several months and involving land, naval, and air forces. Allied forces captured the island and held it against determined attack.

Where: Guadalcanal in the Solomon Islands, in the South Pacific.

When: August 1942– February 1943.

Why: The island was important to both sides as a base for future operations.

Outcome: The Allies won their first major ground victory against the Japanese. Despite heavy losses on both sides, the island was held by the Allies and used as a forward base.

JAPAN

Pacific Ocean

NEW GUINEA
✙ Guadalcanal

then forced away the U.S. offshore supply vessels, leaving the Marines on Guadalcanal alone and with insufficient resources against growing resistance.

The island was harassed by air attacks more or less constantly, but the Japanese commanders were not satisfied. They wanted the Allies driven off Guadalcanal and the rest of the Solomons, and so planned an amphibious attack of their own. The task fell to Seventeenth Army, which arrived in piecemeal fashion and began to launch passionate, but often suicidal, attacks on the U.S. troops. The American troops were by this time not only fighting the enemy, but also the literally gut-wrenching effects of dysentery running through their ranks.

After losing many transports to air attack, Japanese commanders decided that a traditional amphibious operation was not feasible and instead implemented what became known as the "Tokyo Express," whereby destroyers and light cruisers dashed in under cover of night to land relatively small forces and resupply them. The "Tokyo Express" was a clever solution to the problem of getting troops onto Guadalcanal, but it had its limitations. Small warships could not carry heavy equipment or artillery and vessels engaged in these operations were not available for war-fighting missions elsewhere. Nevertheless the "Tokyo Express" ran several thousand Japanese troops into Guadalcanal over the next few weeks until sufficient forces had been built up for an attack.

NEW PHASE

On August 31, General Kiyotake Kawaguchi (1892–1961) arrived to take command of all Japanese forces on Guadalcanal, and he gave the order for an assault on Henderson Field. The ferocious attack nearly succeeded in overwhelming and enveloping the U.S. positions, but after two days of intense fighting, the Japanese pulled back to regroup, nursing heavy losses.

Both sides now rebuilt their forces or defenses as best they could. The U.S. troops received some reinforcements, but by the middle of October the Japanese had brought several thousand men onto Guadalcanal and had repeatedly shelled the airfield. They began to move into position for a major assault against the U.S. positions. Some 20,000 Japanese troops were available, the main attack coming in from the south with additional flanking operations. The attack was dislocated by delays in preparation, and communication problems meant some forces attacked on October 23 and others the day after.

The assault was sustained, however, and in various sectors the Japanese pushed through the outer defenses despite substantial casualties. Although under

pressure, the defenders held their ground, while U.S. aircraft fought off air and naval attacks. Repeated frontal charges were cut up by infantry weapons and artillery firing over open sights. Finally, on October 26, the offensive was called off, and the Japanese retreated.

Land warfare in the Pacific was heavily influenced by the situation at sea. Whichever side had sea control could bring in supplies and reinforcements, tipping the balance of the land engagement. In this field, the U.S. Navy slowly, and painfully, gained the ascendancy. Further Japanese attempts to reinforce their presence on the island were unsuccessful, and U.S. forces began taking the offensive, pushing the enemy away from the airfield. Cut off from resupply and being ground down, the remaining Japanese forces were evacuated in early February 1943, ending the campaign.

Guadalcanal was the first clear-cut land victory over the Japanese and did much to restore Allied confidence. It also deprived the Japanese of an important forward base. The battle had a wider significance too. Japanese commanders realized that the struggle for Guadalcanal was a battle of real strategic significance and gave it great prominence. One consequence of this was that forces advancing on Port Moresby in New Guinea were pulled back and denied reinforcements. Thus the fighting on Guadalcanal indirectly assisted the Allied cause elsewhere.

JAPANESE ARMOR

Japanese tanks were inadequate by European standards and were often deployed in small numbers. On Guadalcanal, the only Japanese tank forces were the 12 vehicles of the 1st Independent Tank Company, with ten Type 95 light tanks (pictured below) and two Type 97 medium models. Two were lost to accidental damage and the others were destroyed at the battle of Matanikau River. The United States had only light tanks available, though these were as good as the Japanese Type 97s. They were useful on the offensive but the jungle terrain restricted their use.

195

IN THE MIDDLE OF THE DEVASTATION OF STALINGRAD, *a German platoon forms up in preparation for an assault on Soviet positions sometime early in the fall of 1942.*

Stalingrad 1942–43

STALINGRAD CHANGED THE FACE OF WORLD WAR II. IN A CATACLYSMIC STRUGGLE, THE *WEHRMACHT* EXPERIENCED ITS FIRST ARMY-SIZED DEFEAT AND THE STRATEGIC ADVANTAGE ON THE EASTERN FRONT BEGAN TO SHIFT TO THE RED ARMY.

In the spring of 1942, Hitler ordered Operation "*Blau*" ("Blue")—a massive offensive by his Army Group South through the Ukraine and into the Crimea toward the Caucasus. Turning away from the capture of Moscow, Hitler's ultimate objective now was to capture the great Soviet oilfields of the Caucasus.

Blau began on June 28, consisting of 1.3 million men (including 300,000 German allies, principally Romanians and Italians) and 1,500 aircraft. Army Group South was divided into Army Groups A and B—Army Group A would strike down into the Caucasus, while Army Group B to the north, would push toward Stalingrad and provide flank protection along the Don River. As with the *Wehrmacht* operations of the previous spring/summer, the Germans

BATTLE FACTS

Who: The German Sixth Army under General Friedrich Paulus (1890–1957), versus the Red Army's Stalingrad Front, principally the Sixty-Second Army under Major-General Vasily Chuikov (1900–82).

What: German forces captured most of the city, but with massive losses. A Soviet counteroffensive trapped 250,000 Germans within the city. About 100,000 of these men were killed and 110,000 went into Soviet captivity.

Where: Stalingrad, southern Russia.

When: September 14, 1942 to February 2, 1943.

Why: The Germans needed to secure the city in their push to occupy the oilfields of the Caucasus.

Outcome: The defeat of the Germans decisively shifted the offensive initiative to the Soviets on the Eastern Front.

made good headway, and by mid-July the Sixth Army under General Friedrich Paulus—the main component of Army Group B—was closing in on Stalingrad.

On July 23, Hitler gave the order to take the city itself. Fourth Panzer Army under General Hermann Hoth (1885–1971) was deployed south of Stalingrad to assist in the assault. On the same day, Stalin issued his own directive stating that Stalingrad would be defended to the last. Soviet forces in the newly designated Stalingrad Front consisted of the Sixty-Second, Sixty-Third, and Sixty-Fourth Armies. Although Stalingrad was an important industrial center, the fact that it bore Stalin's name gave the Soviet leader a definite psychological imperative to see that it did not fall.

The prelude to fighting within the city was a heavy air bombardment by *Luftflotte* 4, which reduced much of the city to rubble and killed more than 30,000 people. By September 12, German troops were already pushing into the city's suburbs, where they faced a defense of almost psychotic vigor from the troops of Chuikov's Sixty-Second Army within the city.

The battle for Stalingrad was to be pure close-quarters street fighting, a form of warfare depriving the Germans of the mobility that was their accustomed route to success in battle. Every building, and every room in every building, became a battleground, the Germans paying for each yard with blood. Nevertheless, at first the Germans seemed to be winning. Between September and mid-November they slowly squeezed the Soviets back, battling through the factory district at appalling cost. By November 18, the Soviets held only a thin, broken strip of territory on the Volga, little more than 10 percent of the city. Winter was beginning, however, and the Germans were shattered and depleted from the last weeks of fighting.

THE SOVIET OFFENSIVE

On November 19, Soviet forces around Stalingrad played their masterstroke, a counteroffensive planned by General Georgi Zhukov (1896–1974). North of Stalingrad, the Soviet Southwest Front and Don Front launched a six-army push southward across the Don, smashing weak Romanian resistance. The next day, the Stalingrad Front attacked north from positions south of Stalingrad, once again overcoming weak German flank protection. On November 23, the two "pincers" met behind Stalingrad, trapping the Sixth Army and much of the Fourth Army—more than 250,000 men—within the city.

A disaster was unfolding for the Germans. Aerial resupply and an attempt by Field Marshal Erich von Manstein (1887–1973) to break the cordon both failed, leaving the German soldiers in Stalingrad to a ghastly fate. Horrific fighting continued in Stalingrad for more than a month as the Soviets steadily crushed the German occupiers. Although 34,000 Germans were evacuated by air before the final airfield fell on January 25, more than 100,000 *Wehrmacht* troops were killed in this period. Finally, between January 31 and February 2, Paulus and some 110,000 German survivors surrendered, destined for Soviet labor camps from which only 5,000 men would emerge alive.

The German defeat at Stalingrad tilted the balance of the war both strategically and psychologically. Strategically, it put paid to Operation *Blau* and began, in effect, the German retreat that would end in Berlin in 1945. Psychologically, it gave the Soviets an enormous boost of confidence and showed they could compete with the invaders on both tactical and strategic levels. For the Germans, it was an undeniable sign that they could be defeated—the glory days of 1939–41 were now forgotten.

FIELD-MARSHAL FRIEDRICH PAULUS

Friedrich Paulus (1890–1957, left) cut his military teeth as an army captain during World War I and showed the ability and ambition that enabled him to rise to the rank of general by 1939. He subsequently served as deputy to General Franz Halder, the German Chief of Staff, before taking his most infamous command, that of the Sixth Army, in 1941. Paulus was an urbane "old-school" officer whose loyalty to the military led him, initially, to obey Hitler's ludicrous "to the last man" defense orders at Stalingrad. On January 31, 1942, Hitler made Paulus a field-marshal, knowing that no field-marshal in German history had ever surrendered or been captured alive. (Hitler was in effect requesting his suicide.) At this point, however, Paulus chose to ignore the precedent and surrendered, going on to be a vocal critic of the Nazi regime while in captivity. His last career posting was as an adviser to the East German Army in the mid-1950s.

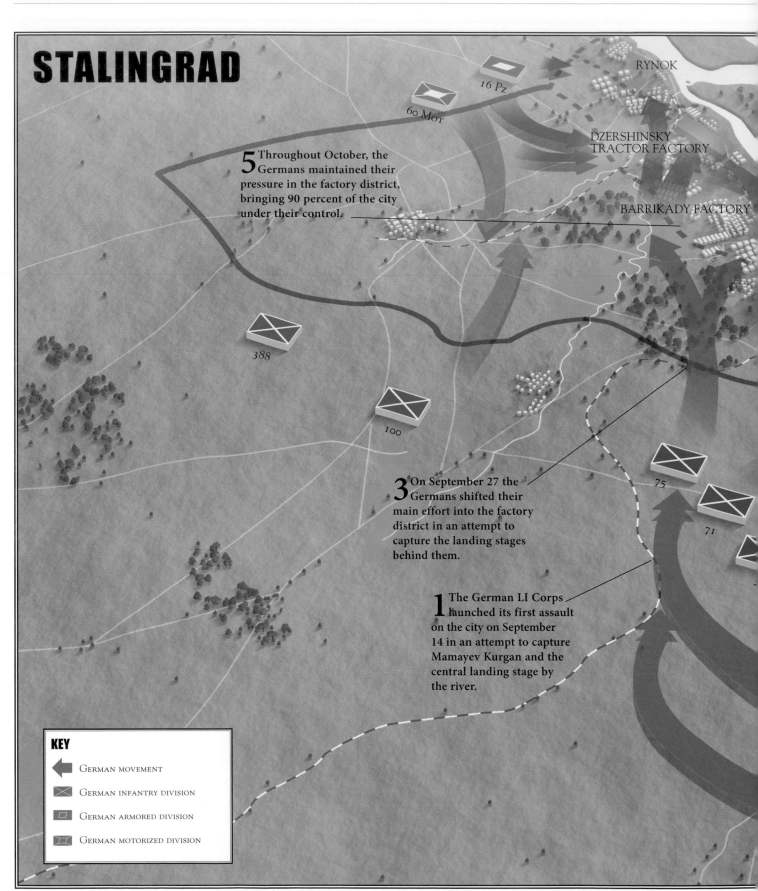

STALINGRAD

RYNOK

16 Pz

60 Mot

DZERSHINSKY
TRACTOR FACTORY

BARRIKADY FACTORY

5 Throughout October, the Germans maintained their pressure in the factory district, bringing 90 percent of the city under their control.

388

100

75

71

3 On September 27 the Germans shifted their main effort into the factory district in an attempt to capture the landing stages behind them.

1 The German LI Corps launched its first assault on the city on September 14 in an attempt to capture Mamayev Kurgan and the central landing stage by the river.

KEY

⬅ German movement

⬛ German infantry division

⬛ German armored division

⬛ German motorized division

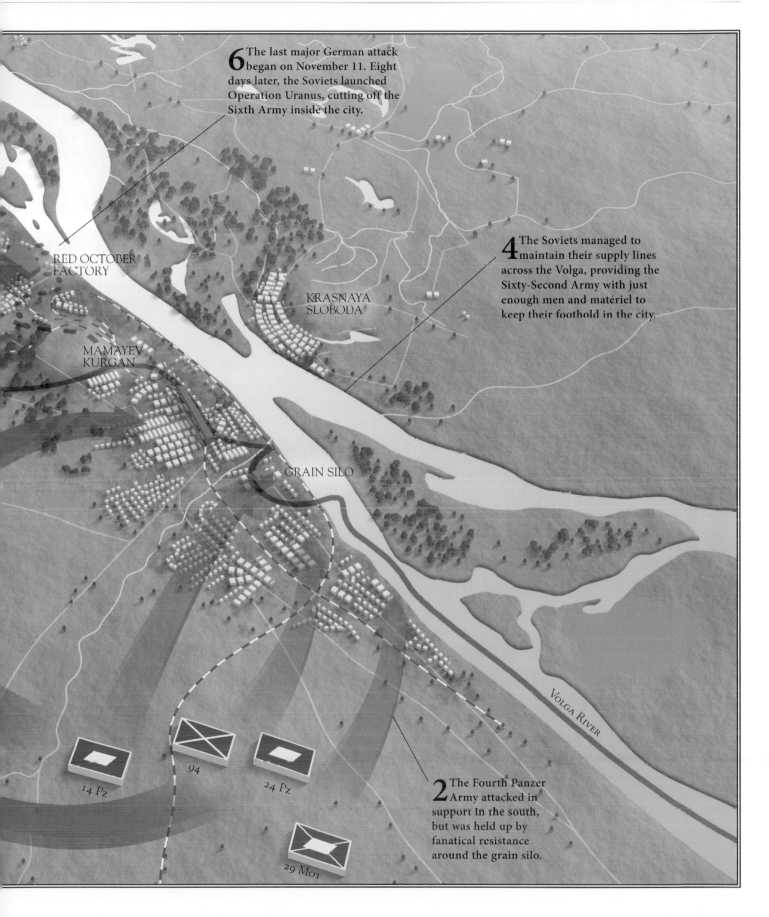

6 The last major German attack began on November 11. Eight days later, the Soviets launched Operation Uranus, cutting off the Sixth Army inside the city.

4 The Soviets managed to maintain their supply lines across the Volga, providing the Sixty-Second Army with just enough men and matériel to keep their foothold in the city.

RED OCTOBER FACTORY

KRASNAYA SLOBODA

MAMAYEV KURGAN

GRAIN SILO

VOLGA RIVER

14 Pz

94

24 Pz

29 Mot

2 The Fourth Panzer Army attacked in support in the south, but was held up by fanatical resistance around the grain silo.

PANZERGRENADIERS OF THE SS DIVISION *DAS REICH* *ride into Kharkov on the engine deck of a Panzer III tank. The SS divisions proved crucial in foiling the Red Army's advance at Kharkov.*

Third Battle of Kharkov — 1943

THE THIRD BATTLE OF KHARKOV IS GENERALLY CONSIDERED TO BE THE LAST GERMAN VICTORY ON THE EASTERN FRONT. IT STANDS AS A CLASSIC EXAMPLE OF ARMORED MANEUVER TACTICS EXECUTED UNDER DIFFICULT CONDITIONS AGAINST A WELL PREPARED AND NUMERICALLY SUPERIOR ENEMY.

The fall of Stalingrad after months of bitter fighting was a serious blow to German morale and prestige, while their opponents were riding a wave of success. Field Marshal von Manstein pulled the short-lived Army Group Don back and the Soviets pushed forward, taking the strategically important city of Kharkov in mid-February. Hitler was enraged, and ordered Manstein to retake the city. For once, the *Führer's* order suited Manstein. A deep salient had appeared in the battlefront where the Soviets had taken ground. This created an ideal opportunity for a

BATTLE FACTS

Who: 160,000 German troops led by Field Marshal Erich von Manstein (1887–1973) versus 300,000 Soviet troops of the Bryansk, Volkhov, and South Western Fronts led by generals Golikov (1900–80) and Vatutin (1901–44).

What: The Soviets stayed on the offensive following their success at Stalingrad, but were pushed back by a well executed German counterattack spearheaded by SS divisions *Leibstandarte* and *Das Reich*.

Where: The city of Kharkov in Ukraine.

When: February–March 1943.

Why: The city was important politically and also as a transportation nexus.

Outcome: The city was captured by the Germans but was lost again in August to a Soviet offensive.

double envelopment against the shoulders of the salient, cutting off, encircling, then destroying the advancing Soviets. Operational plans were made while Manstein's SS and armored formations reorganized themselves after past battles, amalgamating their depleted tanks and other assets into scratch battalions. This method of creating effective battlegroups from the remains of heavily damaged units was a hallmark of the German forces during World War II, and allowed the shrinking formations to go on fighting long after the individual units they were created from had ceased to be useful.

MANSTEIN'S COUNTERATTACK

Manstein's counterattack went in on February 19, 1943. The SS formations spearheaded the northern half of the pincer attack, while regular Panzer units led the southern arm. Despite minefields and foul weather, the SS troops advanced to contact and hit the enemy flank. Early successes included cutting the main road link to the river Dnieper, hampering Soviet movements. Renewing the advance, the SS forces fought several small but sharp encounter battles with Soviet units moving up to the front, capturing the town of Pavlograd on February 24.

Elsewhere, the flanking movements had thrown the Soviets into confusion and their advance to the Dnieper was brought to a halt, then pushed back. The way to Kharkov was now open, and the SS Das Reich division led the way toward the city. The Soviet high command issued "hold at all costs" orders. Reinforcements were rushed into Kharkov and attacks made elsewhere to try to divert German resources. These measures failed. The strategic rail junctions at Lasovaya were taken by the Das Reich and Totenkopf divisions.

Still Soviet reinforcements continued to arrive. The Soviet Third Tank Army (equivalent to a Panzer corps) managed to get between the Das Reich and Liebstandarte divisions. For the Germans this was a perilous situation—or a great opportunity to smash it from both sides, depending on your viewpoint. The SS-Panzer Corps commander, Paul Hausser (1880–1972),

took the latter view and launched an attack that became a three-day slogging match. Despite horrendous weather, a mud-choked landscape, and critical supply shortages, the SS troops gradually came out on top. By the time it was over, three Soviet tank brigades, three infantry divisions, and an entire corps of cavalry were shattered or captured.

Under this punishing onslaught, the Soviet forces pulled back in some areas, and on March 11 a battlegroup of SS troops established itself within the city limits. On March 12, the battle for the city began. Despite extremely stubborn resistance, notably around the train station and the industrial district, the Soviets were gradually pushed out of the city.

By now, the Soviets were in a state of confusion and thoroughly demoralized. Driving ever eastward, the SS divisions, though heavily depleted, smashed up two Guards Tank Corps and four infantry divisions. The last organized resistance was around a tractor factory outside the city. Once this was taken, Kharkov was firmly in German hands by March 15, signaling an impressive, albeit temporary, victory against apparently overwhelming odds.

T-34/76: THE GREATEST TANK OF WORLD WAR II?

The T-34 was among the most important weapons systems in the Red Army in World War II. At the time it was first fielded in 1940, it was easily the finest tank design in the world. Individually, T-34s were workmanlike rather than excellent combat vehicles. They were well protected, mobile, and possessed a good gun that could knock out enemy tanks at a respectable range. However, they were also prone to mechanical problems, especially with the transmission.

One for one, German tanks were generally better, but the phrase "all things being equal" never applies in warfare. Tanks did not fight one on one but as part of a military/technical/industrial partnership in which the fighting capabilities of the vehicle were only one aspect. The ability to repair or replace breakdowns and get tanks back into the fight was also critical, as was the capacity to manufacture them in large enough numbers to make a difference. It was in this context that the T-34 was a world-beater.

201

Kursk 1943

A RARE PHOTOGRAPH OF A CHURCHILL TANK *from the Soviet Fifth Guards Tank Army, a unit equipped with Lend-Lease vehicles from the Western Allies. It is passing a knocked-out German Sd Kfz 232.*

THE JULY 1943 BATTLE OF KURSK WAS THE GREATEST CLASH OF ARMORED FORCES YET SEEN IN WARFARE. THE ORIGINS OF THIS GERMAN OFFENSIVE—OPERATION *"ZITADELLE"* ("CITADEL")—LAY IN THE DISASTROUS START TO 1943, WHEN SOVIET COUNTERATTACKS NOT ONLY DESTROYED THE SIXTH ARMY IN STALINGRAD BUT ALSO IMPERILED FIELD MARSHAL ERICH VON MANSTEIN'S ARMY GROUP DON.

F ollowing von Manstein's effective counteroffensive in February and March 1943, a pause descended over the Eastern Front as the exhausted combatants rebuilt their shattered forces for the looming summer campaign. The earlier battles left a large Soviet-held salient jutting out west into the German lines around Kursk. Hitler ordered his forces to launch a double-pincer attack across the base of this salient to surround and destroy the sizeable Soviet force trapped within. Such an offensive would accomplish this encirclement within a restricted geographical area,

BATTLE FACTS

Who: Elements of Field Marshal G. von Kluge's (1882–1944) Army Group Center and Field Marshal E. von Manstein's (1887–1973) Army Group South faced Marshal K. Rokossovsky's (1896–1968) Central Front and Marshal N. Vatutin's (1901–1944) Voronezh Front.

What: The German strategic offensive of 1943, aimed at eliminating the Soviet salient centered around Kursk.

Where: Kursk in southern Russia, an important railroad junction 497 miles (800 km) south of Moscow.

When: July 4–13, 1943.

Why: The Germans needed to regain the initiative on the Eastern Front.

Outcome: The German offensive failed; the Soviet counterattack provided a launching point for further Soviet operations in 1943.

a sensible plan that reflected the *Wehrmacht's* dwindling operational mobility. For *Zitadelle*, therefore, the Germans achieved a massive concentration of force by assembling 17 Panzer/Panzergrenadier divisions across a total attack frontage of just 102 miles (164 km).

The Germans set *Zitadelle* to begin in early May, but Hitler repeatedly postponed the offensive so small numbers of Germany's latest weapons could reach the front. Hitler believed that with these 340 new "war-winning" weapons (250 Panther medium and 90 Tiger heavy tanks) the massive German forces committed to *Zitadelle* could smash any resistance the Soviets offered, however powerful. Yet when *Zitadelle* commenced on July 4, the Germans were outnumbered by heavily reinforced Soviet forces within the salient—astonishing given that the offensive was of the Germans' choosing in timing, location, and method.

PINCER MOVEMENT

The Germans deployed two main groupings for *Zitadelle*: in the north, elements of Field Marshal Günther von Kluge's Army Group Center; and in the south, forces from von Manstein's Army Group South. In the north, Ninth Army under General Walter Model (1891–1945) had at its disposal six Panzer/Panzergrenadier and 14 infantry divisions. In the south, Fourth Panzer Army under General Hermann Hoth (1885–1971) and Army Detachment Kempf under General Werner Kempf (1886–1969) put into the field 11 Panzer/Panzergrenadier and 10 infantry divisions.

The offensive commenced on July 4–5, with massive armored and infantry surges from opposing sides of the salient. From the start, however, Soviet resistance was ferocious, with artillery, minefields, and large quantities of Soviet armor sapping the energy of both thrusts. The northern German thrust proved a dismal failure. Despite a week of intense and costly attacks, it had managed to advance just 9 miles (15 km). In the south, there was better progress. On July 6, Hoth's XXXVIII Panzer Corps pushed north toward the second Soviet defense line near Oboyan, while farther east II SS-Panzer Corps drove the defenders north toward the village of Prokhorovka.

On July 12, the climax to *Zitadelle* occurred—the titanic clash of armor at Prokhorovka, into which the Soviets committed Fifth Guards Tank Army. With 800 Soviet tanks engaging 600 Panzers, this action was the largest armored battle of the war. For eight hours, the battle raged back and forth, with the tanks throwing up vast clouds of dust that limited visibility to just a few yards.

The Soviets exploited these conditions, closing the range so the Germans could not benefit from their lethal long-range guns. Tactically the battle was a draw, but strategically it was a German disaster. The Germans spent their armored strength, whereas sizeable Soviet armored reserves remained

THE CREW OF A SOVIET T-34 TANK SURRENDER TO AN SS SOLDIER, *presumably during the fighting on the southern side of the Kursk salient.*

available. The Germans also lost the initiative to the Red Army, which then ruthlessly exploited the opportunity to attack.

Prokhorovka convinced Hitler that *Zitadelle* could not succeed, and on July 13 he canceled the offensive. Between July 15 and 25, the German assault forces conducted a slow fighting withdrawal back to their starting positions in the face of ferocious Soviet attacks. On July 12, moreover, the Soviets had also launched an offensive against the German units that protected the northern flank of Model's forces. Catching the Germans by surprise, the Soviets gradually drove them back 80 miles (120 km).

Then, on August 3, the Soviets attacked the German units concentrated along the southern shoulder of the erstwhile Kursk salient. This new Soviet attack swiftly eliminated the German-held bulge to the south of the former salient. After securing rapid success with these two counterattacks, the Soviets escalated their operations into a general strategic counteroffensive across the entire center and south of the Eastern Front.

All things considered, *Zitadelle* was a dire German strategic defeat. Despite their huge concentration of force, all the Germans gained was an advance never deeper than 25 miles (40 km) and through insignificant terrain, for the heavy price of 52,000 casualties and 850 armored vehicles destroyed. Indeed, all *Zitadelle* accomplished was to shatter the German strategic armored reserves, thus making it easier for the Soviets to achieve rapid operational successes with their counterattacks. In fact, Kursk—rather than Stalingrad—was probably the key turning point of the war.

GERMAN PARATROOPERS *man a machine gun in the ruins of the monastery at Monte Cassino. The Allied bombing did little more than create even more defensible positions.*

Monte Cassino 1944

THE BATTLES OF MONTE CASSINO BETWEEN JANUARY AND MAY 1944 REPRESENTED SOMETHING OF AN ANOMALY IN THE CONDUCT OF THE WAR IN EUROPE. IN AN UNUSUALLY STATIC PERIOD OF WARFARE, THE ALLIES TOOK FIVE MONTHS AND FOUR SEPARATE BATTLES TO BREAK THROUGH THE GERMAN GUSTAV LINE, ANCHORED AROUND THE POSITION AT MONTE CASSINO.

The Gustav Line stretched 100 miles (160 km) across Italy from the Adriatic to the Tyrrhenian Sea. The key to the defenses was the entrance of the Liri Valley, which offered the most obvious route to Rome for the Allies. Monte Cassino, surmounted by its famous Benedictine monastery, dominated the approach, overlooking the rivers that crossed the mouth of the valley. The Germans built pillboxes and dugouts across the Liri, established positions in the surrounding mountains, fortified the town of Cassino, and flooded the rivers. It was probably the most formidable defensive position in Europe.

BATTLE FACTS

Who: II U.S. Corps and II New Zealand Corps of General Mark Clark's (1896–1984) Fifth Army and subsequently General Oliver Leese's (1884–1978) British Eighth Army faced Lieutenant-General Fridolin von Senger und Etterlin's (1891–1963) XIV Panzer Corps.

What: A series of offensives against the Gustav Line, a German defensive line anchored around high ground of Monte Cassino.

Where: The area around Monte Cassino, 62 miles (100 km) south of Rome.

When: Jan 24–May 18, 1944.

Why: Cassino controlled the mouth of the Liri Valley and thus the most straightforward route to Rome.

Outcome: Following a long attritional battle, the Gustav Line was finally broken across the front in May 1944.

Operation "Shingle," a planned Allied amphibious landing at Anzio behind the Gustav Line, forced the Fifth Army advancing up the mainland to push on against the Gustav Line to draw the German reserves from the Anzio area. Crossing the rivers in front of the Gustav Line proved to be a harrowing experience for both U.S. and British/Commonwealth forces, with the Germans inflicting devastating losses. The U.S. 36th Division, for example, had two regiments virtually destroyed while attempting to push across the Gari River. Direct assaults on Monte Cassino town were similarly bloody, the Allies throwing themselves against dug-in defenses on numerous occasions in January–March, and typically being repulsed with terrible casualties. Both town and monastery were bombed to destruction, but such destruction often served to provide the Germans—particularly elite German paratroopers—with better defensive positions.

Despite the efforts against Cassino, the Germans launched a massive attack on the Anzio beachhead. Still desperate to maintain pressure on the Gustav Line, the Allied commander in Italy, General Harold Alexander (1891–1969), ordered General Bernard Freyberg (1889–1963), commander of II New Zealand Corps, to attack again. The 4th Indian Division would attack the monastery above the town through Castle Hill, while the Corps' New Zealanders attacked the town from the north. After air raids and a massive bombardment, the two divisions attacked on the morning of March 15 and managed to seize the train station, but were unable to advance farther. Again German paratroopers put up fierce resistance, and even though the New Zealanders managed to clear most of the town and 4th Indian Division took Castle and Hangman's Hills, the Allies were not able to gain complete control of Cassino or capture the monastery. Having achieved very little, Freyberg called off the offensive.

A GERMAN 6 IN (150 MM) s-FH 18 *artillery piece in action. Most German artillery at Cassino was located in the Liri valley. Because the Germans held most of the high ground, they could bring observed fire on the whole battlefield.*

EIGHTH ARMY TAKES OVER

As the weather improved, the Allies reorganized their forces and Cassino became the responsibility of the Eighth Army. Alexander's chief of staff, General John, was the driving force behind Operation "Diadem," the fourth battle of Cassino. He organized a coordinated offensive across the front. In the west, U.S. II Corps would drive up the coastal plain toward Anzio, where U.S. VI Corps had been reinforced and was ready to break out from the beachhead. The French Expeditionary Corps would attack through the Aurunci mountains and break into the Liri Valley behind the Gustav Line. The British XIII Corps would drive up the mouth of the Liri with Canadian I Corps ready to exploit up the valley. The Polish II Corps would take on Cassino, while British X Corps conducted minor operations north of the town.

"Diadem" opened at 11 P.M. on May 11. The main thrust up the Liri by XIII Corps made slow progress, as did U.S. II Corps on the coast. The French, however, achieved excellent results, threatening to turn the German flank. The Poles took terrible losses up on the Cassino massif, but managed to seize Point 593 and the high ground around the monastery by May 17. The Poles entered the abbey the following day to find it abandoned.

Threatened by Allied success in the valley, the Germans finally withdrew north. Alexander ordered VI Corps to break out of Anzio and cut off the German Tenth Army's retreat. However, in an act of gross insubordination, General Mark Clark countermanded Alexander's order and turned his formation toward Rome, which fell to him on June 4. Because of Clark's vainglorious decision to capture Rome rather than defeat the enemy, the Germans were able to extricate their forces and regroup on a defensive line north of Rome. The chance for a decisive victory had been lost.

INDIAN SOLDIER

Soldiers of the British Commonwealth rendered outstanding service during the Italian campaign. Here, a corporal of the 6th Rajputana Rifles is seen in characteristic walking-out uniform. Part of the 4th (Indian) Infantry Division, the unit was closely involved in the battle for Monte Cassino, and sustained heavy casualties. The 6th Rajputana Rifles had previously served with the Eighth Army in Syria and throughout the North African campaign. Awarded many honors and medals, the unit still exists today as part of the modern Indian army.

THE WIDE IRRAWADDY RIVER was a serious obstacle to the logistics services of armies operating in Burma. This makeshift barge turns a disadvantage into an asset, using the river to transport a truck.

Battle of Imphal and Kohima 1944

THE BATTLE OF IMPHAL AND THE ACTION AT KOHIMA REPRESENTED THE HIGH-WATER MARK OF JAPANESE ASPIRATIONS IN BURMA AND INDIA. HOWEVER, AFTER SOME INITIAL SUCCESSES, THE DEFEATED JAPANESE FELL BACK INTO BURMA AND WERE SUBSEQUENTLY DRIVEN BACK THE WAY THEY HAD COME.

The Japanese advance in the early months of World War II seemed unstoppable. Allied forces were driven down the Malay Peninsula to the "fortress island" of Singapore and forced to surrender there. Other formations were pushed back through Burma toward India. A determined rearguard action slowed the Japanese advance and the monsoon brought it to a halt.

This breather gave the Allies a chance to regroup and mount a defense, which the terrain favored. The jungle and hills of the Burmese-Indian border region would funnel an

BATTLE FACTS

Who: British and Indian troops opposed by Japanese forces and elements of the anti-British Indian National Army.

What: Japanese forces encircled the city of Imphal but were driven off and then counterattacked.

Where: The city of Imphal, the capital of the state of Manipur in northeastern India.

When: March 8–July 3, 1944

Why: The Japanese wished to occupy India. This was their

last chance of launching a major land invasion against British India, because their military resources were being rapidly depleted in the war against the United States in the Pacific.

Outcome: The Japanese were decisively defeated and never again threatened British India with invasion.

advance into corridors that could be defended with relative ease. The city of Imphal provided a base and logistics center for the Allies, while the Japanese would have to operate at the end of a long supply line that ran through difficult terrain. Nevertheless, Japanese forces in the region gained a new and aggressive commander, Lieutenant-General Kawabe Masakazu (1886–1965), who thought an attack on Imphal was feasible.

The Japanese campaign opened persuasively on March 8, 1944, with three divisions of the Fifteenth Army assaulting across a broad front. By April 7, the supply route between Imphal and, to the north, Kohima was cut and the two outposts were virtually encircled. The troops of British IV Corps faced a siege warfare situation.

DEFENSE AND COUNTERATTACK

The defenders at Kohima held out in a shrinking perimeter under artillery fire and constant infantry attacks, and by April 17 the situation was desperate. However, the position was relieved the next day by troops of XXXIII Corps moving up from India. The attacks continued unabated, but the chances of Japanese success were ever decreasing.

By early May, more Allied troops had joined the fight at Kohima, and the Japanese, now very short of supplies, came under air attack as well as increasing bombardment. Kohima Ridge, astride the Imphal–Kohima road, was partially cleared of Japanese defenders after a very bitter

fight, but as late as mid-May some high points were still stubbornly held. Yet with Allied troops across their supply line and almost out of ammunition, the now-starving Japanese were forced to pull back and leave the ridge to the British. Not that there was much left of it or the villages there—Kohima has been referred to as the Stalingrad of the East, and with good reason. Many Japanese units broke up, straggling east and south in search of food and unable to play any further part in the campaign. The British now began to push through to the town of Imphal.

JAPANESE DECLINE

Japanese attacks on Imphal itself wound down by May 1. The siege continued, but there was no longer any real chance of a successful assault. As the Japanese supply situation worsened during the campaign, the Allies were resupplied by airdrops at both Imphal and Kohima. Although the Japanese commanders on the spot knew they could not win this battle, a final effort was ordered. A few reinforcements had arrived and these allowed the assault to achieve some limited success. Nevertheless by June 22 the road through to Kohima was opened completely, and the siege was effectively over.

The Japanese divisions around Imphal were at the end of their tether, and more or less ignored orders from above to make a new assault. Bowing to the inevitable, the commanders gave orders for a retreat, and on July 3 the divisions began pulling back. Many of these formations were debilitated by disease and starvation, and were able to do little more than shamble eastward, leaving their remaining heavy equipment and artillery behind.

The ill-advised advance on Imphal was the turning point of the war in Southeast Asia. From then on the Japanese were on the defensive and were steadily pushed back. For the Allies, the dark days of shambolic retreat were long over and they returned to Burma confident that they could take on and beat the Imperial Japanese Army.

MERRILL'S MARAUDERS

Named after its U.S. commander, Brigadier-General Frank Merrill (1903–55), the 5307th Composite Unit (Provisional) became better known as Merrill's Marauders during its long-range raiding exploits in the China-Burma theater.

After training with the highly successful Chindits, the all-volunteer Marauders embarked on a campaign of harassment deep within Japanese territory. Despite heavy casualties and sickness caused by the harsh jungle conditions, they were able to cut Japanese supply lines and inflict serious losses on their opponents in dozens of actions.

At the end of the war, every member of the Marauders was awarded the Bronze Star and the unit was honored with a Distinguished Unit Citation for its contribution to the Burma campaign.

U.S. ASSAULT TROOPS WADE ASHORE *from a landing craft on Omaha Beach, June 6, 1944. The Americans suffered terrible casualties securing Omaha Beach.*

Normandy Landings 1944

D-DAY—THE ALLIED LANDINGS ON THE COAST OF GERMAN-OCCUPIED FRANCE ON JUNE 6, 1944—WAS ONE OF THE MOST CLIMACTIC DAYS OF WORLD WAR II. THE WESTERN ALLIES HAD BEEN PREPARING FOR THIS OPERATION, CODENAMED NEPTUNE/OVERLORD, SINCE THE BEGINNING OF 1943. ON D-DAY, THE ALLIES LANDED 160,000 U.S., BRITISH, AND CANADIAN FORCES (PLUS A SMALL FRENCH CONTINGENT) TO ESTABLISH BEACHHEADS IN NORMANDY.

D-Day began as light faded over England on June 5, 1944. Some 6,939 vessels assembled off the coast of southern England and headed south toward the Normandy coast, while from 11:30 P.M. a total of 1,100 Allied transport planes deployed 17,000 airborne troops to the invasion area. Crossing into France in the early hours

BATTLE FACTS

Who: Supreme Allied Commander General Dwight Eisenhower (1890–1969) commanded the 175,000-strong U.S., British, and Canadian forces that faced Field Marshal Erwin Rommel's (1891–1944) Army Group B.

What: The largest amphibious operation in history, marking the Western Allies' return to northwestern Europe.

Where: The Baie de la Seine in Normandy, France.

When: June 6, 1944.

Why: The Allies wanted to open up a second front against Nazi Germany, and Normandy provided suitable beaches within range of land-based air cover.

Outcome: The Allies successfully established their forces ashore, marking a crucial turning point in the war.

of June 6, British airborne forces landed northeast of Caen and seized key locations to protect the invasion's eastern flank. Simultaneously two U.S. airborne divisions were deployed to provide a similar guard over the invasion's western flank.

At sea, the D-Day armada was laden with tens of thousands of Allied troops, destined for five designated invasion beaches: in the east, the three Anglo-Canadian sectors—"Sword," "Juno," and "Gold" and in the west the two U.S. beaches, "Omaha" and "Utah." As the airborne operations unfolded, the vast fleet stationed itself off the Normandy coast, and began pounding the coastal defenses with devastating fire. Then, between 6:30 A.M. and 7:45 A.M., the Allied amphibious assaults commenced. The "Second Front" had now opened.

At the Anglo-Canadian beaches, the British XXX Corps and I Corps managed to secure beachheads successfully, albeit against pockets of tenacious resistance at strongpoints such as Le Hamel ("Gold" beach). The advances out from "Gold" and "Juno" beaches managed to secure the important road between Creuilly and Bayeux (the latter remained just out of reach of the Allied spearheads by the end of the day), while the "Sword" beach forces pushed toward Caen along the Orne River, albeit against strengthening resistance. During the afternoon of June 6, the 21st Panzer Division made a counterattack into the gap between "Juno" and "Sword," but this was eventually stopped and pushed back.

BLOODBATH AT "OMAHA" BEACH

The assault of 1st and 29th U.S. Infantry Divisions on "Omaha" commenced at 6:30 A.M. Here, however, the operation went far less to plan. Even before the landings commenced, things had gone awry, with the fire support proving less effective than planned. The heavily loaded infantry that managed to struggle through the neck-high water to the shore then encountered murderous enemy fire, which inflicted massive casualties; Allied intelligence had failed to detect the recent reinforcement of the German defenses here. Throughout the morning, U.S. troops strove to fight their way off the beach and into the bluffs beyond,

yet by midday the U.S. grip on enemy-occupied soil still remained precarious. Eventually the American troops secured a tenuous 1-mile (1.6-km) deep foothold on French soil, but at the price of more than 2,000 casualties.

"Omaha" stood in stark contrast to the less costly assault mounted at "Utah," located along the southeastern corner of the Cotentin Peninsula. Here, also at 6:30 A.M., the 4th U.S. Infantry Division commenced its assault after accurate naval gunfire had smashed the relatively weak German defenses; the enemy believed the marshes located behind "Utah" would persuade the Allies not to land there. In the face of moderate resistance, the Americans soon advanced inland to close with the perimeter held by the U.S. airborne forces.

The battles went on throughout the day, but by midnight on June 6, 1944, the 159,000 Allied troops ashore had set up four sizeable beachheads. While the Allied invasion front remained vulnerable to German counterattack, D-Day's success now made it virtually impossible for the enemy to throw the invaders back into the sea. The establishment of the "Second Front" on June 6, 1944, represented a crucial step forward on the Allied march to victory over Nazi Germany.

SHERMAN "FLAIL" TANK

The Sherman Crab was one of a number of specialized armored vehicles used during the D-Day landings. The Crab mounted a flail—a set of heavy chains suspended on a rotating drum in front of the tank—that was used to clear a path through a minefield. The method was first used aboard a Matilda tank, at El Alamein. The Crab, mounted on the standard Allied medium tank the M4 Sherman, could clear a lane about 11 ft (3.3 m) wide at the speed of 1.2 mph (2 km/h). The chains would need replacing after several detonations.

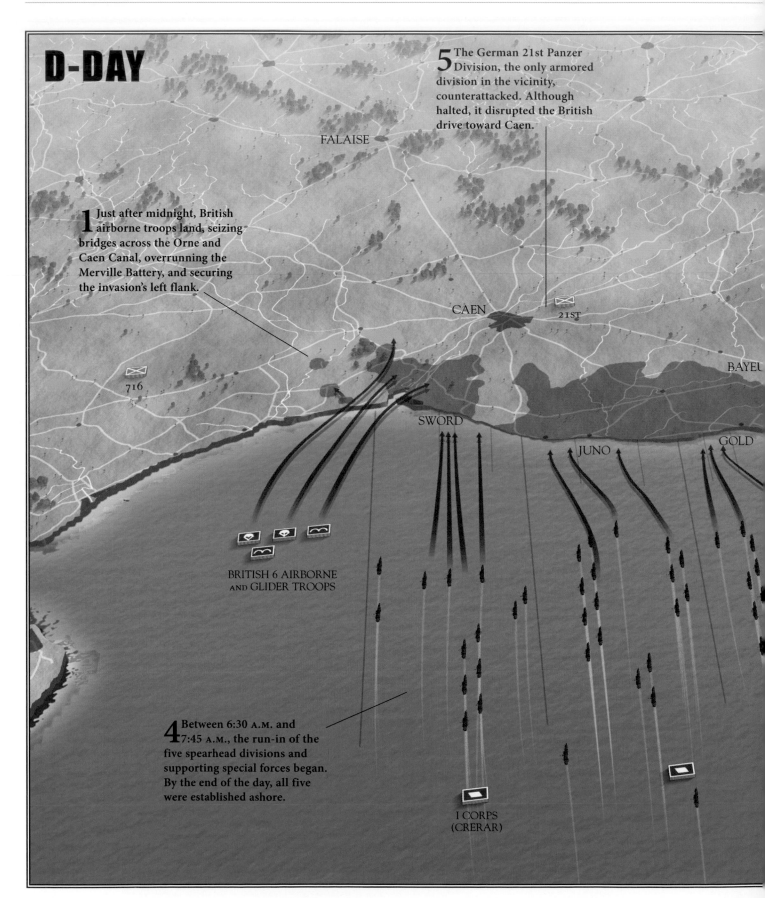

D-DAY

5 The German 21st Panzer Division, the only armored division in the vicinity, counterattacked. Although halted, it disrupted the British drive toward Caen.

FALAISE

1 Just after midnight, British airborne troops land, seizing bridges across the Orne and Caen Canal, overrunning the Merville Battery, and securing the invasion's left flank.

CAEN

21ST

BAYEU

716

SWORD

JUNO

GOLD

BRITISH 6 AIRBORNE AND GLIDER TROOPS

4 Between 6:30 A.M. and 7:45 A.M., the run-in of the five spearhead divisions and supporting special forces began. By the end of the day, all five were established ashore.

I CORPS
(CRERAR)

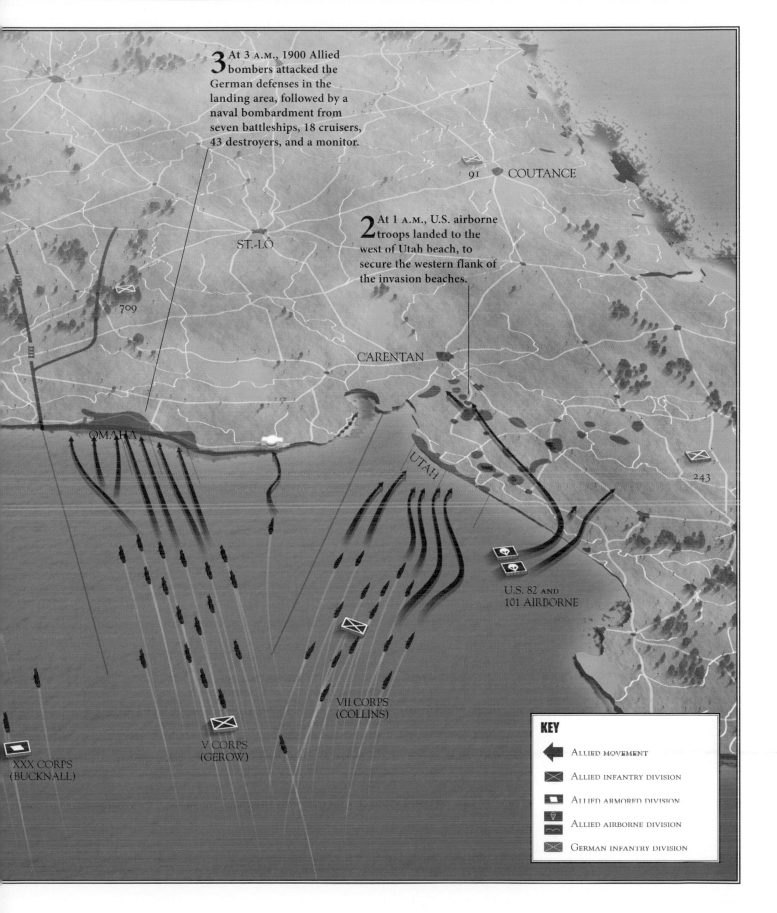

3 At 3 A.M., 1900 Allied bombers attacked the German defenses in the landing area, followed by a naval bombardment from seven battleships, 18 cruisers, 43 destroyers, and a monitor.

91 COUTANCE

2 At 1 A.M., U.S. airborne troops landed to the west of Utah beach, to secure the western flank of the invasion beaches.

ST.-LÔ

709

CARENTAN

OMAHA

243

UTAH

U.S. 82 AND
101 AIRBORNE

VII CORPS
(COLLINS)

V CORPS
(GEROW)

XXX CORPS
(BUCKNALL)

KEY

⬅ ALLIED MOVEMENT

✕ ALLIED INFANTRY DIVISION

▭ ALLIED ARMORED DIVISION

〜 ALLIED AIRBORNE DIVISION

✕ GERMAN INFANTRY DIVISION

A British motorcycle dispatch rider *passes a knocked-out Sherman tank on a churned up road somewhere in Normandy, July 1944. In the background can be seen disabled German AFVs.*

Normandy Breakout   1944

DURING LATE JULY AND AUGUST 1944, THE WESTERN ALLIES SUCCESSFULLY BROKE THE STALEMATE THAT HAD EMERGED IN THE BATTLE FOR NORMANDY, AND SUBSEQUENTLY TRANSLATED THIS INTO A DECISIVE STRATEGIC VICTORY THAT SAW THE GERMAN FORCES EXPELLED FROM THE REGION.

The grinding battles of attrition in Normandy began to bear fruit for the Allies in mid-July, as their numerical superiority wore down the Germans. General Bernard Montgomery launched Operation "Goodwood," an armored assault to outflank Caen from the east. While the operation failed to achieve its objectives, it did facilitate the success of the subsequent U.S. offensive— Operation "Cobra"—initiated on July 25. To sustain their fierce defensive stands against "Goodwood," the Germans had to divert most of their logistical supplies to the eastern

BATTLE FACTS

Who: Two Allied army groups under the command of Lieutenant-General Omar Bradley (1893–1981) and General Bernard Montgomery (1887–1976) faced Field Marshal Günther von Kluge's (1882–1944) German Army Group B.

What: A series of Allied offensives finally cracked the German line and allowed the Allied forces to break out of the bridgehead.

Where: Normandy, France.

When: July 25–August 30, 1944.

Why: Following the D-Day landings, German forces were ordered to hold their ground by Hitler, leading to a six-week attritional struggle.

Outcome: The German position in Normandy was broken and the Allies crossed the Seine River, liberating Paris on August 25.

sector of the front. Consequently, the German forces defending the Saint-Lô front were starved of vital logistical supplies just prior to "Cobra," and their ensuing shortages of fuel and ammunition made it easier for the Americans to achieve success. By July 29, the Americans had ripped the German front asunder, and between July 29 and 31 U.S. forces crossed the Sélune River at Pontaubault, thus rounding the base of the Cotentin peninsula and opening the gateway for further advances west.

On August 2, Hitler reacted to the U.S. breakout by attempting to stuff the genie back into the bottle. He ordered Army Group B to mount a hasty counterattack against the weak western flank of the breakout. By retaking Avranches, this would isolate the U.S. forces located south of the penetration. During the night of August 6–7, a hastily assembled mobile force attacked down the narrow corridor between the Sée and Sélune rivers toward Mortain. Unsurprisingly, after some initial success this German riposte was halted. This failure now presented the Allies with a strategic opportunity to encircle and destroy the German forces in Normandy, either in the Argentan–Falaise area or via a larger envelopment along the Seine.

ADVANCE TO FALAISE

By early August, it had become crucial for the British and Canadian forces bogged down near Caen to advance south. Therefore, starting on August 7 and 8 General Guy Simonds' II Canadian Corps began several halting attacks toward Falaise. But by mid-August the Americans had halted their advance north from Alençon, partly due to supply shortages and fears about friendly fire from Simonds' forces. Instead, Bradley divided his units and directed U.S. V Corps to race eastward to the Seine. Incredibly,

by August 19, this corps had secured a bridgehead across the Seine at Mantes-Gassicourt. Despite the U.S. halt at Alençon, the Falaise pocket was nevertheless well formed by August 16, with the Germans holding just a precarious 10-mile (16-km) wide neck around Trun.

Between August 16 and 19, Simonds' armor thrust southeast toward Trun and linked up with the Americans to close the pocket. This weak Allied blocking position could not withstand the ensuing German breakout. As the battered remnants of Seventh Army desperately fought their way out of the pocket through these blocking positions, SS armor also attacked from outside the pocket. These attacks enabled some 40,000 German troops to escape, albeit without their heavy equipment. With Seventh Army no longer cohesive and with the Americans racing into the interior of France, the Germans now had no choice but to withdraw back to the Seine.

Even before the Falaise pocket had been closed, Montgomery had initiated his own offensive toward the Seine, reflecting his desire to enact the "long" rather than "short" envelopment. By August 21, four corps had struck northeast toward the Upper Seine north of Paris, seeking to catch up with the U.S. advance. However, between August 21 and 30, the battered remnants of Army Group B mounted a controlled withdrawal back to the northern bank of the Seine. At Vernon on August 26, the first British bridgehead was established across the river. Just four days later, all German resistance south of the Upper Seine had ceased and with this the Normandy campaign ended. By this juncture, Paris had fallen and the Americans had raced north beyond the Seine and east into the interior of France. The Allies had won the battle of Normandy and now their thoughts turned to advancing into the German Reich itself.

TIGERS IN NORMANDY

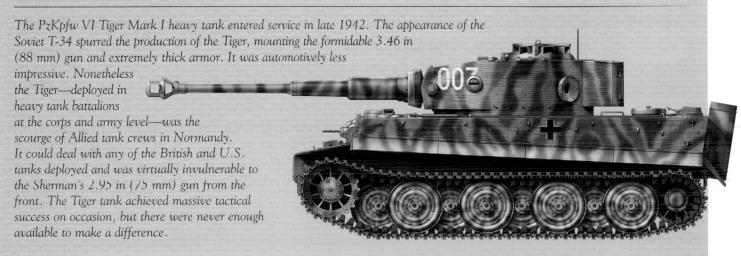

The PzKpfw VI Tiger Mark I heavy tank entered service in late 1942. The appearance of the Soviet T-34 spurred the production of the Tiger, mounting the formidable 3.46 in (88 mm) gun and extremely thick armor. It was automotively less impressive. Nonetheless the Tiger—deployed in heavy tank battalions at the corps and army level—was the scourge of Allied tank crews in Normandy. It could deal with any of the British and U.S. tanks deployed and was virtually invulnerable to the Sherman's 2.95 in (75 mm) gun from the front. The Tiger tank achieved massive tactical success on occasion, but there were never enough available to make a difference.

A DAMAGED U.S. NAVY CURTISS SB2C HELLDIVER *dive-bomber is inspected by officers and crewmen on the flight deck of an aircraft carrier. The Helldiver replaced the aging Douglas SBD Dauntless.*

Philippine Sea   1944

RISING LIKE THE MYTHICAL PHOENIX FROM THE DEVASTATION OF PEARL HARBOR, THE U.S. NAVY HAD BECOME A VERITABLE JUGGERNAUT BY THE SPRING OF 1944. IN SUPPORT OF AMPHIBIOUS OPERATIONS, WHICH HAD WRESTED KEY BASES AND OUTPOSTS FROM THE JAPANESE IN THE GILBERT AND MARSHALL ISLANDS, THE U.S. PACIFIC FLEET WAS POISED TO ACCOMPLISH ANOTHER PRIMARY MISSION—THE DESTRUCTION OF THE IMPERIAL JAPANESE NAVY.

Thirty months of fighting had carried the U.S. armed forces across vast expanses of ocean. On June 15, 1944, amphibious landings took place on the island of Saipan in the Marianas, an archipelago that lay in the path of the American advance toward the Philippines. The capture of Saipan, along with the islands of Guam and Tinian, would disrupt Japanese supply efforts to the far reaches of their empire, while providing bases from which long-range U.S. bombers could regularly attack the Japanese home islands.

BATTLE FACTS

Who: Admiral Toyoda Soemu (1885–1957), commander of the Japanese Combined Fleet, and Admiral Ozawa Jisaburo (1886–1966), commander of the First Mobile Fleet, versus Admiral Raymond Spruance (1886–1969), commander of the U.S. Fifth Fleet, and Admiral Marc Mitscher (1887–1947), commander of Task Force 58.

What: The Japanese committed most of their air power against the U.S. fleet.

Where: The Philippine Sea in the Central Pacific.

When: June 19–20, 1944.

Why: The Japanese hoped to stem the tide of the U.S. advance across the Pacific.

Outcome: A decisive victory for the U.S. Navy resulted in the virtual annihilation of Japanese carrier air power.

Anticipating dire consequences if the Americans succeeded, Admiral Toyoda Soemu, commander-in-chief of the Japanese Combined Fleet, set in motion Operation "A-Go," a desperate gambit. Toyoda dispatched Admiral Ozawa Jisaburo and the First Mobile Fleet to the waters of the Philippine Sea to confront the U.S. naval armada, which was screening the Saipan invasion force and fully expecting such a response from the Japanese. Under his command was a still potentially lethal assemblage of five fleet and four light aircraft carriers, five battleships, 11 heavy cruisers, two light cruisers, 28 destroyers, and more than 500 aircraft. The force included the superbattleships *Yamato* and *Musashi*, the largest warships of their kind ever built.

On the opposing side, Admiral Raymond Spruance, commander of the U.S. Fifth Fleet, was in overall command of a striking force built around the core of Task Force 58, led by Admiral Marc Mitscher. Organized into four battle groups, Task Force 58 included a complement of seven large fleet carriers, eight light carriers, seven battleships, 21 cruisers, 69 destroyers, and nearly 1,000 aircraft.

TURKEY SHOOT

On the morning of June 19, 1944, Ozawa launched 69 planes against the Americans, 45 of which were quickly shot down. A followup strike of 127 planes met a similar fate, 98 of them splashing into the sea under the guns of U.S. Grumman F6F Hellcat fighters. During four raids against Task Force 58, the Japanese managed to inflict only slight damage on one U.S. carrier and two battleships. The slaughter of planes and pilots was so thoroughly one-sided that the action came to be known as the "Great Marianas Turkey Shoot." In effect, Spruance was allowing what remained of Japan's carrier air power to dash itself against the rocks of his formidable air defenses.

Compounding Ozawa's troubles, the newest aircraft carrier in the Japanese fleet and the admiral's flagship, *Taiho*, was struck by a torpedo from the submarine USS *Albacore* on June 19. The damage had not been fatal, but early in the afternoon a young officer ordered the ship's ventilation system to be turned on to clear fumes from ruptured fuel lines, and the *Taiho* quickly became a floating bomb. A spark ignited the volatile fumes, causing a catastrophic explosion, and the carrier slid beneath the waves within an hour. Furthermore, just after noon the submarine USS *Cavalla* slammed three torpedoes into the aircraft carrier *Shokaku*. Hours later, the ship was shattered by a massive internal explosion and sank.

U.S. search planes hunted the Japanese warships throughout the next day, but it was late when Ozawa's force was finally discovered. Mitscher, aware that the enemy ships were steaming at the outermost range of his planes and his returning pilots would probably have to land on decks

ADMIRAL CHESTER W. NIMITZ *served as the U.S. Navy Commander in Chief in the Pacific. Nimitz assumed command days after Pearl Harbor and led the revitalized fighting force to victory.*

in gathering darkness, quickly turned his carriers into the wind and launched 240 aircraft. The sun was low in the west when the U.S. planes found their target. Sweeping in to attack, they seriously damaged the carriers *Zuikaku*, *Ryuho*, and *Junyo* and sank the light carrier *Hiyo*. As combat operations ebbed, the most formidable foe faced by the Americans during the Battle of the Philippine Sea turned out to be darkness. Numerous accidents occurred as planes with nearly empty fuel tanks attempted to land on their carriers. Other pilots were forced to ditch in the open sea and await rescue. Courageously, Mitscher risked attack by enemy submarines by ordering his ships to turn on their lights and fire star shells to assist the returning pilots. Eighty-two planes were lost, but the majority of the downed airmen were plucked from the water the next day.

The Battle of the Philippine Sea resulted in the destruction of Japanese carrier air power. Soemu had lost three carriers and more than 400 planes over two disastrous days. More than 200 land-based planes had been shot down or destroyed on the ground as well. The victory had cost the Americans 130 aircraft and relatively few casualties. After the Philippine Sea, the final defeat of Japan was a foregone conclusion.

Warsaw Rising 1944

IN AUGUST 1944, POLISH VOLUNTEERS *equipped with whatever weapons they could obtain seized much of Warsaw from the German occupation forces, beginning a long and bitter struggle for the city.*

AS WORLD WAR II MOVED TOWARD ITS CONCLUSION, THE ALLIES AGREED TO DIVIDE EUROPE INTO SPHERES OF INFLUENCE. THIS WAS NOT ACCEPTABLE TO THE POLISH PEOPLE, WHO WANTED ONCE AGAIN TO BE A FREE AND SOVEREIGN NATION. TO DEMONSTRATE THEIR INDEPENDENCE, THE POLES PLANNED AN UPRISING TO LIBERATE THEIR CAPITAL BEFORE THE ADVANCING RED ARMY ARRIVED.

By 1944, it was obvious that Poland was going to be "liberated" by the Soviet Union, which meant inevitably falling into its sphere of influence. The Poles did not welcome this prospect. They wanted a free and independent state and that meant doing more than waiting for one foreign army to leave and another to arrive. A Polish plan, named Operation "Tempest," called for orchestrated uprisings in several cities and a campaign of attacks in various regions of the country. This would hopefully drive the German occupiers out before the Red Army arrived. Once

BATTLE FACTS

Who: More than 40,000 Polish irregulars versus German occupying forces of roughly 25,000 troops.

What: The Uprising began on August 1, 1944 as part of a nationwide rebellion. It was intended to last for only a few days until the Soviet Army reached the city. However, it developed into a long urban guerrilla campaign against the occupiers.

Where: Warsaw, Poland.

When: August–October 1944.

Why: The Poles sought to reestablish their sovereignty after four years of Nazi-German occupation.

Outcome: The uprising was crushed with great loss of life. It is estimated that more than 200,000 civilians died, while 700,000 were expelled from the city.

the capital was liberated, members of the Polish government would come out of hiding and assume control. The largest resistance organization was named *Armia Krajowa* (Home Army). It had more than 400,000 members, who were armed with weapons dropped by the Allies or captured from German sources. Thus there was no shortage of willing and experienced fighters available for the operation. The resistance forces had been fighting this kind of guerrilla war for years, albeit on a smaller scale. Now they saw their opportunity to win a decisive victory.

THE UPRISING

The uprising in Warsaw began in earnest on August 1, 1944, against about 11,000 German troops in the city under the overall command of Lieutenant-General Reiner Stahel (1892–1955). Initial progress was promising—by August 4, most of Warsaw was under Polish control. All that was necessary was to hang on until the Red Army arrived. Yet even as the Poles were reaching the high-water mark of their uprising, an organized response began to unfold. German reinforcements arrived. All German forces were placed under a single commander, General Erich von dem Bach (1899–1972), an SS officer who launched a brutal suppression of resistance. Moreover, the uprising had been intended as a short campaign, to end with the Red Army arriving at the city limits. Yet the Red Army remained strangely inactive, suddenly unable or perhaps unwilling to make much progress in its advance. Thus the Poles were forced to fight on.

By September 2, the tide had turned. Under air attack and bombardment by distant artillery to which they had no reply, the Poles had to pull out of the old town, using the sewers to avoid detection. The fighting went on elsewhere, the German forces grinding their way through the city in a manner not dissimilar to the urban hell of Stalingrad.

By the middle of September, the advance units of the Red Army had almost reached the Vistula and were pushing the Germans back once again. Yet the Soviet Army halted short of

Warsaw and stayed there, and withheld their support from Free Polish forces attempting to aid the beleaguered Home Army. For although the Soviets had been calling for a Polish uprising for months, Stalin did not desire the Warsaw insurgency to succeed. He wanted Poland under Soviet control, not independent, and the insurgents had risen in the name of the pro-Western government-in-exile based in London. By waiting until the rising was crushed and then moving in, he ensured that Poland would fall under the sway of Moscow.

On October 2, 1944, the Home Army surrendered what was left of its forces in Warsaw. Some of the insurgents did not turn themselves in, but tried to fade out of sight among the population. Of those who did surrender, some were treated as any other prisoners of war and sent west to camps in Germany. Of the remainder, some were sent to concentration camps, some to labor projects, and most dispersed and released. None was allowed to remain in the city. Warsaw was then systematically destroyed by fire and explosives. Some houses escaped, but all public and historic buildings were deliberately targeted. The Red Army finally entered Warsaw in mid-January 1945, by which time very little remained of the city.

HITLER TOOK A PERSONAL INTEREST *in the battle for Warsaw, allocating large resources and condoning the harsh measures used to suppress the insurgency.*

PARATROOPERS FROM THE U.S. 82ND AIRBORNE DIVISION *await takeoff on board a C-47 transporter as part of Operation "Market Garden." The 82nd successfully seized the bridge at Nijmegen.*

Operation "Market Garden"   1944

THE TWO OPERATIONS "MARKET" AND "GARDEN" WERE COMPLEMENTARY HALVES OF A DARING PLAN TO SEIZE STRATEGIC BRIDGES WITH AIRBORNE TROOPS, THEN RUSH GROUND FORCES UP AND ACROSS THEM TO SECURE THE POSITIONS. HAD IT SUCCEEDED, "MARKET GARDEN" MIGHT HAVE SHORTENED THE WAR BY A YEAR.

O peration "Market Garden" was Field Marshal Bernard Montgomery's (1887–1976) gambit to accelerate the end of the war after the liberation of France and Belgium. The plan was for British, U.S., and Free Polish airborne forces to seize seven key bridges spaced between the Dutch-Belgian border to Arnhem farther north, the paratroopers holding these bridges while the British XXX Corps advanced along the connecting road to relieve them. By so doing, Montgomery hoped to establish a bridgehead over the Lower Rhine, outflanking the German

BATTLE FACTS

Who: Allied airborne and ground forces, including the British 1st Airborne Division and Polish Brigade, opposed by German armored and infantry units.

What: Although at first the advance was a success, German resistance was heavier than expected.

Where: The Netherlands, near the town of Arnhem, on the Rhine River.

When: September 17–25, 1944.

Why: The Allies wanted to get across the Rhine quickly, bypassing major German defenses and trapping large numbers of German forces in the Netherlands.

Outcome: The operation was a failure, prolonging the war in northwestern Europe by at least a few months.

THIS AERIAL PHOTOGRAPH *shows the bridge at Arnhem that the British 1st Airborne Division struggled to hold before withdrawing after a week's bitter fighting in September 1944.*

Siegfried Line defenses that were proving so tenacious. Codenamed "Market Garden" ("Market" was the airborne component, "Garden" the ground advance), the operation was high risk. RAF concerns about the air defenses in the Arnhem region meant that the paras were to be dropped at a distance from their objectives, requiring a forced march and giving the enemy time to react to the threat. XXX Corps had to make smooth progress along a heavily contested road to ensure the airborne units were not cut off and destroyed. Furthermore, the veteran II SS-Panzer Corps was in the region, rebuilding its strength after taking a battering in Normandy. Field Marshal Walter Model (1891–1945) was also in the immediate vicinity. Model had gained a well deserved reputation as an excellent commander on the Eastern Front, where he had staved off defeat again and again by scraping a battlegroup together and improvising a brilliant battle plan. Even though British intelligence was ignorant of many of these factors, there were some Allied commanders who felt that Arnhem might in fact be a "bridge too far."

COSTLY FAILURE

"Market Garden" was launched on September 17, 1944. The first three days of the action brought some encouragement for the Allies. On the first day, the U.S. 101st Airborne Division captured its allocated bridges just north of Eindhoven, while the U.S. 82nd Airborne Division took its bridges over the Maas at Grave. By September 19, XXX Corps had pushed far enough north to link up with all the U.S. paratroopers, and a combined attack on the 20th secured Nijmegen bridge, roughly 10 miles (16 km) from Arnhem itself.

The experience of the British 1st Airborne Division at Arnhem, however, gave little cause for cheer. The British paras had to fight their way into Arnhem against powerful resistance, which included German armor. Model's fast response meant that very few of the paras assigned to take the Arnhem bridges reached the town at all. Elements of 2nd Battalion, the Parachute Regiment under Lieutenant-Colonel John Frost (1912–93), along with an assortment of troops gathered along the way, were able to reach the north end of the bridge and hang on there, but this was the limit of the paras' success. Model assigned part of his force to contain the paras and began gathering everything else he could find to halt the armored attack coming his way.

XXX Corps finally managed to cross the Waal, and advanced to only 11 miles (18 km) from Frost and his paras. A rapid advance might have been in order, but the Allied force was tired and disorganized. It was not possible to put together a sufficient force to break through and achieve anything at Arnhem. The situation was still very fluid, with German forces coming in from the flanks and at times cutting the Allied line of communications. Model's forces at Arnhem were gaining strength and Frost was finally overrun.

AFTERMATH

The operation had obviously failed and it was time to salvage all they could. As many paras as possible were brought across the river in assault boats during the night of September 25–26, but 7,000 remained behind as dead, wounded, or prisoners. The goal of getting across the Rhine quickly and without fighting through heavy defenses had not been achieved. A combination of mischance, poor planning, and the determination of the enemy robbed the operation of success. As a result, the Allies were forced to fight their way in "through the front door" and took heavy casualties as a result.

HALTED ALONG AN ICY ROAD *in Belgium, German Panzer V "Panther" tanks spearhead the German Ardennes offensive. With its large gun, the Panther was one of the best tanks of World War II.*

Battle of the Bulge 1944–45

AT 5:30 A.M. ON DECEMBER 16, 1944, THE THUNDER OF HUNDREDS OF GERMAN GUNS SHATTERED THE STILLNESS OF THE ARDENNES, A RELATIVELY QUIET SECTOR OF THE ALLIED LINES ON THE GERMAN FRONTIER. IT WAS THE BEGINNING OF OPERATION *"WACHT AM RHEIN"* ("WATCH ON THE RHINE"), A LAST GAMBLE BY ADOLF HITLER IN THE WEST.

The *Führer's* objective was to force a wedge between the Allied Twelfth and Twenty-First Army Groups with a fast-moving armored thrust that would drive across the Meuse River and on to the vital Belgian port city of Antwerp. Hitler also hoped subsequently to shift forces to meet a coming offensive in the East, where the Soviet Red Army was poised to strike across the Vistula River into the heart of Germany. Hitler instructed three armies—Sixth

BATTLE FACTS

Who: German forces under the command of *Führer* Adolf Hitler (1889–1945) and his generals versus Allied forces under General Dwight Eisenhower (1890–1969).

What: Hitler hoped to divide Allied army groups in the West, drive to the port of Antwerp, and change the course of the war.

Where: The front lines in Belgium, France, and Luxembourg.

When: December 16, 1944 to January 15, 1945.

Why: Hitler sought to divide the Western Allies and gain time to confront the coming Soviet offensive along the Vistula River in the East.

Outcome: The battle resulted in a disastrous defeat for Nazi Germany. Less than four months later, the war in Europe was over.

Panzer under SS General Josef "Sepp" Dietrich (1892–1966) to the north, Fifth Panzer commanded by General Hasso von Manteuffel (1897–1978) in the center, and Seventh Army under General Erich Brandenberger (1897–1955) farther south—to strike on a 60-mile (97-km) front with 275,000 troops, hundreds of tanks, and nearly 2,000 artillery pieces.

Launched on December 16, the German Ardennes offensive achieved complete surprise, initially overwhelming many inexperienced U.S. units on the way and making good advances through the snowbound landscape. Dietrich's armored spearhead, commanded by SS Colonel Joachim Peiper (1951–76), pushed hard for several key bridges over the Meuse and other waterways, which would facilitate rapid crossings, but his force was eventually surrounded and destroyed. In addition, U.S. troops at the far north of the advance, around Elsenborn, held on doggedly, creating the northern shoulder of the German "bulge."

Brandenberger's thrust ran into the veteran U.S. 9th Armored and 4th Infantry Divisions, and made little or no progress along the southern edge of the offensive. In the center, Manteuffel's tanks came closest to reaching the Meuse near Dinant, roughly 50 miles (80 km) from their start line. A heroic stand by elements of the U.S. 7th Armored Division at the town of St. Vith delayed the Germans for six days. The town did not fall until December 23 and British Field Marshal Bernard Montgomery (1887–1976), placed in command of forces north of the bulge, used the time to consolidate his defenses.

"NUTS!"

Southwest of St. Vith, the Belgian crossroads town of Bastogne proved critical to the outcome of the "Battle of the Bulge." Continued possession of Bastogne by the Americans would deny the Germans use of a key road network and slow their advance considerably. On December 17, the vanguard of Manteuffel's forces reached the outskirts of the town. Unable to capture it by direct assault, the Germans bypassed Bastogne, which was defended by the lightly armed 101st Airborne Division and elements of other units.

The encircled paratroopers held on by their fingernails, but when heavy German forces drew the noose tighter on December 22 they were invited to surrender. The ranking U.S. officer in the embattled town was

Major-General Anthony McAuliffe (1898–1975), and his famous reply to the German ultimatum was simply, "Nuts!" Although he was in dire straits, McAuliffe did have reason to hope. Foul weather, which had benefited the Germans, had begun to clear the previous day and allowed an airdrop of desperately needed supplies, plus the predations of Allied ground-attack aircraft. Of even greater importance, relief for the beleaguered defenders of Bastogne was already on the way in the form of U.S. Third Army under General George Patton (1885–1945). Hardly stopping to rest or eat, the men of Third Army penetrated the German perimeter and Patton's spearhead, the 4th Armored Division, made contact with the 101st Airborne on the day after Christmas.

The relief of Bastogne sealed the fate of the German offensive, while heroic defensive efforts at Elsenborn Ridge, St. Vith, and elsewhere had contained the German thrust within a week. Soon the great bulge began to resemble a gigantic Allied pincer movement rather than a tremendous German threat. As 1944 ebbed away, so too did Hitler's dream of ultimate victory in the West. The offensive had cost the *Führer* dearly. More than 120,000 Germans had been killed, wounded, or taken prisoner during a month of hard fighting. Scores of tanks and other armored vehicles had been destroyed or abandoned. American casualties totaled nearly 80,000, with about 8,500 dead, 46,000 wounded, and more than 20,000 captured. Both sides had suffered terribly. For the Allies, however, the losses could be made good. For the Germans, they could not.

BARRICADES NOW OPEN, AMERICAN TROOPS MOVE THROUGH A VILLAGE *in Belgium that shows signs of heavy fighting, late December 1944.*

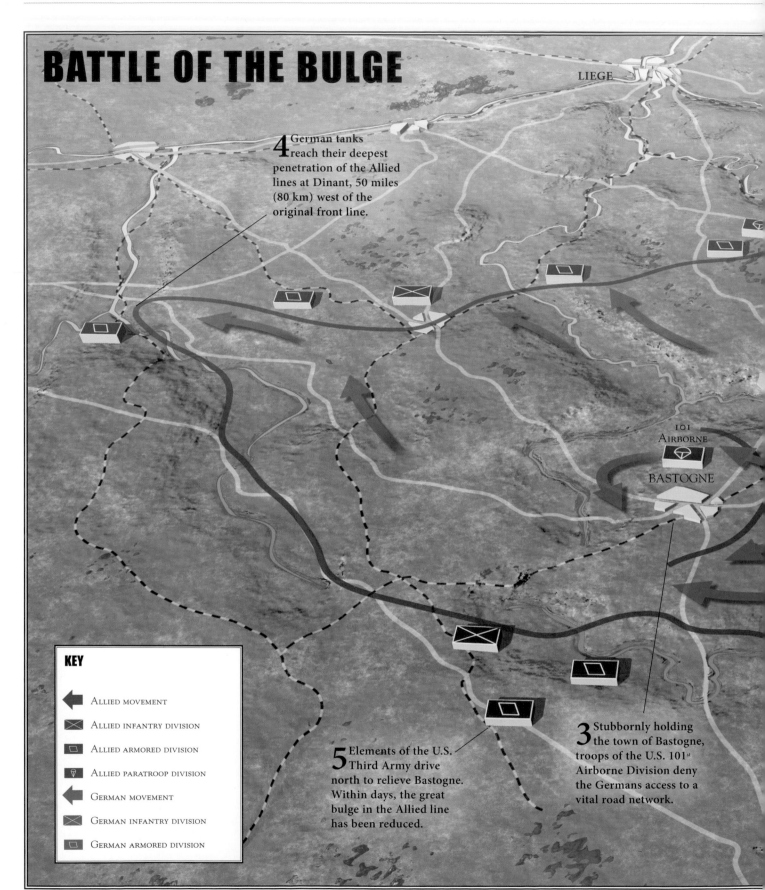

BATTLE OF THE BULGE

LIEGE

4 German tanks reach their deepest penetration of the Allied lines at Dinant, 50 miles (80 km) west of the original front line.

101 AIRBORNE

BASTOGNE

3 Stubbornly holding the town of Bastogne, troops of the U.S. 101st Airborne Division deny the Germans access to a vital road network.

5 Elements of the U.S. Third Army drive north to relieve Bastogne. Within days, the great bulge in the Allied line has been reduced.

KEY

ALLIED MOVEMENT

ALLIED INFANTRY DIVISION

ALLIED ARMORED DIVISION

ALLIED PARATROOP DIVISION

GERMAN MOVEMENT

GERMAN INFANTRY DIVISION

GERMAN ARMORED DIVISION

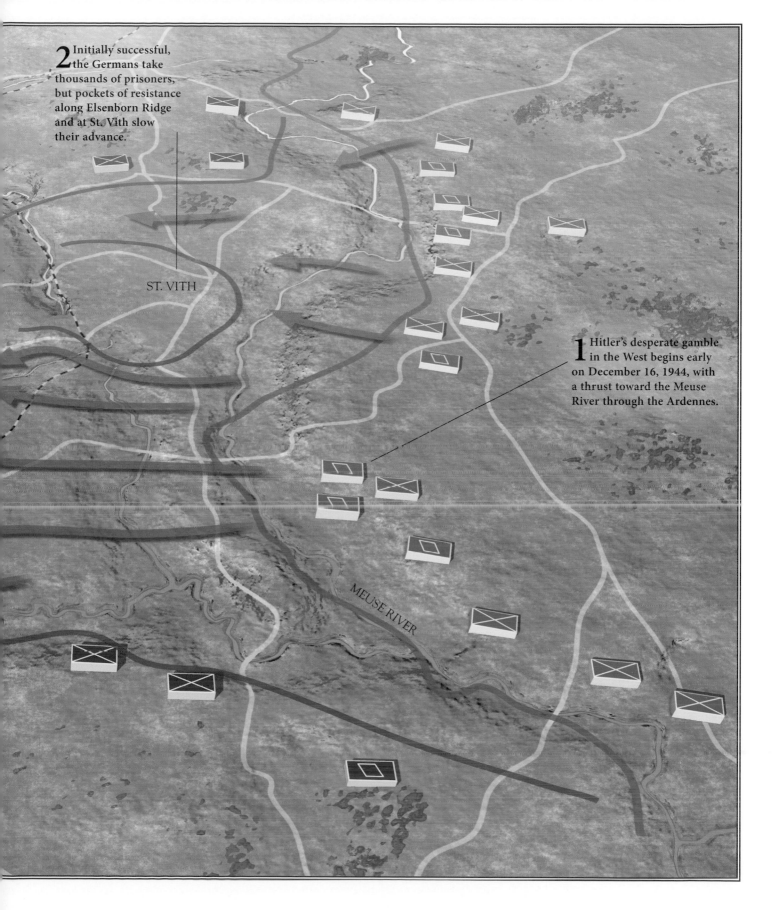

2 Initially successful, the Germans take thousands of prisoners, but pockets of resistance along Elsenborn Ridge and at St. Vith slow their advance.

ST. VITH

1 Hitler's desperate gamble in the West begins early on December 16, 1944, with a thrust toward the Meuse River through the Ardennes.

MEUSE RIVER

AMERICAN ASSAULT CRAFT *approach the black, volcanic-sand beaches of Iwo Jima. The Japanese waited for the landing areas to choke with men and equipment before opening fire.*

Iwo Jima   1945

THE ISLAND ROAD TO TOKYO WAS LONG AND BLOODY FOR THE U.S. MILITARY. ALTHOUGH THE UNITED STATES HAD SEIZED THE INITIATIVE IN THE PACIFIC, IT WAS CLEAR THROUGHOUT THE CAMPAIGN THAT THE JAPANESE WERE RESOURCEFUL AND TENACIOUS FOES—WILLING TO FIGHT TO THE DEATH. AS THE PACIFIC WAR ENTERED ITS FOURTH YEAR, AMERICAN PLANNERS WERE RESIGNED TO THE FACT THAT FINAL VICTORY WOULD NECESSITATE AN INVASION OF THE JAPANESE HOME ISLANDS, INCLUDING IWO JIMA.

Shaped like a pork chop, Iwo Jima is scarcely 5 miles (8 km) long and 4.5 miles (7.2 km) across at its widest point. At the southern tip, the 550-ft (170-m) Mount Suribachi rises to dominate most of the island. Despite its relatively diminutive stature, by 1945 Iwo Jima had been turned into a fortress by more than 25,000 Japanese troops and a large contingent of Korean

BATTLE FACTS

Who: Japanese troops under Lieutenant-General Kuribayashi Tadamichi (1891–1945) versus U.S. Marines under Lieutenant-General Holland M. Smith (1882–1967).

What: U.S. Marines tried to capture the island in the Volcanoes group from the 20,000 strong defenders.

Where: The island of Iwo Jima, less than 700 miles (1,127 km) from the Japanese home islands.

When: February 19–March 26, 1945.

Why: Iwo Jima could provide a staging area for future operations and a safe haven for bombers returning from raids on Japanese cities.

Outcome: U.S. Marines captured Iwo Jima after more than a month of savage fighting, suffering 7,000 killed and 19,000 wounded.

laborers under the command of Lieutenant-General Kuribayashi Tadamichi. Across the island the Japanese had constructed a labyrinth of pillboxes, bunkers, machine-gun nests, artillery emplacements, and spider holes large enough only for a single soldier. Many of the Japanese guns were sited with interlocking fields of fire, their positions reinforced with steel, concrete, coconut logs, and heaps of sand to absorb the shockwaves of American preinvasion bombardment. The Japanese had also honeycombed Mount Suribachi itself with tunnels, and artillery and machine-gun emplacements near the mouths of caves.

INCH BY INCH

The U.S. plan to take the island—Operation "Detachment"—was straightforward. The 4th and 5th Marine Divisions with the 3rd Division in reserve, more than 40,000 strong, were to assault beaches on the southern end of Iwo Jima. From there, they would isolate and capture Mount Suribachi, fight their way across the island, take the airfields, and subdue pockets of Japanese resistance.

On the morning of February 19, 1945, U.S. Marines hit the beach on Iwo Jima. For 20 minutes, there was virtually no reaction from the Japanese defenders—Kuribayashi had told his men to hold their fire until the invasion beaches were choked with American troops and landing craft. Then with a thunderous crash, the eerie silence was broken. Japanese bullets and shells rained down on the Americans and inflicted terrible casualties. To make matters worse, the black volcanic sand of the island made footing difficult and impeded the progress of tracked vehicles. Nevertheless, the Marines braved withering enemy fire and managed

to cut off Mount Suribachi on the first day. Subsequently they fought their way to the base of the extinct volcano and began an arduous climb. Although the high ground was far from secure, on February 23 a patrol worked its way to the top and triumphantly raised a small U.S. flag amid exploding Japanese grenades and sniper fire.

In spite of this early success, more than a month of terrible close-quarters fighting lay ahead for the Americans, whose numbers continued to grow on this small spit of land. Progress was measured in yards, and otherwise nondescript locales earned lasting nicknames such as "Bloody Gorge," the "Amphitheater," "Turkey Knob," and the "Meat Grinder." Marines crawled forward to fling grenades and satchel charges into the firing slits of Japanese bunkers or the mouths of caves. Flamethrowers forced out defenders, or incinerated them where they stood. Some caves were sealed with explosives or bulldozers, burying their enemy occupants alive. Several times, the Japanese hurled themselves against well entrenched Marines in suicidal *banzai* charges and died to the last man.

By February 27, the two completed airstrips were in U.S. hands and a third, which was under construction, had been taken as well. On March 4, with the battle for the island still raging, the first four-engined Boeing B-29 Superfortress bomber made an emergency landing on Iwo Jima. During the remainder of the war, more than 2,200 such landings were made and the estimated number of airmen saved topped 24,000. Fighters soon began flying escort missions with the big bombers as well.

Not until March 26, after 36 days of combat, was Iwo Jima finally declared secure. The Japanese garrison on the island was virtually wiped out during the fighting. The Marines captured only 216 prisoners and some 3,000 holdouts were still being eliminated months later. Although Kuribayashi's body was never found, he was reported either to have committed suicide or to have been killed while leading a final desperate *banzai* charge. The Americans lost more than 6,800 dead and 17,000 wounded at Iwo Jima, but the objectives of Operation "Detachment" had been achieved.

GRUMMAN F4F WILDCAT *fighter planes prepare to take off on a support mission from the deck of the escort carrier USS Makin. U.S. air superiority was complete by this stage in the war.*

225

LARGE ARTILLERY PIECES *such as this tractor-borne 6.5 in (152 mm) gun formed a significant arm of Red Army forces shattering Berlin, along with assault guns, infantry, and support troops.*

Battle for Berlin 1945

BY EARLY APRIL 1945, BERLIN WAS A FORTRESS CITY: ONE MILLION MEN WERE CONCENTRATED IN THE SECTOR WITH 10,400 GUNS AND MORTARS, 1,500 TANKS AND ASSAULT GUNS, AND 3,300 AIRCRAFT. YET BERLINERS, WHO HAD BEEN ASSURED THAT THE RED ARMY WOULD NEVER REACH GERMANY, SOON REALIZED THAT THE ENEMY WAS EDGING INTO THE CITY SUBURBS.

The Soviets who were now preparing to assault Berlin had a massive superiority in strength—2,500,000 men, more than 42,000 guns and mortars, more than 6,200 tanks and self-propelled guns, and 8,300 aircraft. German manpower, by contrast, ranged from 15-year-old Hitler Youth personnel to men in their seventies.

At 3 A.M. Berlin time on April 16, 1945, Soviet artillery opened fire in an unimaginable bombardment, initiating the Battle of Berlin. Red Army infantry north and south of

BATTLE FACTS

Who: Red Army forces led by Marshal Ivan Konev (1897–1973) and Marshal Georgi Zhukov (1896–1974), versus Hitler's designated defender of Berlin, General Karl Weidling (1891–1955).

What: Victory was eventually assured as eight Soviet armies overwhelmed Berlin.

Where: From the Oder River to the capital, Berlin.

When: Between April 16 and May 2, 1945.

Why: The Allies believed that only with the successful assault on Berlin and defeat of the forces controlling it could the war be brought to a final, irreversible conclusion.

Outcome: Nazism was effectively defeated, leaving Berliners to count the cost. The daunting task of rebuilding a shattered Europe lay ahead.

the bridgehead situated near the town of Kustrin plunged into the Oder River, their log boats supporting guns and rafts heavy with supplies. The troops of Marshal Zhukov's First Belarusan Front had been ordered by Stalin to make the attack on Berlin from the bridgehead. At the Seelow Heights, situated some 60 miles (90 km) east of Berlin and overlooking the western floodplain of the Oder, the German reception was fierce and the Soviets were held off until late on April 17. This was in contrast with Konev's First Ukrainian Front, which had crossed the Neisse to the south across open terrain more favorable to tanks and made rapid progress. Stalin ordered Konev to turn two of his tank armies northward to aid Zhukov. The breakthrough to the Berlin suburbs was achieved on April 19.

The next day was the *Führer's* birthday, marked by barrages of exploding artillery shells and the deafening howls of multibarreled rocket launchers. But still there were forces desperately fighting to hold their positions around the city. Ninth Army under General Theodor Busse (1897–1986) had originally been given the task of blocking the Soviets' direct route to Berlin, while Third Panzer Army under General Hasso von Manteuffel (1897–1978) had been positioned farther north. Although von Manteuffel had some success and managed to hang on briefly, it was clear by April 21 that Busse's forces were on the point of total collapse. An appeal went out to Lieutenant-General Hans Krebs (1898–1945) of the High Command of the Army Chief of Staff, that Busse should withdraw or face total destruction. The reply was predictable: Ninth Army was to stay where it was and hold on to its positions.

HOPES OF RESCUE

Hitler's grip on reality slipped further even as the Soviets pushed deeper into the streets of Berlin, fighting for every building and street in the face of a shockingly tenacious, albeit futile, defense. On April 23, Hitler received a blunt report from General Karl Weidling, Battle Commandant of Berlin, that there was only sufficient ammunition for two days' fighting. Nevertheless, Weidling hung on with such forces as he possessed while the Soviet stranglehold grew tighter within the city, now a few blocks from Hitler's bunker. At this time, the remnants of the Twelfth and Ninth Armies, together with as many civilian refugees as possible, were moving westward, attempting to cross the Elbe into U.S. Army-occupied territory, away from the vengeful Soviets. On April 25, the two giant arms of a Soviet pincer closed around the city.

On April 30, Hitler bowed to the inevitable and shot himself in his bunker. By now, Berlin was a raging inferno throughout. For the Soviets, there was a prime objective: the capture of the iconic Reichstag, still heavily defended by its garrison. Even so, by early afternoon the Soviet Red

victory banner was flying from the dome. It was left to Weidling, the last commander of the Berlin defense zone, formally to surrender the city to the Soviets at 1 P.M. on May 2. By 4 A.M., the fighting was over. Figures for the number of dead during the battle could never be calculated precisely, but it is generally thought that up to 100,000 German troops lost their lives and a likely equal number of civilians. Around the same number of Soviet soldiers died. Berlin, in effect, had to be recreated.

MARSHAL GEORGI ZHUKOV

A man of peasant background, Georgi Zhukov emerged as the most outstanding military figure in the Red Army during World War II. He was created First Deputy Supreme Commander in Chief Soviet Armed Forces in August 1942, serving in the post throughout the conflict. Responsible for the attack that relieved Stalingrad, he went on to coordinate the First and Second Belarusan Fronts in the 1944 summer offensive, and he commanded the First Belarusan Front in the final assault on Germany and capture of Berlin, becoming Commander in Chief of Soviet occupation forces. In 1955–57, he served as Soviet Minister of Defense, but had long incurred Stalin's jealousy, and was dismissed and disgraced for allegedly challenging the Communist Party leadership of the Armed Forces. Partly rehabilitated under Khrushchev, he died in June 1974, his ashes buried in the Kremlin wall with full military honors.

U.S. LANDING CRAFT BRING STORES ASHORE *on April 13, 1945, during the battle for Okinawa. The packed horizon gives an indication of the size of the naval armada involved in the operation.*

Okinawa 1945

THE ALLIES' AMPHIBIOUS INVASION OF OKINAWA WAS A MASSIVE UNDERTAKING, AGAINST HEAVY AND DETERMINED RESISTANCE. JAPANESE FORCES ON THE ISLAND WERE AWARE THAT THEY FACED OVERWHELMING OPPOSITION AND WERE DETERMINED TO EXACT AS HIGH A PRICE AS THEY COULD FROM THE INVADERS.

The invasion of Okinawa, the southernmost of Japan's Ryuku group of islands, was going to be different from many of the other Allied campaigns in the Pacific. While some of the islands the Allies assaulted were garrisoned by small forces, often with little artillery or air defense equipment, Okinawa was defended by the Thirty-Second Army under the command of Lieutenant-General Ushijima Mitsuru (1887–1945), with plentiful artillery. The island was also home to nearly half a million civilians, with tragic results.

The Allied ground commander was Lieutenant-General Simon Buckner Jr. (1886–1945), commanding the U.S. Tenth Army. Buckner had a Marine and an infantry

BATTLE FACTS

Who: Allied (mainly U.S.) forces numbering 548,000 soldiers and 1,300 ships, versus 100,000 Japanese ground, air, and naval forces.

What: The Allies launched the largest amphibious operation of the whole Pacific campaign.

Where: Okinawa, in the Pacific Ocean.

When: April 1–June 21, 1945.

Why: The island was to be used as a staging point for the invasion of the Japanese homeland.

Outcome: The Allies captured Okinawa and 90 percent of the buildings on the island were completely destroyed. Okinawa provided a fleet anchorage, troop staging areas, and airfields in close proximity to Japan, allowing the Allies to prepare for the invasion of Japan.

corps under his command, each of two divisions, plus an additional Marine and two more army divisions as a reserve. After preliminary air attacks over a two-week period, and while U.S. Navy vessels battled with *kamikaze* air attacks, U.S. Marines began going ashore on Okinawa on March 31, 1945. The initial landings went well, largely because the defenders knew they could not be strong everywhere and had concentrated their forces where they would be most effective. Okinawa is a long, narrow island running broadly southwest-northeast. The Allies made steady progress in the more lightly defended north, reaching the end of the island by April 13, though the Motobu Peninsula and the island of Ie Shima were stubbornly held and not taken until April 21. Pushing south was more of a problem. Progress was slow and determinedly opposed by well dug-in Japanese troops. High ground, caves, and artificial strongpoints had to be cleared by assault, resulting in hand-to-hand combat. Each position was hotly contested and the Allies took wearying levels of dead and wounded as they pushed onward.

The second half of April established a grim pattern of attack and counterattack that saw little major land gain on either side. This stalemate went on until the end of the month despite fresh U.S. troops rotating into the line. On May 11 Buckner went back over to the offensive, and during the remainder of the month U.S. forces finally broke the imposing "Shuri Line" defenses, pushing the Japanese forces back to a final position on the southern tip of the island.

THE "TYPHOON OF STEEL"

The costly advance was then resumed, with the Marines forced to prize fanatical defenders out of their positions. Many fought to the last or killed themselves to evade capture. Among them were Ushijima and his chief of staff, Lieutenant-General Cho Isamu. The remainder held their final line until June 17, when the defense finally collapsed. This was a rare occasion on which significant numbers of Japanese troops surrendered. The U.S. Marines developed techniques to reduce casualties. For example, one method of clearing a cave involved the mouth being taken under heavy fire, after which a flamethrower tank approached and sprayed burning fuel into the interior, clearing any last defenders. However, despite such measures, losses were very severe.

In the last days of the campaign, General Buckner was killed by enemy shellfire, making him the most senior U.S. officer to be killed in action during the war. Heavy shellfire from both sides was a characteristic of the Okinawa campaign, which became known as the "Typhoon of Steel."

The last organized resistance on Okinawa was from the 24th Infantry Division, which was still fighting on June 21. After this formation was broken, pockets of Japanese soldiers held out for another ten days or so, but were mopped up one by one. The most senior Japanese officer captured alive was a major.

Many of those who survived tried to hide among the local population, but were revealed by the Okinawans, who had no reason to shelter their enemies—Japanese soldiers had used Okinawan civilians as human shields or sent them to collect water under fire. In the closing stages of the battle, the Japanese encouraged locals to kill themselves rather than submit to the Allies.

Okinawa was firmly in Allied hands by the end of June, but the operation had cost U.S. forces 50,000 casualties, including 7,613 dead. By contrast, more than 110,000 Japanese soldiers fought to the death in what was a futile defense.

ALTHOUGH THE JAPANESE DEFENSE OF OKINAWA *collapsed on June 17, clearing out the last pockets of resistance took until the end of the month.*

OKINAWA

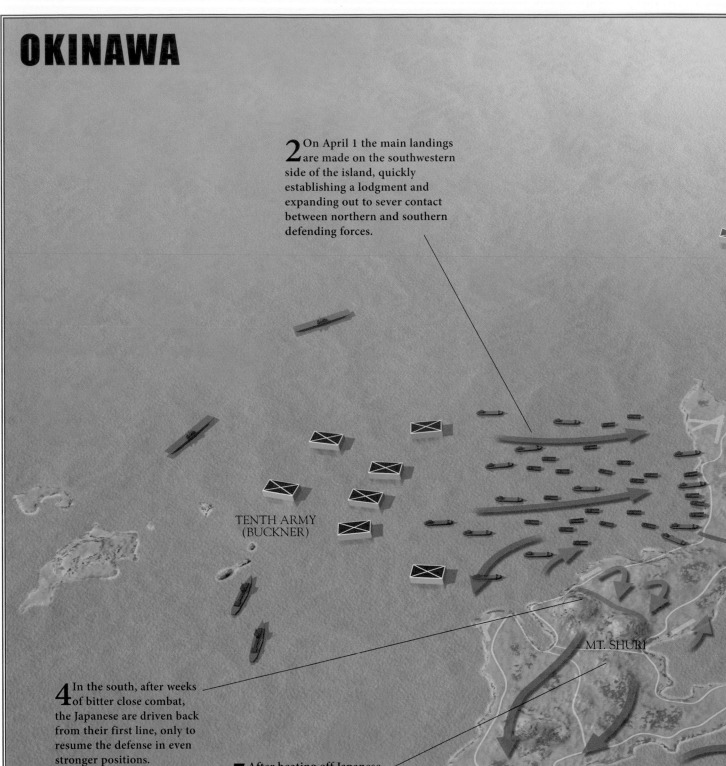

2 On April 1 the main landings are made on the southwestern side of the island, quickly establishing a lodgment and expanding out to sever contact between northern and southern defending forces.

TENTH ARMY
(BUCKNER)

MT. SHURI

4 In the south, after weeks of bitter close combat, the Japanese are driven back from their first line, only to resume the defense in even stronger positions.

5 After beating off Japanese counterattacks, Allied forces finally break the main defensive line around Mount Shuri. Japanese forces prepare to make a last stand.

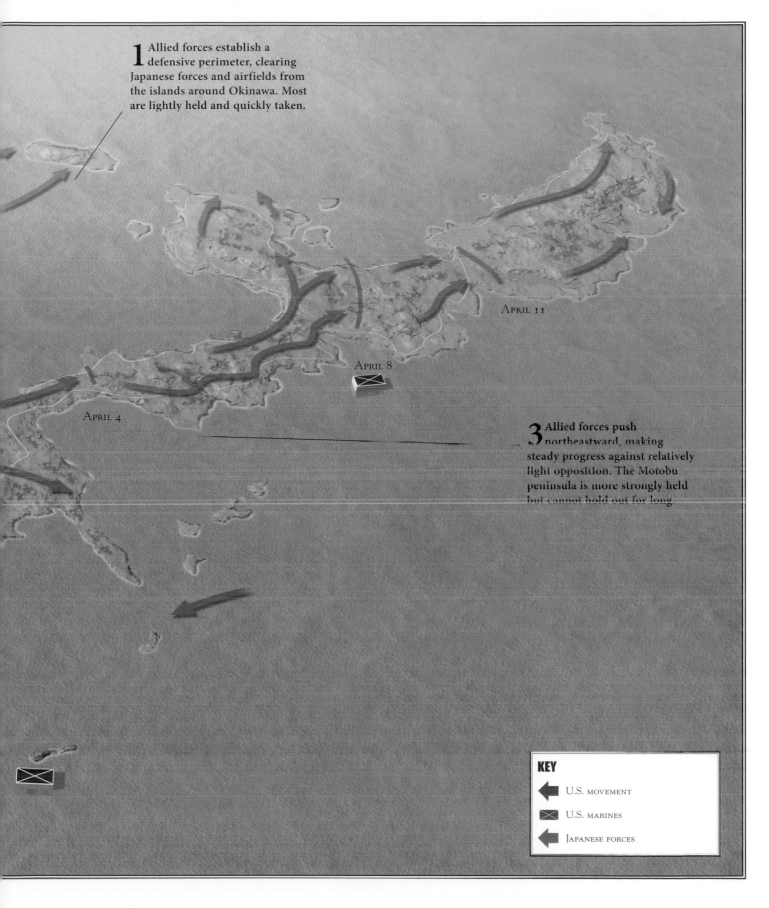

1 Allied forces establish a defensive perimeter, clearing Japanese forces and airfields from the islands around Okinawa. Most are lightly held and quickly taken.

APRIL 11

APRIL 8

APRIL 4

3 Allied forces push northeastward, making steady progress against relatively light opposition. The Motobu peninsula is more strongly held but cannot hold out for long.

KEY

U.S. MOVEMENT

U.S. MARINES

JAPANESE FORCES

U.S. MARINES USING CLIMBING LADDERS *begin an assault against North Korean forces after establishing positions inland from the beach at Inchon, September 1950.*

Inchon 1950

THE UN LANDINGS AT INCHON WERE A STRATEGIC MASTERSTROKE, BYPASSING ENEMY POSITIONS TO CUT THEIR FORCES' MAIN SUPPLY ROUTE.

The North Korean invasion of South Korea on June 25, 1950, was initially a massive success, rapidly taking the capital at Seoul and driving the remnants of the South Korean military southward. United Nations intervention, led by U.S. forces, narrowly succeeded in preventing total victory. The result was North Korean occupation of almost the whole country, with UN forces reduced to defending a toehold in the southeastern corner. The port of Pusan was central to this position.

Although struggling even to hold the Pusan perimeter, UN commanders needed to do more than stand on the defensive. A Communist victory in Korea was not acceptable, and might have political consequences elsewhere. A conventional response would be slow, if it were even feasible, requiring a large buildup of forces and then a costly advance up the country. Drawing on recent experience in World War II, where U.S. forces conducted

BATTLE FACTS

Who: A U.S. Corps comprising one Marine and one Army division under Major-General Edward M. Almond (1892–1979), opposed by around 7,000 North Korean troops under the overall command of Marshal Choe Yong Gun (1900–76).

What: U.S. forces launched a surprise landing at Inchon, permitting a rapid recapture of Seoul.

Where: Inchon, near Seoul on the coast of South Korea.

When: September 15–25, 1950.

Why: Recapturing Seoul would isolate North Korean forces around the Pusan perimeter and tip the strategic balance in favor of UN forces fighting to liberate South Korea.

Outcome: The landing was a total success, leading to the recapture of Seoul.

an island-hopping campaign against the Japanese, UN planners came up with an audacious alternative. A landing at Inchon would allow UN forces to bypass the main enemy positions and recapture Seoul. This was not only a politically critical objective, but it would also cut the main enemy supply line and compromise the entire North Korean effort around Pusan.

HURRIED PREPARATIONS

Inchon was a difficult landing site at best, and fraught with risk. Mudflats made the landing area inaccessible from the sea for 18 hours in every 24, meaning that not only would it be hard to reinforce or resupply the assault force but it might be impossible to withdraw in the event of failure. Inchon had the potential to become a complete disaster if any mistakes were made in planning or execution, which would normally require extensive and careful preparations. However, something had to be done, and fast, so a plan was put together in just a month and vessels were assembled for the attack and its supporting operations. One U.S. Marine division and one Army division were earmarked for the attack.

THE ASSAULT IS LAUNCHED

Unusually high tides on September 15, 1950, allowed relatively easy access to the landing area. The North Koreans had some warning as a result of UN mine-clearance operations and naval bombardment, but their commanders had discounted any possibility of landings near Seoul. There were several thousand troops nearby, but they were not in a state of high readiness. Once alerted, they began to resist as best they could.

The initial objectives were the islands of Wolmi-do and Sowolmi-do. The North Korean commander of the former assured his superiors that he could hold his position, but in the event both islands were overrun by around 7 A.M. This cleared the way for the main assault, but tidal conditions meant that this could not begin until 5:30 P.M.

U.S. MARINE LANDING CRAFT *approach the beach at Inchon as part of the first wave of the assault force, September 15, 1950.*

Going ashore on the mainland, U.S. forces had to deal with a high sea wall behind which were enemy positions. These were not held in strength but still presented a major obstacle. With the benefit of aircraft and naval gunfire support, UN forces were able to drive the enemy from their trenches and bunkers, taking relatively light casualties in so doing.

THE ADVANCE ON SEOUL

After less than 24 hours, U.S. forces were well established ashore and had reached the Inchon-Seoul road. The advance against Seoul itself then began. Benefiting from air support, the UN force was able to reach and surround Seoul, which was then liberated from North Korean control.

With their supply line cut and a major threat in their rear, North Korean forces around Pusan were unable to prevent a UN breakout. Resistance largely collapsed, with 125,000 North Korean troops becoming prisoners. UN forces were able to exploit this situation, pushing into North Korea. However, this triggered a Chinese intervention, which drove the UN back again. Thus began the next phase of the war, a lengthy stalemate along the 38th Parallel.

U.S. MARINE IN KOREA

This U.S. Marine private is carrying ammunition for his M1 .30-caliber rifle in a cartridge belt and also in the cotton bandoliers across his chest— around 200 rounds in total. His main uniform item is a set of olive-drab M1944 fatigues.

FOLLOWING THEIR CAPITULATION AT DIEN BIEN PHU, *French prisoners are marched into captivity, closely watched by attentive Viet Minh guards.*

Dien Bien Phu 1953

DIEN BIEN PHU WAS THE DISASTROUS CULMINATION OF FRANCE'S ATTEMPT TO HOLD ON TO ITS INDOCHINA COLONY. OVER A PERIOD OF NINE YEARS, THE VIET MINH INSURGENTS, LED BY THE INNOVATIVE AND DOGGED GENERAL VO NGUYEN GIAP, WORE DOWN FRENCH CONVENTIONAL FORCES IN HUNDREDS OF MINOR BATTLES AND AMBUSHES.

In late 1953, General Henri Navarre (1898–1983), overall commander of French forces, decided to draw the Viet Minh out into a decisive set-piece battle by establishing a fortified base at the remote northern outpost of Dien Bien Phu, astride the Viet Minh supply lines. As plans for the air-land operation progressed, the abandoned airstrip at Dien Bien Phu, constructed by the Japanese during World War II, was chosen as the landing zone for the launch of Operation "Castor." The initial contingent of 9,000 French airborne troops parachuted or were flown into Dien Bien Phu on November 20, 1953. Crucially,

BATTLE FACTS

Who: Colonel Christian de Castries (1902–91) and 16,000 French and loyal Vietnamese soldiers versus General Vo Nguyen Giap (b. 1911) and 50,000 Viet Minh troops.

What: The two forces fought the decisive battle of the French campaign to retain their colony of Indochina.

Where: The valley and surrounding mountains of Dien Bien Phu in northwestern Vietnam.

When: March 13–May 8, 1954.

Why: The French sought to destroy the Viet Minh in a set-piece battle.

Outcome: Dien Bien Phu was a decisive victory for the Viet Minh, who utilized superior artillery and overwhelming numbers during a successful siege.

CHINA
Dien Bien Phu ✝ • Hanoi
INDOCHINA
• Saigon

VIET MINH COMMANDER *Vo Nguyen Giap discusses strategy with subordinate commanders during planning for operations at Dien Bien Phu.*

they did not attempt to seize the mountainous, jungle-covered high ground that surrounded the base. Instead, the French position was to be defended by a series of nine strongpoints in the valley and lower hills. These were designated "*Gabrielle*," "*Beatrice*," and "*Anne-Marie*" to the north, "*Huguette*," "*Françoise*," and "*Claudine*" to the west, "*Dominique*" and "*Eliane*" to the east, and "*Isabelle*" in the south. Some detractors asserted that the names were those of various mistresses of the French ground commander, Colonel Christian de Castries. The more likely source of their origin is the first nine letters of the alphabet.

Perhaps the most glaring error in the French plan was their underestimation of Viet Minh resolve. Giap ordered communist units in the vicinity to resist as best they could while he marshaled strong forces. As the buildup of French troops at Dien Bien Phu swelled to about 16,000 men during the spring of 1954, the Viet Minh massed five divisions in the rugged mountains. At peak strength, the Viet Minh forces totaled about 50,000. Giap knew that time and terrain were on his side.

In a remarkable feat of logistics, guerrillas and civilian laborers manhandled 200 artillery pieces up steep mountain trails and dug camouflaged emplacements that were virtually undetectable from the valley floor. One Viet Minh veteran of Dien Bien Phu remembered a comrade flinging himself under the wheels of an artillery piece that had broken free of its lines in order to prevent the weapon rolling into a ravine. Large numbers of antiaircraft guns were brought in to counter French airpower and interdict reinforcement and resupply efforts. By the time the first Viet Minh artillery shells came crashing down on Dien Bien Phu in January 1954, the communists outgunned the French four to one and had encircled the lodgment.

THE BATTLE JOINED

After more than three months of preparations, Giap ordered the capture of "*Beatrice*" on March 13. The onslaught began with direct artillery fire. A single shell hit the command post, killing the commander of the 13th Foreign Legion *Demi-Brigade* defending the position, along with his entire staff. At a cost of 600 dead and 1,200 wounded, "*Beatrice*" fell to the Viet Minh in no more than seven hours. Distraught over his inability to direct effective counterbattery fire against the heavy Viet Minh guns, the French artillery commander, Colonel Charles Piroth, committed suicide with a hand grenade. When the communist reduction of the French positions began in earnest, the guerrillas had excavated more than 62 miles (100 km) of trenches around the northern redoubts. After the capture of "*Beatrice*," they tightened the noose further, taking "*Gabrielle*" in two days. The airfield was shut down by concentrated antiaircraft fire, and resupply was sporadic and only by parachute from an altitude that rendered most drops inaccurate. On March 17, "*Anne-Marie*" was abandoned to the communists.

For two more weeks, the Viet Minh continued to dig trenches and harass the tiring French, who were enduring a brutal existence, tending hundreds of wounded with dwindling medical supplies under continuous artillery fire. By March 30, the 1,000 defenders of "*Isabelle*" were cut off. At the end of April, the battered French clung only to portions of "*Huguette*," "*Dominique*," and "*Eliane*." Vigorous Viet Minh attacks on May 7 threatened to overrun the remaining French strongpoints, and de Castries realized that further resistance was futile.

The final fall of Dien Bien Phu on May 8, 1954, was a humiliation for France and effectively ended the nation's involvement in Vietnam. The communists had captured nearly 12,000 prisoners, including 5,000 wounded, and about 1,150 French soldiers had died. Viet Minh casualties were 8,000 dead and more than 15,000 wounded. Giap had paid a high price, but he had achieved a tremendous victory.

Later in 1954, the Geneva Accords divided Vietnam at the 17th parallel. The communist north was supported by the Soviet Union and the People's Republic of China, while the south, which did not ascribe to the terms at Geneva, was backed by the United States. Further conflict was inevitable. The last French soldiers left Vietnam in 1956 as the colonial empire they had bravely defended continued to crumble.

FRENCH PARATROOPER

The airborne forces were an elite component of the French Army, which was defeated at Dien Bien Phu. In full battle dress, this paratrooper carries supplies and ammunition for his automatic weapon, which is slung over his shoulder. Although they fought bravely at Dien Bien Phu, the French underestimated the capabilities of their Viet Minh adversaries.

AN AMERICAN "SKYRAIDER" *ground-attack aircraft bombs North Vietnamese Army (NVA) positions close to the perimeter of the U.S. base at Khe Sanh.*

Khe Sanh   1968

KHE SANH WAS ATTACKED BY NORTH VIETNAMESE FORCES AS PART OF THE 1968 TET OFFENSIVE. HEAVILY SUPPORTED, IT HELD OUT UNTIL RELIEVED.

During the war against the French in what was then Indochina, General Vo Nguyen Giap (b. 1911) led a successful operation against the French base at Dien Bien Phu in 1954. Isolated and surrounded, the base was gradually reduced by artillery fire and ground assaults. Attempts were made to resupply by air, but the deployment of Vietnamese antiaircraft weapons and a shrinking perimeter made this impossible.

The U.S. base at Khe Sanh seemed (to both sides) to be vulnerable to a similar strategy, and so as the 1968 Tet offensive was prepared, North Vietnamese forces surrounded the base and began making probing attacks against the defenses. Considerable numbers of North Vietnamese Army (NVA) troops were either committed to the attacks or held ready nearby. The siege of Khe Sanh may have been intended as a diversion from the main Tet offensive. It is equally possible that the North Vietnamese

BATTLE FACTS

Who: U.S. and Army of the Republic of Vietnam (ARVN) troops numbering 6,000 under the command of Colonel David Lownds (1920–2011), besieged by 20,000 North Vietnamese troops plus supporting forces.

What: The base was besieged and had to be supplied by air. It was bombarded with artillery and forced to repel several ground assaults.

Where: Near the Quang Tri valley in Central Vietnam.

When: January 21–April 14, 1968.

Why: The U.S. base threatened North Vietnamese supply lines and in addition removing it might give the North Vietnamese a political or propaganda advantage.

Outcome: Khe Sanh was relieved by ground forces on April 6.

intended to capture the base to emphasize their successes elsewhere. Either way, fighting had been going on for ten days before the Tet offensive had even began.

The offensive was a success at first. Catching the U.S. and South Vietnamese by surprise, it made significant gains which were nevertheless soon reversed. By the end of March the offensive had failed, but Khe Sanh was still under siege.

THE SIEGE

Despite the large forces available and major efforts being made elsewhere, the North Vietnamese did not immediately attempt to overrun Khe Sanh but instead began a siege that cut off land communications. They were not able to prevent resupply by air, however, and Khe Sanh remained at full fighting efficiency.

Rocket and artillery attacks were conducted against the base, doing considerable damage and causing significant casualties. The outer defenses were also attacked on numerous occasions, but these attacks were not made in the strength required to overrun the base. U.S. forces responded with artillery from the base and from nearby fire bases, firing almost 160,000 shells at the hostiles surrounding the base.

In addition to air resupply, Khe Sanh was also supported by air assets. Fighter-bombers and aircraft as heavy as B-52 bombers delivered 96,000 tons of ordnance on enemy positions around the base. The balance of casualties was heavily on the side of the defenders, but the pressure was kept up nonetheless.

GROUND COMBAT

The only significant North Vietnamese success of the siege was the capture of the Special Forces camp at Lang Vei. Attacked by surprise by a force that included light tanks, the outer defenses of Lang Vei were quickly overrun, though the troops within continued to fight from whatever positions they found themselves in. A rescue mission from the main base at Khe Sanh was successful in extricating the survivors of the attack the next day.

THIS JUNIOR OFFICER IN THE ARMY OF THE REPUBLIC of Vietnam (ARVN) sports a camouflage uniform in the "tiger-stripe" pattern. He carries an M16 assault rifle, with extra ammunition in his chest pouches, while two fragmentation grenades are hooked onto his belt.

U.S. ARMY HU-1 "HUEY" HELICOPTERS LAND *at Khe Sanh base. Helicopters gave U.S. forces a massive advantage in moving men and equipment quickly to counter communist incursions.*

Thereafter the North Vietnamese continued to probe at the base's defenses but despite some local successes were unable to break in. At the time, the U.S. had good reason to fear a repeat of the humiliation suffered by the French at Dien Bien Phu, but the defenses were successfully held until the end of March. By then, the failure of the Tet offensive made the siege of Khe Sanh largely irrelevant, and North Vietnamese troops began to be transferred elsewhere.

OPERATION "PEGASUS"

At the beginning of April, a relief operation codenamed Operation "Pegasus" began. U.S. ground forces advanced toward Khe Sanh while airmobile contingents captured and occupied high ground along the route to prevent ambushes. This was coupled with an increasingly aggressive defense of the base. The relief expedition was able to push through mostly light opposition, though two significant actions were fought against North Vietnamese blocking forces. The lead elements reached Khe Sanh on April 8, and soon afterward the siege was officially declared to be over. There was no clear victory as such; the North Vietnamese were not so much defeated as abandoned the siege, once it ceased to be of benefit to their plans.

237

U.S. ARMORED PERSONNEL CARRIERS *advance into Saigon. The U.S. use of heavy firepower in urban zones, particularly of artillery and air assets, would cause great controversy in the media.*

The Tet Offensive   1968

AS 1967 DREW TO A CLOSE, IT APPEARED THAT THE UNITED STATES WAS GAINING THE UPPER HAND IN THE VIETNAM WAR. THE TET OFFENSIVE OF EARLY 1968, HOWEVER, BEGAN THE STEADY DECLINE OF U.S. FORTUNES IN VIETNAM, DESPITE AN UNDENIABLE MILITARY VICTORY.

In late 1967, Ho Chi Minh (1890–1969) and his military commander, General Vo Nguyen Giap (b. 1911) decided on a radical change in strategy in their war against South Vietnam and the United States. Instead of pursuing the slow, violent grind of revolutionary war, they would gamble on an all-out offensive, hoping to precipitate a general uprising in the South.

The offensive was launched on January 29–30, 1968, during the national Vietnamese Tet Lunar New Year festival, when many Army of the Republic of Vietnam

BATTLE FACTS

Who: The North Vietnamese Army (NVA) and the irregular Viet Cong (VC), versus U.S. forces in Vietnam, plus the Army of the Republic of South Vietnam (ARVN).

What: The Communists launched a major offensive throughout South Vietnam.

Where: The Tet Offensive was launched along the entire length and breadth of South Vietnam.

When: January 29–April 8, 1968.

Why: The Communists hoped to occupy South Vietnam's urban centers and set off an uprising against the South Vietnamese government.

Outcome: Total military defeat for the NVA and VC, although the Western media focused more on the escalation of the conflict rather than U.S. successes.

CHINESE TYPE 56 (AK-47)

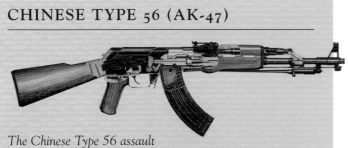

*The Chinese Type 56 assault
rifle was a copy of the Soviet AK-47 and widely deployed by
Vietnamese forces in the Vietnam War. Although it had a
shorter range and lower muzzle velocity than the U.S.-made
M16 assault rifle, it amply compensated by being simple to
operate and firing a larger, more lethal round (0.3 in/
7.62 mm). It was also extremely hardy and technically
robust, making it ideal for difficult jungle fighting conditions.*

(ARVN) troops would be off duty, celebrating with their families. The attack consisted of dozens of simultaneous actions rather than a single campaign. Thirty-six out of 44 provincial capitals, five autonomous cities, 72 district capitals, and 23 military bases came under rocket, mortar, and artillery fire, with followup attacks by either regular North Vietnamese Army (NVA) units of battalion or divisional strength or Viet Cong (VC) assault teams. Most psychologically troubling to the U.S. government were assaults in Saigon on high-value targets such as the U.S. embassy compound, key military headquarters buildings, and the Presidential Palace. In response, U.S. and ARVN forces around Saigon built up ten divisions of combat troops by February 4, and launched a general counteroffensive— Operation *"Tran Hung Do"*—to retake the city. By February 10, all resistance in the capital had been quashed, and it was left to South Vietnamese police to conduct a brutal hunt of VC sympathizers. Crucially for the NVA/VC, the popular uprising it had predicted had not materialized.

THE BATTLE FOR HUE

While the flames of the Tet offensive were being smothered in many parts of South Vietnam, in the exquisite coastal city of Hue, north of Da Nang, the battle would rage until February 25. By the end of January, Hue was entirely occupied by communist troops, and it took some time for U.S.-ARVN forces to begin a counteroffensive. As fighting deepened in Hue itself, the allied forces underwent an appalling introduction to urban warfare, something that had been neglected in many post-World War II training programs. In Hue's New City, the 1st Battalion, 1st Marine Regiment and 2nd Battalion, 5th Marine Regiment managed to make only four blocks' progress in six days of

intense fighting. At first, the historic and architectural status of the city spared it U.S. heavy bombardment. Yet the bitter cost of house-to-house fighting soon changed the policy, and the destruction of Hue began. During the Hue fighting 52,000 rounds of U.S. artillery were fired into the city, along with 7,670 rounds of heavy naval artillery and 600 tons of air-dropped munitions. The consequences for the civilian population were dreadful, but by February 6, most of the major landmarks in the New City had been retaken, and by the 10th its entirety was secured.

The Marines now moved across the Perfume River into the city's historic Citadel, where ARVN units had also been pushing the communists onto the back foot. Gradually ARVN troops blasted the NVA-VC from the northern parts of the Citadel. They eventually retook the airfield and, on February 24, the Imperial Palace on the Perfume River's north bank. By March 2, the whole city was back in Allied hands. In terms of fatalities, the cost of Hue had been 119 U.S. troops, 363 ARVN soldiers, around 8,000 NVA regulars or VC insurgents, and some 6,000 civilians.

END OF THE OFFENSIVE

Hue brought the Tet offensive effectively to a close. For the North, the campaign was a catastrophic failure. Not only had it lost around 54,000 troops (against 11,000 South Vietnamese and 2,000 U.S. troops), but the Viet Cong was almost entirely wiped out as a political and military entity. Furthermore, the lack of a popular uprising destabilized the North's entire belief that the South was simply waiting for the chance to embrace communism. Ironically, however, the Western media saw the offensive as indicating that North Vietnam was far from beaten, contrary to government reassurances, and so increased the pressure for a U.S. pullout.

THIS RARE PHOTOGRAPH SHOWS *a female Vietcong recruit aiming
a Soviet-made RPG-7 rocket-propelled grenade. The RPG proved a
highly effective weapon against vehicles and emplacements.*

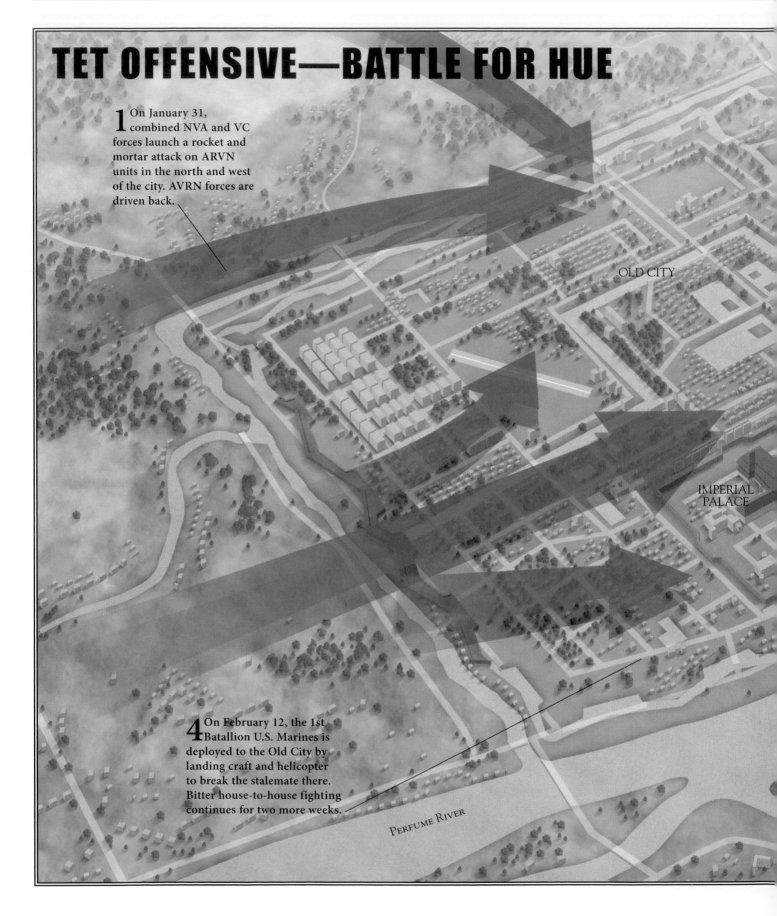

TET OFFENSIVE—BATTLE FOR HUE

1 On January 31, combined NVA and VC forces launch a rocket and mortar attack on ARVN units in the north and west of the city. AVRN forces are driven back.

OLD CITY

IMPERIAL PALACE

4 On February 12, the 1st Batallion U.S. Marines is deployed to the Old City by landing craft and helicopter to break the stalemate there. Bitter house-to-house fighting continues for two more weeks.

PERFUME RIVER

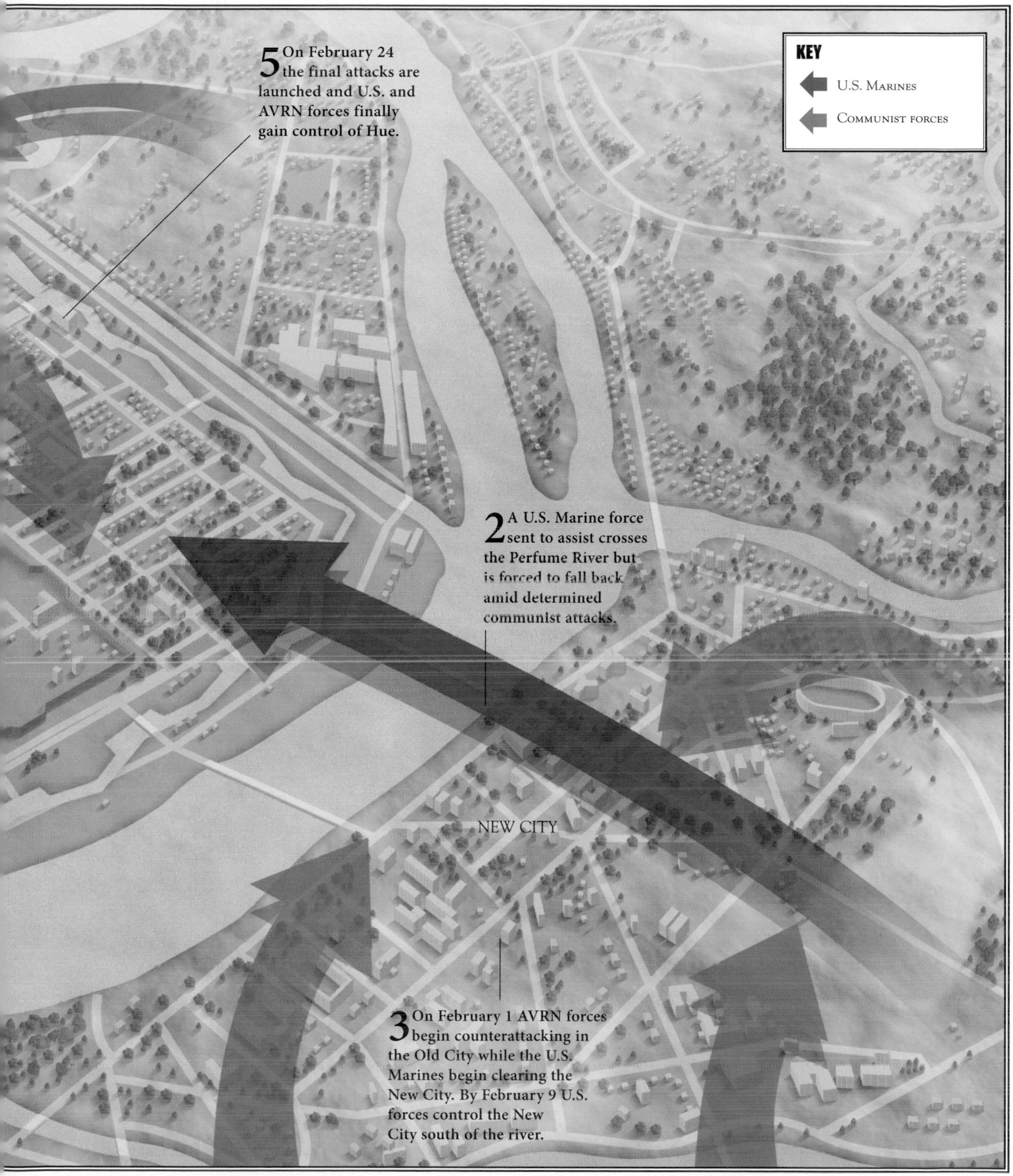

KEY

← U.S. Marines

← Communist forces

5 On February 24 the final attacks are launched and U.S. and AVRN forces finally gain control of Hue.

2 A U.S. Marine force sent to assist crosses the Perfume River but is forced to fall back amid determined communist attacks.

NEW CITY

3 On February 1 AVRN forces begin counterattacking in the Old City while the U.S. Marines begin clearing the New City. By February 9 U.S. forces control the New City south of the river.

THIS PAKISTANI TANK HAS BECOME A TROPHY OF WAR *for the Indian Army. Pakistani armored forces came close to overrunning the outpost at Longewala.*

Longewala 1971

BORDER FORCES SERVE MAINLY IN A SECURITY AND "TRIPWIRE" ROLE, IMPOSING A LITTLE DELAY AND WARNING THE MAIN BODY THAT AN ENEMY IS ON THE MOVE. WHILE IT IS EXPECTED THAT SMALL UNITS WILL TRY TO HOLD THEIR POSITION AS LONG AS POSSIBLE, THE STAND MADE BY "A" COMPANY OF THE 23RD BATTALION OF THE PUNJAB REGIMENT TURNED OUT TO BE ONE OF THE DECISIVE ACTIONS OF THE INDO-PAKISTAN WAR OF 1971.

The British retreat from South Asia in the 1940s left behind two new nations on the Indian Ocean coast. India occupied the subcontinent, while Pakistan was divided into two areas by Indian territory. The political situation in Pakistan was troubled and rife with internal disputes. Elections held in 1970 precipitated a crisis when Sheik Rahman, an East Pakistani leader, emerged with a majority. This threatened vested interests in the west of the country, and General Yahya Khan decided to use the army

BATTLE FACTS

Who: A small Indian force under Major Kuldip Singh Chandpuri, opposed by a much larger Pakistani formation under Brigadier Tariq Mir.

What: Indian defenders fought a hard delaying action until air support and reinforcements turned the battle.

Where: Border post at Longewala on the India–Pakistan border.

When: December 5, 1971.

Why: Pakistani forces needed

to overcome Longewala so they could press on to capture the strategically important town of Jaisalmer.

Outcome: A decisive Indian victory. Major Kuldip Singh Chandpuri was decorated with India's second-highest gallantry award, the Maha Vir Chakra.

to alter the political landscape. The Sheik was arrested and martial law imposed in East Pakistan. The Pakistani Army's habit of chasing insurgents into neighboring India caused a series of clashes with Indian forces. Relations between India and Pakistan were not good anyway, and after trying to get assistance via the United Nations, India decided to go to war with Pakistan.

Pakistan, detecting the slow Indian buildup to war, decided to make the first move. It launched an unsuccessful preemptive air strike on December 3, 1971, intended to cripple Indian air power on the ground as the Israelis had done to Egypt in 1967. Meanwhile, at Longewala, 120 men of "A" Company, 23rd Battalion, Punjab Regiment, held the border post. They had some mortars and two recoilless rifles mounted on jeeps for support. Against this tiny force the Pakistani Army sent an entire infantry brigade backed up by more than 60 tanks and an artillery detachment.

The commander, Major Chandpuri, immediately asked for support from battalion headquarters some 10 miles (16 km) away. Artillery shells were already landing in the Indian positions, killing five camels but doing little other damage. The Pakistani force came into sight at about 1 A.M. on December 5. Battalion headquarters gave Major Chandpuri the option to retreat or make a stand on his own initiative. He announced that he would hold his position to the death.

THE FIRST ATTACK

Antitank defense rested with the two recoilless rifles. These opened fire and disabled an enemy tank, a Chinese-built T-59, almost immediately. A jeep carrying a senior Pakistani officer was also hit. This brought the attack to a halt in some confusion and several more tanks were disabled. Three more lost their tracks to mines thrown in their path by an audacious Indian soldier before he was killed. Meanwhile, Indian machine guns and mortars caused considerable casualties among the infantry. However, some tanks were creeping around the sand dunes, looking for a way to attack from the flank or rear, and the situation was becoming desperate.

At dawn, Hawker Hunters from the nearest Indian airbase were able to take off and found themselves in a target-rich environment. Several tanks were destroyed by rocket and cannon fire, the air strike caused a panic among the Pakistani crews, many driving frantically around in circles to throw off enemy pilots' aim. During the confusion, two companies of Indian infantry and some light tanks with artillery support arrived to reinforce Longewala. Between 11 A.M. and midday the Pakistanis made two more attempts

Lieutenant-general Niazi surrenders Pakistani forces in East Pakistan to Lieutenant-General Aurora, December 16, 1971.

to break the Longewala position. The first was somewhat disorganized and took heavy casualties before being beaten off. The second was a more considered set-piece attack by a battalion of infantry supported by tanks and artillery.

A greatly reinforced defense, backed up by air strikes, met the final attack and soon it was bogged down. After a while the Pakistani forces suddenly pulled back and broke contact, leaving 37 tanks destroyed along with a train that had been bringing reinforcements in when it was spotted by air force pilots and savaged with rockets. Major Chandpuri had sworn to defend his post to the death, but in the event only three Indian soldiers were killed, and three more injured.

Pakistani losses were considerable. In addition to the tanks destroyed outright, many more were abandoned due to damage, mechanical failures, or becoming bogged down in the soft sand. Almost 100 other vehicles were also destroyed or lost, and 200 soldiers were killed. However, it was the operational and psychological results that were most important. A breakthrough at Longewala would have allowed Pakistani forces to strike deep into India, perhaps capturing territory that would have been useful at the negotiating table. However, the entire operation was derailed by failure at Longewala, and morale on both sides was also greatly affected.

The Indo-Pakistani war ended on December 16, 1971, with India victorious. East Pakistan was lost; the only way to retain it would have been to capture Indian territory and trade one for the other at the peace conference. However, Pakistan ended the war with little to trade. Thus East Pakistan became the independent nation of Bangladesh.

A U.S. Army Multiple Launch Rocket System (MLRS) *fires missiles at Iraqi positions in Kuwait from across the border in Saudi Arabia, February 1991.*

Gulf War   1991

THE 1991 GULF WAR DEMONSTRATED THE SUPERIORITY OF WESTERN MILITARY TECHNOLOGY OVER THE ENORMOUS BUT OUTDATED IRAQI ARMY.

Faced with a massive debt to Kuwait and other nations run up during the Iran-Iraq War (1980–88), Iraqi leader Saddam Hussein decided to deal with the problem by invading Kuwait on August 2, 1990. This not only made repayment unnecessary but also gave access to Kuwait's oil reserves. The invasion was effectively complete in a single day; Kuwait is small and could put up little resistance.

Fears that Saddam Hussein might push onward into Saudi Arabia, and the need to eject his forces from Kuwait, prompted a massive international response. The first stage was to build up forces in the region to protect against further aggression and to make ready for the offensive. This was code-named Operation "Desert Shield," and was accompanied by diplomatic pressure on Iraq.

Rather than withdraw his forces, Saddam Hussein resolved to fight and announced that the forthcoming conflict would be the "Mother of all Battles." He certainly

BATTLE FACTS

Who: A U.S.-led coalition of nations under General Norman H. Schwarzkopf (b. 1934), opposed by Iraqi armed forces under the overall command of Saddam Hussein (1937–2006).

What: The Coalition conducted a lengthy buildup followed by an air campaign to wear down Iraqi resistance, then launched a rapid ground advance through Kuwait.

Where: Kuwait and southern parts of Iraq.

When: August 7, 1990– January 17, 1991 ("Desert

Shield"); January 17–February 27, 1991 ("Desert Storm").

Why: Iraqi forces had invaded neighboring Kuwait.

Outcome: Iraqi forces were driven from Kuwait for minimal casualties on the Coalition side.

A U.S. ARMY SOLDIER FROM THE COALITION *guards Iraqi Army prisoners of war following the successful invasion of Kuwait, February 1991.*

had the means to fight a major war; the Iraqi army was one of the largest in the world at that time. However, it was equipped with obsolete Soviet-era equipment and manned by conscripts whose training levels and motivation were not high. The Republican Guard was better equipped and had better morale, but its weaponry was still a generation or more older than that of the forces it faced.

THE AIR CAMPAIGN

Once Operation "Desert Shield" was complete and the forces were in place, Operation "Desert Storm" was launched. This began on February 17 with an air campaign to reduce Iraqi air defenses and then ground capabilities. After suppressing enemy air defenses as much as possible, Coalition aircraft struck at key targets, such as command and control centers, communications facilities, munitions dumps, and ground-combat units. Republican Guard units were the primary ground-force targets.

Iraq could make little response. Much of its air force defected to Iran rather than engage Coalition fighters, and the remainder was no match for the Coalition's superior aircraft. Air defenses had been seriously worn down in the opening days of the campaign, further reducing the Iraqi response. Allied aircraft were lost, but the damage done to Iraq's war-fighting capability was immense. Even those units that remained intact and well supplied were deprived of communications and clear orders, which greatly reduced

their effectiveness. The removal of the Iraqi air force from the equation allowed Coalition helicopter gunships to operate freely, targeting enemy tanks and artillery.

THE GROUND CAMPAIGN

The ground campaign was launched on February 24. Diversionary attacks were made at various points while the main thrust took the form of a left hook, penetrating the Iraqi line and rolling it up. The operation went better than expected. Heavy resistance was anticipated but, in the event, the fast-moving Coalition armored forces overran their initial targets for only a handful of casualties.

Deprived of clear command and control by the air campaign, many Iraqi units were hit by surprise and in a state of relatively low readiness. Some fled their positions; those that fought back did so in a disorganized manner. Their antitank weapons had a low hit rate and were rarely effective when they did strike a target—Coalition weapons were enormously more accurate and effective.

Sandstorms on the second day of the ground campaign slowed the advance but may have worked to the Coalition's advantage. Using GPS it remained possible to maintain the offensive, and Iraqi units were caught by surprise as a result. The ground campaign was halted after 100 hours, by which time the Iraqi army remnants were fleeing back into Iraq.

Although the cease-fire allowed thousands of Republican Guard troops to escape along with their tanks and artillery, and many thought that the advance should continue until Saddam Hussein's regime was crushed, the UN remit for the conflict was to expel the Iraqis from Kuwait and no more. The Iraqi army had, however, lost a large portion of its strength.

Sarajevo   1992

THE SIEGE OF SARAJEVO INVOLVED DELIBERATE ATTACKS ON CIVILIANS, REDUCING THE CITY'S POPULATION TO A DESPERATE EXISTENCE OVER THE COURSE OF THREE YEARS.

The breakup of Yugoslavia resulted in conflict between several factions and ethnic groups, all wanting to create nations in the same territory. Populations were mixed together, making the territorial situation extremely complex. Violence offered a clear path to the goal of gaining control of desirable areas, and in many cases civilians belonging to other ethnic groups were considered to be fair game.

Such was the situation after Bosnia-Herzegovina declared independence from Yugoslavia. Bosnian forces skirmished with Serb militias throughout early 1992 as the new nation sought international recognition and this erupted into full-scale conflict once Bosnia-Herzegovina was recognized on April 6.

Serb forces captured parts of Sarajevo and quickly surrounded the city, occupying the high ground all around. This allowed artillery attacks to which the defenders, a force of ill-equipped Bosnian troops, had no effective reply.

BOSNIAN SECURITY FORCES RETURN FIRE *while civilians crouch in terror as sniper fire crackles overhead somwhere in downtown Sarajevo, 1994.*

By the beginning of May the city was blockaded, cutting off supplies of food and fuel, and a state of siege existed.

THE LONGEST SIEGE
Although the defenders of Sarajevo were outgunned, they possessed sufficient numbers to make an effective defense, and were able to prevent the capture of the city despite attacks from within and without. The besiegers attempted to wear down the defenders' will to resist with shelling and sniper attacks.

The population were forced to try to live under desperate conditions, with snipers deliberately targeting civilians. Some streets became notorious as "sniper alleys" and moving in any open space was highly dangerous. Serb forces controlled many areas within the city, shooting from tall buildings at any target that presented itself.

Starting from June 1992 onward, virtually the only source of food and fuel for the population of Sarajevo was international airlifts into the airport. Deliberate artillery attacks on hospitals and anywhere that people might gather caused a steady toll of casualties, along with deliberate massacres of civilians.

NATO INTERVENTION
After years of troubled peacekeeping efforts, NATO began to intervene actively against Serb forces. This allowed Bosnian troops to take the offensive and force the Serbs to the negotiating table. A cease-fire late in 1995 led to the siege finally being lifted by the withdrawal of Serb forces in February 1996.

BATTLE FACTS

Who: Around 30,000 Serbian troops under a succession of commanders, opposed by possibly 40,000 ill-equipped Bosnian combatants loyal to President Alija Izetbegović (1925–2003). Large numbers of civilians were also deliberately targeted.

What: The city was shelled and subjected to sniper attacks in what became the longest siege of a national capital in modern times.

Where: Sarajevo, capital of Bosnia-Herzegovina.

When: April 5, 1992–February 29, 1996.

Why: The breakup of Yugoslavia led to the encirclement of Sarajevo by Serbian forces seeking the establishment of a Serbian state.

Outcome: The siege was eventually lifted after intervention from NATO.

HUNGARY
YUGOSLAVIA
BULGARIA
BOSNIA
HERZEGOVINA
Sarajevo
Adriatic Sea
ITALY
GREECE
TURKEY

Mogadishu 1993

URBAN COMBAT HAS ALWAYS BEEN A DIFFICULT AND DANGEROUS PROPOSITION. IN THE CLUTTERED TERRAIN OF A CITY, EVEN ILL-ARMED AND UNTRAINED INSURGENTS CAN INFLICT HEAVY CASUALTIES ON REGULAR FORCES. THE BATTLE OF MOGADISHU WAS A SUCCESS IN SOME WAYS FOR U.S. FORCES BUT THE COST WAS CONSIDERED TOO HIGH TO BE ACCEPTABLE.

In October 1993, U.S. forces operating in a peacekeeping support role in Somalia opted to act with force against warlord General Mohamed Farrah Aidid (1934–96), former chairman of the Somali National Alliance. Among other atrocities, Aidid's faction was either responsible for, or at least permitted other insurgents to carry out an attack that killed 24 Pakistani peacekeepers in the Somali capital, Mogadishu. It was decided to launch an operation to capture Aidid's senior staff using a combination of helicopter assault and a ground force moving fast through the streets. The plan, code-named Operation "Gothic Serpent," was to strike rapidly to secure the targets using

THE MOGADISHU SKYLINE IS LIT BY WEAPONS FIRE *as U.S. air assets carry out a raid. Helicopters and C-130 gunships were used in the attacks.*

Special Forces troops rappeling from helicopters, while a support force moved through the streets to pick up and remove the detainees.

The mission was launched on October 3, using a task force of 19 aircraft, 12 vehicles, and 160 men. It soon devolved, however, into a potential disaster. The U.S. troops found themselves locked in gun battles with insurgents; two Blackhawk helicopters were shot down; and a rescue force of 90 U.S. Rangers were themselves trapped in the city, fighting for their lives.

RESCUE MISSION

During the night, a plan was hurriedly thrown together to enter the city and extract the Rangers using ground forces from the U.S. Army, Pakistan, and Malaysia. The Pakistani contingent provided tanks (M48s, which had originally been designed and built in the United States), while the Malaysians deployed armored personnel carriers. The rescue convoy, numbering about 100 vehicles with heavy firepower, made its way through the city and successfully extracted the trapped Rangers. Some 18 Rangers were killed and 79 wounded during the fighting.

It is not known how many Somali insurgents were killed and injured during their attacks on the Rangers or the rescue mission. Estimates of around 800 seem reasonable, though figures upward of 1,000 killed and as many as 4,000 wounded have been suggested. Somali officials claimed a much lower casualty rate. In addition to the U.S. casualties, three men were killed among the Malaysian and Pakistani contingents, and seven wounded. Although in some ways the mission was a success, the Battle of Mogadishu was a new and sobering insight in urban warfare for U.S. forces, and led to future caution about U.S. deployments.

BATTLE FACTS

Who: Fewer than 200 U.S. Army and Special Forces troops, supported by helicopters and Malaysian and Pakistani ground forces, opposed by a total of up to 2,000–3,000 irregular Somalian insurgents.

What: U.S. Rangers became pinned down near a crashed helicopter in the center of Mogadishu.

Where: Mogadishu, capital of Somalia.

When: October 3–4, 1993.

Why: U.S. forces entered the city to capture senior

personnel who were loyal to Mohamed Farrah Aidid, a local terrorist warlord.

Outcome: The trapped unit was rescued but sustained unacceptable casualties, with U.S. forces suffering 18 killed and 79 men wounded during the operation. Up to 1,000 Somalis were killed or wounded.

U.S. MISSILES SLAM INTO KEY TARGETS AROUND BAGHDAD *on 21 March 2003. The air bombardment was in preparation for the land invasion, which began immediately afterward.*

Operation "Iraqi Freedom" 2003

OPERATION "IRAQI FREEDOM" WAS BOLDLY CONCEIVED AND VIGOROUSLY EXECUTED. IN LESS THAN 40 DAYS U.S.-LED COALITION FORCES CRUSHED IRAQI MILITARY RESISTANCE, CAPTURED BAGHDAD, AND REMOVED THE REGIME OF SADDAM HUSSEIN (1937–2006).

O n March 17, 2003, after months of escalating political tension between the United States and Iraq, President George W. Bush gave a clear ultimatum to the Iraqi leadership: "Saddam Hussein and his sons must leave Iraq within 48 hours. Their refusal to go will result in military conflict commenced at a time of our choosing." No Iraqi response was forthcoming, so Operation "Iraqi Freedom" began on March 19.

U.S. attack aircraft and Tomahawk cruise missiles first made precision strikes against key targets across Baghdad. Shortly after, on the night of March 20–21, Coalition forces

BATTLE FACTS

Who: A U.S.-led Coalition force of over 260,000 troops against the national defense forces of Iraq.

What: The invasion of Iraq by the Coalition, with its objective as the destruction of Iraqi forces and the overthrow of Saddam Hussein's regime.

Where: The main theater of the conflict was concentrated between the Iraq-Kuwait border and Baghdad, with a separate theater in the north that was mainly in the hands of Kurdish separatists.

When: March 20–May 1, 2003.

Why: The invasion was in response to the attacks of September 11, 2001, based on claims that Iraq had broken UN sanctions, sponsored terrorist groups, and illegally possessed weapons of mass destruction (WMDs).

Outcome: The successful overthrow of Saddam Hussein's regime.

surged across the Iraq-Kuwait border. The attack plan for the south was three-pronged. The U.S. Army V Corps, led by the 3rd Infantry Division, would drive up toward Baghdad on the western side of the Euphrates River. East of the river, the 1st Marine Expeditionary Force (MEF) would push through An Nasiriyah, cross the Euphrates, and advance on Baghdad from east of the river, thereby forming one arm of a pincer movement with the army formations. Finally, British forces, with U.S. Marine support, would operate in the far south of the country, securing the Al Faw peninsula and taking Iraq's second city, Basra.

The land campaign got off to a brisk start. Late on March 20, British and U.S. Marines stormed and secured the port of Umm Qasr, before the U.S. elements turned northward. The Al Faw peninsula was occupied by a combined-arms amphibious operation, and by March 21 the British 7th Armored Brigade had reached Basra, although the city wasn't completely secured until April 6. The 1st Marine Division secured the Rumaila oilfields in the south of Iraq, before turning west toward An Nasiriyah. The task of actually securing An Nasiriyah, with its vital series of bridges over the Euphrates, fell to Task Force Tarawa, otherwise known as the 2nd Marine Expeditionary Brigade (MEB).

AN NASIRIYAH AND BEYOND

On March 23 a U.S. Army unit, the 507th Maintenance Company, was ambushed around An Nasiriyah by *Fedayeen* fighters, who killed 11 soldiers and took seven prisoners (including the now-famous Private Jessica Lynch). Marines of Task Force Tarawa moved to the rescue, but the day descended into a bloody battle in what would become known as "ambush alley." Eighteen Marines were killed, several by the "friendly fire" of supporting A10 aircraft. It would take until the end of the month to secure An Nasiriyah, although by then the Marine advance northward had resumed.

The U.S. advance was certainly becoming harder. Out to the west, the main U.S. Army advance was facing increasing resistance from four Republican Guard divisions, and by March 25 the 3rd Infantry Division was locked in combat around An Najaf. Furthermore, a huge sandstorm across the region had reduced the Coalition advance to a grinding crawl. An Najaf was steadily brought under control by U.S. forces: encircled on March 26; hammered with artillery and air bombardment; then finally stormed and controlled at the beginning of April by the 101st Airborne Division. By this point, however, the Coalition was closing on the capital.

BATTLE FOR BAGHDAD

The U.S. commanders decided on a bold strategy to take Baghdad. On April 5, the heavily armed 2nd Brigade, 3rd Infantry, made a "thunder run" up Route 8 straight into the

capital. Under heavy fire all the way, the unit then swung out to reach the Saddam International Airport, already in U.S. hands.

On April 7, a second "thunder run" was made, this time plunging into the administrative heart of the capital. By nightfall Saddam's palaces were in U.S. hands, but fighting to secure the supply route was fierce. U.S. Marine units were now entering and securing eastern parts of the city, having forced their way across the Diyala Bridge. By April 8 the Marines had closed up to the Tigris River, effectively completing the occupation of the city. On April 9, in a highly symbolic moment, the towering statue of Saddam Hussein in Firdos Square was pulled down by an American armored vehicle.

The formal land campaign to take Iraq was effectively over. Saddam Hussein's hometown of Tikrit was captured by a U.S. Marine task force on April 15, removing the last significant outpost of resistance in central Iraq, and by April 10 the campaign in the north had secured Kirkuk. On May 1, 2003, President Bush landed on the flight deck of the USS *Abraham Lincoln* and declared—unwisely as the subsequent years of insurgency would prove—an official end to combat operations in Iraq.

A BRITISH SNIPER *serving with the 1st Battalion, Irish Guards, takes up a position close to the city of Basra, April 2003. Snipers were set up to provide protection for British Army engineers employed to put out the numerous oil-well fires started by retreating Iraqi forces.*

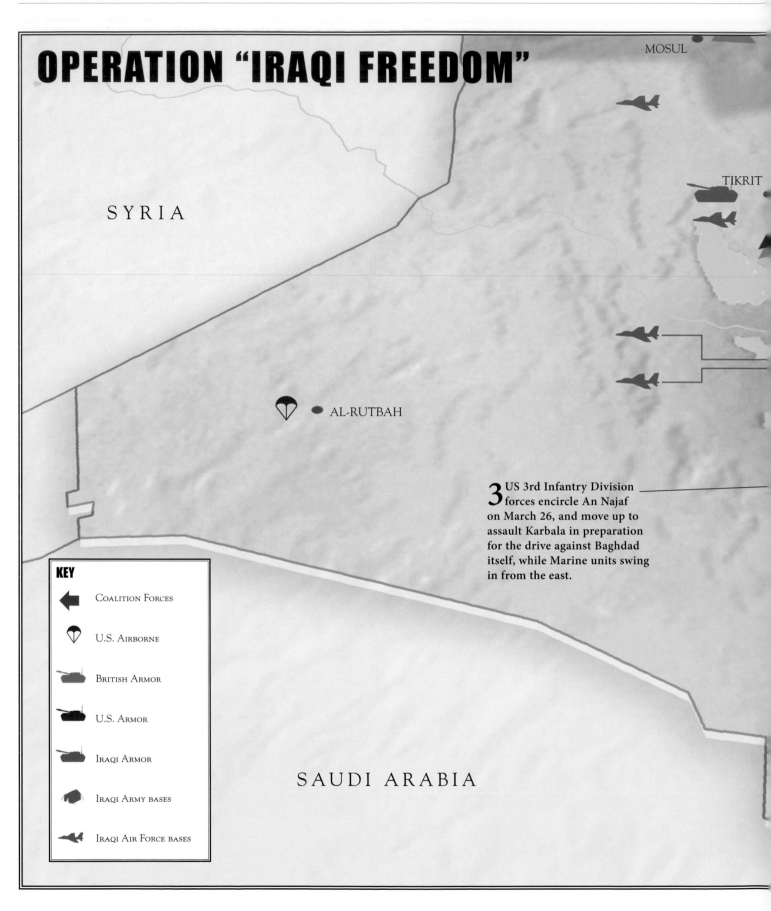

OPERATION "IRAQI FREEDOM"

MOSUL

TIKRIT

SYRIA

● AL-RUTBAH

3 US 3rd Infantry Division
forces encircle An Najaf
on March 26, and move up to
assault Karbala in preparation
for the drive against Baghdad
itself, while Marine units swing
in from the east.

KEY

◄ COALITION FORCES

U.S. AIRBORNE

BRITISH ARMOR

U.S. ARMOR

IRAQI ARMOR

IRAQI ARMY BASES

IRAQI AIR FORCE BASES

SAUDI ARABIA

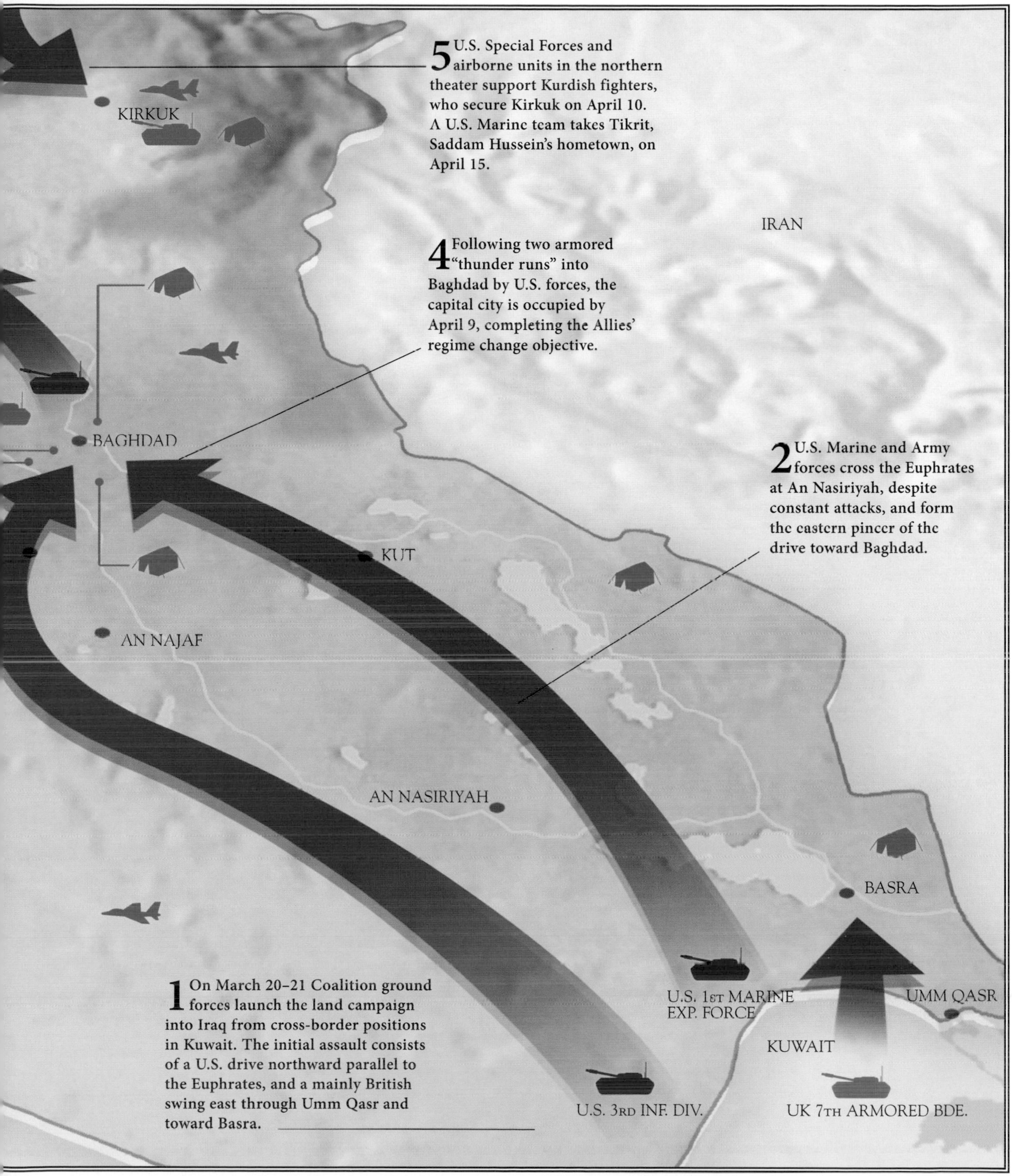

5 U.S. Special Forces and airborne units in the northern theater support Kurdish fighters, who secure Kirkuk on April 10. A U.S. Marine team takes Tikrit, Saddam Hussein's hometown, on April 15.

4 Following two armored "thunder runs" into Baghdad by U.S. forces, the capital city is occupied by April 9, completing the Allies' regime change objective.

2 U.S. Marine and Army forces cross the Euphrates at An Nasiriyah, despite constant attacks, and form the eastern pincer of the drive toward Baghdad.

KIRKUK

IRAN

BAGHDAD

KUT

AN NAJAF

AN NASIRIYAH

BASRA

1 On March 20–21 Coalition ground forces launch the land campaign into Iraq from cross-border positions in Kuwait. The initial assault consists of a U.S. drive northward parallel to the Euphrates, and a mainly British swing east through Umm Qasr and toward Basra.

U.S. 1ST MARINE EXP. FORCE

UMM QASR

KUWAIT

U.S. 3RD INF. DIV.

UK 7TH ARMORED BDE.

251

Fallujah   2004

ATTEMPTS TO CONTROL AND PACIFY FALLUJAH TOOK PLACE IN A COMPLEX POLITICAL SITUATION WHERE IT WAS NOT ALWAYS POSSIBLE TO TELL FRIEND FROM FOE.

A lthough Fallujah was not initially a center of resistance to Coalition forces in Iraq, increasing insurgent activity prompted a decision to withdraw troops from the city and embark on a long-term strategy of building goodwill through humanitarian aid and cooperation with local leaders. This policy was reversed after attacks on aid workers and their security personnel.

FIRST BATTLE OF FALLUJAH

U.S. forces were ordered to enter Fallujah in force and pacify the city. The first step was the establishment of a cordon around the city, beginning on April 4. U.S. forces then began penetrating the city, engaging several groups of heavily armed insurgents who controlled various areas.

By April 9, perhaps one-quarter of the city was in U.S. hands, and a cease-fire was declared to allow humanitarian relief convoys to enter Fallujah. Both sides used this lull to

A U.S. MARINE SQUAD *maneuvers into position during fighting for the town of Fallujah, Iraq 2004. In the background, troops cover their comrades who dash across an open space.*

BATTLE FACTS

Who: Forces of the U.S.-led Coalition, numbering approximately 2,200 and commanded by General James T Conway (b. 1947), opposed by an unknown, but very large, force of insurgents in the first battle. Coalition forces at the second battle numbered around 15,000, opposed by around 3,000 Iraqi insurgents loyal to Abdullah al-Janabi (b. 1951).

What: Coalition forces made two attempts to take control of the city from insurgents.

Where: Fallujah, on the Euphrates River west of Baghdad.

When: April 4–May 1, 2004, November 7–16, 2004.

Why: Fallujah was being used as a base by Iraqi insurgents.

Outcome: The first battle of Fallujah led to partial success, which was quickly eroded by insurgent activity. A decisive victory was obtained in the second battle.

fortify their positions. For the rest of the month, sporadic fighting was interspersed with periods of negotiation until on May 1 the decision was made to hand over operations in the city to a local force.

The "Fallujah Brigade," an Iraqi formation, was given jurisdiction over the city and charged with restoring order. Within a few months this unit had disintegrated, leaving its weapons and the city in insurgent hands.

SECOND BATTLE OF FALLUJAH

Beginning in October 2004, U.S., British and Iraqi troops surrounded Fallujah and blocked road access. On November 7 the first objectives, on the west bank of the Euphrates, were taken and Coalition forces began to penetrate the city. Within two days the main road to Baghdad had been reached and secured, and on November 10 the Coalition declared that it controlled 70 percent of the city.

Heavy urban fighting was further complicated by the extensive insurgent use of booby traps. Coalition forces frequently used tanks as ersatz bulldozers to smash holes in house walls, bypassing booby-trapped doors and windows.

Fallujah was cleared of insurgents by November 16, and the following month residents who had fled began to return home. The region was turned over to Iraqi control in 2007.

Georgia 2008

DECADES AFTER THE BREAKUP OF THE SOVIET UNION, THE TERRITORIAL CLAIMS OF ITS SUCCESOR STATES ARE STILL IN DISPUTE.

Conflict in South Ossetia in 1991–92 resulted in a complex and tense situation, with about half of the region under control of a pro-Russian government and other areas loyal to Georgia. Despite the efforts of peacekeeping forces, armed clashes became more common during the middle of 2008 and on August 7 Georgian forces launched an offensive against South Ossetia.

THE INVASION

Although Russian forces in South Ossetia were forewarned, they were deployed as peacekeepers rather than war-fighters, and thus not ready to face an attack. Nor were the Ossetian militia any match for the highly trained Georgian force, which was led by armored troops.

By the evening of August 8, Georgian troops controlled most of the Ossetian capital, Tskhinvali. However, Russian troops were already entering Ossetia from the north.

A RUSSIAN ARMORED TROOP CARRIER *passes a burning house set on fire by South Ossetian militia in the Georgian village of Kvemo-Achebeti, August 2008.*

BATTLE FACTS

Who: Georgian forces, numbering about 7,500 at the start of the conflict, opposed by 2,500 Ossetian militia and several hundred Russian troops under the command of Major-General Marat Minyurovich Kulakhmetov (b. 1959). Additional Russian forces arrived early in the conflict.

What: Georgian forces entered South Ossetia, triggering Russian intervention.

Where: South Ossetia, in the Caucasus region.

When: August 7–16, 2008.

Why: Ongoing border disputes and skirmishes between Ossetia and Georgia led to the decision to launch a full invasion.

Outcome: After initial success the invasion was decisively defeated by Russian intervention.

THE RUSSIAN RESPONSE

The Russian intervention was spearheaded by an intense and effective air campaign, directed against ground units, bases, and the Georgians' logistics capability. Achieving air superiority, the Russians also attacked Georgian cities. Russian troops engaged Georgian forces through the night of August 8–9 and despite heavy fighting were able to push the Georgians back.

The conflict widened on August 10 as the Russian Black Sea Fleet engaged Georgian naval assets and Abkhazia, an ally of Russia, began to attack Georgia. With Georgian forces driven from South Ossetia, Russian troops pushed into Georgia and reached Senaki on August 11. This suggested that Russia was not content with protecting South Ossetia, but intended to fight a larger war against Georgia. It has been alleged that the conflict was engineered by Russia, whose forces were ready on the north border of South Ossetia.

CEASE-FIRE

International response was generally against Russia. U.S. aircraft began to fly Georgian troops home from their deployment in Iraq. However, there was no real international response beyond calls for a negotiated end to hostilities. A cease-fire was declared on August 12, though fighting continued for a time afterward. The situation remained volatile and complex even after the official end of hostilities, with relations between the belligerents remaining very poor.

Index